UNGOVERNED TERRITORIES

Understanding and Reducing Terrorism Risks

WITHDRAWN

Angel Rabasa · Steven Boraz · Peter Chalk · Kim Cragin · Theodore W. Karasik
Jennifer D. P. Moroney · Kevin A. O'Brien · John E. Peters

Prepared for the United States Air Force

Approved for public release, distribution unlimited

PROJECT AIR FORCE

11000547

The research described in this report was sponsored by the United States Air Force under Contract F49642-01-C-0003. Further information may be obtained from the Strategic Planning Division, Directorate of Plans, Hq USAF.

Library of Congress Cataloging-in-Publication Data

Ungoverned territories : understanding and reducing terrorism risks / Angel Rabasa
... [et al.].
   p. cm.
  Includes bibliographical references.
  ISBN 978-0-8330-4152-4 (pbk. : alk. paper)
  1. Terrorism—Prevention—Case studies. 2. Political stability—Case studies.
3. Security, International. I. Rabasa, Angel.

HV6431.U45 2007
363.325'17—dc22

                                         2007023733

The RAND Corporation is a nonprofit research organization providing objective analysis and effective solutions that address the challenges facing the public and private sectors around the world. RAND's publications do not necessarily reflect the opinions of its research clients and sponsors.

RAND® is a registered trademark.

Published 2007 by the RAND Corporation
1776 Main Street, P.O. Box 2138, Santa Monica, CA 90407-2138
1200 South Hayes Street, Arlington, VA 22202-5050
4570 Fifth Avenue, Suite 600, Pittsburgh, PA 15213-2665
RAND URL: http://www.rand.org/
To order RAND documents or to obtain additional information, contact
Distribution Services: Telephone: (310) 451-7002;
Fax: (310) 451-6915; Email: order@rand.org

Preface

Since the end of the Cold War, failed or failing states and ungoverned territories within otherwise viable states have become a more common international phenomenon. Many of the crises that have required intervention by U.S. or international forces were produced by the collapse or absence of state authority. These ungoverned territories generate all manner of security problems, such as civil conflict and humanitarian crises, arms and drug smuggling, piracy, and refugee flows. They threaten regional stability and security and generate demands on U.S. military resources. The problem of dealing with ungoverned areas has taken on increased urgency since 9/11, which demonstrated how terrorists can use sanctuaries in the most remote and hitherto ignored regions of the world to mount devastating attacks against the United States and its friends and allies.

The objective of this RAND Corporation study is to understand the conditions that give rise to ungoverned territories and their effects on U.S. security interests and to develop strategies to improve the U.S. ability to mitigate these effects—in particular, to reduce the threat posed by terrorists operating within or from these territories. The study is based on an analysis of eight case studies.

Our research approach is as follows: We first identify and analyze the attributes of ungoverned territories, which we refer to as "ungovernability," on the basis of four variables. Second, since not all ungoverned territories are equally hospitable to terrorist and insurgent groups, we identify and analyze what we call "conduciveness to terrorist presence" on the basis of four other variables. Using this two-part framework, we next conduct a comparative analysis of the eight case studies. Finally, we derive the implications of our analysis for the U.S. government, the Department of Defense, and the U.S. Air Force.

In developing the methodology for this study, we entered somewhat of an analytical terra incognita. There is a literature about failed states and civil conflict, and various analysts and policymakers have referred to ungoverned territories as a security problem. But to our knowledge, there has been no concerted effort to define and analyze ungoverned territories as a category of security challenges. We hope that this work, despite its flaws, will serve as a foundation for further research on this important but poorly understood phenomenon.

This research was sponsored by the Deputy Chief of Staff for Air and Space Operations, U.S. Air Force (AF/XO), and conducted in the Strategy and Doctrine Program of RAND Project AIR FORCE as part of a project entitled "Defeating Terrorists in Ungoverned Territories." Research for this project was completed in December 2005. The book should be of value to the national security community and interested members of the general public, especially those with an interest in combating the blight of international terrorism.

RAND Project AIR FORCE

RAND Project AIR FORCE, a division of the RAND Corporation, is the U.S. Air Force's federally funded research and development center for studies and analyses. PAF provides the Air Force with independent analyses of policy alternatives affecting the development, employment, combat readiness, and support of current and future aerospace forces. Research is conducted in four programs: Aerospace Force Development; Manpower, Personnel, and Training; Resource Management; and Strategy and Doctrine.

Additional information about PAF is available on our Web site:
http://www.rand.org/paf/

Contents

Figures

Tables

Summary

This book examines "ungoverned territories" and the challenges that these areas pose to U.S. national security as breeding grounds for terrorism and criminal activities and launching pads for attacks against the United States and Western interests.

For the purpose of this investigation, we define an *ungoverned territory* as an area in which a state faces significant challenges in establishing control. Ungoverned territories can be failed or failing states, poorly controlled land or maritime borders, or areas within otherwise viable states where the central government's authority does not extend. Ungoverned territories can also extend to airspace, for instance, air routes through South and Central America and the Caribbean that the countries affected are unable to control—routes that drug smugglers use to transport illegal drugs.

Research Approach

Eight case studies, covering the range of ungoverned territories, served as our primary research vehicle: the Pakistani-Afghan border region; the Arabian Peninsula; the Sulawesi-Mindanao arc in Southeast Asia; the East African corridor from Sudan and the Horn of Africa to Mozambique and Zimbabwe; West Africa from Nigeria westward; the North Caucasus; the Colombian-Venezuelan border; and the Guatemala-Chiapas (Mexico) border. They are distributed through four continents and include both Muslim and non-Muslim regions. Four of the cases correspond to areas identified as terrorist sanctuaries in the 9/11 Commission Report. Other relevant selection factors included a history of U.S. involvement, whether the area was a theater of ongoing or possible U.S. military operations, the likelihood that U.S. policy or behavior toward the region would affect Washington's relations with other countries, and the region's relevance to the global war on terrorism.

To examine these cases, we identified two dimensions that provide the basic framework for the analysis. We refer to these dimensions as ungovernability and conduciveness to terrorist or insurgent presence. *Ungovernability* means that, in these regions, the state is unable or unwilling to perform its functions. This is not to say that these territories are devoid of governance. Rather, the structures of authority that do exist are not related to the formal institutions of the state. We will have more to say about the relationship between formal and informal forms of authority in our discussion of the dimensions of ungovernability in Chapter Two. We measure ungovernability using four variables: (1) the level of state penetration of society; (2) the extent to which the state has a monopoly on the use of force; (3) the extent to which the state controls its borders; and (4) whether the state is subject to external intervention by other states.

For greater precision, some of the more complex variables are broken down into a number of indicators. For instance, state penetration of society can be measured in terms of the presence or absence of state institutions; the state of the physical infrastructure; the prevalence of the informal or gray economy; and social and cultural resistance to state penetration.

Not all ungoverned territories are equally suitable as terrorist sanctuaries or conducive to the presence of terrorist and insurgent groups. To complete our analytical framework, we added the dimension of conduciveness. *Conduciveness* is measured by the following four variables: (1) adequacy of infrastructure and operational access, (2) availability of sources of income, (3) favorable demographics, and (4) invisibility.

Adequacy of infrastructure means that a terrorist group must have a basic communications and transportation network and the means of transferring funds in order to operate and access its targets. When funding from external sources is not available, terrorists need to raise money locally in order to fund their operations. The variables and indicators used in this study are shown in Tables S.1 and S.2.

Table S.1
Indicators of Ungovernability

Variable
Lack of state penetration
Absence of state institutions
Lack of physical infrastructure
Corruption and the prevalence of the informal economy
Social/cultural resistance
Lack of monopoly of force
Illegal armed groups
Criminal networks
Population with access to arms
Lack of border controls
External interference

Table S.2
Indicators of Conduciveness to Terrorist Presence

Variable
Adequacy of infrastructure and operational access
Transportation and communications
Financial
Sources of income
Favorable demographics
Presence of extremist groups
Supporting social norms
Preexisting state of violence
Presence of favorably disposed NGOs or social assistance programs open to exploitation
Criminal syndicates available for hire
Invisibility

Analysis of the Case Studies

In our analyses, we outline the dominant features of each ungoverned territory and evaluate each region on the basis of ungovernability and conduciveness to terrorists. We scored each region based on the variables and indicators described above, using the following values: 1 = low, 2 = medium, and 3 = high. These scores, summarized in the tables in the appendix, are based on the case studies in Chapters Six through Thirteen. We also provide separate tables for three multicountry case studies: the Arabian Peninsula, the East Africa corridor, and West Africa.

The presence of organized armed groups outside the state's direct control is a common characteristic of three of the two-country regions (the Pakistani-Afghan border, Sulawesi-Mindanao, and the Colombian-Venezuelan border); two cases within the Arabian Peninsula (Saudi Arabia and Yemen); and two cases in East Africa (Somalia and Sudan). (Note that it is not uncommon for the government or ruling factions to rely on extralegal armed groups—for instance, the Janjaweed militia in Darfur—to enforce their will.) Regions that score high for the presence of armed groups also rate medium or high with regard to the absence of state institutions, as we would expect. But most interesting is that they all show a considerable lack of border control. This suggests that border control is a key variable in explaining ungoverned territories and may be a strategic factor in managing them.

Interference by external states does not appear to be an important factor, except to the extent that Russia is an "external state" in some parts of the North Caucasus. Venezuela's interference has the potential to influence the course of the Colombian conflict, but such a level of interference has not yet materialized. Similarly, Iran may have the potential to destabilize some of the Gulf states, and Ethiopia can exert pressure to influence developments in Somalia. However, if political systems are not completely aligned with state institutions and national boundaries, the distinction between state interference and the interference of foreign networks (e.g., Saudi "charities") may be blurred.

Our research also shows that favorable demographic and social conditions are a key factor in a region's conduciveness to terrorist presence. This complex variable comprises the presence of extremist groups, supportive social norms among the population, a preexisting state of violence, the presence of informal social networks that can be exploited by terrorists, and the presence of criminal syndicates that can serve as contractors to terrorist groups.

Supportive social norms, a key indicator of favorable demographic and social conditions, are closely related to social and cultural resistance, which in turn indicate the lack of state penetration. The following ungoverned territories score high with regard to these two indicators: the Pakistani-Afghan border, the North Caucasus, and Mindanao. This combination of conditions is characteristic of a class of ungoverned territories that we denominate as cases of *contested governance*. These territories are also among the areas of highest concern with regard to their potential for becoming sanctuaries for international terrorist groups.

In contrast, the Latin American and African cases score low or medium for social and cultural resistance and supportive social norms (although some score high for other aspects of favorable demographic and social conditions as well, such as the presence of criminal syndicates). This suggests a class of ungoverned territories in which ungovernability derives less from local resistance than from state neglect or incompetence. We call this *incomplete* or *abdicated* governance.

Contested, Incomplete, and Abdicated Governance

Although regions can have similar scores for a given indicator, the underlying bases for those scores may be quite different. For example, two regions may each score poorly for state penetration of society, but in one instance the score would reflect active resistance to the state, while in the other the score would reflect the government's decision to abdicate its responsibility to govern. Ungoverned territories, therefore, depending on the circumstances that gave rise to their present condition, align with a three-part typology: contested, incomplete, and abdicated governance.

Contested Governance. Chechnya, Mindanao, and Colombia are prominent examples—regions in which local forces, actively disputing government control, seek to create their own state-like entity, either to realize aspirations of independence and self-rule or to profit from illegal activities without the interference of state authorities.

Incomplete Governance. For a host of reasons, governments in the Afghan-Pakistani border region, parts of the North Caucasus, Central Sulawesi, and along the Mexican-Guatemalan frontier cannot maintain a competent, qualified presence that is stronger than competing power centers. They lack the resources and the competence to project effective rule into the region. Local officials, where they exist, are inept or are co-opted by criminal organizations.

Abdicated Governance. Instead of producing public goods—such as safety, order, infrastructure, and services—the central government abdicates its responsibilities for marginal provinces and regions because it believes that nothing cost-effective can be done or because ethnic minorities with whom it shares little affinity predominate. In some instances, Saudi Arabia, for example, the central government cedes border security to the local tribes. The North Caucasus also illustrates this type of abdicated governance and the nature of the ungoverned spaces that result, especially when security services collude with illegal armed bands in the region.

Implications and Recommendations

For the U.S. Government

Although ungoverned territories may have different sources that require different policy mixes, U.S. policy must always address the two sets of attributes that make some of these territories actual or potential terrorist sanctuaries: the lack of an effective state presence and the conduciveness of these territories to the presence of terrorist groups. Recommendations deriving from our analysis include the following:

Reevaluate the role of development assistance. Helping to strengthen governance is critical. Currently, the United States tends to emphasize security cooperation and military assistance in dealing with the security problems that ungoverned territories generate. But extending the reach of government should involve other activities too. One possible option could be to use development assistance as a tool to encourage recipient governments to invest in infrastructure and institutions in regions where they have abdicated their governing responsibilities (see pages 33–34). This task is harder when the regime itself is the source of the problem (see "Address profound, official corruption directly," below).

Promote competent government practices. Lack of coordination among agencies is a major obstacle to the authorities' ability to improve governance in these regions. Therefore, providing expert advice to officials on how to coordinate their actions across departments and minimize bureaucratic competition would be an important step in strengthening public sector capabilities (see page 34).

Improve infrastructure. Improving the transportation infrastructure could have profound effects in many ungoverned territories considered in this study by improving the overall mobility within society (see page 34).

Promote regional security architectures. Action attempted through formal international organizations has a mixed record at best. The members may not share a set of interests, which can confound cooperation and timely, effective collective action. As an alternative, the United States might promote less formal "regional architectures" to coordinate the efforts of those states that do share similar concerns about the effects of ungoverned territories on their security. Interested countries and other influential stakeholders need only agree to work constructively to create initiatives that could limit the corrosive effects of ungoverned territories. The regional architecture approach might similarly enlist local cooperation to coordinate infrastructure development to project authority, order, economic activity, justice, and other public goods into areas of ungovernability (see pages 34–35).

Mobilize regional organizations. Emphasizing the role of regional organizations despite their unpromising records might prove beneficial, especially when trying to reduce incomplete or abdicated governance or resolve contested rule (see pages 35–36).

Address profound, official corruption directly. The United States must exercise caution to ensure that its assistance efforts are not wasted by entrenched corruption in the public administration of recipient countries and that it does not provide lethal aid that enables a corrupt regime to prolong its grasp on power. We may have to recognize that some regimes may not be salvageable (see page 36).

Some of the policy prescriptions aimed at addressing ungovernability will also reduce a region's conduciveness to terrorist activities: for example, building the capacity of the local military and counterterrorism forces (see page 37). Other steps that the United States could take to address the conduciveness side of the equation include the following:

Reduce terrorist exploitation of infrastructure. Terrorists typically need two types of infrastructure for their activities: transportation and the means to move funds. The United States might, therefore, make training and assistance available to the local government so that it could deploy well-trained officers in sufficient numbers to detect and apprehend terrorists trying to move about on public transportation. Terrorists also need to move money and pay for their purchases, so modern monetary and banking systems with safeguards against money laundering and software for tracking financial transactions could prove to be an impediment to terrorist transactions (see page 38).

Deny terrorists local sources of income. Terrorists derive income from criminal activity or from the black market or gray economies of the countries they inhabit. The United States therefore might help a government's efforts to suppress or reduce the criminal activities that fund terrorists. Counterdrug assistance in regions where terrorist groups are involved in the illicit drug trade can also have a counterterrorism effect (see pages 38–39).

Prevent exploitation of assistance programs. The more states fail to produce public goods—public health services, education, social welfare services—and become dependent upon nongovernmental organizations (NGOs) and private, volunteer organizations to provide these functions, the greater the probability that money from assistance programs will be funneled by sympathizers to terrorists or extremists. Therefore, U.S.

programs that help governments build capacity to produce public goods would eventually reduce terrorist exploitation of NGO services (see page 39).

Make invisibility more difficult to achieve. U.S. assistance that improves a state's ability to exert control over its borders, e.g., instrumentation to detect illegal entrants, coastal surveillance systems, counterfeit-resistant passports, border-crossing watch lists, and biometric identification technologies, reduces the probability that terrorists can cross borders undetected. U.S. assistance in the form of intelligence-sharing and warnings could also be important in reducing a terrorist's anonymity. Ways to expedite communication between intelligence agencies should therefore be a priority (see page 40).

It goes without saying that the problem of ungoverned territories reflects deep-seated, long-standing problems in the societies where they occur, and our recommendations are unlikely to render a region completely inhospitable to terrorism. However, taken collectively, these recommendations would make the region less appealing and more dangerous for terrorists and a more difficult place for them to operate.

For the U.S. Department of Defense

The Department of Defense (DoD) seeks to address specific problems arising from ungoverned territories: terrorism; narcotics trafficking; illegal arms trafficking; and proliferation of chemical, biological, radiological or nuclear (CBRN) materials and weapons. Given the pervasiveness of ungoverned territories throughout much of the Middle East, Asia, Africa, and Latin America, an alternative approach should be considered: treating ungoverned territories comprehensively as a distinct category of security problems. In designing responses to the security effects of ungoverned territories, DoD and other components of the U.S. national security community might want to use the three-part typology of ungoverned territories as an organizing principle. DoD (and the U.S. government) might review the capabilities it needs to address the requirements of handling different types of ungoverned territories (see pages 40–41). For example, what capabilities and resources would it need in cases of contested rule? To remediate incomplete governance? To encourage governments that have abdicated their governance responsibilities to assume them again?

One place to start would be to make ungoverned territories a design point in the Strategic Planning Guidance (SPG). In addition, the Security Cooperation Guidance (SCG) should also highlight ungoverned territories as a focus of security cooperation. The current formulation of defense challenges—traditional, irregular, disruptive, and catastrophic—does not capture the potential effects of ungovernability in an area sensitive to terrorist influence. A new taxonomy would have to be invented, one that would account for the phenomenon of state failure and ungoverned territory as a source of instability that is not currently captured in the SPG. However, to the degree that understanding the origins of ungovernability in a given area sheds light on potential solutions, the department may find that dealing with ungoverned territory directly—rather than as a symptom of protracted violence, crime, and poverty—might prove useful (see pages 41–42).

The 2005 Quadrennial Defense Review (QDR) highlighted the training of foreign security forces as a critical component of DoD's security cooperation strategy. Much of the QDR discussions in this narrow area focused on the ungovernability problem. The training of foreign internal defense (FID) forces has been given a high priority with the aim of improving the defense self-sufficiency of certain countries around the world. The idea is to assist our allies and partners in securing their own borders, thus improving their ability to deal with terrorist threats and incidents and reducing the burden on U.S. forces in the event that the employment of U.S. military forces is required in the future (see pages 43–44).

For the U.S. Air Force

The U.S. Air Force (USAF) faces two sets of concerns regarding ungoverned territories: operational issues and Title 10 considerations concerning USAF interaction with other air forces. The operational concerns center on the challenges that the Air Force faces when it is required to operate in ungoverned territories. The Title 10 questions have to do with the Air Force's requirements to raise, train, equip, and maintain forces suitable for the missions and tasks that ungoverned territories might precipitate.

Operational Issues. The typology of contested governance, incomplete rule, and abdicated rule casts the Air Force in one of two operational roles: (1) supporting a beleaguered government in its attempts to defend its rule in the face of opposition and insurgency and to project its authority into an ungoverned region or, less frequently, (2) supporting opposition factions as they seek to displace a hostile government, as was the case in Operation Enduring Freedom in Afghanistan.

When supporting friendly foreign governments, the Air Force may be called upon to operate from forward operating sites in government-controlled territory. These facilities may be vulnerable to enemy attack, especially in circumstances when the Air Force is performing security, stability, and counterinsurgency operations. The quality of host-nation support will be critical, especially where security, both on and off the installation, is concerned. In planning for host-nation facilities, the Air Force will also have to consider whether the United States will deploy a significant ground force. Depending upon the terms of the agreement between the host nation and the U.S. government, the Air Force may not enjoy full freedom of action against insurgents or in the implementation of its force protection measures, some of which may fall within the domain of the host nation. These considerations will be important in designing any force package for deployment in support of the host-nation government. In circumstances when there is a substantial threat to an operating location, U.S. security force personnel may have to deploy in significantly larger numbers and perform more difficult and dangerous tasks. Where the host nation can offer only limited intelligence about threats to a forward operating location, the USAF Office of Special Investigations may have to deploy additional personnel so that the base can develop better situational awareness (see pages 44–45).

FID activities may be central to U.S. efforts to help states with contested governance problems or states seeking to strengthen governance in areas of incomplete rule. The Air Force may find that it must perform advice and assistance roles with the indigenous air forces or other military or security forces—roles requiring cultural sensitivity and language skills. Where counterinsurgency activities figure prominently, the Air Force Special Operations Command (AFSOC) may have to deploy forces in support of host-nation ground forces to assist in targeting terrorists or insurgents. There may also be requirements for civic action to restore the legitimacy of, and popular confidence in, the host government (see page 45).

Security Cooperation Implications. In October 2004, the Department of the Air Force's International Affairs Office (SAF/IA) issued the first ever U.S. Air Force Security Cooperation Strategy to provide guidance to the U.S. Air Force major and component commands. The new strategy is intended to contribute to developing the capacity of allies and friendly nations by "building cooperative relationships to ensure international access and interoperability to enable present and future expeditionary air and space operations."[1] The document provides guidance to optimize USAF security cooperation programs and lays out a framework to facilitate transparency and improve coordination.

The Security Cooperation Strategy does not identify ungoverned territories as a key theme or even a key issue. But this is not surprising, given that this issue is not identified in executive-level guidance, e.g., the Strategic Planning Guidance or the Office of the Secretary of Defense's Security Cooperation Guidance. However, issues such as "combat proliferation of WMD" and "cooperating with parties to regional disputes" are two themes that are related to ungoverned territories.

The Air Force is somewhat limited in its ability to build partner capacities on its own without the involvement of other DoD or U.S. government-level programs and resources. Air Force Headquarters seems to recognize this reality. The new strategy calls for program managers to leverage security cooperation efforts to the maximum practical extent. However, that document does not provide the specifics on other U.S. and DoD activities where synchronization to advance USAF Title 10 objectives may be possible (see pages 46–47).

Title 10 Issues. The Air Force is prepared doctrinally to contend with ungovernability resulting from contested, incomplete, or abdicated governance. Where organizational issues are concerned, the Air Force is also generally well prepared. There are limited concerns about organizational preparedness to deal with territories where there is incomplete governance, but the Air Force will generally be operating in a supporting role in such places. The greatest organizational challenge relates to managing cases

---

[1]   Department of the Air Force (2004), p. 2.

arising from contested governance. Contested governance cases—usually involving insurgencies—are commonplace, as our case studies show; at issue is whether high-demand units (some of them unique), such as the 6th Special Operations Squadron, are adequate given the number of cases the Air Force might be directed to deal with.

Although most airmen are highly trained in their specialties and units routinely do well on their operational readiness inspections, there are some concerns about training relative to ungoverned territories. These concerns center on additional training that might be required if airmen are to be effective in training and advisory capacities. Cultural sensitivity and language facility could become requirements for airmen working in such capacities with a host-nation air force or in a supporting capacity with opposition forces. These requirements could influence both the USAF's special operations forces and its general-purpose forces.

Equipping becomes an issue principally where ungoverned territory results from contested governance and the Air Force must help a beleaguered government develop infrastructure relatively quickly in order to establish a presence in a contested region. Opening, operating, and sustaining airfields could be an important Air Force contribution. Manpower is always a concern when the Air Force contemplates future operations. Building government capacity and expanding the government's writ into ungoverned territories can be the work of generations. When contemplating the challenges posed by ungoverned territories, the Air Force must ensure that it can generate the trained, capable manpower that addressing the challenges of ungoverned territories will demand (see pages 47–48).

Acknowledgments

The authors wish to thank all those who made this study possible. First of all, we thank our sponsors in the U.S. Air Force and particularly Lt Col John Jerakis, our point of contact in Office of Regional Plans and Issues (USAF HQ A5XX) and the staff of the U.S. Embassies and Defense Attaché Offices who facilitated our work overseas.

We wish to thank the reviewers of this study, former Secretary of State George Shultz, William Reno, William Rosenau, and Richard H. Solomon, president of the U.S. Institute of Peace, for their corrections and suggestions, which greatly improved the quality of the book. Any shortcomings are entirely the responsibility of the authors. We also express appreciation for the collaboration that we received in our work on this study from the State Intelligence Agency of Indonesia (BIN), the Security and Intelligence Division of the Ministry of Defence of Singapore, the Intelligence Service of the Armed Forces of the Philippines, and other agencies.

We also thank the High Commissions of the United Kingdom, Nairobi, Kenya, and Dar es Salaam, Tanzania; the University of Zanzibar, Tanzania; the Ministries of Interior and Foreign Affairs, the Inter Services Intelligence (ISI) Directorate, the Federal Investigative Agency, and the Anti-Narcotic Force (ANF) of Pakistan; the British Broadcasting Corporation (Pakistan Bureau); the Intelligence Bureau and the National Security Council Advisory Board of India; the Security Service, United Kingdom; and the Control Risks Group, London, United Kingdom.

We are also indebted to our former RAND colleague C. Christine Fair, now Coordinator of South Asian Research, U.S. Institute of Peace, for her assistance with the research on the Pakistani-Afghan border region; Zachary Abuza and RAND Summer Associate Cleo Calimbahin for their contribution to the chapter on the Mindanao-Sulawesi arc; John Colarusso of McMaster University and Mikhail Alexseev of the University of San Diego for their firsthand insights into the North Caucasus region; Jusuf Wanandi and the staff of the Jakarta Center for Strategic and International Studies (CSIS); for our discussion of the Philippines we thank Eugene Martin of the U.S. Institute of Peace; Under Secretary of Defense of the Philippines Antonio Santos; Brigadier General Marlu Quevedo, Chief of the Intelligence Service of the Armed Forces of the Philippines; Carolina Hernandez and the Institute for Strategic and Development Studies of the Philippines; Amina Rasul-Bernardo; and Ustadz Esmael Ebrahim.

Within RAND we cannot fail to acknowledge the important contributions by RAND Navy Fellow Lieutenant Commander Steven Boraz, coauthor of two Latin American case studies; RAND Research Assistant Donald Temple for his contribution to the East Africa chapter; Michael Tseng, who conducted the geospatial work for this project; and Kristin McCool for her indefatigable data collection on infrastructure in the regions included in the case studies.

We also thank Andrew Hoehn, Vice President and Director of RAND Project AIR FORCE, under whose auspices this research was conducted; David Shlapak, acting director of PAF's Strategy and Doctrine Program; Cynthia Cook and Alan Vick, who oversaw the quality assurance process for this volume; and our assistant Natalie Ziegler. Finally, we would like to express our gratitude to our production editor, Joanna Baker, and to our editor, Miriam Polon, for helping to turn the manuscript into a finished product; and to John Warren, marketing director. Credit for the cover design goes to Maritta Tapanainen.

Abbreviations

ACI	Andean Counterdrug Initiative
ACOTA	Africa Contingency Operations Training Assistance
ACRI	Africa Crisis Response Initiative
ACSS	Africa Center for Strategic Studies
AFL	Armed Forces of Liberia
AFMIC	Armed Forces Medical Intelligence Center
AFP	Armed Forces of the Philippines
AFRICOM	U.S. Africa Command
AFSOC	Air Force Special Operations Command
AF/XO	Air and Space Operations, U.S. Air Force
AIAI	Al-Itihaad al-Islaami (Somalia)
AKI	Anti-Kidnapping Initiative
ANF	Anti-Narcotic Force (Pakistan)
AQAP	Al-Qaeda in the Arabian Peninsula
ARMM	Autonomous Region in Muslim Mindanao
ASEAN	Association of Southeast Asian Nations
ASG	Abu Sayyaf Group (Philippines)
ATAP	Anti-Terrorism Assistance Program
ATT	Afghan Transit Trade (agreement)
AU	African Union
AUC	United Self-Defense Group of Colombia
BIN	State Intelligence Agency of Indonesia
BSEC	Black Sea Economic Cooperation Organization
BSI	Black Sea Initiative
CAFTA	Central American Free Trade Agreement

CBRN	chemical, biological, radiological, and nuclear
CCP/NPA	Communist Party of the Philippines/New People's Army
CENTCOM	U.S. Central Command
CIA	Central Intelligence Agency
CICIAS	Commission for the Investigation of Illegal Groups and Clandestine Security Organizations (Guatemala)
CICPC	Police forensics corps (Venezuela)
CILSS	Committee for Drought Control in the Sahel
CJTF-HOA	Combined Joint Task Force-Horn of Africa
CNIES	Cooperating National Information Exchange System
CPI	Corruption Perception Index
CSIS	Center for Strategic and International Studies (Jakarta)
CTAP	Counter-Terrorism Assistance Program
CTFP	Counter-Terrorism Fellowship Program (U.S.)
CTR PPI	Cooperative Threat Reduction Proliferation Prevention Initiative
DAO	Defense Attaché Office
DAS	Administrative and Security Department (Colombia)
DCG	Defense Consultative Group (U.S.-Pakistan)
DHS	Department of Homeland Security (U.S.)
DISIP	National Intelligence Service (Venezuela)
DOAN	Anti-Narcotics Operation Department (Guatemala)
DoC	Department of Commerce (U.S.)
DoD	Department of Defense (U.S.)
DoE	Department of Energy (U.S.)
DoJ	Department of Justice (U.S.)
DoS	Department of State (U.S.)
DS	Defense Strategy
EACTI	East Africa Counter-Terrorism Initiative
ECOMOG	Economic Community of West African States Monitoring Group
ECOWAS	Economic Community Of West African States
EDA	excess defense articles
ELN	National Liberation Army (Colombia)

EO	Executive Outcomes
EPA	People's Army in Arms (Venezuela)
EPL	People's Liberation Army (Colombia)
EU	European Union
EUCOM	U.S. European Command
EXBS	Export Control and Related Border Security Program (U.S.)
FARC	Revolutionary Armed Forces of Colombia
FATA	Federally Administered Tribal Areas (Pakistan)
FBL	Bolivarian Liberation Forces (Venezuela)
FCR	Frontier Crimes Regulation (Pakistan)
FIA	Federal Investigation Agency (Pakistan)
FID	foreign internal defense
FMF	foreign military financing
FMS	foreign military sales
FSB	Federal Security Service of the Russian Federation
FUR	Revolutionary United Front (Liberia)
FY	fiscal year
GAULA	Unified Action Groups for Personal Liberty (Colombia)
GCC	Gulf Cooperation Council (Arabian Peninsula)
GDP	Republic of the Philippines
GSM	Global System for Mobile Communications
GTEP	Georgia Train and Equip Program
HM	Hizbul Mujahidin (Pakistan)
HuM	Harakat-ul-Mujahidin (Pakistan)
IAA	Islamic Army of Aden Abayan
ICG	International Crisis Group
ICP	International Counterproliferation Program
IDP	internally displaced persons
IJM	Islamic Jihad Movement
IMATT	International Military Assistance Training Team
IMB	International Maritime Bureau (London)
IMET	International Military Education and Training
INL	international narcotic and law enforcement (Pakistan)

INM	Mexican National Migration Institute
ISAF	International Security Assistance Force
ISI	Interservices Intelligence (Pakistan)
ITP	Islami Tehreek Pakistan
JAH	Jamiat Ahle Hadith (Pakistan)
JATG	Joint Anti-Terrorist Group (England)
JEM	Justice and Equality Movement (Sudan)
JeM	Jaish-e-Muhammad (Pakistan)
JI	Jemaah Islamiyah (Southeast Asia)
JUI	Jamiat Ulema-e-Islam (Pakistan)
JUP	Jamiat Ulema-e-Pakistan
LAPES	low altitude parachute extraction system
LeT	Lashkar-e-Taiba
LTTE	Liberation Tigers of Tamil Elam (Sri Lanka)
MANPADS	man-portable air defense system
MCAPS	Multi-Year Capabilities Planning System (Philippines)
MEPI	Middle East Partnership Initiative
MILF	Moro Islamic Liberation Front (Philippines)
MMA	Mutahidda Majelis-e-Mal (Pakistan)
MNLF	Moro National Liberation Front (Philippines)
MOD	Ministry of Defense (Philippines)
MOI	Ministry of the Interior (Pakistan)
NA	Northern Alliance
NADR	nonproliferation, antiterrorism, demining, and related programs
NAFTA	North American Free Trade Agreement
NIC	National Intelligence Council
NMS	National Military Strategy
NPA	New People's Army (Philippines)
NSC	National Security Council (U.S.)
NSS	National Security Strategy
NTR	National Telecommunication Region
NWFP	Northwest Frontier Province (Pakistan)
OAS	Organization of American States

OEF	Operation Enduring Freedom
OIF	Operation Iraqi Freedom
OSCE	Organization for Security and Cooperation in Europe
OSD	Office of the Secretary of Defense (U.S.)
OTM	other-than-Mexican
PA	Political Agent (Pakistan; FATA)
PACAF	Pacific Air Forces
PAF	Project AIR FORCE
PATT	Planning and Assistance Team
PGT	Guatemalan Labor Party
PIA	Pakistan International Airlines
PML-Q	The King's Party (Pakistan)
PNC	National Police Force (Guatemala)
PSI	Pan-Sahel Initiative
QDR	Quadrennial Defense Review
RCD	Regional Cooperation for Development (Iran)
RSA	Republic of South Africa
RUF	Revolutionary United Front (Sierra Leone)
RUSI	Royal United Services Institute
SAF/IA	Office of International Affairs (USAF)
SAIA	Anti-Narcotics Analysis and Information Services (Guatemala)
SANG	Saudi Arabian National Guard
SAT	Tax Collection Agency (Guatemala)
SCG	Security Cooperation Guidance
SCS	Security Cooperation Strategy (USAF)
S/CT	Office of the Coordinator for Counter-Terrorism
SIM	Subscriber Identity Module (Kenya; Tanzania)
SLM	Sudan Liberation Movement
SOCCENT	Special Operations Command Central
SOCEUR	Special Operations Command Europe
SPG	Strategic Planning Guidance (DoD)
SPLM/A	Sudan People's Liberation Movement/Army
TFG	Transitional Federal Government (Somalia)
TI	Transparency International

TSC	Theater Security Cooperation
TSCTI	Trans-Sahara Counter-Terrorism Initiative
UAE	United Arab Emirates
UN	United Nations
UNAMSIL	United Nations Assistance Mission to Sierra Leone
UNDP	United Nations Development Program
UNHCR	United Nations High Commissioner for Refugees
UNMIL	United Nations Mission in Liberia
URNG	Guatemalan National Revolutionary Union
USAFE	U.S. Air Force Europe
USAID	U.S. Agency for International Development
USCENTAF	U.S. Central Command Air Forces
USSOUTHAF	U.S. Southern Command Air Forces
WAEMU	West African Economic and Monetary Union
WARP	West Africa Regional Program
WMD	weapons of mass destruction
ZANU-PK	Zimbabwe African National Union-Patriotic Front
ZAPU	Zimbabwe African People's Union
ZDI	Zimbabwe Defense Industries

CHAPTER ONE

Understanding Lack of Governance

Angel Rabasa and John E. Peters

Introduction

This study examines ungoverned territories and the challenges that these areas pose to U.S. national security as breeding grounds for terrorism and criminal activities and launching pads for attacks against the United States and Western interests. For the purpose of this investigation, we define an *ungoverned territory* both with respect to physical space and to the level of state control, the degree to which the state has control of normal government functions. Ungoverned territories can be failed or failing states; poorly controlled land or maritime borders or airspace; or areas within otherwise viable states where the central government's authority does not extend. Ungoverned territories can thus be found along a continuum of state control.

At the benign end of the continuum are otherwise healthy states that have lost control of some geographic or functional space within their territories. For instance, a state that otherwise functions reasonably well could be plagued with a high level of illegal immigration across poorly controlled borders and the presence of criminal gangs involved in that activity. At the other end are failed states, in which the institutions of the central government are so weak that they cannot maintain authority or political order beyond the major cities and sometimes not even there.[1]

Until recently, ungoverned territories were of little interest to the U.S. national security community, unless, like the coca-growing areas of South America during the 1990s "war on drugs," they generated problems that required some degree of intervention. In the post-9/11 world, however, national security experts are coming to the consensus that threats to U.S. security may arise from areas within states or at the boundaries between states that, for various reasons, are not controlled by state authority. According to this view, the front lines of the war on terrorism lie in these ungoverned territories.[2]

Not all ungoverned territories, however, pose the same level of threat. In order of descending importance, the hierarchy of threats generated by ungoverned territo-

---

[1] See Esty et al. (1998).

[2] *The 9/11 Commission Report*, pp. 361, 366–367.

ries is as follows: (1) ungoverned territories that harbor terrorists affiliated, associated, or inspired by al-Qaeda—what we refer to as the global jihadist movement;[3] (2) areas containing terrorists, insurgent forces, or criminal networks that, while not part of the global jihadist movement, nevertheless threaten U.S. regional interests and the security of U.S. friends and allies; (3) areas that may not harbor terrorists but that can produce humanitarian crises—refugees, epidemics, and famine—that generate demands for U.S. resources.

We are primarily concerned with the first category of threat, ungoverned territories that are used, or have the potential to be used, as logistical, training, and operational bases by al-Qaeda and other groups in the global jihadist movement. Of lower priority are ungoverned territories used as hubs for financial, logistical, or criminal activity by militant Islamist organizations that have no known association with al-Qaeda but that nevertheless threaten or could threaten U.S. interests (Hezbollah's criminal activities in West Africa come to mind in this regard). Of lowest priority are ungoverned territories harboring terrorist or insurgent groups that threaten the stability of U.S. friends and allies, e.g., contested areas in Colombia.

The results of this analysis have important implications for U.S. counter- and anti-terrorism priorities. They provide a basis for assessing the effectiveness and relevance of existing policies and programs and help to identify potential targets for intervention in each territory. They thus can serve as a guide for military planning and operations.

Methodology

For this investigation, we compare eight regions that are generally regarded by terrorism and regional experts as having the potential to become terrorist sanctuaries. *Terrorist sanctuaries* are geographic areas, infrastructure, and facilities where terrorists can conduct training and indoctrination; develop networks that may subsequently serve as a source of operational, financial, and other support; and plan and launch operations. They may also include financial, cyber, and propaganda nodes that allow terrorists to advance their cause.

The goals of this study are to describe the characteristics of ungoverned territories and the attributes that make some of them seedbeds for terrorist groups. Through a review of the literature on failed and weak states and discussions among the regional experts involved in this research, we have identified two dimensions—ungovernability and conduciveness to terrorism—that provide the basic elements of a framework for characterizing the territories that represent a risk of hosting terrorist organizations. These dimensions are, in turn, reflected in a set of four variables that capture the key attributes of ungoverned territories and a second set of four variables that capture the

---

[3] Rabasa et al. (2006a).

attributes that make particular ungoverned areas conducive to the presence of terrorist or insurgent groups.

Before entering into a discussion of the nature of ungoverned territories, it is important to distinguish between two types of armed challenges to the state's control of these territories: terrorism and insurgency. *Insurgency* is defined by the Department of Defense as "an organized movement aimed at the overthrow of a constituted government through the use of subversion and armed conflict."[4] Insurgents often use terror as a method, but they generally conduct military operations against government formations and seek to seize and hold territory and create "liberated zones," where they establish a "counter-state." Unlike terrorists, who in most cases are isolated from the mass of the population, insurgents sometimes have substantial popular support and achievable aims. Therefore, political solutions in some cases can bring an end to insurgencies. Terrorists, on the other hand, operate in small clandestine cells, lack mass support, sometimes have millenarian, unachievable aims, and attack primarily non-combatants. Their methods, in many cases, alienate the population and result in the ultimate defeat of the terrorist movement.

Indicators of Ungovernability

We use the following variables to describe the extent to which territories are ungoverned: (1) the level of state penetration of society; (2) the extent to which the state has a monopoly on the use of force; (3) the extent to which the state can control its borders; and (4) whether the state is subject to external intervention by other states. For greater precision, some of the more complex variables are broken down into a number of indicators. For instance, state penetration of society can be measured in terms of the presence or absence of state institutions, the state of the physical infrastructure, the prevalence of an informal or shadow economy, and social and cultural resistance to state penetration. We refer to these as *indicators of ungovernability*.

By this we do not imply that the territories in question are ungovernable. A territory may in fact be governable, but the state apparatus may not be equal to the task. We mean that in these regions the state is absent, unable, or unwilling to perform its functions. Neither do we argue that no governing structure exists in such territories: Groups like Hezbollah in Lebanon and the Tamil Tigers in Sri Lanka establish parastatal institutions that are often better organized than those of the formal government. (Indeed, nearly all insurgencies seek to establish a "counter-state" in the areas under their control.) Thus, *ungoverned* means that these territories are outside the control of the government that holds nominal sovereignty over the territory in question.

---

[4]   Joint Staff (2006).

Indicators of Conduciveness

Conduciveness, the second major dimension that we use to characterize ungoverned territories, is important because not all such territories harbor terrorists or insurgents. We use conduciveness to differentiate ungoverned territories that are likely to provide terrorist havens from ungoverned territories that are unlikely to provide such havens. In describing conduciveness, we use four other main variables: (1) adequacy of infrastructure and operational access; (2) sources of income; (3) favorable demographic and social characteristics; and (4) invisibility. As with our consideration of ungovernability, some of the more complex variables are broken down into a number of indicators. For instance, favorable demographics can be measured in several ways: the presence of extremist groups or communities vulnerable to co-option or intimidation; supportive social norms among the population; a preexisting state of violence that could be engineered to fit with extremist agendas; informal social assistance programs or networks open to exploitation; and the presence of criminal syndicates available for hire. Thus, *conduciveness* means the extent to which these territories lend themselves to exploitation by terrorist or insurgent groups.

Case Studies

Using the indicators described above as a framework, we analyze a number of areas that might be considered ungoverned. The case studies we discuss here encompass variations in geography and in the religious heritage of the population. They are distributed across four continents and include both Muslim and non-Muslim areas. Four of the cases correspond to areas identified as terrorist sanctuaries in the 9/11 Commission Report (the Pakistani-Afghan border, the Arabian Peninsula, Southeast Asia, and West Africa). They also reflect other factors (Table 1.1). In particular, four cases involve regions in which the United States has a history of involvement, and five cases involve regions that are the scene of ongoing or potential U.S. military operations. In all the ungoverned territories examined, U.S. policy and behavior toward the region is likely to affect relations between the United States and other countries, including countries beyond the region.[5]

---

[5] We could have selected many other cases for this study. In Latin America, we could have included the tri-border areas of South America; the Upper Huallaga Valley in Peru; the Darien gap between Colombia and Panama; and, one could argue, some parts of the Mexican border with the United States. In Asia, the "golden triangle" in Southeast Asia; the Muslim provinces of Southern Thailand; the Tamil areas of Sri Lanka; Southern Lebanon; and much of Iraq. In Africa, certainly the Great Lakes region and much of the Congo. There are also urban ungoverned zones, such as large parts of Karachi or Sao Paulo, and Muslim "ghettos" in some Western European cities.

Table 1.1
Characteristics of Selected Case Studies

	Afghan-Pakistan Border	Arabian Peninsula	Sulawesi-Mindanao Arc	East Africa	West Africa	North Caucasus Region	Colombia-Venezuela Border	Guatemala-Chiapas Border
Historic U.S. involvement	X	X	X		X		X	X
Area of potential or ongoing U.S. military operations	X	X	X	X	X		X	
Area likely to affect U.S. relations with others	X	X	X	X	X	X	X	X
Highly relevant to global war on terrorism	X	X	X	X	X	X		

Our case studies are the following:

1. The Pakistani-Afghan border area, with a focus on the Federally Administered Tribal Areas (FATA) and Baluchistan province
2. The Saudi Arabian borders with Yemen, other Arabian Peninsula states, and Jordan
3. The Sulawesi-Mindanao arc in Southeast Asia
4. The East Africa corridor from Sudan and the Horn of Africa to Mozambique and Zimbabwe
5. West Africa westward from Nigeria to Sierra Leone and Liberia
6. The North Caucasus region
7. The Colombian-Venezuela border
8. The Guatemala-Chiapas (Mexico) border.

In each case study, we score the territory on each variable and its indicators. Distinguishing the territories from each other and, in particular, analyzing their salient characteristics—both in terms of ungovernability and conduciveness to terrorism—yield insights that have important implications for U.S. counter- and antiterrorism priorities. They provide a basis for assessing the effectiveness and relevance of existing policies and serve as a guide for military planning and operations.

CHAPTER TWO

Dimensions of Ungovernability

Angel Rabasa and John E. Peters

In this chapter, we describe in detail the four variables that we use to assess levels of governance, or lack thereof, and the indicators associated with some of these variables.

State Penetration into Society

The first attribute of an ungoverned territory is the lack of penetration by state institutions into the general society.[1] Lack of state penetration could be measured by absent or nonfunctioning state institutions. For example, law enforcement entities may only be present in the capital or major cities of a state, leaving substantial territory outside the state's purview. State health and welfare institutions may not reach into a substantial portion of the state's rural areas or inner cities. This lack of presence allows other organizations to take precedence in determining the rules of everyday life.[2] Thus, individuals may look to warlords, mullahs, or tribal leaders rather than state entities for judicial processes. Or insurgent groups may offer the only health care or other social services available to individuals residing in ungoverned territories.

Lack of state penetration is also reflected in low compliance with existing laws.[3] When state penetration is low, residents may ignore local laws with little or no penalty. For instance, they may not pay taxes or may engage in smuggling or illegal extraction of natural resources with little fear of arrest or prosecution. Empirically, the effects of low compliance can be hard to distinguish from the effects of lack of enforcement, but the two concepts are not the same. Compliance implies citizens' collaboration with the state and a sense among the populace that the state's rule and its laws are legitimate. Compliance can also take an active meaning, as when citizens in democratic societies participate in elections because they consider it to be their civic duty or in their interest—not because they are forced to the ballot box. Some constituencies may favor

---

[1] Migdal (2004).

[2] See the introductory chapter of Zartman (1995).

[3] Migdal (2004).

higher taxes to fund higher levels of social services because they believe their taxes deliver value for money.[4]

In an ungoverned territory, the state is not the primary source of authority. It is no more likely than other social institutions (e.g., tribes and clans) to be perceived as legitimate or to be able to elicit compliance with its laws. Indeed, the state is simply one actor within an ecosystem in which many groups and entities interact with each other and evolve through adaptation to changes in the environment. In this situation, a "survival of the fittest" dynamic emerges, in which the health of whatever institutions that may be present—particularly judicial and law enforcement—is a key determinant of the state's ability to penetrate the society.[5] To make such an assessment, one must determine whether those institutions are subverted by corruption or competing local allegiances; if so, how advanced the decay is; and whether the state can reassert control. In some cases, as we discuss in Chapter Four, ungoverned territories are the outcome of political decisions by those in power to operate through informal channels—militias or criminal networks—outside the formal structures of the state.

Aside from the overarching issue of the presence, or lack thereof, of state institutions in ungoverned territories, there are three indicators that can be treated separately for analytical purposes.

Lack of Physical Infrastructure

This indicator refers to the physical dimension of the state's presence in a territory: the infrastructure linking the region to the political and economic heart of the state. Much of the ungovernability associated with the areas we studied is the result of inaccessibility. Ungoverned territories are often found in difficult terrain: mountains, jungles, or desert. These areas are generally economically marginal and sparsely populated—conditions that retard economic development and diminish the state's incentives to develop the infrastructure necessary to maintain a robust state presence.

Even where physical infrastructure is least developed, however, there are options for travel and communications. Parts of Somalia have the semblance of a working surface transportation system, for instance. Small airstrips and regional airports provide the possibility of air transport. Cell phones are widely available in some of these regions. Nevertheless, especially in states with weak administrative structures, such limited infrastructure might actually aggravate governability problems because anti-state forces can use it for their own purposes. (See "Adequacy of Infrastructure" in the section on Conduciveness to Terrorism).

---

[4] In discussing the conditions of weak states, analysts often refer to a state's lack of legitimacy in the eyes of its citizens. But it is difficult to measure perceived legitimacy on its own.

[5] Adapted from an unpublished paper by David Kilcullen, "Irregular Warfare—A Systems Assessment," September 2004.

Corruption and the Prevalence of the Informal Economy

Corruption is endemic in most, if not all, of our case studies. This corruption is structural—not just a question of corrupt individuals—and it reflects, as we discuss in the cases of Indonesia and the Philippines, the low level of income of government officials, the cultural norms that require them to take care of subordinates and relatives, and the resulting need to raise money in unconventional ways. Widespread corruption delegitimizes the state and may have severe security consequences. For instance, corruption in the Russian law enforcement and border security agencies has allowed terrorists and would-be terrorists to move around the Russian Federation relatively freely. In some cases criminals and state employees are one and the same.[6]

The prevalence of the informal economy refers to the extent to which the informal economy overshadows the formal economy and escapes the control of the state.[7] The informal sector is composed of economic actors in a variety of commercial activities operating beyond the realm of formal employment or economy. Typically, this sector does not generate tax revenues for the state the way the formal economy does.

Social and Cultural Resistance to Penetration by State Institutions

Social and cultural resistance usually means that the populace disputes the legitimacy of the state and its institutions, and prefers to have other entities—ethnic groups, clans, tribes, extended families—serve as the basis for social, judicial, and political organization. This is a key factor in several of our case studies. In the Federally Administered Tribal Areas of Pakistan, the Pashtun tribes have a long history of resistance to outside authority and a distinct legal and administrative system dating back to colonial times. The Muslim inhabitants of Mindanao, commonly known as Moros or Bangsamoro (the Moro nation) have contested the authority of the Manila government—and its religious and cultural influence—since the Spanish colonial period. The Sulu Sultanate, in fact, maintained an independent existence until the nineteenth century. Likewise, in the North Caucasus there has been a history of resistance to Russian domination on the part of some of the Caucasian peoples. The current Chechen insurgency is simply the latest episode of a conflict going back to tsarist times.

Monopoly on the Use of Force

Strong states have a monopoly over the means of coercion within their own borders. In some remote areas, especially in environments with a low penetration of law enforcement into society, alternatives to this state monopoly emerge. If the central government

---

6   For instance, Dr. William Reno, in his review of the manuscript of this book, notes that at the Mineralnye Vody airport in Stavropol Kray, the customs personnel are the mafiya.

7   Adapted from Zartman (1995).

does not have a monopoly on the use of force, it is important to determine what level of control it is able to exert in the contested jurisdiction and how effectively government agents can protect or coerce the local population relative to competing power centers. We have identified three indicators of the lack of a monopoly on the use of force.

Presence of Organized Armed Groups Outside the State's Control

The presence of armed groups outside the state's control is a primary indicator of the extent to which a territory is ungoverned. The activities of illegal groups, particularly when they are trafficking in a lucrative and socially destructive commodity such as cocaine, tend to weaken and corrupt political and social institutions. To the extent that these groups are successful, they also displace state and government institutions—usually weak to begin with—in the areas where they establish a foothold. Unchecked, illegal armed groups will expand their resource base, increase their recruiting pool, and generate greater capacity at the expense of the state. Such groups also threaten individual citizens, requiring them to pay "taxes" or protection money or compelling them to participate in illegal activities. These actions further weaken the state because citizens come to view the state as ineffective or irrelevant.

To a greater or lesser degree, all our case studies manifest the presence of organized armed groups outside the state's control. In some cases, these armed groups are full-blown insurgent movements with thousands of fighters—for instance, the Moro Islamic Liberation Front in Mindanao, the Revolutionary Armed Forces of Colombia (FARC), the Sudanese People's Liberation Movement/Army (which is now part of a coalition government) and Somali militias. At times, these groups have actively contested control of territory against government forces. Other terrorist groups, such as al-Qaeda and related jihadist groups on the Afghan-Pakistani border region and al-Qaeda in the Arabian Peninsula, have sanctuaries in those regions but do not seek territorial control. Other groups, such as the Mara Salvatrucha on the Guatemalan-Mexican border region, are gangs without a particular ideology or political agenda that are nevertheless destructive of public order.

Presence of Criminal Networks Linked to Terrorist or Insurgent Groups

The presence of criminal networks also represents an intrusion on the state's monopoly over the legitimate use of force. In numerous cases, terrorist or insurgent groups develop opportunistic alliances with these networks. This convergence may be facilitated by the following factors:

- a common enemy—the government[8]
- similar logistical and operational requirements

---

[8]   Except in those cases where the ruling faction is coeval with a criminal enterprise.

- synergies produced by sharing a common infrastructure, e.g., runways, logistical corridors, safe havens, and financial and money laundering networks
- mutually reinforcing activities.

Even where this convergence of insurgency or terrorism with crime has not occurred, there seems to be a feedback mechanism in which the activities of criminal groups in turn create greater social disorder.[9] The prototypical case of the convergence of crime and insurgency is, of course, Colombia, where over the past two decades the FARC—a Marxist guerrilla force that has operated in the backlands of Colombia since the 1960s—has emerged as a narco-guerrilla group, deeply involved at various stages in the cocaine trade, from which it derives about half of its income.[10] Another compelling case is the Revolutionary United Front (RUF), a loosely organized guerrilla force seeking to retain control of the lucrative diamond-producing regions of Sierra Leone and notorious for its violence and gruesome maiming of civilians.[11]

Population with Access to Weapons

Access to weapons also represents competition with the state over the legitimate use of force. It is no accident that many of the regions that we examine in this study are awash in small arms (and sometimes crew-served weapons) in the hands of civilians. For instance, a recent United Nations survey estimated approximately 40 weapons per 100 people in Yemen. The Yemeni Interior Ministry, however, estimates that the country's approximately 19 million people own some 50 million personal weapons.[12] In the FATA of Pakistan there is an entrenched "Kalashnikov culture" that extends beyond adults to teenagers and even children. This culture has made it necessary for the local population to both have guns and possess the requisite knowledge of how to use them.[13]

A high influx of illegal weapons also suggests the presence of an alternative source of power in ungoverned territories. Usually the demand for illegal weapons comes from tribes or rebel groups that operate outside the effective control of the central authorities. The North Caucasus, the Afghan-Pakistani frontier, portions of the Arabian Peninsula, and large swatches of Africa share this attribute.

---

[9] See the considerable literature developed by the World Bank Project on Civil Conflicts, Crime and Violence, in particular, Collier (1999); Collier (forthcoming); and Collier and Hoeffler (2000).

[10] The other half of the FARC's income is derived from extortion, kidnappings, and funds diverted from municipal governments in the areas where the FARC operates. See Chapter Twelve, "The Colombian-Venezuelan Border;" and Rabasa and Chalk (2001).

[11] See Chapter Ten, "West Africa."

[12] Jane's Information Group (2004c).

[13] See Chapter Six, "The Afghan-Pakistani Border Region."

Control over Borders

Lack of control over borders could logically be considered as an indicator of lack of state penetration, but it is of sufficient importance to be treated as a separate variable. Border areas are spaces with unique characteristics that present unique problems—issues of functional cooperation among neighboring states, for instance.[14] In theory, borders mark the interface between nation-states; they serve as functional barriers where states control the transnational movement of people and goods. In practice, borders are dynamic. They shift in response to disputes among neighbor states and often reflect the preference of the victor in the last war. Regulating cross-border movements by individuals with tribe, clan, or family ties on both sides of the border is particularly problematic. This is the case with the Wazir tribes in FATA, many of whom neither recognize nor respect the Durand Line that formally marks the frontier between Afghanistan and Pakistan.[15]

Borders are also gateways through which insurgent and terrorist groups trade resources and receive critical inputs. In many cases, they are areas in which the state is least likely to exercise a monopoly on the use of force. Almost without exception, ungoverned territories are found in border areas, remote from the capitals of their respective states, where neither regime can successfully exert control over them and where the exact location of the frontier is not obvious. The exceptions are ungoverned territories in archipelagic states, e.g., in Southeast Asia, where the "borders" are the seas.

In addition, as former Citicorp chairman Walter B. Wriston observed at the beginning of the 1990s, as the technologies of print, broadcast, and telephone converge and expand, national borders cease to be boundaries for information. The explosion in information technology reduces the power of governments to regulate the knowledge and behavior of people and institutions within national boundaries and raises risks to existing power structures.[16]

External Interference

A characteristic of some ungoverned territories is outside interference that prevents or diminishes a state's ability to control its territory. In some situations, an external power—usually a neighboring state—exerts control over the domestic political and economic space within a state or prevents a government from asserting control over that space. This interference could be direct, as in the case of Rwandan military incur-

---

[14] See Geneva Centre for Democratic Control of Armed Forces (2004).

[15] See Chapter Six.

[16] Wriston (1992).

sions into the eastern Congo. Or it could be carried out by local proxies or allies or by a combination of both—for instance, Syria in Lebanon or Russia in the Caucasus, where both Damascus and Moscow maintain an overt presence and influence. External states can also take subtler, sub-rosa actions, backing preferred local candidates and officials and undermining others. In cases where political systems are not completely aligned with state institutions and national boundaries, the distinction between state interference and the interference of foreign networks (e.g., Saudi "charities") may be blurry.[17]

Since external interference has important implications for the characteristics of an ungoverned territory (and is amenable to diplomatic or political measures), we need to consider the role of external actors where pertinent. In particular, it is important to consider how much influence external actors have on the internal activities of a given state, the extent to which external actors exacerbate or, alternatively, mitigate problems of state weakness, and whether external involvement is a cause or symptom of the problem. In some cases, external interference means that an outside power has recognized a power vacuum and has moved in to fill it, but the "solution" may not produce long-term stability.

In sum, our framework involves four indicators of the extent to which a territory can be regarded as ungoverned: levels of penetration into society by state institutions; state monopoly on the use of force; control over borders; and external interference that prevents or diminishes a state's ability to control its territory. In the next chapter, we describe a similar set of indicators of the extent to which areas can be regarded as conducive to the presence of terrorist groups.

---

[17] Dr. William Reno, in his review of this manuscript, reports that he recently returned from Somalia, where he was able to see large numbers of Saudi "experts" and "philanthropists" who were deeply engaged in the local situation. Given the relationship between religious organizations and state officials in Saudi Arabia, he asks, how should one judge the status of these visitors to Somalia?

CHAPTER THREE

Dimensions of Conduciveness

Angel Rabasa and John E. Peters

Several environmental factors allow terrorist and insurgent groups to flourish in particular places. As stated in Chapter One, we are concerned with a hierarchy of threats: from al-Qaeda and its affiliated and associated groups in the global jihadist movement to insurgent groups that do not threaten the United States directly but threaten U.S. regional interests and the security of U.S. friends and allies.

Al-Qaeda and other groups in the global jihadist movement use ungoverned territories as financial, logistical, and training bases or as operational bases. Each of these activities poses a different set of requirements. An ungoverned territory that lends itself well to use for logistical or training purposes or as a transit area for terrorists may not be suitable as an operational base; it may be too remote from potential targets or may lack an adequate communications infrastructure. Certain ungoverned territories could themselves be the theater in which jihadist terrorists conduct attacks, but in other ungoverned territories such attacks might be limited by the relative absence of lucrative targets. Or a territory could be suitable as an operational base, but the terrorists may not want to jeopardize its use as a logistical base by using it in that way.

Insurgents operate in particular ungoverned territories for different reasons. In most cases, of course, the ungoverned territory is simply the insurgents' home area. Moro insurgents, whom we discuss in Chapter Eight, operate in Mindanao because it is the historic homeland of the Moro people and the place in which they seek to establish their political entity. Southeast Asia's Jemaah Islamiyah—although it is a terrorist group associated with the global jihadist movement—operates in that area because that is where the group has its historic roots, support networks, and cultural affiliation. Other insurgents, such as Nepalese neo-Maoists, the New People's Army of the Philippines, and the FARC in Colombia, have built their strength in rural strongholds as part of a Maoist "people's war" strategy to overthrow the central government.

Our primary concern, of course, is with international jihadists who have the wherewithal and volition to choose operating and support areas, rather than with terrorists or insurgents who are regionally anchored and have local objectives. Beyond the natural tendency of terrorist or insurgent groups to operate in the areas in which they were formed, we have identified four key variables that seem to influence the extent to which territories are conducive to the presence of terrorist and insurgent groups:

adequacy of infrastructure and operational access; availability of sources of income; favorable demographic and social characteristics; and invisibility—the ability of terrorists (and insurgents in government-controlled territory) to blend into the population and escape detection by the authorities.

Adequacy of Infrastructure and Operational Access

A key requirement of a terrorist operational base is the existence of an infrastructure that allows terrorist groups to perform basic functions. The elements of such an infrastructure include (1) communications facilities, (2) an official or unofficial banking system that allows for the transfer of funds, and (3) a transportation network that provides access to urban centers and potential external targets.

There is a certain tension between the terrorists' requirements for invisibility and for operational effectiveness. To the extent that a territory lacks the basic infrastructure required for government surveillance, terrorists can move around with impunity. But if the territory is so undeveloped that individuals cannot communicate across distances, move funds, or travel from remote locations to urban areas, it will be difficult for terrorists to organize themselves and support their operations. Take, for instance, the case of the FATA of Pakistan. The FATA have few paved roads and rudimentary public transport, but it is possible to travel from urban centers in Pakistan to points along the Afghan border, and vice versa, by train, bus, automobile, and minivan. Completely ungoverned territories lacking even those basic assets would hold little appeal for a terrorist group that, like any organized entity, requires at least a semblance of structure if it is to pursue meaningful designs and endeavors.

Related to the idea of adequate infrastructure is the idea of reasonably easy access to terrorists' desired attack venues, which we call *operational access*. In the case of al-Qaeda and groups in the global jihadist movement, this means locating in areas that have or are in proximity to visible U.S. or Western targets. Targets could take the form of diplomatic missions and military facilities; Western-owned banks and businesses; Western tourists; or such cultural symbols as international schools, universities, or foreign aid offices. Thus, an ungoverned territory, such as Somalia and surrounding areas, that is contiguous to a zone of jihadist operation—in this case, Kenya and Tanzania—would be more attractive to jihadist groups than one that is a long distance away or separated by difficult terrain from potential targets.

Sources of Income

Unless they can tap into external sources of income (e.g., remittances from sympathizers or diaspora communities), terrorists and insurgents need to generate revenue from local sources to finance their activities. World Bank studies have documented a linkage between areas producing high-value commodities and the growth of rebel movements.[1] As noted in the RAND study *Beyond al-Qaeda*,[2] these commodities provided easy targets of opportunity for terrorists and insurgents. Such groups have the firepower to deal themselves into the trade. They can trade the commodities themselves, as in the case of the Liberia-backed Revolutionary United Front (FUR) of Sierra Leone and "conflict diamonds," or they can protect and "tax" them, which is the preferred approach of the FARC to the cocaine industry. Table 3.1 summarizes the sources of income that fuel terrorism and insurgency in some of our case studies.

Table 3.1
Sources of Income for Terrorist Groups, by Region

Region	Sources of Income
Pakistani-Afghan border	Drugs, weapons smuggling, human trafficking, stolen vehicles, money laundering, trafficking in false documents
Arabian Peninsula	Charities, money laundering, weapons smuggling, personal wealth
North Caucasus	Drugs, energy, weapons smuggling, human trafficking, kidnapping, charities
West Africa	Fraud, drug trafficking, diamonds
Colombian-Venezuelan border	Drugs, energy (protection payments), weapons smuggling, kidnapping
Sulawesi-Mindanao arc	Drugs, piracy, weapons smuggling

SOURCES: Bagley (2002); Cragin and Hoffman (2003); Douthat (2005); Farah (2004b); Steve Jackson (2002); Pasha (2007); Roth, Greenburg, and Wille (2004).

Favorable Demographic and Social Characteristics

Ungoverned territories are not demographic blank slates. They are home to complex societies, some of which lend themselves to terrorist penetration while others do not. Indicators of demographic and social characteristics that would make an ungoverned territory attractive to a terrorist group include the presence of extremists groups or communities vulnerable to co-option or intimidation; the existence of supportive social norms among the population; a preexisting state of violence or ethno-religious cleavages that could be engineered to fit with extremist agendas; the presence of favorably disposed nongovernmental organizations (NGOs) or social assistance programs that are open to exploitation; and criminal syndicates available for hire.

---

[1]   See Chapter Twelve of this study and Rabasa and Chalk (2001).

[2]   Rabasa et al. (2006b).

Presence of Extremist Groups or Communities Vulnerable to Outside Co-Option or Intimidation

Successful penetration of an area by outside terrorists requires a base of support, willing or coerced, in the local community. Local extremist groups or minorities within the population that have become alienated could serve this function. The prototype of the symbiosis of foreign terrorists and local communities is Pakistan's FATA. Throughout the area there are Arabs who fought in the anti-Soviet jihad in Afghanistan, along with Uzbeks and other Central Asians, all sharing sanctuaries and cooperating. Many have married local women and acquired status as members of local clans and extended families. Dislodging these foreign fighters thus poses serious social and cultural problems.

Supportive Social Norms Among the Population

Terrorist groups are more likely to penetrate an ungoverned territory if the surrounding population abides by a set of social norms that are either similar to or at least can be manipulated by the terrorist organization. A broad range of cultures, mostly in places where central authority has always been weak, exhibits characteristics susceptible of exploitation. The most clear-cut example that we have identified is al-Qaeda's manipulation of the all-embracing Pashtun code of conduct known as *Pashtunwali*. The code requires that any supplicant should enjoy the host's protection and should neither be harmed nor surrendered to an enemy. This communal norm has been strengthened over the past two decades as a consequence of the interaction noted above between foreign fighters and the local population during the Afghan war. Western intelligence analysts believe that these cultural traits, as well as tribal affinity, were critical determinants in shaping the strategic relocation calculus of both the Taliban and al-Qaeda following the Tora Bora operation in late 2001.[3] In the case of the southern Philippines, which is often singled out as an area of interest to al-Qaeda and its regional affiliate, Jemaah Islamiyah, only the outlying, underdeveloped rural provinces and the smaller islands of the Sulu archipelago have harbored these groups because the more urbanized, largely Christian, regions of Mindanao do not provide a favorable social environment for jihadist activity.

A Preexisting State of Violence or Communal Ethno-Religious Cleavages

Regions where there are grievances against the regime or a preexisting state of communal conflict are attractive to international jihadists. This is the case in the North Caucasus, where Islamist militants have co-opted the Chechens' struggle for independence from Russia. There is also significant overlap between the conflict in Kashmir and the global jihad. Since Pakistan's involvement in the global war on terrorism, some of the Kashmiri mujahidin groups, originally formed and trained by Pakistan's Interservices Intelligence (ISI) Directorate to prosecute a war of attrition against India, have increas-

---

[3]   RUSI (2005).

ingly reoriented the focus of their aggression inward toward targets in Pakistan and Pakistani government interests.

In the Moluccas and the region of Poso, in Sulawesi, which we examine in the chapter on the Sulawesi-Mindanao arc, jihadists from other parts of Indonesia introduced themselves into local conflicts and turned them into full-blown jihads. These "local jihads" not only enable extremists to gain support among the broader Muslim population by presenting themselves as defenders of endangered Muslim communities, but also, according to Southeast Asia terrorism expert Zachary Abuza, provide new members with a "rite of passage" which is the functional equivalent of the founding generation's experience in Afghanistan.[4]

Informal Social Assistance Programs Open to Exploitation

Social assistance programs, in which the motives of the providers—whether religious, ideological, or cultural—are congruent with those of terrorists or insurgents, can often be subverted or exploited to support terrorist and insurgent objectives. Throughout areas of conflict in the Muslim world, Islamic NGOs have provided funding and support for Islamist fighters and their families.

Criminal Syndicates Available for Hire

In the preceding chapter, we identified the presence of criminal networks linked to insurgent or terrorist groups as an indicator of ungovernability because it breeds social disorder and detracts from the ability of the state to enforce its jurisdiction. In a different context, it is also a factor in the conduciveness of an ungoverned territory to the presence of terrorists or insurgents. The presence of criminal networks opens the possibility of strategic alliances through which terrorists or insurgents and criminal groups can share logistical corridors, safe havens, and access to sources of funding and money-laundering arrangements. Pragmatically exploiting these conduits, terrorists can entrench themselves in ungoverned territories and use them to plan operations, train and battle-test cadres, scout for new "talent," stockpile weaponry, and move personnel and materiel.

Invisibility

Terrorism is a form of asymmetric warfare. By definition, terrorists are weaker than the governments they challenge and can be destroyed if they are found and engaged. Being invisible to the local authorities (if there are any) and to international counterterrorist forces is therefore a survival requirement for terrorists.

---

[4] Rabasa discussion with Zachary Abuza, Washington, D.C., May 2004.

Invisibility is not the same as operational security. Operational security is a set of procedures. Being invisible is a function of the environment in which terrorists operate and which reduces the requirement for rigorous operational security. Invisibility may be a product of similarity in appearance, language, and behavior between terrorists and the host society, which allows them to blend in. Alternatively, invisibility may be a consequence of the anonymity provided by modern, cosmopolitan mass society, in which diversity in appearance, language, and behavior is the norm, rendering terrorist operatives no more remarkable than the usual run of human heterogeneity.

Invisibility manifests itself in two ways: In ethnically homogeneous areas, terrorists do not stand out and can blend into the general population. In contrast, widely heterogeneous areas, such as metropolitan centers in the West, confer a different kind of invisibility. But even in the latter case, terrorists need support communities to keep them from being noticed and discovered for what they are. The fact that ungoverned territories may receive only a low level of official attention is likely to make such territories more conducive to the presence of terrorist groups than are regions or countries that are high on the international security agenda. For instance, while East Africa has become a focal point of the global war on terror, little attention has been devoted to Zimbabwe or Mozambique, and intelligence on prevailing conditions in Somalia is extremely thin. Similarly, the area that encompasses the northern coast of South America and the eastern Caribbean has only emerged recently as an area of concern. In general, areas that have no international peacekeeping presence are more opaque to the intelligence agencies of major powers and provide easier environments for terrorists to rebuild and restructure, make up losses, and plan future attacks.

There are of course, limits to invisibility. Terrorists need to communicate; recruit new members; and survey, access, and attack targets—and those activities make them vulnerable. However, terrorists can enhance their invisibility (and reduce their vulnerabilities) when they use areas removed from population centers for training or other support functions. A case in point is the jihadist training camp that operated in Poso, a remote part of Sulawesi, Indonesia, and only came to light because of the discovery of documentation relating to the camp after the arrest of an al-Qaeda cell in Spain in 2001.

A key question concerns the relationship between invisibility and operational access—the terrorists' ability to access and strike their targets. Withdrawal to remote areas reduces terrorists' visibility but also impedes their access to the infrastructure and resources that they need to operate, so there is a trade-off between security and effectiveness. Are there periods in terrorists' operational cycle when they seek publicity (preferring operational access) rather than protection (preferring invisibility)—periods that would offer officials significantly improved opportunities to discover them and take action against them? The answer is not clear-cut and may depend on such factors as the nature of the terrorists' sanctuary, their target, the demographics around the target, and other environmental factors.

CHAPTER FOUR

Comparative Analysis of Case Studies

Angel Rabasa and John E. Peters

In this chapter, we analyze the results of eight case studies of ungoverned territories in terms of the dimensions identified in our framework—ungovernability and conduciveness to a terrorist presence. We do this in two ways. First, we describe the dominant characteristics of each of the case studies, that is, those features that are most relevant to a specific ungoverned territory and that differentiate it from others. Second, we compare the values that we have given to the indicators of ungovernability and conduciveness in each of these territories. On the basis of this analysis, we seek to determine how ungoverned territories cluster in ways that might provide insights into the phenomenon that is the subject of this study. We then develop a three-part typology of ungoverned territories, each with different policy implications.

Dominant Characteristics of the Case Studies

The Pakistani-Afghan Border Region

The Pakistani-Afghan border region can be regarded as the prototypical ungoverned territory. Ungovernability in this region, the suspected hideout of the core al-Qaeda leadership, derives from an almost complete lack of state penetration into tribal societies and high social resistance to government authority. The presence of the state in the Federally Administered Frontier Areas has always been tenuous. Under the Raj and after Pakistan emerged as an independent nation, the central government allowed the tribes in the region to run their own affairs under the supervision of Political Agents appointed by Islamabad. Pakistani laws did not formally extend to the tribal areas, which were governed under their own colonial-era legal codes. Disputes between individuals and tribes were adjudicated in accordance with Pashtunwali, the Pashtun tribal code of conduct.

Until the military sweeps against militants in the spring of 2004, Pakistan also refrained from sending its military forces into the region. The population is heavily armed and resistant to outside interference, as demonstrated by the strong armed resistance to the 2004 Pakistani military incursions. The poorly controlled Afghan-Pakistani border, called the Durand line, bisects the Pashtun homeland. Similar conditions prevail in the border areas of Baluchistan province. Although central government representatives have the ability to influence tribal behavior up to a point through coercion or monetary and other inducements, the state is merely one of a number of competing power centers.

Although almost all the factors that are conducive to terrorist groups are present on the Pakistani-Afghan frontier, the most salient factor is favorable social norms, in particular elements of Pashtunwali that mandate hospitality and sanctuary to those seeking refuge with the tribes. Combined with religious affinity and social ties developed during the Afghan war, these factors make the region an ideal haven for terrorists fleeing U.S., coalition, and allied forces.

The Arabian Peninsula

The governments on the Arabian Peninsula have devoted substantial resources to the physical infrastructures of their countries. Nevertheless, the sparse population and geographic constraints posed by mountain ranges and deserts make penetration into the more remote outposts of these countries difficult. Moreover, state penetration of society has not been uniform. Urbanization, too, has brought its own problems. In the years since the end of the Persian Gulf War, slums have emerged on the outskirts of Jeddah and Riyadh in Saudi Arabia, giving rise to ungoverned urban spaces. Similar patterns can be detected elsewhere on the peninsula.

The fact that tribal relationships dominate life in most of the Arabian Peninsula complicates these states' ability to expand their reach and authority throughout their countries. The Yemeni government, for instance, admits that it does not have control in 16 of the country's 19 provinces. Lack of border control appears to be another important element of ungovernability in the peninsula. Many of the tribes of the region have ignored international boundaries to continue a way of life that involves social, political, and trade relationships on both sides of the border.

The Arabian Peninsula states—in particular, Saudi Arabia—are faced with expanding political violence on the part of terrorist groups associated with al-Qaeda. These groups interact and cooperate with each other throughout the Gulf littoral. A population explosion and an ethic that considers physical work demeaning have resulted in a large number of unemployed youth. These young people are unattached to the reality of the marketplace and are therefore easy victims to conspiracy theories and radical ideologies.[1] Organized crime networks are present on the peninsula, but they are not a major factor influencing the governability of the area. Criminal networks are not believed to be tied to terrorism.

Porous borders, pockets of weak government control, and religious extremism among sectors of the population make the peninsula conducive to terrorist activities.

---

[1] We are indebted to former Secretary of State George Shultz for this observation in his review of this manuscript.

Collectively, these factors provide terrorists with access to both remote and urban areas of operation and the infrastructure to move people and materiel. The region also includes targets attractive to jihadists, such as facilities of the governments they seek to overthrow and the offices and personnel of Western governments and oil corporations.

The Sulawesi-Mindanao Arc

The Sulawesi-Mindanao arc—the region comprising the Celebes and Sulu Seas and the land areas bordering on them—constitutes a single geopolitical area that affects the political stability of the larger Southeast Asian maritime region. Nevertheless, the sources of ungovernability in Sulawesi and Mindanao are somewhat different. In Mindanao, massive movements of people from the northern and central Philippines and conflicts over land have been key factors in the polarization of ethnic and religious groups and the outbreak of armed conflict. Weak law enforcement and a weak justice system manifest themselves in the privatization of justice. Clan and family feuds, known as *ridos*, are rife. Corruption is high in the Autonomous Region of Muslim Mindanao (ARMM), which remains by far the poorest region in the Philippines, with a poverty rate of an astounding 92 percent in the province of Sulu.

The Indonesian province of Central Sulawesi, the other region we consider in our assessment of the Sulawesi/Mindanao arc, has suffered largely from government neglect. The weakness of the state is evident in the communal violence that wracked the province after the downfall of the Suharto government. Incidents of violence have continued even after the signing in 2001 of a peace accord, known as Malino I, between Muslim and Christian factions. As in other parts of Indonesia, corruption among local officials is endemic and fuels illegal logging and other illegal activities.

Unlike the borders of other ungoverned territories considered elsewhere in this report, the borders of this region are maritime and have their own special characteristics. Poorly policed sea borders make the lands bordering on this maritime space, including Sulawesi, Mindanao, and the Malaysian State of Sabah, vulnerable to infiltration by Islamic extremists, as well as by smugglers and common criminals. The region is home to a multitude of religious, ethnic and criminal entities, many of which have proven susceptible to or vulnerable to co-option by terrorists. With vast tracts of inhospitable terrain and areas that are effectively outside the central government's purview, particularly in Mindanao, the Sulawesi-Mindanao arc offers conditions of invisibility that allow terrorists to stay hidden from national law enforcement and counterterrorism agencies.

The East Africa Corridor

Ungovernability in East Africa results in large part from active resistance to attempts by central governments to penetrate some sectors of society; insurgencies; civil wars and collapsed governments; and the inability of governments to assert their authority because they lack the necessary resources. Somalia, for example, lacks a legitimate government; the acting authority, the Transitional Federal Government, has no army to enforce its will and no revenue with which to produce public goods. Border control lies beyond the capacity of Sudan and Kenya, and Tanzania has had to acquiesce to Zanzibar's semiautonomy. The regime in Mozambique has limited ability to assert its authority beyond the capital. In Zimbabwe, corruption has become so profound as to distract government officials from any serious attempt at governance.

The most interesting feature of this region is the extent to which governments have used insurgent forces as proxies. At least since the 1970s, governments have commonly sponsored rebel groups in neighboring countries in an attempt to destabilize them or to deter separatists in their own countries. This has led to a chain of interlocking conflicts extending from Congo's eastern regions to Uganda, Sudan, Ethiopia, Eritrea, and Somalia.

The region's conduciveness to terrorism lies in its relatively robust financial and transportation infrastructure; its weak airport security; its abundance of arms and explosives; a widespread, indigenous Islamist network; ease of entry and exit; good sanctuaries in proximity to appealing targets; and a widely held popular perception that the future lies with outside benefactors, e.g., Islamic charities, rather than with the regimes in power. Some of the outside benefactors, of course, are sympathetic to and supportive of extremist groups. Terrorists can therefore move about the region easily and satisfy their requirements for arms, explosives, and operating bases with little fear of the authorities. To the degree governments try to exercise their authority, they are often preoccupied with local criminal networks. Geographic features such as the Jebel Kurush mountains offer terrorists secure bases with proximity to lucrative targets in the broader region. Oftentimes, Islamist fighters can expect indigenous support or at least passivity on the part of the population and active assistance from regional Islamist networks.

West Africa

In West Africa, the dominant feature of ungovernability is the exceptionally low level of state penetration, even when compared to other ungoverned territories we studied. It is no exaggeration to say that, outside the capitals and other major cities, West Africa is a vast swath of ungoverned territories, requiring repeated external interventions over the last decade—by the Nigerian-led Economic Community of West African States Monitoring Group (ECOMOG) peacemaking force in Liberia; the international United Nations Assistance Mission to Sierra Leone (UNAMSIL) force and the British in Sierra Leone; the French in Cote d'Ivoire; and the U.S. Marines in Liberia—to stabilize violent and chaotic situations or rescue foreign nationals. The exception is Nigeria, the region's hegemon, which has relatively functional state institutions compared with other regional states. Even there, however, corruption and crime are pervasive; Islamic radicalism is on the rise; and currency, arms, drugs and people are trafficked through its poorly controlled borders.

From the standpoint of West Africa's conduciveness to a terrorist presence, the dominant favorable features for terrorists are the availability of income from the trade in illegal commodities and the chaotic conditions and absence of authority that allow criminals and terrorists to operate in relative safety. Although some sectors of the population could provide a pool of potential recruits, there appear to be few indications that even ethno-religious conflicts have resulted in recruitment by international jihadist groups. This could be explained by the prevalence of Sufi traditions and other cultural factors that make West Africa less hospitable to radical messages than other regions of the Muslim world.

Nevertheless, this does not mean that terrorist operatives would not find West Africa fertile ground, particularly if extreme Islamist ideology makes further inroads. Given the porous borders between states and loose controls within states, along with an extensive gray economy that supports all kinds of illegal activity, terrorists could find West Africa a favorable environment as a sanctuary and base for operations. Recruits could potentially be generated easily through economic inducements, and those communal conflicts that do exist could be exploited to stir up further conflict.

The North Caucasus

The factors producing ungovernability in the North Caucasus are historical, ethnic, economic, religious, and cultural. Some are new; others have become deeply rooted over time. The latter include the ethos of warrior societies and a history of resistance to Russian domination dating back to tsarist times, when the expanding Russian empire conquered the region. Disaffection with Moscow's rule lay buried for decades under Soviet repression, but reemerged more pronounced than ever with the collapse of the Soviet Union. The end of the Soviet state also meant the weakening of the Russian Federation's instruments of control: the Ministry of the Interior, the Federal Security Service of the Russian Federation (FSB) (the former KGB), the local police, and the Russian army.

The North Caucasus manifests a low level of state penetration into local societies. It is estimated that over half of its economy is informal. Corruption and crime are rife. Law enforcement is dysfunctional, and the judicial system does not deliver impartial justice. The police are often on the payroll of criminal groups, and crimes committed by security forces are not investigated. The relationship between terrorists and organized criminals remains primarily a matter of business. Most criminals do not have terrorist goals but concentrate instead on making money through illegal trade of highly taxed commodities. As in other ungoverned territories in this study, there is no concept of border security in the North Caucasus. The Chechen-Dagestani border is particularly problematic because vans filled with weapons pass easily across this border with a small bribe.

Not only is the North Caucasus a theater of operations for rebel and jihadist forces, it is also a platform for operations beyond the Caucasus region—for what we refer to as operational access. The Chechens and other jihadist groups have been able to organize, train, and equip themselves freely and conduct numerous terrorist attacks within and outside the region. These groups are sustained by an increasingly radicalized vision of Islam that has taken root over the last decade of the Chechen war. Finally, the ability of terrorists to move around freely without being noticed illustrates what we refer to as invisibility. Many recruits to the Chechen cause have the appearance of ethnic Russians and are able even to enter Moscow unnoticed to carry out terrorist attacks.

The Colombia-Venezuela Border

Colombian instability derives from the interaction and resulting synergies of a 40-year insurgency against the Colombian state and the development of drug networks and a pervasive underground drug economy. The FARC, smaller anti-government guerrilla groups such as the National Liberation Army (ELN), the so-called paramilitaries, and drug traffickers all interact and exacerbate deeper problems of Colombian society, including the decay of government authority and lack of social cohesion. These problems are magnified in the border region that is the subject of this study. Numerous municipalities remain isolated by poor infrastructure, and all the illegal armed groups mentioned above maintain a sizeable presence. State penetration, though far from perfect, is better on the Venezuelan side of the border. The border is difficult to monitor and secure and provides significant opportunities for the illegal armed groups to smuggle weapons, drugs, and other contraband. Colombian insurgents have operated on both sides of the frontier and have received support from Venezuelan sources.

It is worth noting that both Colombia—despite its problems with insurgency and drug trafficking—and Venezuela have far greater state capacity than any other case considered in this book. Security indicators in Colombia have been improving, compared with previous years. The corruption perception index in Colombia is better than that of China, not to speak of the African cases, and there has been significant progress in tax reform. This means that Colombia has the institutional foundation for reform that is lacking in other states with ungoverned areas, but it also raises the question of why Colombia has been more susceptible to the development of criminal networks than other, less well governed, states.

The illegal armed groups have had years to develop smuggling routes and are able to generate hundreds of millions of dollars in illegal activities, primarily related to the drug trade but also involving kidnapping for ransom, extortion, arms trafficking, and gasoline smuggling. Existing infrastructure, such as the Pan-American Highway and developed ports on both the Caribbean and Gulf of Maracaibo, provide significant opportunities for terrorists, insurgents, and criminal networks to move materiel and personnel. Their ability to use intimidation and bribery and their knowledge of the areas in which they have been operating for years allows them to evade government forces.

The Guatemala-Chiapas Border

Poor governance is endemic in Guatemala and even more so in the rural border departments. A recent World Bank study notes that Guatemala performs at or near the bottom of several governance indicators, including political stability, government effectiveness, regulatory quality, rule of law, control of corruption, and accountability.[2] Worse, government effectiveness and the rule of law have been steadily declining since 2002. Gangs, or *maras*, as they are known throughout Central America, pose a staggering problem. The maras are exceptionally violent and, according to some reports, outnumber the police. Gangs and other criminal organizations control considerable portions of the illegal border networks that transport people, drugs, and weapons into Mexico and onward to the United States. Border guards are more likely to be involved in crime than in security. The greatest threat these gangs and criminal organizations pose is that they become increasingly powerful in a weak state, turning it into a criminal state or "narco-state." This process is under way in Guatemala, and even the vice president of the country has warned about the "Colombianization" of Guatemala.

Some aspects of the border area may be conducive to a terrorist presence. Although the region may not represent the most appealing area for Islamist terrorists (the Muslim population in Guatemala and Mexico is insignificant), its lawlessness may be exploitable by terrorists. As noted above, Guatemala provides an important staging point for entry into the United States. Possible linkages between members of the MS-13 gang and al-Qaeda surfaced in statements by U.S. and Honduran officials, as well as various news sources, but they have not been given credence by U.S. law enforcement and intelligence personnel.

The Guatemalan experience also illustrates the problem of ungoverned airspaces. There is significant airborne drug trafficking from Colombia to the Petén region of Guatemala and thence to Mexico and the United States.

Toward a Typology of Ungoverned Territories

Having outlined above the dominant features of the ungoverned territories in our case studies, the next step in the analysis is to develop a typology of ungoverned territories. We do this by evaluating each of the regions on the basis of the variables and indicators of ungovernability and conduciveness that we described in Chapters Two and Three. The methodology and some of the patterns that emerge from this analysis are described in the Appendix.

Depending on the circumstances that gave rise to their present condition of absent or ineffective governance (which in some cases go back to the process of state forma-

---

2   World Bank (2005b).

tion, as we discuss in the historical sections of the case studies), ungoverned territories align with a three-part typology: contested, incomplete, and abdicated governance.

Contested Governance

In contested governance, a group refuses to acknowledge the legitimacy of the government's rule and pledges loyalty to some other form of social organization, such as an insurgent movement, tribe or clan, or other identity group. Chechnya, Mindanao, and Colombia are prominent examples. In most cases, the groups contesting the state's authority are seeking to establish their own state-like entity. These insurgencies may be of different kinds: separatist, Islamist, or Marxist. (Although separatists usually cloak their goals in ideology, their primary goal is establishing their own state in their ethnic homeland rather than imposing their rule on the rest of the country.) In Mindanao, Muslim sultanates fought intermittent wars against the Spanish from the sixteenth to the nineteenth century, and resistance continued under the U.S. colonial rule and against the Republic of the Philippines since the 1960s. In Colombia, the goal of the rebels is to control territory as a stepping-stone to wresting control of the whole country, or to profit from illegal activities without the interference of state authorities.

Incomplete Governance

In incomplete governance, a state seeks to exert its authority over its territory and produce public goods for its populace, but lacks the resources to do so. In the Afghan-Pakistani border region, Central Sulawesi and other parts of Indonesia, throughout West Africa, and along the Guatemalan-Mexican frontier, governments lack the competencies to project effective rule into the region. Where local officials are present, they are inept at their jobs or give higher priority to other pursuits—bribes from smugglers, for example—than to enforcing the laws and border-crossing regulations. For a host of reasons, government in these areas cannot maintain a competent, qualified presence that is stronger than the sources of violence and order, such as clans, tribes, terrorists, or criminal syndicates. Other forces, some tribal, some criminal, move in to fill the vacuum that results. They intimidate and corrupt the few local officials who remain in the region.

Abdicated Governance

In abdicated governance, the central government, instead of operating to produce public goods such as safety and order, infrastructure and services, abdicates its responsibilities for poor provinces and regions where it concludes that maintaining a presence is not cost-effective or where ethnic minorities with whom the government shares little affinity predominate. In some instances, such as Saudi Arabia, the central government cedes border security to the local tribes. The Dutch, who ruled the main islands of present-day Indonesia in colonial times, ignored the interior areas of Celebes (Sulawesi) for centuries, and the region remained marginal under the Republic of Indonesia. In the North Caucasus, the collusion of security services with illegal armed bands also illustrates this type of abdicated governance and the nature of the ungoverned spaces that result.

Abdicated governance is sometimes the outcome of political decisions by those in power to operate outside the formal agencies of the states. As Dr. William Reno points out, in these cases abdication of state authority is not abdication of political control. For instance, Sierra Leone's prewar dictator, Siaka Stevens, was uninterested in building his state's bureaucracies and seemed to have taken active steps to tear them down. But he did rule, mostly through the enterprises and militias associated with his business partner, Jamil Said Mohamed, who also was the neighbor of Sierra Leone–born Nabih Beri, the head of Lebanon's Amal militia and now head of Lebanon's legislature. From the point of view of this study, this "alternative authority" network shaped (and shapes) Sierra Leonean commercial connections to Hezbollah. The situation was similar in Liberia under Samuel Doe and Charles Taylor, but with different actors.[3]

These types of ungoverned territory are not mutually exclusive. Often, regions suffer from two or all three of them. There is value, however, in identifying their causes, because they point to viable policy options for addressing the resulting problems. Understanding the causes of an ungoverned territory can also illuminate which policy options are likely to be ineffective or inappropriate. For example, where abdicated governance lies at the heart of the problem, policies that emphasize official development assistance and encourage foreign direct investment and government reform are probably sound choices. These policies would give officials an incentive to make investments in the region when they would otherwise conclude doing so was prohibitively expensive and not cost-effective. This policy assumes that the state's leadership wants to increase the capacity of state institutions. If, on the other hand, the governing style and methods of the ruling group are at the root of the problem, strengthening the state would require instigating more profound social and political change. Such states might not be salvageable through the usual institutional reform mechanisms. To change the character of such a state, if it is to be attempted at all, would be risky and expensive, with uncertain chances of success.[4]

---

[3] We are indebted to our reviewer, Dr. William Reno, for this insight and the West African examples given above. For the role of Jamil Said Mohammed and Nabih Beri in the Sierra Leone illegal diamond trade, see "For a Few Dollars More" (2003).

[4] Dr. William Reno's review of the manuscript.

When contested rule is the source of the trouble, U.S. officials face a basic decision of whether to support the incumbent government. A decision to support the government might lead to policies of counterinsurgency, official development assistance, foreign military financing and assistance, foreign military training and education, and similar options.

CHAPTER FIVE

Conclusions and Recommendations

John E. Peters and Jennifer Moroney

This chapter considers some specific options and implications for U.S. government policies, using our three-part typology of ungoverned territories to inform the discussion.

Although ungoverned territories may have different sources that require different policy mixes, U.S. policy must always address the two sets of attributes that make some of these territories actual or potential terrorist sanctuaries—the lack of an effective state presence and the conduciveness of these territories to the presence of terrorist groups. Two approaches are possible: the direct approach, targeting terrorists directly with military force, and the indirect approach, helping friendly governments extend state control and improve governance in these territories.[1] This study focuses on the second approach, but we also consider operational considerations related to possible U.S. Air Force forward deployments in ungoverned territories.

In making our recommendations, we take into account several important questions. One—which must be answered on a case-by-case basis—is, How amenable to U.S. approaches are conditions in regions of concern? For example, the United States can play only a very limited role with regard to the North Caucasus, which is part of the Russian Federation, but it can have a major impact on the Colombian government's efforts to regain control of its territory. We address this question in this chapter and in the body of the study, with regard both to the policy tools available to the U.S. government and to the U.S. Air Force under its Title 10 responsibilities. A second important question is, How are the United States government, the Department of Defense, and the services organized to address the security challenges posed by ungoverned territories?

Implications for the U.S. Government: Addressing Ungovernability

Reevaluate the Role of Development Assistance

As several of our case studies show, strengthening governance is critical. Currently, the United States tends to emphasize security cooperation and military assistance in

---

[1] See Ochmanek (2003).

dealing with the security problems that ungoverned territories generate because the capabilities of the combatant commands and the individual services that support them are substantial. But extending the reach of government should involve other activities too. One possible option could be to use development assistance as a tool to encourage recipient governments to invest in infrastructure and institutions in regions where they have previously abdicated their governing responsibilities.

Our case studies show that lack of coordination among agencies is a major obstacle to governments' ability to improve governance in ungoverned territories. Therefore, providing expert advice to officials on how to coordinate their actions across departments and minimize bureaucratic competition would be an important step in strengthening public-sector capabilities.

Upgrading the transportation infrastructure could have profound effects in many ungoverned territories considered in this study because it would improve overall mobility within society. Improved mobility means that the police and judicial officials can expand their activities to remote areas; that legal crops can be brought to market at competitive prices, reducing the attractiveness of narcotics and other illicit crops; and that other utilities—electricity and water—can reach remote regions of a country, as can health care, public education, and the rule of law. Of course, as we note throughout this study, improved infrastructure may also make these areas more attractive to terrorists.

Teaching competent government practices and building infrastructure have been military tasks in the past. Indeed, these projects occupied the U.S. Army through its early years in the Philippines, and many years later during U.S. assistance to the Republic of Vietnam. These projects might be more efficiently pursued through civilian agencies, nongovernmental organizations, and commercial firms—especially given the number of firms available to do international development work.[2]

It is worthwhile, therefore, to reevaluate development assistance to determine its role in addressing the problem of ungoverned territories. Almost certainly, there are instances where shifting the work toward development assistance and civilian agencies and away from military channels can provide relief from high military operation tempos (intensive use of military opertions) and perhaps generate other important benefits, such as allowing the Defense Department to concentrate on the military dimensions of national security and defense.

Promote Regional Architectures

International cooperation, attempted through formal international organizations, has a mixed record at best. If member organizations do not share a set of interests, it can confound cooperation and timely, effective collective action. As an alternative, the United States might promote less formal "regional architectures" to coordinate the efforts of

---

[2] For example, USAID alone lets about $4 billion annually in contracts. See USAID (2006).

those states that do share similar concerns about the effects of ungoverned territories on their security and regional stability. Such arrangements need not produce elaborate secretariats and bureaucracies. Interested countries and other influential stakeholders need only agree to work constructively to create initiatives that would in some measure limit the corrosive effects of ungoverned territories.

Because, as the case studies demonstrate, the effects of ungoverned territories—transnational crime, arms trafficking, illegal migration—may cross borders to infect neighboring states, a regional architecture might be an especially useful way to enlist neighbors for collective action. This type of international cooperation has been infrequent, but it might be feasible with strong leadership from the United States (in some instances from behind the scenes) and the constructive involvement of others in the region.

A regional-architecture approach might be particularly effective at organizing neighbors of a state where ungovernability results from contested rule. Here, the regional architecture could coordinate efforts among governments and influential local players to exert positive control over borders to prevent fighters from using neighboring territory as sanctuaries, and to deny combatants protection behind international frontiers. The regional-architecture approach might similarly enlist local cooperation to coordinate infrastructure development to project authority, order, economic activity, justice, and other public goods into multistate regions of ungovernability.

A regional architecture could also reduce a region's conduciveness to terrorism by enhancing popular perceptions of government effectiveness and competence. Members of a regional architecture could pool their resources to improve governmental practices, strengthen channels between the populace and government officials, and delegate decisionmaking to local governmental bodies, such as local councils and village advisory groups. Regional architectures also enjoy the virtue of being adaptable to circumstances. They can embrace new participants and can adjust to state failure and other changes in the security environment.

Mobilize Regional Organizations

The United States, of course, has been deeply engaged with many of the regions suffering from ungoverned territory for decades, so policy does not have to be crafted from scratch. Many of the countries involved already benefit from various forms of security assistance and broader economic assistance.

That said, emphasizing the role of regional organizations despite their unpromising records might prove beneficial, especially when trying to reduce incomplete or abdicated governance or resolve contested rule. Organizations such as the Organization of American States (OAS), the African Union (AU), the Association of Southeast Asian Nations (ASEAN), perhaps the Gulf Cooperation Council (GCC), the Organization for Security and Cooperation in Europe (OSCE), and the Black Sea Economic Cooperation Organization (BSEC) could provide forums for tackling mutual problems arising from ungovernability, forging cooperative strategies, and organizing resources for collective action.

Some international organizations will obviously have greater utility than others. The United States should evaluate all potential candidates to see what they might contribute and engage the most promising ones. For example, member countries might be induced to support a regional border security regime; support a regional police and public administration academy to train and deploy more effective, competent officials; or make additional surveillance aircraft or naval assets available for border security. The United States performs many of these functions in various regions already, but internationalizing the effort could bring more assets to the project.

Address Profound, Official Corruption Directly

This kind of corruption is commonplace in the developing world. It diverts public funds for private use, perverts due process to undermine the law, protects officials and their cronies from prosecution, and otherwise destroys the effective functioning of institutions of government for the public good. There are few prospects for reform in countries where holding office is one of the only pathways to prosperity. In fact, the incentives run the other way—toward more ruthless, repressive behavior and human rights violations to preserve one's privileges and position. In such circumstances, the United States must exercise caution to ensure that its assistance efforts do not provide lethal aid that enables a corrupt regime to prolong its grasp on power or more effectively brutalize its populace.

Security Cooperation Implications

At the level of the U.S. government, numerous capabilities-building programs can help to build the capacity of partner countries with ungoverned territories problems. U.S. agencies that oversee and execute these activities around the world include the following: Department of State (DoS), Department of Defense (DoD), Department of Energy (DoE), Department of Homeland Security (DHS) (specifically, the Coast Guard and the Department of Customs and Border Patrol), Department of Justice (DoJ), Department of Commerce (DoC), and the intelligence community.

The DoS oversees a large number of the programs focused on combating terrorism, improving border security (weapons of mass destruction [WMD]/drugs/terrorist trafficking in arms and illegal drugs, and countering the proliferation of chemical, biological, radiological or nuclear (CBRN) weapons and materials, but other agencies (DoD, DoE, DHS, etc.) typically execute the specific activities. Some of the major programs focused on these areas include the following (the executive agent is in **bold**; the executing authority is in *italics*):

- Export Control and Related Border Security Program (EXBS) **DoS,** *DoE, DHS, DoC*

- Anti-Terrorism Assistance Program (ATAP) **DoS,** *contractors*
- International Counter-Proliferation Program (ICP) **DoD,** *DoD/DoJ* (investigative side), *DoD/DHS* (interdiction side)
- Cooperative Threat Reduction Proliferation Prevention Initiative (CTR PPI) **DoD,** *DoD*
- International Military Education and Training (IMET) **DoS,** *DoD*
- Enhanced IMET (for civilians) **DoS,** *DoD*
- Foreign Military Financing (FMF) **DoS,** *DoD*
- Counter-Terrorism Fellowship Program (CTFP) **DoD,** *DoD*.

This list of U.S. government capability-building programs is not exhaustive. Multiple agencies have a role (either as the executive agent or executing authority or both in some cases) in these programs. Thousands of U.S. officials, both military and civilian, living in the U.S. or overseas, are involved in the planning and execution of U.S. security cooperation activities.

After 9/11, there has been an increase in overall security cooperation resources to some regions of the world. If emergency funding is considered, program resources allocated to Eurasia have doubled in the past few years and tripled in some cases. For example, in fiscal year 2001 FY01, Georgia received $23 million; in FY02, that allocation was increased to $50 million. Uzbekistan received about $3 million in FY01 with a sharp increase to $66 million in FY02.[3]

Currently, there are redundancies among the various programs as well as gaps, particularly in the area of border security. In terms of redundancies, several of the programs identified above, such as EXBS, FMF, CTR-PPI, and ICP, provide both border security training and equipment to foreign countries. Better coordination among them would help to identify overlaps. In terms of gaps in border security, emphasis has been given primarily to upgrading border security on land rather than to air or maritime border security. Overall, there is a need for the agencies and their program managers and executors to work together to accomplish the goals set forth in the Security Cooperation Guidance to leverage program resources and maximize impact. DoD and the USAF have a large stake in security cooperation at the U.S. government level to address ungoverned territories, but DoD program managers need to be aware of the broader picture of interagency capability-building activities, particularly because the State Department oversees and finances a large number of these programs.

---

[3] These figures include total allocation for FMF, EXBS (nonproliferation, antiterrorism, demining, and related programs [NADR]) and IMET only (Federation of American Scientists, 2007).

Implications for the U.S. Government: Addressing Conduciveness

Some of the policy prescriptions aimed at addressing ungovernability will also reduce a region's conduciveness to terrorist activities, for example, building capacity in the local military and counterterrorism forces that would allow them to stop or prevent outbreaks of violence. Other dimensions of conduciveness deserve specific policy treatments, however. This section highlights those aspects of conduciveness that might be responsive to specifically tailored U.S. policy initiatives. That said, reducing a region's conduciveness to terrorist activity could be a Herculean task, depending upon the dimensions of the problem. Therefore, some of the recommendations below are unlikely to make a region completely inhospitable to terrorism. Taken collectively, however, they may make the region less appealing, more dangerous for terrorists, and more difficult to operate in; thus, they may prompt some to look elsewhere for a support base or area of operations. Our specific recommendations follow.

Reduce Terrorist Exploitation of Infrastructure

Terrorists typically need two types of infrastructure for their activities: transportation and the means to move funds. U.S. assistance that improves airport security and the security of such forms of public transportation as bus and rail service would make it more difficult for terrorists to exploit this type of infrastructure. For example, if terrorists knew that there was a reasonable chance that police or security personnel would be patrolling train and bus stations or actively searching for suspects and persons of interest in airports, some of them might be deterred. Making training and assistance available to local governments so that they could deploy well-trained officers rapidly and in sufficient numbers, as the United States is doing in several of the regions in this study, increases the probability of detecting and apprehending terrorists who are trying to move about on public transportation.

Terrorists also need to move money and pay for purchases, so a modern money and banking system with safeguards against money laundering and software for tracking financial transactions could prove to be an impediment to terrorist transactions. Of course, the traditional *hawala* system—an informal remittance system that leaves no paper trail—still operates in some societies but may over time be supplanted by a modern banking system. Thus, any investment that the United States makes in helping countries move toward modern banking might eventually pay dividends by impeding terrorist transactions or identifying them and aiding in their prosecution.

Deny Terrorists Local Sources of Income

Some terrorists derive income from criminal activity or from the black or gray economies of the countries they inhabit. The United States therefore might help a government's efforts to suppress or reduce the criminal activities that fund terrorists. Counterdrug assistance in regions where terrorist groups are involved in the illicit drug trade can also have a counterterrorism effect. The United States might support belea-guered governments by helping them reduce their gray and black markets to deprive terrorists of local sources of income. U.S. help could include training for law enforce-ment and tax and revenue police. Other steps might include financial assistance to enable a government to pay incentives or price supports for growing legal crops or to build roads, making legal crops economically competitive to grow.

U.S. development assistance might also seek to enlarge the legitimate economy and expand employment opportunities. Policies that encourage countries to partici-pate in free-trade agreements would thus have an antiterrorism dimension.[4] Well-supervised free trade zones near borders and in port cities might also enhance the legit-imate economy and job opportunities and thus shrink the gray and black markets and, with them, the sources of income available to terrorists. Policies supporting a healthy, growing legitimate economy with expanding job opportunities might also help miti-gate another dimension of conduciveness to terrorism, specifically, demographic and social characteristics that might otherwise make a demographic cohort—unemployed young men, for instance—or other social groups available to terrorist groups.

Prevent Exploitation of Assistance Programs

The more that states fail to produce public goods—public health services, education, social welfare services—and become dependent upon programs from nongovernmen-tal organizations and private, volunteer organizations to provide these functions, the greater the probability that some assistance will be provided by organizations sympa-thetic to extremists, or that those programs will be exploited by terrorists. Therefore, U.S. programs that help governments build capacity to provide these public goods would eventually reduce the scope of terrorist exploitation. This is not to imply that civil society should not be allowed to develop. Our concern is that if government is unable to provide such services, organizations with radical agendas—for instance, Saudi-funded foundations in Somalia and Indonesia—might fill the gap.

U.S. assistance might also help in instances of incomplete governance, where a regime lacks the resources to extend services uniformly throughout the country. Uni-form, reliable delivery of public goods throughout the state's territory would in some instances help reduce the appeal of extremist groups, undermine their messages, and shrink the size of alienated communities within the populace inclined to sympathize with them.

Support the Local Campaign Against Criminal Syndicates

U.S. policies that help other states fight organized crime—for instance, assistance in developing sound police and investigative practices and an effective and impartial judi-

---

4 However, these policies could undermine the governments' legitimacy if corruption or other factors prevent the benefits of trade liberalization from reaching most of the population.

cial system—reduce a country's conduciveness to terrorists. They undermine the criminals' ability to serve as contractors to terrorist groups by supplying them with weapons and other commodities, moving their personnel and equipment safely, or providing other services. Supporting a state's efforts to destroy criminal networks and syndicates also has the effect of reducing the black and gray economies, thus reducing the opportunities for terrorists to raise funds.

Make Invisibility More Difficult to Achieve

As the case studies describe, both homogeneous and heterogeneous societies can provide invisibility to terrorists. U.S. assistance can reduce this dimension of conduciveness in several ways. First, terrorists lose their invisibility if they must present an official form of identification to authorities when entering and departing a country. Therefore, U.S. assistance that improves a state's ability to exert control over its borders—instrumentation to detect illegal entrants, coastal surveillance systems, counterfeit-resistant passports, border-crossing watch lists, biometric identification technologies, and counterintelligence capabilities—reduces the probability that terrorists can cross borders undetected.

Second, terrorists will find it more difficult to remain invisible if government officials know what to look for. Thus, U.S. assistance in the form of intelligence-sharing and warnings could be important in reducing a terrorist's invisibility and anonymity. Such intelligence-sharing is already part of U.S. counterterrorism cooperation with many countries facing terrorist threats, but transmission of intelligence across intelligence agencies is sometimes a slow process. Ways to expedite transmission in the "synapses" between intelligence agencies should therefore be a priority.

As noted at the outset of this section, many of these policies are difficult to implement and even more difficult to make significantly effective. Nevertheless, if the United States works with its partners to implement them, then—despite individual failings and inefficiencies—the overall results would help to make ungoverned areas less hospitable to terrorists and much less conducive to their activities. Taken in tandem with policies to reduce the number and size of ungoverned territories, the results could mean enhanced constraints on terrorism, the global jihad, international organized crime, and other plagues that traditionally have been spawned and nurtured in ungoverned territories.

Implications for the Department of Defense

Today's Defense Department involvement typically seeks to address specific problems arising from ungoverned territory: crime, terrorism, narcotics trafficking, and similar threats. The DoD may benefit from dealing with the phenomenon of ungoverned territory directly through the typology described in the preceding chapter. Given the pervasiveness of the phenomenon—in the Middle East, much of Asia, Africa, and South and Central America—DoD might review the capabilities it needs to address the ungoverned territory typology directly: What resources would it need in cases of contested, incomplete or abdicated governance?

Consider Ungoverned Territory in DoD Guidance

One place to start could be to make ungoverned territory a design point for the Strategic Planning Guidance (SPG). The current formulation of defense challenges—traditional, irregular, disruptive, and catastrophic—does not capture the potential influence of ungovernability. A new taxonomy would have to be invented, one that would account for the phenomenon of state failure and ungoverned territory as a source of instability that is not currently captured in the SPG. However, to the degree that understanding the origins of ungovernability in a given area sheds light on potential solutions, the department may find that dealing with ungoverned territory directly—rather than as a symptom of protracted violence, crime, and poverty—might prove useful.

For example, planning force structure to exert control over an ungoverned space could have a significant effect on end strength. Force-to-population and force-to-space ratios suitable to establish control and maintain order would be much denser than similar ratios necessary to prevail in combat and would require larger overall military forces. Substituting technology for manpower might prove to be problematic as well.

The force mix would also probably be somewhat different if ungoverned territory were a design consideration in the Strategic Planning Guidance. In addition to the usual mix of combat and combat support units, forces optimized to restore order would probably contain larger combat service support elements, perhaps with emphasis on civil engineers, military police, medical units capable of providing public health services, civil affairs personnel with deep expertise in public infrastructure, contractors for construction support, and similar capabilities.

Force packages designed for ungoverned territory contingencies would arguably tend toward standing joint/interagency task forces. They would feature linguists and interagency working groups trained for the specific cases that worried the United States. The Defense Department would surely play a central role, but it would find itself planning and exercising with a rich mix of actors from other executive branch departments: DOS, DOJ, DOE, DOC, and the Intelligence Community. A task force structure would have the flexibility to accommodate allies with a shared interest in managing ungovernability.

Another place to highlight the phenomenon of ungoverned territories around the world would be in the Office of the Secretary of Defense (OSD) Security Cooperation Guidance (SCG). The SCG directs the regional combatant commands, the services, and the other DoD agencies (e.g., the Defense Threat Reduction Agency, National

Guard Bureau, etc.) to conduct security cooperation activities in certain regions and countries pursuant to U.S. national security interests.

The SCG establishes broad priorities for security cooperation activities conducted by any of the department's elements. These priorities vary from year to year, but they generally include building allied and partner country capabilities, enhancing military-to-military relationships, and promoting access for contingency operations. The SCG also sets policy-level goals for security cooperation with a limited number of high-priority partners. The SCG does not, however, provide activity-level guidance for security cooperation. This detailed planning is left to the combatant commands and to the services.

The SCG in recent years has highlighted the threat of WMD proliferation and the movement of WMD and related materials, drugs, and of course, terrorists, across porous border regions around the world. Therefore DoD agencies are encouraged to focus their activities in countries of emphasis with border security problems to help to alleviate these threats.[5] By highlighting the specific issues associated with ungoverned territory, OSD would encourage DoD agencies to think creatively about ways to address this problem, for example, through combined exercises, specific training and equipment, and staff talks and workshops.

Security Cooperation Implications

DoD security cooperation planning is not complicated as far as strategy-to-task management is concerned. As shown in Figure 5.1, the OSD Security Cooperation Guidance is derived from several key documents developed and promulgated by the Executive Office of the President and the National Security Council (NSC). These documents include the National Security Strategy (NSS), Defense Strategy (DS), National Military Strategy (NMS), and the Strategy Planning Guidance as discussed earlier.[6]

The SCG is the derivative document for all subsequent DoD security cooperation plans and strategies at lower levels (combatant commands and services, as shown in Figure 5.1). From the SCG, the combatant commands develop their regional strategies and country-specific plans for the year. The services, also develop their strategies from a Title 10 perspective. Some of the services' strategies (e.g., the U.S. Army International Activities Plan) are program- rather than country-focused because the services control programs, not regional areas of responsibilities. Although there is a dialogue between the combatant commands and the services as the guidance is developed, the guidance comes together at the component/major command (execution) level, which for the Air Force is at U.S. Air Force

---

[5] OSD identifies specific countries of emphasis for a given year in the SCG.

[6] The Defense Strategy gives OSD-level guidance; the National National Military Strategy gives Joint Staff–level guidance.

Figure 5.1
DoD Security Cooperation Planning Process

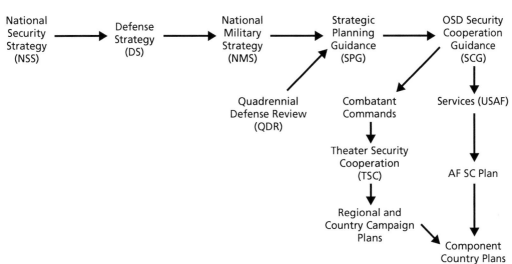

RAND *MG561-5.1*

Europe (USAFE), U.S. Central Command Air Forces (USCENTAF), Pacific Air Forces (PACAF), and U.S. Southern Command Air Forces (USSOUTHAF), respectively.

On the programmatic side, DoD executes many capability-building programs relevant to dealing with ungoverned territory. Some of these programs reside in DoD as the executive agent (in the sense that DoD has policy and resource oversight); others are executed by DoD in consultation with another executive agent, usually the State Department. Many of the capability-building programs focus on border security, counter- and nonproliferation, counter-narcoterrorism, and combating terrorism.

Because of the increase in resources, activities, and players in recent years, it is difficult to keep track of the specific events—even, for example, in an area as narrow as border security. However, similar to the broader U.S. government–level perspective of security cooperation, DoD policymakers and program managers should strive to identify redundancies and gaps in programs to improve security in ungoverned territories. Currently, there are stovepipes within DoD as well as in the broader interagency process.

The 2006 *Quadrennial Defense Review* (QDR) highlighted the training of foreign security forces as a critical component of DoD's security cooperation strategy.[7] Much of the emphasis of the QDR discussions in this narrow area has focused on the ungovernability problem. The training of foreign internal defense (FID) forces has been given a high priority with the aim of improving the defense self-sufficiency of certain countries around the world. The idea is to help our allies and partners secure their own borders and improve their ability to deal with terrorist threats and incidents,

---

[7] U.S. Department of Defense (2006).

thus reducing the burden on U.S. forces. If the need for direct U.S. combat operations arises, U.S.-trained FID personnel would be a critical complement to U.S. forces as providers of local knowledge. FID forces capable of holding their own against antistate forces are key to any viable exit strategy.

Implications for the U.S. Air Force

The U.S. Air Force faces two groups of concerns regarding ungoverned territories: operational issues and Title 10 considerations. Operational concerns center on operating from locations in or near ungoverned territories and the challenges they present. Title 10 concerns have to do with the effect of ungoverned territory on the Air Force's requirements to raise, train, equip, and maintain forces suitable for the missions and tasks that such territories precipitate.

Operational Issues

Our typology—contested governance, incomplete rule, and abdicated rule—casts the Air Force in one of three operational roles: supporting the beleaguered government in its attempts to defend its rule in the face of opposition and insurgency; assisting the government as it tries to project its authority and extend its public goods into an ungoverned region; and (rarely, but not out of the realm of the possible, as Operation Enduring Freedom showed) supporting opposition forces as they seek to displace a rogue regime.

Ungoverned territories can also extend to airspaces, for instance, air routes through South and Central America and the Caribbean that the countries affected are unable to control—routes that are utilized by drug smugglers to transport illegal drugs. Therefore, a primary role for the Air Force when supporting friendly governments, where such conditions exist, is to assist in monitoring and controlling airspaces.

The Air Force may be called upon to operate from facilities that, although they are in government-controlled territory, are nevertheless vulnerable to enemy attack. This could be especially true in circumstances where the Air Force is performing security and stability and counterinsurgency operations. Quality of host-nation support will also be a matter of interest, especially where security, both on and off the installation, is concerned. Air Force planning for foreign operating locations will also have to consider whether the United States deploys a significant ground-force presence. Depending upon the terms of the agreement between the host nation and the U.S. government, the Air Force may not enjoy full freedom of action against insurgents or in implementation of its force protection measures, some of which may fall within the domain of the host nation. These considerations will be important in designing any force package for deployment in support of the host government, especially where security forces are concerned.

In circumstances where the facilities face substantial threats, security force personnel may have to deploy in significantly larger numbers and perform more difficult and dangerous tasks than they have typically had to undertake in recent operations—for example, extended-duration combat patrols in the base security zone. Indeed, under circumstances in which the ground-force presence beyond the perimeter is limited, security force personnel may have to exert greater control over the base security zone. Where the host nation can offer only limited intelligence about threats to a forward operating location, the Air Force Office of Special Investigations may have to deploy additional personnel so that the base can develop more complete situational awareness.

Foreign internal defense activities may be central to U.S. efforts to help states with contested governance problems or those seeking to improve in areas with incomplete rule. The Air Force may find it must perform advice and assistance roles with the local air forces or other military or security forces, requiring cultural sensitivity and language skills. The Air Force may also have to coordinate its advisory and assistance functions with those of other U.S. military services, such as Army Special Forces, and Executive Branch agencies, such as the Department of State and the U.S. Agency for International Development (USAID).

Where counterinsurgency activities figure prominently, Air Force Special Operations Forces (AFSOC) may have to deploy in support of host-nation ground forces in strikes against insurgents. There may also be requirements for civic action to restore the legitimacy and popular confidence in the host government. In cases where the opposition forces are especially capable and robust, the Air Force may have to conduct combined air operations against enemy strongholds and sanctuaries, perhaps in adjacent states. These operations could involve all the supporting activities necessary for effective attack operations against major states, such as suppression of enemy air defenses and jamming support.

When supporting opposition forces, the Air Force would be functioning in an unusual role, but one that could become reality if significant U.S. interests are threatened or if American interests would be best served when the incumbent regime does not prevail over its rivals. The USAF could have an especially important role in unconventional warfare, training and equipping opposition forces. In such circumstances, AFSOC units might find themselves inserting special operators deep inside government-held territory and resupplying U.S. special forces and their local allies in remote regions, while at the same time avoiding government air and air defense forces.

It seems unlikely that support to an opposing faction would fall solely to special operations forces. General-purpose units might also find themselves supporting opposition forces from remote, perhaps third-country, airfields. Airmen accustomed to the expeditionary mindset might nevertheless face demanding circumstances if they have to operate in smaller elements and under conditions more austere than usual.

Support for opposition forces might also involve clearing landing zones, airstrips, and low altitude parachute extraction system (LAPES) zones to facilitate resupply operations.[8] Working closely and effectively with irregulars could require cultural and language skills for the airmen who will make the interface. Supporting opposition forces may also involve long, circuitous flight routes and increased maintenance requirements under difficult conditions.

Security Cooperation Implications

In October 2004, the Department of the Air Force's International Affairs Office (SAF/IA) issued the first ever USAF Security Cooperation Strategy, which is intended to provide guidance to USAF major and component commands. The USAF strategy is intended to contribute to developing the capacity of allies and friendly nations by "building cooperative relationships to ensure international access and interoperability to enable present and future expeditionary air and space operations."[9] The document provides guidance to optimize USAF security cooperation programs and a framework to facilitate transparency and improve coordination.

Like the other services' documents, the USAF strategy points out that DoD is moving toward effects-based security cooperation activities. It is no longer centered on what kinds of equipment should be provided to a specific country, but on what effects can be achieved and what activities can best help achieve those effects.[10] USAF security cooperation activities include, but are not limited to the following:

- foreign disclosure activities and technology transfer policies
- Personal Exchange Program
- AFSOC aviation advisors
- International Military Standardization Program
- counterpart visits and staff talks.

The USAF Security Cooperation Strategy does not identify ungoverned territories as a key theme or even as a key issue. But this is not surprising, given that this issue is not separated out in the executive-level guidance (e.g., SPG or SCG). However, issues such as "combat proliferation of WMD" and "cooperating with parties to regional disputes" are two themes that are related to the security effects of ungoverned territories.

The USAF is rather limited in its ability to build partner capacities on its own without the involvement of other DoD or U.S. government–level programs and subsequent resources. Air Force Headquarters seems to recognize this reality. The strategy calls for program managers to leverage security cooperation efforts to the maximum

---

[8]   These zones are runway-like strips designed to receive cargo delivered via LAPES.

[9]   Department of the Air Force (2004), p. x.

[10] Department of the Air Force (2004), p. 2.

practical extent. However, the document does not provide the specifics on other U.S. and DoD activities where synchronization to advance USAF Title 10 objectives may be possible.

Title 10 Issues

Table 5.1 summarizes the effect of ungoverned territories on several key dimensions of the Air Force's Title 10 responsibilities. The white cells are meant to indicate that the Air Force faces no major concerns, and the shaded cells indicate those areas where the Air Force should look carefully to evaluate its capabilities. As the table indicates, the Air Force's doctrine is adequate, no matter what type of ungoverned territory the service encounters.

Where organizational issues are concerned, the Air Force is generally well prepared. There are some limited concerns about organizational preparedness to deal with ungoverned territories resulting from incomplete governance but, as the table notes, the Air Force will generally be operating in a supporting role. The greatest organizational challenge relates to managing cases arising from contested governance. Contested governance cases are commonplace, as the case studies in this report demonstrate; at issue is whether the low-density, high-demand units (some of them unique), such as the 6th Special Operations Squadron, are adequate given the number of cases the Air Force might be directed to deal with.[11]

Although most airmen are highly trained in their specialties and units routinely do well on their operational readiness inspections, there are some concerns about training relative to ungoverned territories. These concerns center on additional training that might be required if airmen are to be effective in a training and advisory capacity where cultural sensitivity and language facility are required. These requirements could influence both the special-operations and general-purpose Air Force.

Equipping becomes an issue in cases of contested governance where the Air Force is directed to help a beleaguered government develop infrastructure quickly to establish a presence in a disputed region. Although this is an area of concern, contingency contracts could be placed so that units such as the Florida Air National Guard 202nd Red Horse Squadron and civil engineering units could expand their capacity to render assistance quickly if directed to do so.[12]

Although manpower is not reflected in the table, it is always a concern when the Air Force contemplates future operations. Stemming ungovernability that results from contested governance or incomplete or abdicated rule can be a long-term project. It can take years to resolve disputes over who shall rule and what form that rule shall take.

---

[11] Vick et al. (2006).

[12] The mission of the 202nd Red Horse Squadron is to provide a highly mobile, rapidly deployable civil engineering response force. The unit performs heavy damage repair for recovery of critical Air Force facilities and utility systems following enemy attack or natural disaster.

Table 5.1
Impact of Ungovernability on USAF Title 10 Responsibilities

	Contested Governance	Incomplete Governance	Abdicated Governance
Doctrine	Air Force doctrine provides for counter-insurgency activities in support of a friendly foreign government and unconventional warfare in instances where U.S. policy supports an anti-government faction. AFDD2-1, *Counterair Operations*; AFDD2-1.3, *Counterland*; AFDD2-3, *Military Operations Other Than War*; AFDD2-3.1, *Foreign Internal Defense*; AFDD2-4, *Combat Support*; AFDD2-5.2, *Intelligence, Surveillance, and Reconnaissance Operations*; AFDD2-6, *Air Mobility Operations*; AFDD2-7, *Special Operations*.	Doctrine currently addresses counterinsurgency, counterterrorism, counternarcotics, and development support, AFDD2-1.3, *Counterland*; AFDD2-3, *Military Operations Other Than War*; AFDD2-3.1, *Foreign Internal Defense*; AFDD2-4, *Combat Support*; AFDD2-5.2, *Intelligence, Surveillance, and Reconnaissance Operations*; AFDD2-6, *Air Mobility Operations*; AFDD2-7, *Special Operations*.	Doctrine currently addresses counterinsurgency, counterterrorism, counternarcotics, and development support, AFDD2-1.3, *Counterland*; AFDD2-3, *Military Operations Other Than War*; AFDD2-3.1, *Foreign Internal Defense*; AFDD2-4, *Combat Support*; AFDD2-5.2, *Intelligence, Surveillance, and Reconnaissance Operations*; AFDD2-6, *Air Mobility Operations*; AFDD2-7, *Special Operations*.
Organization	Air Combat Command can provide forces for combat and combat support operations. Flexible unit type codes facilitate modular deployments sized to the particular task. Air Force Special Operations Forces also generate forces. At issue is whether high-demand, low-density assets, such as the 6th Special Operations Squadron, are adequate given the number of ungoverned territories resulting from contested rule.	Same basic concerns as with ungoverned territories resulting from contested rule. The Air Force typically functions in a supporting role in addressing incomplete governance issues and would not usually have to shoulder the leading role in helping a government extend its presence and authority into undergoverned territory. State Department, USAID, and others would have primary role.	Same basic concerns as with ungoverned territories resulting from abdicated rule. That said, the Air Force typically functions in a supporting role in addressing abdicated governance issues and would not usually have to shoulder the leading role in helping a government extend its presence and authority into undergoverned territory. State Department, USAID, and others would have primary role.
Training	Airmen typically are highly trained in their specialties and units pass their operational readiness inspections. Additional training may be required, however, if airmen are expected to carry out training and advisory functions as part of a counterinsurgency or similar campaign. Specifically, additional language and cultural training, and advisory training may be required. Specialized training of this sort is a concern for the general-purpose as well as the special operations forces.	Additional training may be required if airmen are expected to carry out training and advisory functions as part of a counterinsurgency or similar campaign to extend the government's authority. Specifically, additional language and cultural training, and advisory training may be required. Specialized training of this sort is a concern for the general-purpose as well as the special operations forces.	Additional training may be required if airmen are expected to carry out training and advisory functions as part of a counterinsurgency or similar campaign to extend the government's authority. Specifically, additional language and cultural training, and advisory training may be required if airmen are to help government officials reassert their authority in regions where it has previously been abdicated. Specialized training of this sort is a concern for the general-purpose as well as the special operations forces.
Equipping	Air Force units are equipped for their functions. However in circumstances where the government under pressure needs help extending infrastructure into ungoverned space, Red Horse and civil engineering units may require contractor augmentation or support to manage the workload. In cases of contested government, the task may be more demanding, depending upon the quality of the opposition that disputes control of a given area.	Air Force units are equipped for their functions. However in circumstances where the government under pressure needs help extending infrastructure into ungoverned space, Red Horse and civil engineering units may require contractor augmentation or support to manage the workload. The requirement for contractor support presents few issues because an entire industry has developed to provide this type of assistance.	Air Force units are equipped for their functions. However in circumstances where the government requires incentives to extend infrastructure into spaces where it has abdicated its responsibilities, Red Horse and civil engineering units may require contractor augmentation or support to manage the workload. The requirement for contractor support presents few issues because an entire industry has developed to provide this type of assistance.

Likewise, as the U.S. experience in the Philippines and elsewhere illustrates, building government capacity and extending government authority—especially in countries facing difficult terrain—can be the work of generations. Among the many considerations the Air Force faces when contemplating the challenges posed by ungoverned territories is ensuring that it can generate the trained, capable manpower that will be essential for addressing the long-term challenges of ungoverned territories.

CHAPTER SIX

Case Study: The Pakistani-Afghan Border Region

Peter Chalk

The Pakistani-Afghan border is the prototype of an ungoverned territory that serves as a sanctuary for terrorist groups. The British annexed the area during the nineteenth century but never fully pacified the area. There were major rebellions in 1919, when Wazir tribesmen briefly drove the British out of the South Waziristan Agency capital of Wana; and in 1936–1938, when a charismatic Muslim cleric, the Faqir of Ipi, led a popular uprising in Waziristan that the British subdued by resorting to extensive aerial bombardment. The two decades of war in Afghanistan that began with the Soviet invasion in 1979 also shaped the politics and economy of the border region. It was during this period that the foundations of the networks that sustain today's terrorist and extremist groups were laid. In the years after Operation Enduring Freedom, the border region became an area of central concern in the global war on terrorism because of the presence there of remnants of al-Qaeda and of the former Taliban regime. This chapter assesses the degree of functional and geopolitical order in this border area, focusing on the agencies that constitute the Federally Administered Tribal Areas of Pakistan (FATA) and Baluchistan province, and delineates those facets of the region that seem to be conducive for harboring or otherwise facilitating terrorist activity.

The Border Region as an Ungoverned Territory

The Pakistani-Afghan border region is a 2,400-kilometer stretch of territory that comprises, on the Pakistani side, the northern reaches of Baluchistan, the FATA, and parts of the Northwest Frontier Province (NWFP). Baluchistan, which has a total land area of 347,190 square kilometers, is the largest province in Pakistan. It is made up of six administrative divisions—Quetta, Sibi, Kalat, Mekran, Zhob, and Nasirabad. It incorporates the full length of the country's border with Iran and, together with the NWFP, shares the frontier with Afghanistan.[1]

Baluchistan is the largest and least developed province in Pakistan, and much of its interior remains both unopened and unadministered (half of the population lives

---

[1]   Government of Pakistan (2001). Baluchistan covers nearly 44 percent of Pakistan's land mass.

within 85 kilometers of the capital city, Quetta). Since 2002, it has been politically dominated by the Mutahidda Majelis-e-Mal (MMA), a loosely organized religious coalition that rules in conjunction with the King's Party (PML-Q).[2] Stability in Baluchistan, already considered one of Pakistan's more dangerous regions, has further worsened over the past two years as a result of a local insurgency that seeks to secure a more equitable share of the area's sizable gas reserves.[3]

The NWFP lies contiguous to Baluchistan, with a total land area of 74,521 square kilometers. It consists of seven administrative divisions—Hazara, Malakand, Peshawar (the capital), Dera Ismail (DI) Khan, Bannu, Mardan, and Khot—and is bounded on the north and northwest by Afghanistan, on the northeast by the Northern Areas (NA), on the east by Azad (Pakistani Kashmir), on the southeast by Punjab, on the south by Baluchistan and on the west by the FATA.[4] Essentially Pashtun in ethnic makeup and overwhelmingly Muslim in religious orientation (99.4 percent), the NWFP is run according to strict Islamic precepts with a strong Pashtun tribal flavor and rejects much of the secular and modernist leanings of the Musharraf regime. Like neighboring Baluchistan, the NWFP has been politically dominated by the MMA since 2002, although in this case the religious coalition rules outright.[5]

FATA covers roughly 25 percent of the NWFP and consists of seven agencies—Bajaur, Mohmand, Kyber, Orakzai (the only agency that does not share a border with Afghanistan), Kurram, North Waziristan, and South Waziristan. Although geographically part of Pakistan, FATA is run according to a distinct colonial-era legal and administrative system. The tribal areas do not formally recognize federal or provincial laws and political parties cannot operate in the region.[6] Established bureaucratic police and judicial powers in each agency are vested in a political agent (PA), who is appointed by the governor of the NWFP as a representative of the president. These local administrators retain both an executive and legal right to ensure regulation in

---

[2]   The MMA includes Jamiat Ulema-e-Islam (JUI)–Fezlur Rehman faction; Jamiat Ulema-e-Islam–Sami Ul Haq faction; Jamaat-I-Islami (JI); Jamiat Ulema-e-Pakistan (JUP); Jamiat Ahle Hadith (JAH); and Islami Tehreek Pakistan (ITP). The coalition shares power with the PML-Q and rules the neighboring provincial assembly of the NWFP outright. See Fair (2004a), p. 287; Fair (2004b), p. 501, footnote 17; Khan (2002a); and Khan (2002b).

[3]   See Khan (2004a), pp. 50–54.

[4]   Government of Pakistan (2000).

[5]   Chalk interviews, British Broadcasting Corporation (hereafter BBC), Pakistan Bureau, Islamabad, January 2005. See also Fair (2004b), p. 501.

[6]   Although no political parties are legally allowed to operate in FATA, it is important to note that Pakistani religious groups are able to influence and sway public opinion through proxies in madrassas and mosques. The ultra-conservative JUI, for instance, particularly the Fazul Rehman faction, remains a favorite among tribal mullahs in Waziristan.

FATA and rule via a system of patron-client relations with respective tribal leaders (or *maliks*) and influential clerics.[7]

Pakistani State Penetration into the Border Regions

In many ways, the areas that constitute the Afghan-Pakistan border region remain beyond the formal functional, geographic, and technical writ of the central government in Islamabad. As noted above, FATA has a peculiar constitutional status within Pakistan because its internal governing arrangements are based on a distribution of tribal power originally established during the Raj. No federal or provincial laws are applied in the tribal areas and, although administrative and developmental funds are routed through the Ministry of State and Frontier Regions, all decisions as to how these monies are actually used are determined at the agency level.[8] Moreover, prior to the Pakistani army's 2004 offensives in South Waziristan, FATA had not had any military presence within its territorial boundaries, with the exception of the Frontier Corps, a paramilitary outfit that recruits locally but is staffed with regular army officers.[9]

In Baluchistan and the NWFP, state penetration has been complicated by the political dominance of the MMA. The Islamist coalition has played a particularly important role in blunting federal efforts aimed at education reform and at curtailing the militant and logistical activities of local Islamist armed groups known as *tanzeems*. The MMA has helped spawn an environment in both provinces (more marked in the NWFP than in Baluchistan) that espouses policies fundamentally at odds with the Musharraf government's guiding concept of "enlightened moderation."[10]

---

[7] Comments made during the Royal United Services Institute (RUSI) conference (2005). See also ICG (2004a), pp. 27–29. The essence of the PA's authority stems from the 1901 Frontier Crimes Regulation (FCR), a set of imperial-era British laws designed to stabilize the Pakistani-Afghan border areas. The FCR sanctions collective punishment of tribes and villages through the seizure of property and individual detentions.

[8] RAND field research in Pakistan, spring of 2004.

[9] Chalk interviews, Ministry of the Interior (hereafter MOI), Islamabad, January 2005. See also ICG (2004a), pp. 27–29; and RUSI (2005). Following the initiation of Operation Enduring Freedom (OEF), Pakistani troops were dropped on the borders of the Khyber and Kurram (both of which abut Tora Bora) to seal FATA from al-Qaeda and Taliban militants fleeing the coalition operations in Afghanistan. However, the military presence was confined to the frontier only and did not entail any territorial intervention into either agency.

[10] "Enlightened moderation" is the stated goal of the current Pakistani government. It aims at domestic internal reform and renewal (focusing especially on the health, education and judicial sectors); encouragement of the international community to both help resolve drivers of Islamist radicalism and engage countries seeking economic development. President Musharraf has explicitly touted enlightened moderation as the guiding framework for the future direction of Pakistani domestic and foreign policy. Chalk interviews, Ministry of Foreign Affairs and MOI, Islamabad, January 2005. See also Rashid (2003a); Fair (2004a), pp. 286–290; Fair (2004b), p. 493; Kronstadt and Vaughn (2004), pp. 8–9; and Rizvi (2005).

At the local level, there has also been a perceptible reluctance to engage or work with the central government. In FATA, the agencies tend to relate to the bureaucracy in Islamabad as an outside, largely unknown body that they neither understand nor are able to influence in a meaningful manner. Indeed, at a very basic level, the central administration is viewed as not only different but—more intrinsically—as an entity in fundamental conflict with the interests of the tribe (*qaum*). Under such circumstances, the local population has almost always supported local leaders and customs first, irrespective of what benefits the central government may be offering.[11] The government in Islamabad rules in a way that strengthens these local powerholders, with patronage channeled to intermediaries.

In the NWFP, popular identification with the center has been further undermined by the Musharraf government's active collaboration with the U.S.-led global war on terrorism. Reports of alleged American hot-pursuit raids against suspected al-Qaeda and Taliban militants hiding in the border region have further fueled discontent. These operations have prompted many, including elements of the local elite and educated strata, to claim that President Musharraf has sacrificed the country's sovereignty and is now acting at the behest of Washington.[12]

In Baluchistan, most of the indigenous population are semi-nomadic pastoralists and shepherds who adhere to a hierarchical power structure that gives preeminence to local tribal leaders or *sardars* rather than the formal structures of government.[13] As Paul Titus explains, the source of Baluch identity in contemporary Pakistan stems largely from "mobilization behind political figures who attain their standing initially from the tribal sphere and retain strong links to it."[14] Layered on this substratum of tribal particularism is resentment over the failure of the central government to provide a sufficient share of revenue from the province's natural resources.[15]

The lack of formal state penetration into the border regions is reflected in at least three respects: (1) The existence of parallel socioeconomic systems and structures; (2) lack of a monopoly of force on the part of the state; and (3) compromised sovereignty and lack of border control. We discuss each of these in more detail below.

Parallel Socioeconomic Systems and Structures

Various parallel or alternative socioeconomic systems and structures exist in the border region. Baluchistan, FATA, and NWFP currently account for the highest concentra-

---

[11] RAND research in Pakistan, spring of 2004.

[12] Fair (2004b), p. 493.

[13] Spooner (1998).

[14] Titus (1998), p. 681.

[15] According to Kachkol Ali, the leader of the opposition in the Baluchistan Assembly, state-sector gas transmission companies are generating profits in excess of 84 billion rupees each year, from which the province receives a meager 5 percent in royalties. See Khan (2004a), p. 52.

tion of madrassas in Pakistan.[16] Although these institutions vary in the type of education they impart, they all share a common trait—they are not registered with the Ministry of Education in Islamabad, nor do they adopt or recognize standard curricula as set forth by the central government.[17] While it is estimated that only 4 percent of school-aged children currently attend madrassas—a recent study by the World Bank has shown popular figures of 33 percent and higher to be exaggerated—it is noteworthy that the bulk of these schools are located in a region where the mandate of the central government is weakest.[18] Indeed, it is this very correlation that has led several commentators to advance cause-and-effect arguments that pertain to an explicit "failed state" theory.[19] To be sure, there may well be other reasons for the popularity of madrassas in the border region.[20] However, the possibility that their prominence is indicative, in at least some respects, of the government's general inability to advance viable educational alternatives cannot be dismissed.

Prevalence of an Informal Economy

Widespread tax evasion and a thriving black market in consumer goods have sprung up as a result of illicit smuggling and non-declaration of duty-payable items imported through the Afghan Transit Trade (ATT) agreement.[21] The World Bank estimates the overall value of this "stealth" economy (which has been institutionalized by corrupt customs, border, and police officials) at over $30 billion, roughly a tenth of the country's official gross domestic product (GDP) and one of the highest ratios of any state in the world.[22]

At the heart of much of this underground trading is the *hawala*—a network of finance brokers and lenders who transmit funds to and from Pakistan without physically moving money across borders or creating a paper trail. According to Citigroup, hawala flows into Pakistan are so robust that the informal economy they support defies

---

[16] Chalk interviews, MOI and ISI, Islamabad and Rawalpindi, January 2005.

[17] The proper plural of madrassa is madari, but we use the Anglicized plural for convenience. The Pakistani government has stipulated that all madrassas in Pakistan must be registered with the Ministry of Education and that these institutions should teach a fully rounded curriculum that mixes religious studies with such conventional subjects as mathematics, science, and reading/writing. In addition, individual institutions must inform the Ministry of all foreign students attending classes, each of whom is required to have a "no objection certificate" issued by his home country before being admitted. Chalk interviews, MOI, Islamabad, January 2005.

[18] See Andrabi et al. (2005).

[19] See Singer (2001).

[20] For an overview of possible alternative theories see Andrabi et al. (2005), pp. 19–21.

[21] The ATT was originally instituted in 1950 to allow land-locked Afghanistan to transport certain listed goods across Pakistan duty-free so they could then be exported through the port of Karachi. Over the years, however, these arrangements have been systematically exploited to avail the illicit smuggling of a vast array of goods and commodities ranging from electronics and truck tires to tea. See Rashid (2000), pp. 189–194.

[22] "Dark Days for a Black Market" (2001); Behar (2002), p. 84; Ahmad (2004).

"fiscal gravity" in terms of normal inflationary pressures and adverse foreign capital exchange rates.[23] Although the hawala network has been somewhat restricted following the 9/11 attacks on the United States, it remains the preferred means of transferring money among Pakistanis on account of its cheapness, convenience, and efficiency.[24]

Endemic corruption among local bureaucrats and members of the security forces exacerbates and institutionalizes the informal economy in the border regions. Over the past ten years, Pakistan has consistently been ranked in the upper 10 percent of Transparency International's Corruption Perception Index (CPI),[25] with scores ranging between 2.1 to 2.7 (out of a possible maximum "clean" of 10).[26] In common with the rest of the country, bribes are routinely paid in Baluchistan and the NWFP for everything from being relieved of a traffic fine, ensuring connectivity to an electricity supply, having a case heard by a sympathetic judge, and availing access to medical care to settling land disputes and altering exam results.[27] Alarmingly, most citizens appear to accept corruption as an unavoidable fact of life, resigning themselves to a system that is viewed as largely unfixable and wholly bereft of any effective legal recourse.[28]

Lack of a Monopoly of Force

Presence of Organized Armed Groups

The Afghan-Pakistan border areas are beset with numerous alternative centers of power. Foreign Islamist militants have been active in the border regions, particularly in FATA, which is believed to have hosted al-Qaeda, Taliban, and Central Asian extremists since Operation Enduring Freedom (OEF). Evidence of this external involvement became clear in the wake of Pakistani military sweeps through South Waziristan in 2004.[29]

The 2004 capture of Abu Farraj al-Libbi, a close confidant of Osama Bin Laden who is believed to have coordinated various assassination attempts against President Musharraf, further underscores FATA's relevance for external militants. Indeed, in many ways, al-Libbi typifies the so-called Afghan Arab that has been at the forefront of Western attention since 9/11. Although he was arrested in the Northwest Frontier

---

[23] Behar (2001), p. 84.

[24] Chalk interview, MOI, Islamabad, January 2005.

[25] The CPI provides a comparative assessment of national integrity systems based on interviews and surveys— both resident and nonresident—aimed at gauging perceived levels of corruption among politicians and public officials. Scores of 2 or less generally reflect a pervasive problem that is not being met with any concerted countermeasures.

[26] See, for instance, Transparency International (2002).

[27] Transparency International (2003a), p. 8; Haqqani et al. (2004), p. 7.

[28] Transparency International (2003a), p. 27.

[29] Comments made during RUSI conference (2005). See also Khan (2004c), pp. 60–67.

town of Mardan, he had been hiding in Waziristan for eight years, had married a local Pakistani, was fluent in Pashto, Urdu, and Arabic and had been fully integrated into the communal structure of the tribal areas.[30]

According to the Central Intelligence Agency (CIA), the tribal areas continue to form the crux of the residual bin Laden network, allegedly including the base for an "elite" unit dedicated to preparing for and coordinating major anti-Western attacks. Analysts contend that the cell, which is dispersed but able to communicate with regional affiliates around the world, now acts as the central operational hub of al-Qaeda.[31] Pakistani security sources reject these assertions, arguing that the 2004 offensives in South Waziristan (which were reportedly undertaken with the explicit support of local tribal elders) decisively eroded any foreign jihadist presence in FATA. That said, they do concede that some Waziris probably continue to give succor to al-Qaeda elements. For this and other reasons, there is general agreement that the region needs to remain a focus of ongoing counterterrorism efforts.[32]

Islamist Kashmiri tanzeems are especially prominent, including Jaish-e-Muhammad (JeM),[33] Harakat-ul-Mujahidin (HuM), Lashkar-e-Taiba (LeT)[34] and Hizbul Mujahidin (HM). While many of these groups were originally formed and trained by Pakistan's ISI Directorate to prosecute a war of attrition against India, since Pakistan's involvement in the global war on terrorism they have increasingly reoriented the focus of their aggression inward toward targets in Pakistan and Pakistani government interests.[35] Attacks such as the suicide strike on Delhi's Federal Parliament in 2001 (a joint operation undertaken by JeM and LeT that almost triggered an Indo-Pakistani war) and assassination attempts on Musharraf in 2004 (attributed to splinter cells of HuM) and senior Army leaders clearly show that these groups are neither under the control of the state nor necessarily prepared to limit their actions in deference to Islamabad's national security interests.[36]

---

[30] RAND interviews in Pakistan in June 2005 with journalists based in Lahore, Islamabad, and Peshawar. See also Haven (2005).

[31] See Risen and Rohde (2004).

[32] Chalk interviews, Interservices Intelligence (ISI) Directorate and Ministry of the Interior), Rawalpindi and Islamabad, January 2005.

[33] JeM, which was banned in 2002, now operates under the name of Khudam-ul Islam.

[34] LeT, which was also proscribed in 2002, now operates under the name of Jamaat al-Dawat.

[35] For further details on the Kashmir conflict see Varshney (1991); Wirsing (1994); Bose (1997); Ganguly (1997); Blank (1999); and Evans (2000).

[36] Two splinter groups were connected to the Musharraf assassination attempts: Jamiat-ul-Ansar and Harakat-ul-Jihad-e-Islami. The former was led by Qari Saifullah Akhatar, a senior Islamic militant accused of running training camps under the Taliban in Afghanistan, until his arrest in August 2004; the latter is currently under the charge of Fazlur Rehman Khalil, a long-time jihadist "chief" who cosigned Bin Laden's 1998 Khost fatwa affirming that it a Muslim duty to kill Americans and Jews. Chalk interviews, Intelligence Bureau and National Security Council Advisory Board, Delhi, September 2002. See also Chandrasekaran (2001); Chandrasekaran

In addition, militant ethnic groups, particularly in Baluchistan, witnessed a major resurgence of violence during 2004. As noted above, renegade tribal militias have been at the forefront of much of this unrest. In 2005, groups such as the Baloch Liberation Army, the Baloch People's Liberation Army, and the Baloch Liberation Front, were linked to no less than 141 attacks between January and June, killing 56 and injuring 190.[37]

Presence of Criminal Networks

Organized drug groups have also been active, reflecting the border region's importance as a central point for the trafficking of heroin and related substances. Officials with Pakistan's Anti-Narcotics Force (ANF) believe that as much as a quarter of the unrefined, refined and morphine-based opiates produced in Afghanistan pass through Pakistan, entering the country via FATA, the NWFP, and Baluchistan and exiting through points scattered along the Makran coast and the land frontier with Iran. Syndicates in Karachi and Quetta are believed to handle the bulk of these shipments, utilizing a network of cells, subcontractors, and brokers based throughout the northwest frontier area.[38]

Population with Access to Arms

Heightening the force projection capabilities of these groups is a profusion of illegal weaponry, ranging from assault rifles to rocket-propelled grenades. These munitions, which stem from stocks left over from the anti-Soviet mujahidin campaign in the 1980s, as well as back-street vendors on the outskirts of Peshawar, have been effectively employed to directly challenge Islamabad's monopoly on coercive violence in the border regions. The widespread availability of arms has provided criminal, religious, and politically motivated elements with tactical options that were formerly available only to the government and its armed forces. Not only has this situation allowed these alternative power centers to inflict considerable losses on government forces, it has also

---

and Lakshmi (2001); U.S. Office of the Coordinator of Counterterrorism (2002), p. 110; Masood (2003); Lancaster and Khan (2004); Terzieff (2004); Waldman (2004); Zaidi (2004).

[37] See Khan (2004a), pp. 51–63; Rahman (2004); "Baloch Will Resist Military Offensive, Warns Senator," (2005); "Four Explosions Rock Balochistan" (2005); and "Six Blasts Rock Pakistan" (2005).

[38] The overall volume of trafficked opiates has steadily increased since 2001 in line with the rapid expansion of the Afghan drug trade, with a record 34 metric tons of heroin seized in 2003. This represents a 283 percent increase over 2002 figures and a massive 466 percent increase over the 2001 total. Chalk interviews, Anti-Narcotic Force (hereafter ANF), Rawalpindi, January 2005. See also "Southwest Asia" (2004); and "Tonne of Heroin Worth $8.4 Million Seized in Pakistan" (2003).

generated a highly problematic security gap by changing the balance between state and nonstate actor to the detriment of the former.[39]

Besides empowering criminal and militant groups, ready access to weaponry has helped to give rise to a pervasive martial culture across FATA—entrenching a so-called "Kalashnikov culture" that extends beyond adults to teenagers and even children. This culture reflects the harsh living conditions found in the tribal areas, which, while not constituting a Hobbesian "war of all against all," has made it necessary for the local population to both have guns and possess the requisite knowledge of how to use them.[40]

Compromised Sovereignty and Lack of Effective Border Control

In many ways, Pakistan has been unable to assert effective control over its border with Afghanistan. The frontier is mostly bereft of roads, greatly limiting the scope for security force deployment. In addition, immigration and customs procedures are almost nonexistent and reflect the stationing of officials who, for the most part, are corrupt, underresourced, and untrained.[41] Exacerbating the situation is the difficulty of regulating cross-border movements by individuals with tribe, clan, or family ties on both sides of the border. This is particularly true of the Wazir tribes in FATA, many of whom neither recognize nor respect the Durand Line that formally marks the frontier between Afghanistan and Pakistan.[42]

In Baluchistan, there have also been claims that tribal groups have benefited from Indian training and support. Last year, the province's chief minister went so far as to assert that Delhi's external intelligence organization—the Research and Analysis Wing—had established an entrenched presence in the region and was operating at least 40 camps across the province.[43] Assertions such as these must be assessed in the

---

[39] See Chalk (2000c), pp. 7–10. Overviews of the trade in and proliferation of light weapons throughout Pakistan and South Asia can be found in Smith (1993); Gunaratna (1999); Khan (1999); Naik (1999); and Krott (2000).

[40] Chalk interview, MOI, Islamabad, January 2005. Similar comments averring to the martial spirit of FATA were made during the RUSI conference in 2005. In a briefing at RAND in October 2005, a U.S. commander in Afghanistan noted that relatively sophisticated Soviet-era weaponry is as ubiquitous in villages as SUVs and trucks in the American Southwest and that the locals hang onto these weapons "just in case" they might need them.

[41] Chalk interviews, U.S. State Department, December 2004.

[42] Chalk interviews, MOI, Islamabad, January 2005. Similar points concerning the informality of FATA's border with Afghanistan were raised during the RUSI conference in 2005. Britain drew the Durand Line in 1893 as a buffer against Afghanistan, which it believed constituted the main external threat to its empire on the Indian subcontinent.

[43] Khan (2004a), p. 55.

wider context of the Indo-Pakistani strategic rivalry, but, if accurate, they would sig-
nify an additional aspect of compromised sovereignty—external interference.

Mitigating Factors

Despite the conditions outlined above, it would be wrong to portray the Afghan-
Pakistan frontier region as devoid of any state presence or semblance of order or open
to unrestricted cross-border movement.

State Penetration
The Pakistani government has demonstrated both willingness and ability to use forcible means to extend its control over the region, including the autonomous tribal areas
formally outside Islamabad's day-to-day writ. This was perhaps most evident in February 2004, when President Musharraf successfully pressured tribal elders into endorsing
sweep-and-destroy missions against jihadists in South Waziristan. Over the course of
the subsequent 11 months, some 302 militants were killed and 656 arrested.[44] The Pakistani military has also since managed to retain a visible ground presence in the agency
as the results of the launching of an infrastructure and socioeconomic development
program. The principal components of the program are construction of roads, schools,
colleges, and basic health units; the installation of windmills, solar geysers, and micro
hydropower stations; and forestation, focused on olive grafting, tea planting, and the
preservation of oak trees.[45] Government and nongovernment commentators concur
that, if maintained, this program will provide a viable way to foster positive attitudinal
changes that could lift the tribal areas out of their current state of isolation.[46]

In Baluchistan, the reach of the central government has been extended by the
large security presence in the province, which includes major army and air bases, the
military's Staff College and specialized forces responsible for protecting Pakistan's
nuclear infrastructure (most of which is located in this part of the country). Not only
do these assets symbolize the formal, established reach of the Islamabad government,

---

[44] Figures supplied during the RUSI conference (2005). See also LeMiere (2004), p. 6; Idris (2004); and Hussain (2004).

[45] According to comments made during the RUSI conference in 2005, $39 million has so far been committed to these projects. It should be noted that central government has been attempting to open up the tribal areas and integrate them into the federal structure for several years. The events of 9/11 and the ensuing influx of Taliban and al-Qaeda fighters following OEF, however, effectively suspended these efforts until they were reinvigorated in the wake of the 2004 Waziristan operation.

[46] Chalk interviews, ISI, BBC and MOI, Rawalpindi and Islamabad, January 2005. For interesting and insight-ful analyses of the military incursions into Waziristan and their impact and possible implications see Khan (2004b), pp. 59–62; and Khan (2004c), pp. 60–64.

they also provide a platform from which to extend more concerted action, should it become necessary, for instance, to quell an escalating Baluch insurgency.[47]

Localized Governing Arrangements

Likewise, the border regions do not exist in the complete absence of localized governing arrangements. As noted above, the central government's authority in each of the FATA's agencies is represented by the political agent. The PA is responsible for administering civil, criminal, and revenue cases consistent with the Frontier Crimes Regulation and customary law. The PA is assisted by assistant political agents, for each of the agency's subdivisions and *tehsil* (district) officials (political *tehsildars* and political *naib tehsildars*), who are responsible for controlling the tribes and maintaining law and order within their tehsils.

The system of maliks, inherited from the Raj, also operates. The *malik* (leader) is the government-recognized tribal leader. He is the mediator between the government and the tribe. The position is hereditary and passes down through sons. Historically, the mullah or religious leader was subordinated to the tribal elder. The mullah's main function is to run the village mosque and conduct "rites of passage" as appropriate. However, as the result of the dislocations brought about by the Afghan war, some mullahs have developed their own power bases and spheres of autonomy.[48] Decisions are made through tribal assemblies or *jirgas*.[49] Jirga decisions are binding and, for the Wazirs at least, have the same force as dictates of Islamic law.[50]

Political parties are also part of the governing structure. The NWFP is subject to the rule of the MMA, which has a high degree of popular support in the frontier region, partly because of dissatisfaction with the Musharraf government's cooperation with Washington in the global war on terrorism. This grassroots support has been instrumental in allowing the coalition to consolidate its power base and develop a policy platform that, while not necessarily consistent with the central government's policy priorities, has ensured a relatively high degree of functional order throughout the province.[51]

---

[47] Chalk email correspondence with C. Christine Fair, May 2005.

[48] Ahmed (1991) p. 26.

[49] The jirgas exercise executive, judicial, and legislative functions and frequently act as instruments for arbitration or conciliation. They can be convened at any level of tribal organization, from the smallest group to an entire confederation and make their decisions by consensus. See Spain (1963); and Hart (1985).

[50] Hussain (2004), p. 138.

[51] "MMA Opposes Pak-US Military Drive" (2003); "MMA Says Check on Seminaries to Be Resisted" (2003); "US Trying to Destabilize Pakistan, Iran: MMA" (2003); Fair (2004b), p. 493; Khan (2004b); Kronstadt and Vaughn (2004), p. 9; Rizvi (2004).

Border Control

The Pakistani government has attempted to tighten control over the border with Afghanistan but not, it appears, with a great deal of success.[52] The United States has sought to assist Islamabad in this effort by orienting a significant proportion of its International Narcotics Control and Law Enforcement (INCLE) assistance to frontier surveillance and control. Current funding priorities include construction of border security (and antinarcotic) access roads; provision of land patrol vehicles, five Huey II helicopters and three fixed-wing surveillance ("Caravan") aircraft for a newly created air wing in the Ministry of the Interior; point-of-entry upgrades, including planned installations of computerized terrorism watch lists at all major land crossings (the institution of which fall under the PISCES program);[53] training of customs and immigration officials; and expansion of the Frontier Corps, the main security detachment in the region.[54]

Besides these initiatives, Washington has targeted components of its foreign military sales (FMS) to strengthen extended border security. Notable in this regard has been the decision to make eight P-3C Orion aircraft available to the Pakistani military, the main purpose of which is to augment aerial surveillance over Karachi and the Makran coast—the two main exit points for much of the illegal human and commodity traffic that originates in Afghanistan and passes through NWFP and Baluchistan.[55]

Despite this focus on Pakistan's borders, the Afghan-Pakistan border remains the least regulated region of Pakistan and the one where the legitimacy of the Musharraf regime is most questioned. Moreover, although U.S. security assistance has helped the Pakistani authorities to seal parts of the NWFP border, significant tracts of the 2,400-kilometer frontier remain subject to uncontrolled movement, especially in areas that are not currently the focus of INCLE programs. This is especially true of regions in Baluchistan, which, as noted above, is one of the least developed areas in Pakistan.

The various attributes of ungovernability discussed above are summarized in Table 6.1. Indicators are graded according to the following scale: high = 3; medium = 2; and low = 1. While the border region is not totally bereft of formal governing arrangements and despite moves by the Pakistani state to extend its physical presence in the area, this part of the country continues to be marked by the existence of numerous

---

[52] Information developed in other RAND studies of FATA suggests that efforts at enforcement of border controls at the local level are at best desultory.

[53] PISCES was established in January 2002 as a screening system that uses a digital photograph to check incoming visitors and residents against an established terrorism watch list that can be accessed in real-time. The program currently covers Pakistan's three major international airports at Karachi, Lahore, and Islamabad, the Port of Karachi, and the country's main land crossing with India at Wagah. The long-term aim is to have the system up and running across all Pakistan's 20 main exit points. Chalk interviews, U.S. State Department, December 2004 and Federal Investigation Agency (hereafter FIA), Islamabad, January 2005.

[54] Chalk interviews, U.S. State Department, December 2004, and MOI and FIA, Islamabad, January 2005.

[55] Chalk interviews, U.S. State Department, December 2004.

Table 6.1
Indicators of Ungovernability,
Pakistani-Afghan Border

Variable	Score
Lack of state penetration	
Absence of state institutions	2
Lack of physical infrastructure	2
Social and cultural resistance	3
Lack of monopoly of force	
Organized armed groups	3
Criminal networks	2
Population with access to arms	3
Lack of border controls	3
External interference	1

alternative centers of power, a palpable resistance to the policies and institutions of the central administration and notoriously weak frontier control.

Attributes of the Pakistani-Afghan Border Conducive to the Presence of Terrorist Groups

As noted elsewhere in this book, just because a territory is marked by a degree of ungovernability does not necessarily mean it will emerge as a base for terrorist activity. For that to occur, the region in question must have attributes that make it conducive to the presence of terrorist groups. The following section takes up these considerations more fully as they apply to the Pakistani-Afghan border and the cost-benefit calculations of al-Qaeda.

Adequacy of Infrastructure

A reasonably reliable communication, financial, and transportation infrastructure is in place along the Afghan-Pakistan border. Internationally connected banks, frequently equipped with automatic teller machines (ATMs) are visible in such major cities as Peshawar and Quetta, and a thriving hawala network exists across the region. According to the federal finance ministry, the hawala system "handles" on average $4.8 billion of the $6 billion sent from overseas to Pakistan every year.[56] A major trait of

---

[56] Behar (2002). The intensive use of the hawala network reflects a pervasive cash culture that transcends Pakistani society. Hawala has three important advantages: (1) It is cheap—broker fees usually run around 2–5 percent compared with the 15 percent commission typically charged by standard financial institutions. (2) It is convenient—funds are often delivered directly to people's home, even in remote villages. (3) It is efficient—the system is not subject to the normal bureaucratic requirements associated with international money transfers. For further details see Chandrasekaran (2001); "Cheap and Trusted" (2001); and Dewan and Saccoccio (2001).

this latter informal remittance system is its invisible quality. Because money does not physically move between locations,[57] there is no telltale paper trail for law enforcement authorities to follow. Thus, transfers are largely untraceable, offering anonymity, and hence security, to both the originator and receiver of remitted funds. The hawala is, in other words, perfectly suited to the covert designs of terrorists (and criminals), providing a secure and speedy medium through which to send and receive operational and logistical capital.

A relatively functional transportation network additionally characterizes parts of the frontier region. While most roads in Baluchistan are rudimentary and prone to frequent flooding during the rainy season, functional routes link the province with Sindh (the Loralai-Dera-Ghazi road), Iran (the Regional Cooperation for Development [RCD] highway), and Afghanistan (the Quetta-Chaman highway).[58]

Conditions are far better in the NWFP; there are some 9,440 kilometers of road in the province, of which 6,737 kilometers are paved.[59] Infrastructure development projects currently taking place in FATA will extend road links to the tribal areas, with 1,354 kilometers of highway scheduled for construction by the end of 2005 (989 kilometers have already been fully or partially built).[60] Moreover, there are at least four major highways and motorways in the NWFP, including

- the Grand Trunk, the largest national highway in Pakistan, allowing travel between the Federal capital and Peshawar (167 kilometers) in around two and a half hours [61]
- the N-55, which starts in Peshawar and passes through Kohat, Bannu, and DI Khan, traversing the entire length of the province
- the N-35, which starts at Hassan Abdal and ends at the Hunjrab Pass border point in China, passing through the NWFP between Jarikas and Tahkot

---

[57] Dewan and Saccoccio (2001) describe operation of the hawala system in the following terms:

> The operator of a hawala is a thadekar. A fee, traditionally, five percent of the amount to be transferred, is charged for the service. When a person wishes to transfer money, the thadekar of one hawala contacts his counterpart in the other location. This is now usually done via e-mail. Within minutes, the originating thadekar gets a response from the recipient thadekar, confirming that there is enough cash on hand to complete the transfer. To verify the transaction, a password is shared among the donor, recipient, and the two thadekars. The recipient must provide his thadekar with the password to receive the money. The system is based on trust between the two thadekars, in a relationship that develops over the years. The cash debt is settled later between the two thadekars.

[58] Government of Pakistan (2001).

[59] Government of Pakistan (2000).

[60] Comments made during the 2005 RUSI conference.

[61] The Grand Trunk highway starts in Kabul, Afghanistan, and ends in Calcutta, India; the portion that falls in the NWFP lies between Khairabad and Torkhum and constitutes the main trade route between Pakistan and Afghanistan.

- the M2, which consists of four vehicular lanes, intended to form Pakistan's main motorway. Construction has been completed on the Islamabad-Rawalpindi-Lahore section, with plans calling for the road to be eventually extended to Peshawar over the next several years.[62]

A reasonably robust public transport system is also in place, both in Baluchistan and the NWFP. Buses, minivans, and trains allow for travel between villages and towns in each of the provinces and from there to other locations in Pakistan.[63] Railways provide additional inter- and intraprovincial connections; although slow and infrequent in Baluchistan, branch lines in the NWFP cater to express as well as inter-city trains.[64] There are also several airports and landing strips in the two provinces, six in the NWFP, and 11 in Baluchistan.[65] The principal hubs are Peshawar and Quetta. The former serves eight airlines: Pakistan International Airlines (PIA), Qatar Airways, Emirates, Gulf Air, Shaheen, Aero Asia, Bhoja, and Saif Air, with 114 departures and 113 arrivals per week.[66] The latter offer regular schedules, via PIA, to Karachi (daily), Lahore (four days a week) and Islamabad (five days a week) as well as one international route to Sharjah; international connections to Muscat and Oman are also available from Gwadar and Pasni.[67]

Besides finance and transportation, there is a range of options for communications. Internet cafes are plentiful and cheap in such cities as Quetta and Peshawar; postal and DHL offices provide outlets for surface mail, airmail, and freight; and there are numerous telephone and telegraph bureaus from which to make national and international calls. There is comprehensive satellite coverage across the region, providing wireless connectivity that extends to even some of the more rural, outlying areas of the NWFP and Baluchistan (see Tables 6.2 and 6.3).

Combined, these traits provide a functional infrastructure that is quite clearly capable of sustaining various terrorist support activities. Not only do hubs exist for facilitating inter-cadre contact and physical movement, the hawala system provides a sec-

---

[62] Government of Pakistan (2000).

[63] Author observations and interviews, Peshawar, January 2005.

[64] The Sibi-Harnai rail link, for instance, has the unenviable reputation of being the slowest in the world—it takes between 7 and 12 hours to cover a distance of only 52 miles.

[65] The NWFP's are in Peshawar, DI Khan, Saidu Sharif, Chitral, Bannu, and Parachinar; Baluchistan's are in Quetta, Khuzdar, Sibi, Zhob, Loralai, Turbat, Sui, Gwadar, Pasni, Jiwani, and Dalbandin. Most of these take the form of landing strips rather than formal airports.

[66] Government of Pakistan (2000); author observations during field research, January 2005.

[67] Government of Pakistan (2001).

Table 6.2
National Telecommunication Region (NTR) Capacity in NWFP

Exchanges	Total	Digital	Analog	Manual
Installed exchanges	515	335	35	145
Installed capacity	435,836	384,156	37,700	13,980
Working connections	333,520	300,225	22,721	10,574

SOURCE: Pakistan Telecommunication Corporation Limited, Peshawar, 1998.
NOTE: 1998 figures are the latest currently available.

Table 6.3
Telephone Capacity in Baluchistan

Exchanges	Total	Digital	Analog	Manual
Number of exchanges	229	88	15	126
Capacity	114,484	99,134	7,100	8,250
Working connections	83,214	74,958	4,148	4,108
Spare capacity	31,270	24,176	2,952	4,142

SOURCE: Western Telecomm Region, Quetta, 2000.

ure and speedy medium through which to transmit operational and logistical capital. Western intelligence sources particularly emphasize the importance of this latter facet, asserting that Pashtun thadekars (hawala operators) based along the frontier have long been used to facilitate al-Qaeda's covert monetary transfers and continue to play a pivotal role in financially underwriting the operations of jihadist networks.[68]

Operational Access

Areas in the immediate vicinity of the border generally lack attack venues that would be of interest to al-Qaeda or its affiliates—foreign tourists, symbolic government buildings and diplomatic missions, Western-owned banks, businesses and hotels, international schools, and foreign aid offices. However, the existence of a functioning transportation network means that the border region can serve as a base from which to launch strikes in other parts of the country where more lucrative targets are located. Several high-profile attacks attributed to al-Qaeda and affiliated indigenous and foreign groups operating out of the border region have taken place in Pakistan over the past three years, including two bombing attacks against President Musharraf's motorcade in Rawalpindi (December 2003); and the bombings of the Karachi Sheraton Hotel (May 2002); the U.S. Consulate, again in Karachi (June 2002); an international

---

[68] Chandrasekeran (2001); "Cheap and Trusted" (2001).

church in Islamabad (May 2002); a Christian missionary school in Jhika Gali (August 2002); and the Islamabad Marriott Hotel (October 2004).[69]

Sources of Income

The Afghan-Pakistan border is replete with revenue sources that can be tapped to underwrite and support logistical and operational activities. Apart from a thriving underground trade in commodities and consumer items ranging from tractor tires to clothes and chinaware, an entrenched drug economy has been established throughout the NWFP and Baluchistan. As previously noted, these provinces form the primary conduit through which Afghan narcotics are trafficked to major international airports at Lahore, Islamabad, and Karachi, as well as exit points located along the Makran coast and Iranian border.[70]

The temporary ban on poppy cultivation instituted under the Taliban in 2000, combined with the subsequent failure of eradication policies enacted in the absence of viable alternative development programs, made the farm-gate cost of opium soar between 2002 and 2003 to an average of $650 per kilogram. Although prices declined in 2004, they remain at least double the median of $30–$40 during the 1990s.[71] More significantly, the overall markup of Afghan opiates remains as great as ever. The cost of a kilogram of refined heroin that might fetch around $1,000 after passing into Pakistan rises to between $130,000 and $150,000 when sold on the streets of Europe.[72]

While it is not known to what extent al-Qaeda has exploited the Afghan drug trade, there is widespread speculation that the network has pragmatically engaged in trafficking as a means of funding.[73] Affiliated Islamist groups have shown no compunction in engaging in criminal endeavors that are ostensibly prohibited by Islam, arguing that such pursuits are fully legitimate if used to prosecute the war against "nonbelievers."[74] This is perhaps best illustrated by jihadists in Chechnya and Uzbekistan, who are currently believed to net approximately $120 million from opiates smuggled out

---

[69] Adil (2002); Matri (2002); "Pakistan Bombing Bears Stamp of Bin Laden," (2002); "Musharraf Survives Second Assassination Attempt in Two Weeks" (2003); Shahzad (2004).

[70] Chalk interviews, ANF, Rawalpindi, January 2005.

[71] Gall (2004); McGirk (2004); Chouvy (2005), p. 27; Gall (2005). Afghanistan currently accounts for roughly 80 percent of the world's supply of opiates, generating profits that, in 2004, were in the range of $2.8 billion (which equals approximately 60 percent of the country's legitimate GDP).

[72] Galeotti (2005), p. 34.

[73] Al-Qaeda is not thought to engage in opiate production; rather, it enters the drug chain at the trafficking level where markups and associated profits are far higher. See Gall (2004).

[74] See, for instance, Rotella (2004).

of Afghanistan.[75] Western officials contend there is little, if any, reason to believe that al-Qaeda is not similarly benefiting from direct involvement in narcotics sales, particularly given the sustained international effort that has been directed at dismantling its quasi-legitimate global financial empire after 9/11.[76] Indeed, according to a U.S. congressional fact-finding mission to the Pakistani-Afghan border region in 2004, bin Laden is presently reaping as much as $24 million a year from just one heroin network based in Qandahar.[77]

Even if this estimate is high, there is strong circumstantial evidence pointing to at least residual involvement in drug trafficking by al-Qaeda. Documenting some of the more notable cases that have been established in this regard, Tim McGirk of *Time Asia* observes that Afghanistan has emerged as the crux of a heroin-trafficking enterprise that is a principal source of funding for the Taliban and al-Qaeda terrorists:

> [A] smuggling network [is now in place] that is peddling Afghan heroin to buyers across the Middle East, Asia and Europe, and in turn is using . . . drug revenues to purchase weapons and explosives. . . . Recent busts have revealed [the scope of these activities]. On New Year's Eve [2003], a U.S. Navy vessel in the Arabian Sea stopped a small fishing boat that was carrying no fish. After a search, says a western antinarcotics official, "they found several al-Qaeda guys sitting on a bale of drugs." In January [2004], U.S. and Afghan agents raided a drug runner's house in Kabul and found a dozen or so satellite phones. They had been used to call numbers linked to suspected terrorists in Turkey, the Balkans and Western Europe. "It was an incredibly sophisticated network," says the official. In March [2004] U.S. troops searching a suspected terrorist hideout in Oruzgan province after a firefight found opium with an estimated street value of $15 million.[78]

Favorable Demographic and Social Features

Presence of Extremist and Criminal Groups

As noted above, the border region is home to a multitude of extremist religious, ethnic, and criminal entities, many of which have proven susceptible or vulnerable to co-option by outside jihadists. This is perhaps best reflected in the contemporary stance

---

[75] Ghafour (2004); Galeotti (2005), p. 34. In similar vein, the Taliban financed the bulk of its war effort against the Northern Alliance (NA) on profits gleaned from Afghan opiates. According to the Paris-based Observatoire Geopolitique de Drouges, the movement netted at least $60 million from the heroin trade between 1996 and 2000, which was used to purchase everything from weapons and ammunition to food, fuel, clothes, and transportation. See "Iran's Muscle Flexing" (1998); "Islamic Nerves" (2000); Leader and Wiencek (2000), p. 52; Rashid (2000), Chapter 9; and Chalk (2003a), p. 201.

[76] Gall (2004).

[77] Scarborough (2004).

[78] McGirk (2004).

of groups such as JeM and HuM. Traditionally oriented toward local objectives in Kashmir, these groups have quite clearly shifted their ideological focus to a more international agenda that both buys into and seeks to propagate the broader global Islamist war against the West.[79]

According to Indian intelligence sources, indigenous and foreign jihadist organizations have also managed to establish pragmatic links with criminal groups based in Pakistan, both to facilitate the purchase of arms and explosives and to aid the covert movement of operational cadres within and beyond the country's borders. Indian government and security officials continue to assert that the 2003 bombings in Mumbai[80] and the earlier 2002 attack on the federal parliament building in Delhi were, at least partly, the result of an intimate Islamist-criminal nexus that connected Kashmiri and sectarian extremists to criminal elements in Peshawar, Quetta, and Karachi.[81]

Supportive Social Norms

FATA and Baluchistan are each characterized by established codes of conduct that regulate and constrain behavior within the wider community. In the tribal areas, Pashtunwali predominates. Pashtunwali comprises all the values and social norms that determine the way of life of the Pashtuns. It is an all-embracing regulator for the preservation and conservation of the society and for the behavior patterns of the individual, as well as the means of identification and differentiation in relation to other ethnic groups. In other words, Pashtunwali includes everything a Pashtun should or should not do.[82] Pashtunwali places a primary injunction on the individual to avoid bringing shame on himself or herself, their families or clan.

Some scholars maintain this code should be viewed as "tribal law," noting that it encompasses a wide range of reciprocal obligations, including *melmastia*, which requires showing hospitality to all guests without expectation of reward; *badal,* a duty to avenge an insult or injustice, even if unintended; *nanwata* (literally, "going along with the elders to the place of one's enemy"); magnanimity in reciprocation for the abasement of the offending party, leaving the offended party no option but to accept

---

[79] Chalk interview, BBC, Islamabad, January 2005.

[80] The Mumbai attacks left 52 people dead and more than 150 injured and, according to Indian sources, were an attempt to reenact the March 1993 bombings that killed almost 300 people. See, for instance, Luce and Merchant (2003).

[81] Chalk interviews, Research and Analysis Wing (RAW) and National Security Council, Delhi, September 2003.

[82] Steul (1981).

the petitioner's entreaty.[83] Finally, *nang* formalizes a responsibility for Pashtun males to defend the honor of their women, family, and clan.[84]

The concept of melmastia requires that any supplicant should enjoy the host's protection and should neither be harmed nor surrendered to an enemy. This communal norm has been strengthened over the past two decades as a consequence of the large foreign presence in FATA since the Afghan war. Many of these outsiders, which included ex-mujahidin fighters, married local women and settled in the tribal areas, creating a social fabric replete with a strong Arab influence.[85]

In Baluchistan, a similar concept of honor operates. Stemming from the nomadic tradition of much of the province's indigenous population, this code establishes a hierarchical order that encompasses, unifies, subsumes, and orders otherwise weak or destructive groups and individuals. Integral to the notion of Baluch "character," this code embodies and formalizes the virtues of honesty, loyalty, faith, and hospitality.[86]

Western intelligence analysts believe that these cultural and demographic traits were critical determinants in shaping the strategic relocation calculus of both the Taliban and al-Qaeda following the Tora Bora operation in late 2001. The border provinces—especially the remote agencies of FATA-were judged to be the most desirable place from which to recover and recoup losses inflicted at the hands of the U.S.-led coalition on account of their tribal affinity with people living west of the Durand Line.[87]

In addition to specific militant and criminal groups, the frontier regions appear to account for the highest concentration of unregistered madrassas in Pakistan.[88] Moreover, while the majority of madrassas in Pakistan are associated with the Barelvi school, with its Sufi and syncretic influences, in the border region most madrassas inculcate the more puritanical Deobandi and Ahl-e-Hadith interpretations. Because most of these schools are not registered with the Ministry of Education, there is little way of knowing what they teach, where their students come from, or what activities might be

---

[83] Once the petitioner has humbled himself, tribal elders determine the size of either the indemnity to be paid or the land to be given by the petitioner to the offended party. The offended party often refuses any compensation from the petitioner, offering the offender an unconditional pardon. Anything less is regarded as ungracious. Hussain (2004), pp. 23–24.

[84] See Ahmed (1991), p, 24; Hussain (2000), pp. 23–24; and Beattie (2002), p. 8.

[85] Because Pashtuns are endogamous in their marriage arrangements, they are quite prepared to allow their daughters to marry Afghan Arabs—whom they trust and respect as freedom fighters. As Chris Fair pointed out in a May 2005 email to Chalk, this is one of the main reasons explaining the prominence of foreigners in the FATA.

[86] Spooner (1987), p. 63; Titus (1998), p. 670.

[87] Comments made during the RUSI conference, 2005. See also Khan (2004c), pp. 60–67.

[88] Estimates of the total number of unregistered madrassas in Pakistan range from 25,000 to 50,000. However, these figures are based on unverifiable sources and the exact number has yet to be empirically validated. See Andrabi (2005), pp. 7–8.

taking place there.[89] Some madrassas—for instance, the Uloom Haqqania madrassa east of Peshawar, were set up to supply fighters for the anti-Soviet jihad in Afghanistan; Haqqania's alumni include at least eight senior Taliban leaders. There is a highly concentrated patchwork of these institutions across Baluchistan and the NWFP, a number of which are known or widely suspected to have hosted radical Arab extremists whose teachings and sermons have been geared solely toward jihadist recruitment and indoctrination. Moreover, there is speculation that at least some Middle Eastern–funded schools provide a measure of more-directed military training—both to Pakistani and foreign students—under the veneer of spiritual guidance and instruction.[90] A 2003 World Bank study estimated that as many as 15 to 20 percent of Pakistan's madrassas may be engaged in "extra-curricular" activity of this type.[91] According to Samina Ahmed and Andrew Stroehlein of the International Crisis Group, extremist schools account for about 15 percent of the madrassas in Pakistan.[92]

Invisibility

As noted above, U.S., Afghan, and Indian sources believe that FATA and Baluchistan have been systematically penetrated by al-Qaeda, Taliban, and Central Asian militants since 9/11 and that the border districts continue to serve as important basing and recruiting grounds for extremists. The environment in the border region certainly gives foreign jihadists what we refer to as invisibility, that is, the ability to blend into the local population and escape detection by the authorities. Nevertheless, because the region constitutes a main focus of the global war on terrorism, its residents cannot be considered invisible in terms of international security concerns. There are also aspects of the jihadist presence on the border region that might be visible to the Pakistanis. The ISI is widely held to have the best overall picture of the scope and dynamics of Islamist radicalism in the wider South Asian theater, not least because of its active role in supporting groups such as LeT, HM, and JeM in Kashmir and fostering the growth of the Taliban between 1996 and 2001.

Table 6.4 summarizes the conduciveness of the Afghan-Pakistan border region to a terrorist presence. As before, the indicators are graded according to the following

---

[89] Chalk interviews, MOI, Islamabad, January 2005.

[90] Chalk interviews, U.S. State Department Office of the Coordinator for Counterterrorism and MOI, Washington, D.C., and Islamabad, December 2004–January 2005. See also Stern (2000), pp. 115–126; ICG (2004c); and Kronstadt and Vaughn (2004), pp. 7–9.

[91] "Editorial: Retreating on the Madrassas" (2002); Looney (2002); Malik (2002); Fair (2004b), p. 494.

[92] Ahmed and Stroehlein (2005).

Table 6.4
Indicators of Conduciveness to Terrorist Presence, Pakistani-Afghan Border Region

Variable	Score
Adequacy of infrastructure	
Communications	2
Financial transactions	2
Transportation	2
Operational access	2
Favorable demographics	
Presence of extremist groups	3
Supportive social norms	3
Preexisting state of violence	2
Criminal syndicates	2
Sources of income	3
Invisibility	2

scale: high = 3; medium = 2; and low = 1. Factors that seem particularly important in terms of facilitating a militant extremist presence are favorable demographics combined with viable income-producing opportunities and an infrastructure that can be used to avail operational access to other parts of the country. The high visibility of the area in terms of the global war on terrorism does not yet seem to have decisively affected the area's perceived conduciveness for terrorist activities.

U.S. Policies and Programs

Scope of U.S. Counterterrorism Assistance Program

The importance of Pakistan in the war on terrorism is reflected in the dense network of U.S.-Pakistani military-to-military relations that has developed since the onset of coalition operations in Afghanistan, and in the size of the U.S. security assistance program. The main vehicle for bilateral military cooperation is the U.S.-Pakistan Defense Consultative Group (DCG). The DCG, moribund since 1997, was reestablished during President Musharraf's visit to Washington in 2002. The DCG is co-chaired by the U.S. Under Secretary of Defense for Policy and Pakistan's Defence Secretary and has working groups on military cooperation, counterterrorism, and security assistance.[93]

A wide range of activities is also carried out under the auspices of the U.S. Central Command (CENTCOM). These include official visits; bilateral Joint Staff talks; multinational service conferences—including, on the part of U.S. Air Forces, U.S. Central Command Air Forces (USCENTAF), an Applied Communications and Information

---

[93] Congressional Research Service (2005).

Networking conference, a coalition safety conference, and ten safety staff visits in FY05—combined exercises; USCENTAF combined exercises (Falcon Talon); Special Operations Command Central (SOCCENT) exercises and Joint Combined Exchange Training, and intelligence exchanges, among other activities.[94]

Three billion dollars in security assistance have been proposed for the country over the five-year period after 2005, which is to be split equally between foreign military financing (FMF) and economic support funds. FMF for Pakistan was $74,560,000 in FY04, $148,800,000 (estimated) in FY05, and $300,000,000 (requested) in FY06, making Pakistan, for each of these years, the largest recipient of FMF after Israel and Egypt.[95] In addition, the funding for the IMET program in Pakistan was $1,353,860 in FY04, $2,999,213 in FY05, and $2,044,000 (requested) in FY06.[96] The purpose of this assistance is to sustain Pakistan's cooperation in the global war on terrorism, and beyond that, to lay the groundwork for a long-term bilateral relationship that fosters and consolidates an internal environment hostile to militant extremism—one of the key recommendations of the 9/11 Commission Report.[97]

In addition to the FMF package, the United States has devoted funds to help support specific counterterrorism and law enforcement initiatives in Pakistan, primarily through the State Department's Bureau of International Narcotics and Law Enforcement and the Office of the Coordinator for Counter-Terrorism (S/CT), which were respectively allocated $31.5 million and $11 million for programs in Pakistan in FY04. Funds have been directed toward the following principal areas:

- construction of border security (and antinarcotic) access roads
- development of a newly created air wing in the Ministry of the Interior, specifically through the provision of five Huey II helicopters and three fixed-wing "Caravan" spotter planes to augment aerial surveillance
- training of customs and immigration officials
- expansion of the Frontier Corps, the main security detachment in the Afghan border region
- formulation of a comprehensive system of command and control to strengthen frontier control in the NWFP
- establishment of a dedicated Counter-Terrorism Special Investigation Group at the National Police Academy in Rawalpindi

---

[94] Unclassified parts of CENTCOM Theater Security Cooperation Implementation Plan, FY05.

[95] Not counting Afghanistan and Iraq.

[96] FMF figures in U.S. Department of State (undated-b). IMET figures in U.S. Department of State (2005).

[97] Chalk interviews, U.S. Department of State, December 2005. See also The National Commission on Terrorist Attacks Upon the United States (2004).

- installation of computerized terrorism watch lists at all major points of entry (the PISCES program)
- establishment of an automated national fingerprinting identification system.[98]

Pakistan also participates in the Counter-Terrorism Fellowship Program (CTFP), an international Defense Department program to provide nonlethal counterterrorism training to foreign military officers. Under this program, Pakistani officers received training with a dollar value of $1,136,302 in FY04 and $469,769 in FY05.[99]

For its part, the Pakistani state, within its limitations, was willing to work with the United States after 9/11 in prosecuting the global war on terrorism. This was especially evident following two assassination attempts against President Musharraf in 2003, which were apparently part of a wider radical Islamist plot to provoke a crisis that would lead to the fall of the government.[100] Perhaps the clearest indication of the Pakistani government's resolve came in 2004 with the army sweeps in South Waziristan, marking the first time that Islamabad had intervened directly in the territory of the tribal areas. The operations were conducted at considerable cost to the military. Between their initiation in February and termination in December, a total of 221 government soldiers lost their lives, with a further 482 sustaining serious battlefield injuries.[101]

Partner Country Willingness, Capabilities, and Deficiencies

Although Pakistan affirms that it remains fully committed to the war against terrorism, questions have been raised over the sincerity of the central government's resolve to limit jihadist activities along the Afghan border. American intelligence officials have claimed there are increased indications that al-Qaeda has been allowed to reconsolidate an operational hub in North Waziristan that is now being used to train and direct operatives. According to these sources, one of the principal factors responsible for this worrisome development was the 2006 decision by Musharraf to redeploy troops in FATA to designated camps as part of an negotiated deal with tribal leaders to end support for cross-border Taliban attacks into Afghanistan. That said, informed observers contend that jihadist elements have conspicuously moved to exploit the heightened

---

[98] Chalk interviews, U.S. State Department, Washington D.C., December 2004, and FIA, Islamabad, January 2005.

[99] U.S. Department of State (2005).

[100] Chalk interview, British Security Service Joint Anti-Terrorist Group (JATG), London, January 2005.

[101] Professor Richard Bonney, Director of the University of Leicester's Program for South Asian Security Studies, points to this operation and the Pakistani army's willingness to take casualties as indications of Pakistan's resolve to play a firm and decisive role in rolling back the operational and logistical jihadist hubs that are located within the country's borders. Comments made during RUSI conference, 2005.

latitude afforded by the demilitarization of FATA and that this has been availed with either the backing, or at least indifference, of the ISI.[102]

Beside the issue of political will, there is reason to doubt the ability of Pakistan to maintain an active counterterrorist footing. The police have little knowledge about basic skills in collecting evidence, following chains of custody, or undertaking other necessary operations to conduct investigations. Law enforcement agencies also have few technical resources at their disposal. The state has no centralized criminal database and, until recently, no forensics laboratories were available for assembling evidence against criminal or terrorist suspects.[103]

In addition, the Pakistani government lacks both the human and technical means to monitor and maintain the integrity of its rugged and porous border with Afghanistan and Iran. Although immigration procedures at major points of entry are somewhat more comprehensive, international airports have only recently begun operationalizing a digitized system for tracking those arriving in and leaving the country.[104]

In recognition of these materiel and personnel shortcomings, the United States has moved to invest considerable resources in helping to bolster and improve Pakistan's civil security infrastructure. The bulk of this assistance takes the form of FMF, INL, and S/CT funding, which is designed to achieve four interrelated objectives:

- Bolster Pakistan's counterterrorism capabilities.
- Fortify the policy instruments that can be brought to bear against the criminal and other enterprises that support militant radicalism.
- Address the underlying dearth of security and governance that creates a permissive environment for extremism.
- Enable the national government to effectively project authority and the rule of law throughout its national territory.

To be sure, U.S. aid is helping to address some of the more glaring deficiencies in Pakistan's domestic security setup. The automated PISCES border screening system, the national fingerprint identification system, and the dedicated Counter-Terrorism Special Investigating Group have been particularly useful, providing the foundation for a far more robust regime of frontier control as well as the means to undertake decisive terrorist and related criminal investigations.[105] However, two interrelated problems exist with the assistance package as currently configured: First, programs have been

---

[102] These judgments are based on RAND fieldwork in Afghanistan in 2006 and 2007.

[103] The United States provided Pakistan with its first forensics laboratory in 2002; the functional level and capacity of this facility remains to be seen.

[104] For an overview of Pakistan's deficient internal security arrangements, see Fair and Chalk (2006). See also Schaffer (2004).

[105] Chalk interviews, MI and FIA, Islamabad, January 2005.

formulated in an ad hoc fashion and continue to proceed in the absence of a wider integrative framework. Second, in the absence of metrics to compare results, the effectiveness and relative utility of specific components of U.S. support has been difficult to determine.[106]

Policy Implications and Conclusions

The Pakistani-Afghan border area remains plagued by a multitude of security and governance challenges. Numerous well-armed alternative centers of power exist across the region, including Baluch ethno-nationalist militants and Kashmiri jihadists. The latter are proving to be especially problematic, not least because the focus of their violence has increasingly taken on a directed antigovernment slant since President Musharraf aligned his government with the United States in the war on terrorism. The main danger is that these groups will make a common cause with extraregional extremists, confronting Islamabad with a radical Islamist challenge that its security forces may be unable to control.[107]

In addition to extremist threats, an endemic culture of organized criminal activity exists in the frontier region, embracing everything from documentation forgery and money laundering to drugs and commodity smuggling. The narcotics trade has proven to be an especially favored pursuit, with dealers and subcontractors in NWFP and Baluchistan playing a key role in the movement of Afghan heroin to markets in Central Asia, Russia, and Europe. The trafficking of opiates carries dangers in its own right—both in terms of fostering addiction and corruption and providing a viable source of income to extremists. American security officials remain concerned about the possibility that al-Qaeda has already moved to profit from the sale of heroin and is now using this revenue to sustain its ongoing war against the West.

Further complicating the security situation is a limited formal state presence throughout much of the border area, something that is particularly apparent in FATA, where the government's writ has been no more than tenuous at best and, as noted, at the time of writing has been effectively curtailed altogether.

In spite of these challenges, there is little doubt of the importance that the United States attaches to Pakistan.[108] Indeed, since reversing its policy in Afghanistan, Pakistan has emerged as a central partner to the United States in the war on terrorism,

---

[106]Chalk interviews, U.S. Department of State, Washington D.C., November 2004.

[107]This view is widely held by U.S. officials, both in Washington and at the American embassy in Islamabad, who were interviewed by the author of this chapter.

[108]Officials at the U.S. Department of State interviewed in December 2004 universally acknowledged the importance of Pakistan's role in the global war on terror and praised its general willingness to work with Washington in pursuit of this campaign.

playing a critical role in helping to degrade the operational capabilities of al-Qaeda and Taliban elements fleeing Afghanistan in the wake of Operation Enduring Freedom. Arguably more significantly, Islamabad has rendered more terrorist suspects to America than any other coalition partner, including several high-profile commanders such as Khalid Sheikh Mohammad, Abu Farraj al-Libbi, and Ahmed Ghalini.[109]

There are, thus, two prime challenges for the United States as it seeks to define future policy toward Pakistan: First is how best to ensure the government's will in continued counterterrorist efforts; second is to identify ways of encouraging and supporting the establishment of effective state control of the border regions. This will be necessary in the context of both the United States' counterterrorism and security assistance programs. Of course, U.S. assistance strengthens not just the state but also the regime. Although General Musharraf's government is considered a key U.S. partner in the global war on terrorism, its apparent tolerance of armed militant groups—including jihadists operating in FATA—has contributed to the growth of extremism and lawlessness. As Hassan Haqqani points out,

> [F]rom the point of view of Pakistan's Islamists and their backers in the ISI, jihad is only on hold, but not yet over. Pakistan still has unfinished business in Afghanistan and Kashmir and, given its lack of military and economic strength, subconventional warfare with the help of Islamists remains one of the Pakistan's options.[110]

Washington has a fair degree of leverage with regards the first challenge simply by virtue of the billions of dollars of security aid that has been earmarked for the country to the end of 2008. Provision of this assistance could and should be made conditional on Islamabad meeting specific measurable objectives, such as decisively moving to close identified militant camps or arresting or killing middle- and high-ranking Taliban and al-Qaeda operatives.[111] By the same token, because a meaningful crackdown on extremist elements is likely to carry domestic political risks for the Musharraf government, positive progress in these areas needs to be recognized and rewarded.

In terms of capability-building, and to maximize the impact of resources made available to Pakistan for counterterrorism and law enforcement, key areas of immediate priority should be identified and assessed in terms of their cost-effectiveness per dollar spent.[112] Integral to this will be the delineation of a comprehensive, long-term

---

[109] Mohammad was one of al-Qaeda's most senior operational planners; al-Libbi was allegedly the number three in the organization at the time of his arrest (2005); Ghalini remains the chief suspect behind the 1998 East Africa embassy bombings.

[110] Haqqani (2004), p. 308.

[111] Cohen (2004), pp. 301–329; Fair and Chalk (2006), p. 75.

[112] For a detailed assessment of U.S. internal security and law enforcement assistance to Pakistan, see Fair and Chalk (2006), pp. 61–81.

program of internal security development that can be used to guide future investments in counterterrorist and crime-fighting initiatives.[113]

Finally, thought should be given to the military dimension that defines the U.S.-Pakistani relationship. Although Washington has gone some way toward rehabilitating its lost bond with the Pakistani defense establishment, residual distrust remains both from the period when Islamabad was under a U.S. military embargo and from ongoing Pakistani concerns that the Bush administration's developing ties with India could accelerate a strategic imbalance on the subcontinent. The United States needs to foster and deepen its military links with Pakistan, not only to create a solid basis for cooperation on regional security (which should, by default, reduce the incentive for using militant proxies as a tool of foreign policy), but also to appropriately influence the direction of Pakistani civil-military relations—not least by helping to ensure that the army does not hinder the country's political process from developing in a democratic direction.

The U.S. Air Force already plays an important role in the overall scheme of U.S.-Pakistani military-to-military relations, as well as in advancing broader U.S. policy and humanitarian objectives in South Asia. After the October 2005 earthquake that devastated areas in northeastern Pakistan, the Air Force supported earthquake recovery operations by airlifting more than 133,000 pounds of aircraft parts, turbine engines, tents, and other equipment, and more than six million pounds of relief supplies.[114] As U.S.-Pakistani military-to-military relations expand, the role of the U.S. Air Force is likely to grow, particularly in light of the U.S. decision to resume the sale of F-16 aircraft to Pakistan after a 16-year hiatus—a high Pakistani defense priority. Therefore, in its interaction with the Pakistani government and military, the U.S. Air Force will have an opportunity to play an increasing role in advancing U.S. policy objectives in the region.

---

[113] This could take place under the auspices of the existing U.S.-Pakistan Joint Working Group on Counter Terrorism and Law Enforcement. Main issues covered at the forum's initial meeting included counternarcotics, counterterrorism, extradition, money laundering, human trafficking, reducing demand for illegal substances, alternative development, poppy eradication, and police and legal system reform. For further details see U.S. Department of State (2002).

[114] U.S. Central Command (2005).

CHAPTER SEVEN

Case Study: The Arabian Peninsula

Theodore Karasik and Kim Cragin

This chapter focuses primarily on the border regions of Saudi Arabia, Yemen, Oman, the United Arab Emirates (UAE), Qatar, Bahrain, and Kuwait. Our research explores the governing capacity of states in the Arabian Peninsula and the movement of goods across their borders, with the goal of gaining a better understanding of remote borders. We also include a brief look at Jordan and Iraq because the movement of persons and goods across their borders presently affects stability in the Arabian Peninsula. However, we do not discuss Operation Iraqi Freedom (OIF) or the ongoing insurgency in Iraq in detail in this report, since the security issues regarding Iraq are much broader than the potential threats presented by Iraq as an ungoverned territory. Our research addresses four overarching questions:

- What is the configuration of ungoverned territories on the Arabian Peninsula?
- What factors generate ungoverned territories in this region, including the development of terrorist hubs and insurgencies?
- What is the nature of the threats posed to the United States and its friends and allies by this ungoverned territory?
- How can the United States government, particularly the U.S. Air Force, address the potential threat of ungoverned territories on the Arabian Peninsula?

This study is not the only one that identifies potential instability in the Arabian Peninsula as a cause for concern. The U.S. National Intelligence Council's *Middle East in 2015* study identified the birth of a new destabilizing regime on the Arabian Peninsula as one of several possible negative futures. Similarly, the U.S. National Defense University Near East and South Asia (NESA) Center has identified the collapse of state authority and the development of a radicalized regime in Saudi Arabia as the worst "wild card" scenario that the Middle East might face in the coming decade.[1] In this

---

[1] "Saudi Arabia Faces Instability" (2004).

chapter, we explore the potential factors that could lead to increased instability, not only in the Kingdom of Saudi Arabia, but also in other states in the Arabian Peninsula.

Geopolitical and Historical Context

The Arabian Peninsula, with an estimated total population of 50,000,000 in 2004, is bordered on the west by the Gulf of Aqaba and the Red Sea, on the south by the Gulf of Aden and the Arabian Sea, on the east by the Gulf of Oman and the Arabian Gulf, and on the north by Iraq and Jordan. (See Figure 7.1). The peninsula's principal cities are Jeddah, Makkah (Mecca), and Medina in Saudi Arabia; Sana'a, Aden, and Mukalla in Yemen; Abu Dhabi and Dubai in the United Arab Emirates; Muscat

Figure 7.1
The Arabian Peninsula and Vicinity

SOURCE: RAND.

RAND *MG561-7.1*

in Oman; Manamah in Bahrain; and Kuwait City in Kuwait. Except for the inland cities of Riyadh and Hail in Saudi Arabia, most of the region's large urban centers are on or near the coast. Mountain ranges and vast, barren deserts make up large parts of the interior of the peninsula. All the countries on the peninsula have the same basic language, religion, and cultural backgrounds, but important differences exist. These differences are a key point of analysis in our discussions of the region's ungoverned territories and their conduciveness to the presence of terrorist groups.

The geopolitical importance of the region derives, of course, from its energy resources. The Arabian Peninsula has the largest oil and natural gas reserves in the world; in fact, they dwarf other existing oil reserves.[2] Until the early 1970s, oil firms from the United States, Great Britain, and—to a lesser extent—Japan, had a monopoly on drilling concessions. However, the Gulf states acquired much greater control over oil exploration, production, and price controls after 1970. Modern technology and the huge wealth generated by oil resources have profoundly altered traditional life in Arabia. Flourishing private enterprise, new transportation links, rapidly growing cities, a large foreign labor presence, and rising education and living standards characterize much of the Arabian Peninsula.[3]

Like many of the other regions analyzed in this report, the Arabian Peninsula has faced sporadic instability in modern times. To some extent, the instability was due to the geopolitical history of the region: Most modern states and their ruling authorities were imposed by European colonial powers when the Middle East was reorganized after the end of World War I.[4] Prior to that period, the area was loosely ruled by the Ottoman Empire, with de facto authority in the hands of tribal elders. We discuss tribal relations in subsequent sections of this chapter. At this point, it is important to note that the tribes played a key role in the emancipation of the region from Ottoman

---

[2]   According to the Department of Energy's Energy Information Administration, which quotes *Oil & Gas Journal* and *World Oil*, Saudi Arabia had 261.8 billion barrels of crude oil as of January 1, 2003. Iraq had between 112.5 and 115 billion barrels of crude oil, Kuwait had 96.5–98.9, UAE had 63–97.8, Oman had 5.5–5.7, Qatar had 15.2–19.6, Bahrain had negligible amounts to 0.1 billion barrels and Yemen had 2.9–4.0 billion barrels. Canada has the next closest amount of oil reserves (180 billion barrels), only if one includes the unconventional source of Alberta's oil sands (174.8 billion barrels). Other countries that come close include Venezuela with 53.1 to 77.8 billion barrels, Russia with 58.8 to 60 billion barrels, Iran with 89.7 to 100.1 billion barrels, Nigeria with 24 to 32 billion barrels, Libya with 29.5 to 30 billion barrels, and the United States with 22.7 billion barrels (U.S. Department of Energy, 2005a).

[3]   For more information, see Gause (1994).

[4]   During this period, Iraq and Trans-Jordan were established as Hashemite monarchies under indirect British control, and Aden (or southern Yemen) was a British protectorate; the British government also retained significant informal influence in Oman and held treaty relations with Bahrain, Qatar, and Kuwait. Northern Yemen and Saudi Arabia were technically independent, although surrounded by British-controlled or influenced areas. Syria was a French mandate and Tunisia and Morocco were considered "protectorates." See Owens (1993), map on p. 12.

rule—the Arab Revolt of 1916—and in the subsequent development of the modern nation-states in the peninsula.

The discovery of oil and the subsequent expansion of the oil industry in the Gulf transformed the political economy of the region and strengthened its tribe- and family-based regimes by enabling them to develop the state infrastructure, subsidize employment, and buy off dissidents. But paradoxically the oil wealth also worked to the advantage of extremists, who capitalized on the social dislocations and the corruption generated by the oil economy to gain support for their more radical views. One of the effects of the development of the oil economy was the development of a large expatriate labor force, as shown in Table 7.1.

These workers include not only Western oil experts but also workers for the regional oilfields drawn from other Arab populations (e.g., Palestinians, Egyptians, Moroccans) as well as from across the Muslim world. This transient labor force, combined with the fact that some of the countries on the peninsula, such as Saudi Arabia and Oman, do not collect income taxes but instead provide stipends to its citizens drawn on oil revenue, creates a unique dynamic between citizens, other residents, and state officials.[5] Rather than drawing its legitimacy from a social contract between citizens and governments, therefore, many of these states rely on a combination of tribal and religious authorities as well as economic incentives to establish their legitimacy.

In the 1950s and 1960s, a tide of pan-Arab nationalism throughout the Arab world threatened to overcome the Gulf region. The Iraqi monarchy was overthrown in a bloody coup in 1958; after the overthrow of Yemen's Imamate in 1962, Egyptian President Abd al-Nasser's government sustained the Yemeni republican side in a civil war that drew in the Saudis on the side of the monarchists.[6]

The Iranian revolution put new pressure on the ruling elites of the peninsula. The success of the Islamic revolutionaries in Iran in overthrowing the Shah's supposedly strong regime encouraged extremists throughout the region—Sunni as well as Shi'a— notably in Saudi Arabia, where the takeover of the Grand Mosque in Mecca by Saudi extremists shook the Saudi monarchy to its foundations.

The Saudis responded to the ideological challenge of Khomeinism by seeking to bolster their religious legitimacy. They tightened religious observances at home and, of greater consequence, stepped up the propagation of the official Wahhabi ideology abroad. The Saudi effort to co-opt extremists has not prevented, and may have accelerated, the rise of a neo-Salafi jihadist movement, a more virulent brand of extremists seeking to overthrow "apostate" regimes in the region that currently constitutes the most serious threat to stability on the peninsula.

---

[5] Gause (1994).

[6] See Goldschmidt (1991); and Hourani (1991).

Table 7.1
Arabian Peninsula Work Force, 2002

Country	National Population	Expatriate Population	Total Population	Population Growth Rate (%)	National Workforce	Expatriate Workforce	Total Workforce
Saudi Arabia	15,500,000	7,300,000	22,100,000	3.3	2,800,000	5,300,000	8,100,000
Bahrain	400,000	270,000	670,000	1.6	100,000	200,000	300,000
Jordan	Unknown	48,411	5,100,000	3.0	643,661	48,411	700,000
Kuwait	900,000	1,500,000	2,400,000	3.3	200,000	1,100,000	1,300,000
Oman	1,900,000	600,000	2,500,000	3.4	300,000	600,000	900,000
Qatar	200,000	500,000	700,000	2.9	30,000	250,000	280,000
UAE	900,000	2,700,000	3,600,000	1.6	200,000	1,700,000	1,900,000

SOURCES: "Saudi Arabia: A Show of Force" (2004); Hashemite Kingdom of Jordan (2003).

The Arabian Peninsula as Ungoverned Territory

Although the previous paragraphs provide only a brief overview of the history and geography of the Arabian Peninsula, it is easy to see how this region could be vulnerable to exploitation by illegal groups, whether criminal or political. For example, the large number of laborers moving out of the region could conceal similar movement by militants. Expatriate workers also provide anti-Western militants with proximate targets. The following sections examine these and other characteristics more thoroughly, beginning with a discussion of factors that may contribute to the expansion of ungoverned territory and that enable militant groups to flourish.

In the introduction to this book, we discussed factors that pertain to "failed states," "weak states," or—as we term it—"degrees of ungovernability." We identified three major variables: (1) lack of state penetration, (2) lack of a monopoly of force, and (3) compromised sovereignty, which includes lack of effective border control. We discuss these factors below as they relate to the Arabian Peninsula, as well as Saudi Arabia's borders with Yemen, the Gulf states, and Jordan.

Lack of State Penetration

The degree to which a centralized government can actually "govern" relies heavily on its presence in rural as well as urban areas. As implied previously, the low populations (see Figure 7.2) and basic geographic constraints of the Arabian Peninsula make penetration into the more remote outposts of these countries difficult. For example, the Yemeni government has admitted that it does not have control over 16 of 19 provinces in that country. And that claim is optimistic—most experts believe that the central government in Yemen only has a strong presence in Aden and Sana'a.[7] But beyond these more general observations, it is possible to get some indication of how much these centralized states touch their citizenry on a day-to-day basis.

Perhaps the most evident indicator of state penetration is the physical infrastructure that exists on the Arabian Peninsula. The governments on the peninsula have devoted, in fact, substantial resources to the physical infrastructures of their countries. The purpose of these programs has been the transformation of what was once a predominantly pastoral society into a modern state with a diversified industrial economy in which the export of crude oil will not be the sole source of wealth. These projects have been impressive, at the very least. Saudi Arabia alone had spent 344 billion riyals (US$100 billion) on infrastructure development by 2000, including four ports, 28 dams, 24,000 kilometers of roadway (14,913 miles), more than 175,000 new homes, the world's first nationwide computer-controlled telephone network, and an airport

---

[7]   "Yemen Feels the Backlash (2002). For more information on rural Yemen, see Mackintosh-Smith (2000); and ICG (2003f).

Figure 7.2
The Arabian Peninsula—Population

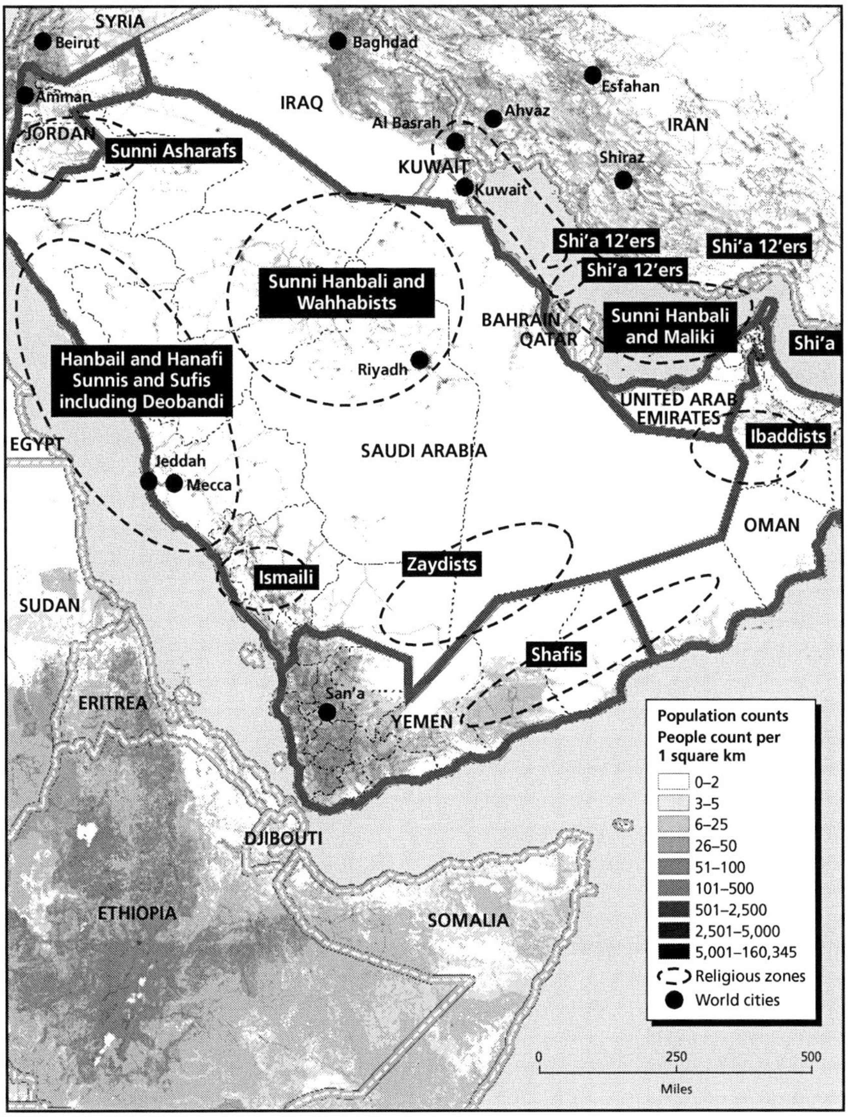

SOURCE: RAND.
RAND *MG561-7.2*

approximately the size of New York's Manhattan Island. Today, as a result, modern transportation routes—air, road, and rail—link the far-flung provinces of Saudi Arabia with the country's main population centers (See Figure 7.3). The physical foundations

Figure 7.3
The Arabian Peninsula—Infrastructure

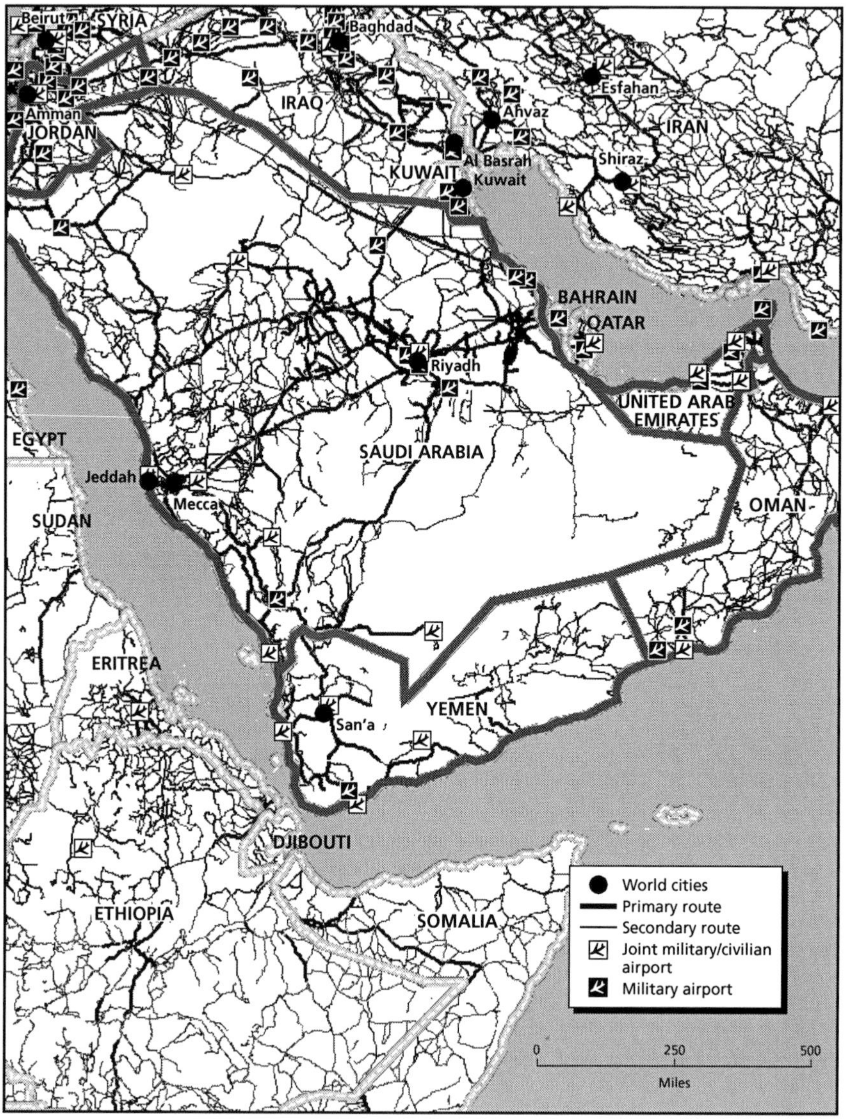

SOURCE: RAND.
RAND *MG561-7.3*

for industrial development have been laid. This type of infrastructure development is also seen in Qatar and UAE. Both have been building what represents the most impressive infrastructure and supply line projects in those countries ever. Doha, Abu Dhabi, and Dubai rival each other in hub facilities. Perhaps unique among other countries on the peninsula, Saudi Arabia has also had to accommodate overland transportation for the Hajj. Thus, the Saudi government has constructed hundreds of miles of all-weather, four-lane highways, particularly between Arafat and Mina. It has also fully computerized its traffic control system. Each year, portable tent cities are set up at Arafat and Mina to provide housing, food, water, health and sanitation, banking facilities, transportation, telecommunications, public safety, and markets—all the amenities needed for a city of two million people. Nearly every Saudi government agency and ministry becomes involved one way or another in making the Hajj an administrative success.[8]

Saudi Arabia's neighbors to the south have also invested in projects to expand their infrastructure. Yemen and Oman, for example, opened a new cross-border route between Al-Ghayada (Yemen) and Shihan (Oman) in May 2000 that includes a major roadway.[9] Similarly, Jordan has invested in the expansion of its infrastructure, building the Desert Highway, which connects the port city of Aqaba to Ma'an and Amman and continues north to Damascus, as well as the King Hussein Highway to the west. Dubai is also rapidly challenging all other actors in the region with ambitious plans for transport options.

In addition to infrastructure, citizen compliance—defined here as the willingness of citizens to abide by laws and regulations and participate in civic activities without official compulsion—could also be viewed as a measure of state penetration of society. Compliance is a difficult concept to measure. We have chosen citizens' participation in elections as one indicator of compliance because it also relates to the legitimacy of the state. Some of the Arabian Peninsula states have made important strides in fostering citizen participation in elections. In Qatar, the country's first elections were held in 1999 when citizens elected a 29-member municipal council. Women were allowed to vote and stand for office in this election. Kuwait holds regular elections; Saudi Arabia conducted elections for municipal councils in 2005. In Bahrain, citizens have voted several times for a 40-member consultative council; among those elected were women as well as one person of Jewish ancestry. In the summer of 2003 Jordan held parliamentary elections—the first elections since King Abdullah dissolved the parliament in 2001.[10] Approximately 57 percent of registered voters participated; notably, turnout was decidedly lower in urban areas compared with the more rural, tribal-controlled regions of Jordan.[11]

The trends in state penetration of society are not uniform, however. Urbanization has brought its own problems. In the dozen years since the conclusion of the Persian Gulf War, slums have emerged on the outskirts of Jeddah and Riyadh in Saudi Arabia. Many of the inhabitants of these quarters are illegal immigrants not eligible for employment or government aid. But some are Saudis who have slipped through the

---

[8]   Long (2005).

[9]   Jane's Information Group (2004c).

[10]   Ryan and Schwedler (2004).

[11]   Ryan and Schwedler (2004).

normal aid channels, such as people from poor regions in the south who never went to school and are not qualified for skilled work, divorced women with children, tribesmen who for various reason do not have Saudi nationality, and the children and grandchildren of immigrants who were born and grew up in Saudi Arabia but remain ineligible for work or aid because they are not citizens.[12] Although it is difficult to derive exact poverty levels in these areas, the growth in the number of child beggars—estimated to be in the thousands—on the streets of urban centers in Saudi Arabia is illustrative of the problem.[13] Perhaps more significantly, at least for our purposes, slums in major cities throughout the Arabian Peninsula increasingly appear to be outside the purview of authorities.[14]

Similar patterns exist elsewhere on the peninsula, although for different reasons. For example, approximately 700,000 Yemeni workers were expelled from Gulf states during the Persian Gulf War and the 1994 civil war in Yemen. These deportations dealt a crushing blow to the Yemeni economy and put significant pressure on the already war-burdened authorities in north and south Yemen.[15] In Jordan, the youth population has exploded in recent years, with approximately 75 percent of the country's population under the age of 30; more important, less than half of those able to work participate in the official labor market.[16]

Second, there is evidence that certain populations are resistant to expanding state authority. Popular uprisings have occurred as central governments attempt to expand their reach. These uprisings have occurred in Ma'an (Jordan) in 2003, in Manama (Bahrain) in 2003 and 2004, and in Ta'if (Saudi Arabia) in 2004.[17] The details of the Ma'an unrest, which involved the police and army battling masked gunmen, are sketchy. Authorities attempted to portray the operation as a crackdown against a criminal gang that used religion and politics as a front for its smuggling activities. However, the short time between U.S. Embassy official Laurence Foley's murder and the fighting in Ma'an led to speculation that the two events were connected. It turned out that the authorities' aim was to apprehend an Islamist leader, Mohammed Shalabi, but the large-scale nature of the operation suggests a wider objective. Notably, the cities of

---

[12] In November 2002, Crown Prince Abdullah made a surprise visit to Riyadh's slums—the Al Aoud, Sebala, and Shamissi area—to take stock of the situation; little has been done since. See Murphy (2003).

[13] M.G.A. Khan (2002).

[14] Karasik interviews, Qatari military personnel, February 2004, UAE security analysts, March and April 2005. See also Murphy (2003).

[15] Jane's Information Group (2004c).

[16] "Jordan Set to Launch Youth Strategy" (2004).

[17] The Ta'if riots were over the sale of land to outsiders including Qataris who traveled specifically to Ta'if for the sale.

Ma'an and Karak have a history of rebellion and the Ma'an uprising should be viewed in this context.[18]

Third, the fact that tribal relationships dominate life on most of the Arabian Peninsula complicates these states' ability to expand their reach and authority throughout the country. Although Saudi Arabia has developed remarkably over the past decades and has become more urbanized, its tribal system is still strong and deeply rooted. There are hundreds of tribes in Saudi Arabia, but tribal politics generally revolve around a few major tribes.

The relationship of these tribes with the ruling al-Saud family in the modern Saudi state is a cyclical process, alternating between outbreaks of violence and relative harmony enforced with a strong hand. The founding of the state itself was due to King Abdul Aziz's ability to control the tribes. The 1979 takeover of the holy sites in Mecca by an Ikhwan movement composed of Saudi Arabian National Guard (SANG) personnel and members of the Shammar, Harb, and Utaybah tribes was a pivotal moment in tribal relations with the al-Saud. Four years after his father's assassination by a nephew in a dispute over Westernization, Prince Turki bin Faysal (former intelligence chief and now Saudi Ambassador to the United States) led the counterattack to crush the rebels and restore order. This event began the process of deemphasizing tribalism, although it now appears that the kingdom's 2005 three-part municipal elections allowed some tribes to win in rural areas, triggering a new round of tribal identity and pride.

The Saudi bureaucracy is full of tribal offices and positions. Each senior al-Saud prince has a tribal affairs office through which specific tribes are cared for. Tribal leaders frequently attend diwan sessions (audiences) with key Saudi princes at which the leaders will ask the prince for favors. Tribal leaders also sit in regional governmental offices so there is a link between the royal governor and the tribe. Yet it is important to remember that in decisionmaking the state always trumps the tribe.

Tribes in Saudi Arabia are increasingly moving away from their traditional areas into the main cities. Media, Internet, and cell phones are erasing some aspects of tribal identity. Tribal relations currently consist of al-Saud leaders overseeing the well-being of the tribe by providing stipends for developing and maintaining social services, schools, and so forth. When a key al-Saud leader dies, responsibility for the tribe is transferred or inherited by another al-Saud leader; this important fact can have immense implications for family squabbles. Finally, the SANG, which is staffed by members of key tribes, helps to solidify power in the hands of the leader who heads it (at present, former Crown Price, now King, Abdullah and his son, Mit'ab). The SANG is a sizable and capable security force that is loyal to the elite who control and pay them.[19]

---

[18] For more information, see ICG (2003a, 2003d); and Jane's Information Group (2004a).

[19] The above description of state-tribal relations is based on extensive 2004–2005 RAND work on Saudi tribes.

Saudi Arabia is not the only country on the Arabian Peninsula with deep-rooted tribal politics. We briefly mentioned the role of tribes in Jordan's political system. The tribes of the UAE and Oman are also significant players at odds with each other. Tribes in the northern part of the UAE are the most frustrated with Abu Dhabi's rule because of historical tribal grievances and the distribution of funds from the federal center.[20] In Qatar, there are twelve major tribes. One tribe, the al-Murra, is increasingly being displaced because of its historical support for the current emir's father, who was ousted in a palace coup in 1995. Since November 2004, when the emir's father was allowed to return to Doha for his wife's funeral, the al-Murra have been losing their Qatari citizenship; over 3,000 have been expelled to Saudi Arabia.[21]

In Oman, the tribes are divided by religious allegiance. Ibadist tribes are becoming more prone to planning and executing violence because of a lack of an accepted succession formula in Oman.[22] These tribes, which inhabit the center of the country, argue against primogeniture succession or successors appointed by the sultan. Instead, they seek a leader who would be selected by an Ibadist imam who is not a Sunni. The trial and conviction of more than 30 Omanis for planning a coup in this regard is a warning sign of struggles to come within Oman after Sultan Qaboos passes from the political scene.[23]

Yemen also has a strong tribal culture, with the Hashids representing the strongest tribal conglomerate. Tribes retain significant autonomy in Yemen and have considerable influence over trade and access to the oil in Ma'arib province. President Salih has managed to retain their loyalty—at least to a degree—since the October 2002 attack on the French oil tanker *Limburg*. His success appears to be due to his approach of co-option, specifically with regard to support for Islamists, rather to than coercion and disarmament.

In sum, state penetration of society on the Arabian Peninsula has been aided through infrastructure projects and the development of representative politics. But the tribal structure, urban poverty, and limited yet important popular support for extremists all appear to be key barriers.

---

[20] Karasik interviews, UAE security analysts and cultural officials, February–March 2005.

[21] Karasik interviews, UAE security analysts and cultural officials, April 2005.

[22] Ibadism is an outgrowth of the Kharijite movement, a variant form of Islam practiced by descendents of a sect that seceded from the principal Muslim body after the death of the prophet Muhammad in AD 632. Kharijites reject primogeniture succession of the Quraysh, the tribe of Muhammad, and assert that leadership of Islam, the caliphate, should be designated by an imam elected by the community from candidates who possess spiritual and personal qualities. Ibadi leadership is vested in an imam, who is regarded as the sole legitimate leader and combines religious and political authority. The imam is elected by a council of prominent laymen or shaykhs. Adherence to Ibadism accounts in part for Oman's historical isolation. Considered heretics by the majority Sunni Muslims, Ibadis were not inclined to integrate with their neighbors.

[23] Karasik interviews, UAE security analysts and cultural officials, March 2005.

Lack of a Monopoly of Force

A lack of a monopoly of force indicates that another competing power center may have the means to challenge the state's use of coercion. On the Arabian Peninsula, extremist groups and criminal networks challenge many of the regional states' monopoly of force.

Terrorist Presence

Perhaps the most important pressure on states' monopoly of force on the peninsula, or at least the one most critical to U.S. national security interests, is the presence of terrorist groups associated with al-Qaeda. These groups interact and cooperate with each other all around the Gulf littoral. One key to these groups' ability to operate successfully is access to both remote and urban areas of operation. Thus, it appears that al-Qaeda has found pockets of weak government control on the Arabian Peninsula where terror can proliferate in ungoverned spaces—even in urban areas, including certain neighborhoods of the Saudi capital, Riyadh.

Al-Qaeda on the Arabian Peninsula (AQAP) emerged in Saudi Arabia in the wake of Operation Iraqi Freedom.[24] Since that time, AQAP has launched several successful attacks against both the monarchy and Westerners in Saudi Arabia.[25] The following attacks took place in 2003 and 2004:

- May 12, 2003: four simultaneous suicide bombings against Western targets in Riyadh that killed 34 people
- November 8, 2003: a suicide car bombing that killed 17 people and injured 120 in Riyadh
- May 30, 2004: a hostage standoff in al-Khobar that killed approximately 22 people and injured an additional 25
- June 13, 2004: the assassination of Kenneth Scroggs, an American who worked with Advanced Electronics Company
- June 20, 2004: the assassination (beheading) of Paul Johnson, an American engineer
- December 20, 2004: a suicide car bombing at the Interior Ministry that killed one and injured an additional six people.

AQAP suffered some criticism as a result of its May 30, 2004, al-Khobar attack, which caused a number of casualties to local Muslims. Since that time, AQAP has apparently adopted smaller and more focused attacks to minimize collateral Muslim deaths. In addition to attacks against Western targets and symbols of the monarchy,

---

[24] In Arabic, Al-Qaeda in the Arabian Peninsula is Tanzim al-Qaida fi Jazirat al-Arab.

[25] *Al Qaida in the Arabian Peninsula* (2004).

AQAP has conducted attacks against Muslims working on defense-related projects. Apparently, AQAP members believe that these attacks against Muslims are justified because the victims were working for the enemy. At the time of this writing in the summer of 2005, the Saudi government released a third list of suspected AQAP members, promptly found the leader of AQAP, and killed him at the beginning of July 2005.

Al-Qaeda cells have also emerged in other countries. In October 2002, a Kuwaiti police sergeant pulled two U.S. soldiers in a civilian vehicle off the road and shot them at close range. In December 2003, al-Qaeda terrorists shot at U.S. soldiers and expatriate workers employed at a Kuwaiti port used by the U.S. military. And in July 2004, in a more troubling development, authorities arrested a number of Kuwaiti nationals on suspicion of planning terrorist attacks as part of a robust al-Qaeda network in that country.

On July 14, 2004, Bahraini security forces arrested seven suspected terrorists accused of planning "to carry out bombings on some government, economic, and tourist facilities to spread chaos and fear and harm the national economy and foreign investments."[26] The arrests targeted a group of extremists who had received their religious training in Saudi Arabia.[27] This development—along with the aforementioned attacks in Kuwait—marks an important geographical expansion of the terrorist threat in the Gulf. It also highlights the potential for an emerging link between radical Islamist elements from Saudi Arabia, a growing sense of Sunni disentitlement, and traditionalist backlash in the modernizing smaller Gulf states.

Al-Qaeda cells have also emerged in Jordan. Of course, most people are aware that the late Abu Musab al-Zarqawi, former leader of al-Qaeda's affiliate in Iraq, was born and began his terrorist career in Jordan. He was involved in the plot that resulted in the assassination of American diplomat Laurence Foley in October 2002. Since Operation Iraqi Freedom, Jordanian authorities reportedly foiled another major ter-

---

[26] Between July 1 and July 4, 2004, the U.S. State and Defense Departments alerted American citizens to avoid unnecessary travel to Bahrain and withdrew approximately 900 nonessential personnel and their families. The stated reason for these actions was that the United States had "received information that extremists are planning attacks against U.S. and other Western interests in the Kingdom of Bahrain"; specifically, "credible information indicates that extremists remain at large and are planning attacks in Bahrain." See Knights and Solomon-Schwartz (2004).

[27] The precautions appeared to have been given added justification with the rearrest on July 14 of six suspected Bahraini members of the Salafist Muslim community, which is considered to be close to al-Qaeda. The suspects (who were first picked up on June 20) were said to have been preparing to target Western installations, including U.S. military personnel, and were thought to have been linked to a cleric in Bahrain aligned with al-Qaeda, Shaykh Muhammad Salih, who had been recently released after spending nine months in prison. Two of the suspects, Yasir Kamal and Muhammad Salih Muhammad, had already come to the attention of the authorities, in Kuwait and Saudi Arabia, respectively, while another three, Bassam Bukhuwa, Bassam al-Ali, and Muhyiddin Khan, had been temporarily detained in a weapons case in February 2005. Another suspect, Ali Mahmud Khan, a British passport holder released with the others in June, appears to have slipped through the net and exited the country. See Knights and Solomon-Schwartz (2004).

rorist plot against the Jordanian General Intelligence Department and possibly the U.S. embassy. In April 2004, authorities arrested six suspects driving five trucks filled with explosives. The alleged leader of the plot, Azmi al-Jayusi, claimed that he was trained in al-Zarqawi's camp near Herat, Afghanistan.[28] The most spectacular attack in Jordan was, of course, the November 9, 2005, suicide bombing at a Palestinian wedding reception in Amman by an Iraqi man associated with al-Zarqawi's network. (The man's wife, who was expected to participate in the attack, survived when her explosives belt failed to detonate, She was captured a few days later.) The attack was widely condemned in the Muslim world and, according to Pew polls, led to a decline in support for jihadist movements.[29] In addition, some militant groups outside al-Qaeda's orbit, mostly Palestinian, have also maintained at least a political presence in Jordan.[30]

In addition to its loosely affiliated cells in Kuwait and Bahrain, al-Qaeda has maintained close ties with some groups active in Yemen: the Islamic Army of Aden-Aden/Abyan Islamic Army (IAA), the Islamic Jihad Movement, and the Abu Hafs al-Masri Brigade. The IAA, in particular, announced in October 2003 that it was formally "joining" al-Qaeda.[31] Scholars believe that most of the key members of the IAA returned from Afghanistan in the 1990s to continue the fight in Yemen. Militants from IAA and the Islamic Jihad Movement (IJM) apparently maintain training camps in Yemen's more rural areas and provided logistical support to al-Qaeda members in the USS *Cole* attack in October 2000.[32] The IAA has also claimed responsibility for a suicide boat attack against the French oil tanker *Limberg* in 2002.[33] Yemen has progressed from passively tolerating these groups to actively opposing them. In 2005, the Yemeni government implemented a program to reconvert or persuade arrestees to renounce the ideology of these groups.

Criminal Networks and the Shadow Economy

Organized crime networks are present on the Arabian Peninsula, but they are not a major factor influencing the governability of the area. The one exception is the presence of international criminal networks in the UAE, where Chinese, Indian, and Russian criminals have organized a hub of operations. From India's point of view, the UAE-Pakistan relationship is one fraught with danger. LeT terrorist Abu Hamza, whom Mumbai police suspected of involvement of terrorist blasts in the city, lived in the

---

[28] Jane's Information Group (2004a).

[29] Al-Shishani (2005).

[30] Al-Shishani (2005). Since King Abdullah II ascended to the throne, Jordan has taken a stronger stance against Hamas, deporting Hamas figures Khalid Mishal, Musa Abu Marzuq, and Ibrahim Ghawshah in 1999.

[31] Marzuk (2003).

[32] "Yemen Quakes in Cole's Shadow" (2000).

[33] ICG (2003e).

UAE. Indian Deputy Prime Minister Advani said that India was in touch with UAE authorities "to secure the deportation of more Indian terrorists and criminals" residing there.[34]

Organized Chinese and Russian crime networks are not believed to be tied to terrorism but instead concentrate on human trafficking (from sex workers to scientists and technicians) and contraband smuggling operations.[35] The UAE's improving performance in counterterrorism points to increased cooperation in helping to slow or stop the evolving international networks of organized criminals and Islamist extremist terrorists.[36]

Beyond international criminal networks, and perhaps exacerbated by the increase in urban poverty, a shadow economy appears to be expanding on the Arabian Peninsula. This shadow economy represents the Arabian Peninsula's second major barrier to further state penetration of society. Smuggling is rampant throughout and between the major ports on the Red Sea and in the Arabian Gulf.[37] The UAE acts as a hub for the transfer of goods to Iran through illegal trafficking routes. Because the rail and road infrastructure between Bandar Abbas and Chabahar is poor, speedboats smuggle the bulk of the goods in and around Oman's Musandam Peninsula.[38] Farmers' markets and souks also are an unmeasured part of the shadow economy because they are not counted in official statistics.[39]

Weapons trafficking networks appear to extend from West Africa, across the Sahel, through Somalia, and into Yemen.[40] There are different estimates of the availability of weapons in Yemen, but the number is significant. A Small Arms Survey report estimated approximately 40 weapons per 100 people in Yemen.[41] Some analysts

---

[34] In what was seen as a partial breakthrough by India, the UAE announced on December 8, 2002, the arrest of Anees Kaksar Ibrahim in Dubai. (He was arrested on December 3, three days after his reported arrival from Pakistan). Anees is one of the fugitives on the list of 20 most wanted terrorists that had been handed over to Pakistan in the wake of the December 13, 2001, attack on India's Parliament. Also in 2003, the UAE deported Mustafa Mohammed Umar Dossa, a key suspect in the 1993 Mumbai serial blasts. He is accused of supplying arms and ammunition used in the blasts. South Asia Terrorism Portal (2002, 2003).

[35] An important development from outside the region is the emergence of human trafficking operators. These people prepare all paperwork and build mock-ups to train their "cargo" how to react in interviews with customs or security officials. Karasik interviews, UAE security analysts, April 2005.

[36] Karasik interviews, UAE security analysts, April 2005.

[37] Index of Economic Freedom (2005).

[38] Karasik interviews, UAE security analysts, March 2005.

[39] Some souks are being shut down and replaced with modern malls as part of a process to bring illegal business behavior under legal supervision. Karasik interviews, UAE security analysts, February–March 2005.

[40] See ICG (2004f, 2004h). On the role of Yemen in the regions' weapons trafficking routes, see "Saudis have intercepted 100,000 infiltrators this year" (2004).

[41] Miller (2003).

think that that number is too low.[42] The Yemeni Interior Ministry, however, estimates that the country's approximately 19 million people own some 50 million weapons.[43] Saudi authorities have claimed that approximately 90 percent of the illegal weapons in that country come through Yemen.[44] Although some of the weapons and bombs used by Saudi terrorists are believed to have accumulated illegally inside Saudi Arabia for years, other weapons with the mark of the Saudi Ministry of Interior have been found in Iraq.[45] This might be the result of collusion on the part of elements of the Saudi security forces, but it could be also part of an indigenous black market.[46]

So far we have noted that the presence of militant groups, criminal organizations, and easy access to weapons all undermine the governments' monopoly of force on the energy sector has provided the motivation for these governments to boost internal security in rural areas significantly. For example, in late April 2004, Aramco's chief executive, Abdullah Jumah, said, "there is nowhere in the world that oil facilities are protected as well as in Saudi Arabia."[47] According to Jumah, Aramco employs 5,000 security guards to protect its oil facilities. In addition, the SANG, regular Saudi military forces, and Interior Ministry officers are tasked with protecting oilfields, pipelines (the country has around 10,000 miles), ports (Ras Tanura, Al Juaymah, Yanbu), refineries, and other oil facilities (e.g., gathering centers and gas-oil separation plants). In May 2004, Nawaf Obaid, an advisor to the Saudi royal family, said that the Saudi government had added $750 million to its security budget over the past two years to beef up security in the oil sector. According to Obaid, the Saudis spent $5.5 billion in 2003 on oil security. In addition to direct security, Saudi Arabia is known to maintain "redundancy" (e.g. multiple options for transportation and export) in its oil system, in part as a form of indirect security against any one facility being disabled.[48]

Lack of Effective Border Control

In the previous section, we discussed smuggling routes on the Arabian Peninsula. Clearly, these smuggling routes also indicate a low level of control over borders. Pressures on the border between Yemen and Saudi Arabia, in particular, derive from tribal

---

[42] Comment by Dr. William Reno, review of manuscript.

[43] Jane's Information Group (2004c).

[44] Jane's Information Group (2004c).

[45] *Al-Jazirah* (2003); Habtar (2005).

[46] Finn (2003).

[47] U.S. Department of Energy (2005b).

[48] U.S. Department of Energy (2005b). One report says that Saudi Arabia has rigged the entire petroleum infrastructure with radioactive dispersal devices to be used specifically to prevent any anti-royal or American intervention from seizing operational control of the fields. See Posner (2005), pp. 119–134.

conflict and historical memory. Many of the tribes of the region have ignored international boundaries in order to continue a way of life that involves social, political and trade relationships on both sides of the border. Frequently, state officials interpret these interactions as destabilizing and then apply pressure on the tribes—through such means as threats and cuts in subsidies.[49]

Yemen and Saudi Arabia did not negotiate a formal agreement determining the exact border between them until 2000. In 2004, Saudi Arabia began to build a wall to better protect its border from smugglers in Yemen but halted this project when the Yemeni government protested. Subsequently, Yemen agreed to joint patrols along the border. It is difficult for these governments to maintain control over the border, not only because it is some 1,500 kilometers long but also because some of the smaller tribes, especially in Saudi Arabia's Asir province, have historically been outside central control. Once the joint patrol program is implemented, Saudi Arabia and Yemen will be able to develop a more formalized border protection program.[50] The southern and eastern borders of Saudi Arabia are shown in Figures 7.4 and 7.5.

Until recently, the Saudi-Iraqi border was extremely porous. Many Saudi nationals traveled to Iraq to participate in the jihad against U.S. and coalition forces in Iraq.[51] As of June 2005, at least 2,500 Saudis were estimated to be fighting in Iraq.[52] The Saudi-Iraqi border area, however, is not particularly hospitable to Saudi jihadists seeking to infiltrate Iraq. The border is closer to Shi'ite communities in southern Iraq than to the Sunni areas in central and western Iraq. Most Saudi jihadists are believed to infiltrate Iraq through Syria, which is closer to the Sunni heartland.[53] Moreover, to prevent movement of fighters, the Saudis have been fortifying their borders. General Al-Anqawi, an official with the Saudi Ministry of Interior, stated, "1,721 kilometers of roads have been constructed in the Jizan, Najran, Asir and Eastern Provinces." He added: "Several new contracts have also been executed to modernize border guard equipment through high-speed mediums to reinforce the security control over the kingdom's coastlines, with observation posts that are equipped with the most modern means of surveillance, communications and guidance."[54]

A wide array of technologies and personnel has been brought to the Saudi border with Iraq, including satellite-based tracking systems and a squadron of light survey

---

[49] For more information, see "Stereotypes and Political Styles" (1995).

[50] Habtar (2005).

[51] "Article Discusses Number, Motives of Saudi Combatants in Iraq" (2005).

[52] Abedin (2005).

[53] Nir (2005).

[54] "Interview with Director-General of the Saudi Border Guard" (2004).

Figure 7.4
Southern Border of Saudi Arabia

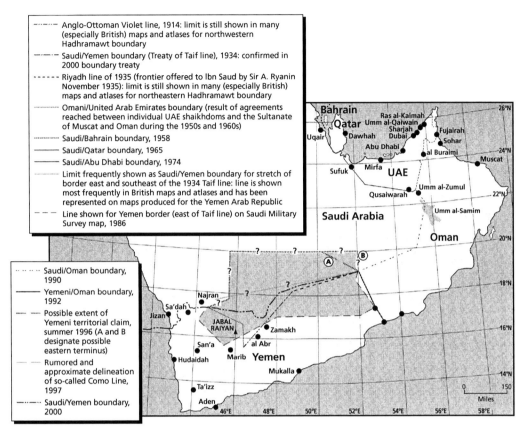

SOURCE: Schofield (2001), p. 217.
RAND *MG561-7.4*

aircraft.[55] The Saudi Border Guard has placed more than 110 thermal cameras along the border to detect infiltrators and smugglers.[56] Yet, despite technology, it is important to remember that border disputes on the Arabian Peninsula represent hatreds that span decades. Many of the borders were delineated by the colonial power during the period of direct or indirect British rule, and security for these borders was handed directly to the tribes that reside on both sides of the imposed border.[57]

---

[55] "Defense of the Realm" (2005), p. 25.

[56] *Abha Al-Watan* (2004).

[57] Karasik interviews, UAE legal scholars and media representatives in Dubai, July 2005.

Figure 7.5
Eastern Border of Saudi Arabia

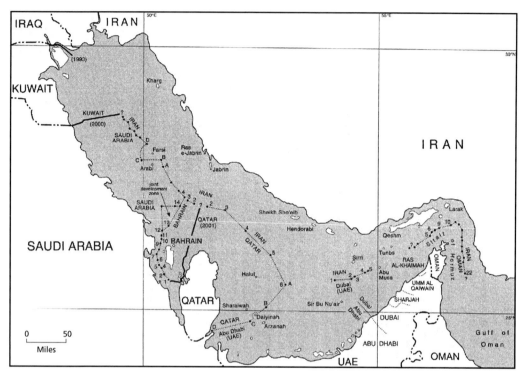

SOURCE: Schofield (2001), p. 215.
RAND *MG561-7.5*

External Interference

Through its relationship with Shi'ite populations in the region as well with the countries and emirates themselves, Iran is an influential actor on the peninsula. It should not be assumed, however, that Iran would necessarily have a hostile relationship with the Arabian Peninsula states. These states and Iran have a mutual interest in ensuring the safe extraction of natural gas deposits from the large offshore field that Qatar shares with Iran in the Gulf. Nevertheless, Iran's history of periodic meddling in the internal affairs of Gulf emirates, its desire to reduce U.S. influence in the region, its evolving role in Iraq's internal affairs, and its ongoing military modernization all have the potential to threaten the sovereignty of the Arabian Peninsula states.[58]

---

[58] For background on Iran's current foreign policy outlook, see Ehteshami (2004).

Currently, there do not appear to be any Iranian proxy groups operating openly on the Arabian Peninsula.[59] However, Bahrain's 70 percent Shi'ite population, long restive under the rule of the Sunni Khalifa family, especially in light of widespread perceptions of corruption at the highest levels of government, appears to be a likely target of destabilization.[60] Although most Shi'ite violence against the established order in Bahrain is unorganized street violence against foreign-owned businesses (as occurred in 1994–1996 and again in the spring of 2004), there are some organized Shi'ite militant groups in that country that might have the potential to spread their operations into Qatar. One is the group known as Bahraini Hizballah, which is apparently funded to some degree by the Iranians.[61] Bahraini Hizballah was active during the 1994–1996 period, when Iran made a conscious effort to destabilize Bahrain. After a number of arrests by Bahraini authorities, the organization disappeared from view, but it is possible that it could reemerge.

Kuwait, where Shi'ites make up 30 percent of the population,[62] has not been a hotbed of Shi'ite discontent because of its relatively vibrant civil society. Nevertheless, over the years a shadowy group called Kuwaiti Hizballah has periodically surfaced.[63] Although it seems to be an umbrella for a range of Islamist groups and has not posed any real threat to the ruling Al-Sabah family, it cannot be discounted as a threat in the current era of heightened tensions over the unsettled situation in Iraq as well as the election of Mamoud Ahmadinejad as Iranian president and the ascendancy of hard-liners in Iran.

Assessment of Ungovernability

The preceding discussion analyzed the factors that affect the governability of border areas in the Arabian Peninsula. When combined with a complicating tribal structure, the barriers to state penetration to society appear to outweigh the enablers. On the lack of monopoly of force, again the Arabian Peninsula is faced with expanding political violence in the form of jihadist terrorism and a significant illegal weapons trafficking network. At the same time, the presence of international criminal networks is not as much of a risk to stability on the Arabian Peninsula as in other regions in this study. Finally, border security is an ongoing problem on the Arabian Peninsula, yet central governments are in the process of mitigating these risks. These indicators, and some of

---

[59] There is a small Shi'a presence in Sharjah that could become a proxy under the proper circumstances. Karasik interviews, UAE security analysts and cultural officials, April 2005.

[60] See Byman and Green (1999), pp. 32–33.

[61] Byman and Green (1999), pp. 34–35.

[62] *CIA World Factbook* (2005).

[63] Byman and Green (1999), pp. 37–38.

their components, are summarized in Table 7.2. The values are as follows: 1 = low; 2 = medium; and 3 = high. Thus, in terms of lack of state penetration, 1 would indicate a high level of penetration in Kuwait, and 3 a low level in Yemen.

Table 7.2
Indicators of Ungovernability, Arabian Peninsula

Variable	Saudi Arabia	Oman	UAE	Bahrain	Qatar	Yemen	Kuwait	Jordan
Lack of state penetration								
Absence of state institutions	2	2	1	1	1	3	1	2
Lack of physical infrastructure	2	1	1	1	1	3	1	1
Social/cultural resistance	2	2	1	2	1	3	2	2
Lack of monopoly of force								
Organized armed groups	3	2	1	2	1	3	2	2
Criminal networks	2	1	3	1	1	3	1	3
Population with access to arms	3	2	1	1	1	3	2	3
Lack of border controls	2	1	1	1	1	3	2	3
External interference	2	1	1	1–2	1	2	2	3

Attributes of the Arabian Peninsula Conducive to the Presence of Terrorist Groups

The overarching purpose of this study is to provide a framework for thinking about the new and emerging threats presented by weak states or ungoverned territory. In this context, understanding the factors that produce a given ungoverned space is unlikely to be sufficient. That is, some areas may be highly ungovernable but may not pose a threat to U.S. national security. Ungovernability measures, therefore, must be combined with some measure of the conduciveness of a given area to a terrorist presence or of the utility that the area presents to militant groups that want to attack the United States or U.S. interests abroad. This section of the chapter addresses the issue of conduciveness to a terrorist presence.

Given the extent of U.S. and Western strategic and economic interests on the Arabian Peninsula, it is clear that potential instability alone on the Arabian Peninsula is sufficient for concern. But beyond the threat that the collapse of an existing state could pose to these interests, there is also a high risk that extremist groups, especially al-Qaeda, could continue to find the Arabian Peninsula an attractive operational hub. As such, ungoverned territories on the Arabian Peninsula present a potential threat to U.S. national security.

Adequacy of Infrastructure and Operational Access

Paradoxically, while the development of the physical infrastructure is a measure of the degree to which central governments have been able to penetrate into local society, it also is a key factor in a territory's attractiveness to terrorists. Terrorists need a basic infrastructure to establish support facilities, train, transport weapons and personnel, and plan and conduct attacks. Thus, the complete absence of physical infrastructure greatly hinders their operations. So as Saudi Arabia, for example, expands its infrastructure to accommodate pilgrims for the hajj, it also makes it easier for terrorists to move about to conduct attacks and recruit new members. Indeed, U.S. officials have warned that a very small but dangerous number of terrorist operatives are using pilgrimages to Mecca as a cover for some of their activities.[64] Similarly, the use of dhows for trade and travel in the Arabian Gulf and the Red Sea provides ample cover for the transport of personnel, weapons, and commodities for terrorist networks in the region.[65]

It is clear that AQAP and al-Qaeda central have been able to take advantage of the expanding physical infrastructure on the peninsula. Eleven of the perpetrators of the October 2000 attack against the USS *Cole* were Yemeni, but six of these returned to Yemen from abroad to conduct this attack.[66] According to a study by Israeli counterterrorism expert Reuven Paz, from September 2004 through February 2005 over 60 percent of suicide bombings in Iraq were conducted by Saudis.[67] So, as noted in the section on border control, Saudi citizens have continued to be able to cross the border into Iraq. Similarly, AQAP apparently seeks to create networks across these countries for the migration of tactics, techniques, and procedures in order to destabilize other Gulf states.[68] These tactical innovations take advantage of the robust transport infrastructure as well as the presence of explosives and weaponry that can be used in attacks. A case in point was the March 2005 suicide car bombing of a British theater in Doha in March 2005. Although never clearly explained by Qatari authorities, the bombing is illustrative of a small al-Qaeda cell in Qatar or a "lone wolf" who was able to get the materials he needed for the attack from construction sites in Qatar. Thus, it appears that AQAP, al-Tawhid (an Islamic terrorist cell that originated in Jordan) and al-Qaeda central have all been able to use the expanding physical infrastructure on the Arabian Peninsula to their advantage.

---

[64] Robinowitz (2004).

[65] Karasik interviews, UAE security analysts, March 2005. See also "U.S. Navy Seizes Scores of Militants in Gulf" (2005).

[66] See "Cole Bombers Identified" (2000); "Double Whammy" (2000); Schmidt and Priest (2002); and "U.S.: Top al Qaeda Operative Arrested" (2002).

[67] Glasser (2005).

[68] Paul (2003).

At the same time, however, there is another trend of importance with regard to operational access—the ability of terrorists to reach and attack targets. Since many U.S. interests, including military facilities, have been hardened against terrorist attack, terrorists are directing their attacks against softer targets. The majority of terrorist attacks on the Arabian Peninsula are likely to continue to be against soft targets accessible to dispersed groups of young men who receive their inspiration from the pronouncements of global and regional terrorist leaders and who have little or no contact with regional facilitators. These atomized groups make their own calculations about what kinds of targets they can engage with the limited means at their disposal.

The attack against the U.S. consulate in Jeddah serves as an example of this pattern. Although AQAP has demonstrated its ability to task a local cell with a symbolic attack on a hard target, the execution of the Jeddah attack contained further indicators of declining terrorist capabilities in the kingdom. According to a U.S. Department of State official involved in post-attack analysis, a review of the consulate's gate camera footage showed that the terrorists undertook "days rather than weeks" of reconnaissance, failing to understand how the delta barriers worked or to gain any deeper insight into the internal layout of the compound or the security measures barring entry to the chancery. The location of the consulate on a busy road allowed hundreds of cars to loiter close to the gates, precluding any meaningful countersurveillance against the simple surveillance effort of the assailants. The attack plan was both flawed and under-resourced.[69] While indigenous, younger followers of al-Qaeda ideology display the motive but neither the means nor the opportunity to strike serious blows, instances of anti-Western kidnappings, shootings, knifings, deliberate vehicle ramming, and physical or verbal assaults at roadblocks will likely be the norm.[70]

Favorable Demographic and Social Characteristics

Vulnerable Populations and Supportive Social Norms

There are advantages for terrorist groups that want to use the Arabian Peninsula as an operational hub. It is possible, for example, to find refuge, if not support, in groups or clusters of individuals already outside the mainstream who are vulnerable to co-option or intimidation. For example, al-Zarqawi has reportedly been able to establish strong ties with the Bedouins along Jordan's borders with Syria and Iraq. Similarly, residents of cities with strong religious convictions, antiroyalist sentiments, and overt anti-Americanism could be vulnerable to cooption, by AQAP in particular. Buriada in Saudi Arabia, for instance, is a hotbed of resentment against the al-Saud and the United States. Even in the 1990s, riots were frequent in the city. What proved notable

---

[69] Knights (2005a).

[70] Knights (2005a).

was the extent to which a number of residents echoed strains of the case against the monarchy that were advanced by dissidents abroad and militants in Saudi Arabia, many of whom are now in prison. It is within this population, and those who served time in jail, that terrorists can find refuge.

Also in Saudi Arabia, differences in political, religious, tribal, and cultural outlook between the Najd, the Eastern Province, Hejaz, and southern regions of that country are subject to exploitation by extremists. At the center of Saudi Arabia is the Najd, the heartland of Saudi religious orthodoxy. The tribes there adhere to the Hanbali school of Islamic jurisprudence and take pride in their close links to the current regime. The Eastern Province, on the other hand, is predominantly Shi'ite. There, Saudi authorities suppress Shi'ite religious expression as anathema to proper Islamic practice. To the west, along the Red Sea coast, is the more liberal Hejaz, where the preference is for the Maliki and Shafi'i schools. Along the southern border with Yemen, one finds an eclectic blend of sects, foremost among them the al Zaydiya and Ismaili Shi'a. It is the tribes in these regions that al-Qaeda and radical Wahhabis seek to expose as apostates.

Clerics represent another population that is potentially vulnerable to co-option by al-Qaeda and likeminded groups. Saudi "reforms" have included the demand that clerics avoid extremes in their sermons. There are now constant warnings against extremism or excessiveness (*ghuluww*) and a promotion of *wasatiyyah* (literally, centrism, but in Saudi Arabia it means moderation) in the propagation of the faith. Toward that end, the Supreme International Council of Mosques, which falls under Saudi patronage, issued the Mecca declaration in September 2003, in which it sought to combat "the deviationist thought, in clear reference to the extremist ideology of bin Laden and similar militants."[71]

Nevertheless, clerics continue to speak out on the need for jihad and call for the death of Americans in Iraq.[72] These clerics, for instance, the *sahwa* or "awakening shaykhs," a group of former dissidents who have come to support the regime for the time being, also have a support network.[73] Of particular interest are two of the sahwa's most prominent and remarked-upon members, Salman al-Awdah and Safar al-Hawali, both of whom enjoy considerable notoriety as hard-liners who allegedly continue to support al-Qaeda.[74] That they have provided inspiration for radicals in the past is unquestionable, although their present role in providing spiritual comfort to militants is less certain. The role of the sahwa in the current political order is complex. At various times, its members can be said to be both supporters and critics of the regime—a remarkable accomplishment considering both the short leash given by the

---

[71] AbuKhalil (2004), p. 133.

[72] Myers (2005).

[73] Jones (2005).

[74] Hawali suffered a stroke in June 2005. His future is uncertain.

ruling family to dissenters as well as some of the clerics' personal history of anti-regime political activism.

Exploitable Ethno-Religious Cleavages

Finally, ethno-religious cleavages on the Arabian Peninsula can be exploited to produce dissension between the religious establishment and the more radical clerics who help terrorist recruitment. Terrorists can exploit tribal tensions by exposing the co-option of tribal shaykhs aligned with the ruling regime. For instance, favored tribal shaykhs of the al-Saud in Tarabjal and al-Jawf in the north and Abha and Najran in the southwest received benefits from state agencies.[75] As discussed, Saudi Arabia's rigid political system and chronic budget deficits limit the House of Saud's ability to deal with these pressing issues. Outside observers note that regional disparities in Islamic beliefs across the Arabian Peninsula also set the stage for separatism should the country show signs of failing. In addition, there are supportive social norms in the population because the neofundamentalist streak finds strong support from robust, hidden networks.

It is important to understand historical events in terms of the relationships between various regions of the country. But it is often more important how mysticism, magic, poetry, storytelling, and hadith (traditions relating to the words and deeds of Muhammad) are interpreted by elites and other components of society.[76] Throughout this chapter, we have been discussing the role that tribes play in politics. Yet the leadership itself is a "tribe" subject to the same laws that govern other tribes: conflict, marriage, role of mothers and wives, place of birth and support. Repression as part of enforcing rules and norms radicalizes some of the population. In many of the Arabian Peninsula states, specifically in Saudi Arabia itself, religion (Wahhabism) has left its imprint on the culture, heritage, and symbols of the state over time. When debate erupts over religion and its role in society, historical analogies are used to justify today's positions. In short, history matters, and people's perception of historical events plays an important role in the shaping of current policy agendas. The role of historical memory is critical to understanding the broader dynamics of leanings and sympathies for the activity of terrorists.

Criminal Syndicates

Criminals of various levels of sophistication are present throughout the Arabian Peninsula. Petty crime is largely indigenous; foreigners do not play an important role in crime. For the most part, they see their economic livelihood as bound up with in the Gulf economy, and they do not want to threaten the income that supports their families back in South or Southeast Asia.[77] The exception, interestingly, is Saudi Arabia.

---

[75] AbuKhalil (2004) p. 96; Karasik interviews, UAE security analysts, April 2005.

[76] Karasik interviews, UAE cultural officials and religious scholars, April 2005.

[77] Karasik interviews, Qatar military officials, February 2004; UAE security analysts, March 2005.

The kingdom has always suffered from rampant crime including assaults and car theft, not just pickpockets and other forms of petty crime as in other countries such as Bahrain.[78] In May and June 2005, Saudi police launched a countrywide sweep of criminal groups and illegal immigrants to the kingdom that resulted in a 50 percent drop in crime. Police found gangs in remote areas, including the Abu-Arish forest in Jizan, who were smuggling contraband from Yemen and Ethiopia.[79] As noted earlier, however, crime does not appear to be a major factor threatening governability in the Arabian Peninsula.

Invisibility

On the Arabian Peninsula, it is possible for terrorist groups to maintain a low profile and hide. Large spaces are hidden as a result of the hostile environments for nonindigenous visitors. Media representatives and some NGOs, especially those that deal in human rights abuses, are not allowed to operate in some parts of the region.[80] Terrorists can take advantage of this situation by staying where outsiders and law enforcement cannot see them. This "invisibility" factor is especially valuable when combined with close proximity to desired targets, such as the U.S. military presence in Kuwait and Qatar, as well as Western business interests and expatriate workers, such as oil workers in Saudi Arabia.

The expanding Salafi jihadi movement on the Arabian Peninsula also provides a welcoming environment to potential terrorists. As we mentioned at the beginning of this chapter, a number of studies address how, why, and the degree to which radical Salafism has taken hold in the Muslim world. As mainstream—albeit underground—support continues to grow for radical Islamic ideology, it bolsters Islamist terrorists' ability to recruit new members and to gain legitimacy among sectors of the population. Youth are increasingly being recruited into terrorist cells.[81] Recruitment has moved from mosques and other public venues, such as cybercafes and bookstores, to homes.[82] Frequently, jihadists turn to armed robberies for funding.[83] There is also evidence to suggest that sympathizers exist within many military, security, and energy institutions and installations, as demonstrated by the ease of access in terrorist attacks as well as the

---

[78] United Nations Office on Drugs and Crime (2001).

[79] *Abha Al-Watan* (2005); Bin-Falah (2005); "Crime Watch: Crime Rate Drops by 50 Percent" (2005).

[80] Iraq under Saddam Hussein comes to mind. NGOs operated in the north and the south but never in the core center.

[81] Karasik interviews, Dubai media representatives, July 2005.

[82] Karasik interviews, Dubai media representatives, July 2005.

[83] "Allowing Crime and Recruiting Those Who Have Strayed (2005).

procurement of security vehicles, passes, and clothing.[84] Once Saudi-dominated cells or "entourages" return from the jihad in Iraq, many will be well suited to restarting their campaign against ruling families throughout the Arabian Peninsula.[85]

Assessment of Conduciveness to Terrorism

Table 7.3 summarizes how we have categorized these factors when it comes to conduciveness to terrorism. The significance of this table is the strong "high" and "medium" showing, thereby posing uncertainty regarding the situation of these critical states.

Table 7.3
Indicators of Conduciveness to Terrorist Presence, Arabian Peninsula

Variable	Saudi Arabia	Oman	UAE	Bahrain	Qatar	Yemen	Kuwait	Jordan
Adequacy of infrastructure	2	2	3	3	3	1	2	2
Operational access	3	1	1	2	2	2	3	3
Favorable demographics	3	1	1	2	2	2	2	2
Sources of income[a]	1	1	1	1	1	2	1	1
Invisibility	3	2	1	2	2	3	2	2

[a] Difficult to determine directly because of lack of reliable data.

U.S. Policies and Programs

This section is divided into three parts: (1) the U.S. global defense posture in the Arabian Peninsula; (2) partner country capability deficiencies and security cooperation tools available to address threats; and (3) democracy and reform programs.

U.S. Global Defense Posture Implications for the Arabian Peninsula

The U.S. Global Defense Posture for the Arabian Peninsula is flexible enough to quickly adjust to state threats but not to threats deriving from the factors analyzed in this study. The United States seeks to maintain or upgrade, and in some cases to establish, forward operating sites and cooperative security locations for rotational and contingency purposes, along with strategically placed prepositioned equipment and forward command and control elements. This equipment includes U.S. missile defense assets as part of basing arrangements in order to protect cities, ports and other areas impor-

---

[84] See, for example, Bradley (2005), p. 114.

[85] Karasik interviews, UAE security analysts and media representatives in Dubai and Abu Dhabi, July 2005.

tant to the host governments.[86] Additionally, the United States continues to identify advanced training opportunities with Arabian Peninsula states for capacity-building in areas such as counterterrorism and broader military interoperability. In this way, it seeks to maintain a presence without the heavy footprint that impinges on regional sensitivities—thereby reassuring allies and partners.[87]

CENTCOM's Theater Security Cooperation program builds essential cooperative security relationships with the Arabian Peninsula states in the face of evolving terrorist and extremist threats. The TSC program improves allied military self-defense capabilities, boosts interoperability with U.S. forces, encourages military transformation, enhances intelligence-sharing and information exchange, and reinforces U.S. military access when required. The pillars of the TSC program are IMET, foreign military financing and sales (FMF/FMS), and the U.S. Department of Defense's Counter Terrorism Fellowship Program.[88] The TSC also helps to posture U.S. forces for stability operations in the future including forward operating sites and cooperative security locations to provide capabilities to assist regional states in the war against terrorism and extremism.[89]

Almost all countries in the region continued significant international counterterrorism cooperation and undertook efforts to strengthen their counterterrorism capabilities. Many countries continued to provide support to coalition efforts to bring peace and stability to Iraq and Afghanistan. The United States continued to provide training throughout the region to assist U.S. allies to enhance their counterterrorism capacity. For instance, in November 2004, Bahrain hosted the first meeting of a newly established regional body, the Middle East and North Africa Financial Action Task Force, which is strengthening members' efforts to combat money laundering and terrorist financing.[90] The Bahraini government has committed itself to establishing a Counter-Terrorism Operations and Intelligence Center.[91]

Finally, the United States has a very active Cooperative Defense Initiative and Consequence Management program with the Arabian Peninsula states and they have made this effort an annual exercise of agreement and importance. In 2000, a U.S.–Gulf Cooperation Council Conference on Cooperative Defense Initiative and Consequence Management convened. Senior military and government officials from the GCC and the United States met in Bahrain to address a series of issues concerning

---

[86] These host governments prefer land-based systems as opposed to over-the-horizon. See Kramer and Nelson (2005), p. 11.

[87] Feith (2004), p. 13.

[88] Abizaid (2005).

[89] Abizaid (2005).

[90] U.S. Department of State (2005a).

[91] Abizaid (2005).

WMD-related crises, including protecting the civilian population. These programs, sponsored by CENTCOM, are part of a larger U.S. effort to engage the GCC militarily in an effort to present a united front against possible external threats.[92] This effort has been further expanded through the annual GCC Conference of Military Medicine and Protection against WMD. The conference brings together military officers, civilian professionals, and industrial organizations working in the field of detection and decontamination.[93]

Partner Country Capabilities Deficiencies[94]

Each of the Arabian Peninsula states faces some type of weakness, and it is not necessarily military or security based. In fact, these weaknesses include tribalism, ties between dynasties, and border security issues that will complicate coordination and cooperation in the years to come. As noted earlier, tribalism goes to the heart of Gulf politics.[95] Even within the armed forces of the GCC states, tribalism can be a source either of state stability or of rivalry between services. Frictions between the al-Saud and ruling families in other Gulf states are another source of weakness. Since 9/11, Doha and Riyadh have escalated their war of words over al-Jazeera commentaries that criticize Saudi royals. Although local media claimed that these are part of "normal relations" between the two countries, they are not. In October 2002, Saudi Arabia floated rumors of a Qatari coup attempt as a punishment for allowing anti-Saud commentary to be broadcast across the region from Doha. Border disputes are rife. A border dispute erupted in July 2005 between Saudi Arabia, the UAE, and Qatar over an Abu Dhabi–Doha plan to build a bridge between the two countries—signaling a fresh new round of tensions over boundaries.

Yet, military capabilities do matter. The overall military capabilities of the Gulf states have been greatly enhanced through their acquisition of sophisticated systems that enable them to engage the enemy with precision, lethality, and speed. For example, in most contingencies with Iran, the Gulf states' superb air assets, capable naval sys-

---

[92] Institute for Foreign Policy Analysis (undated).

[93] "Qatar to Host GCC Conference" (2002). The third such conference, held in Doha in October 2002, focused on educating and training young GCC army officers on protecting against WMD attacks. A fourth conference was held in Doha in May 2005, which helped Qatar respond to explosive attacks on a sports arena. Other GCC states and their first responders participated in this exercise. Seraphin (2005).

[94] This section is based on Karasik interviews with Qatari military officials through 2004 and related RAND work since 2001.

[95] The shared Anazi tribal roots of the al-Saud and al-Sabah ruling families among the Shammir were an important part of GCC attempts at unity. In the UAE, the leading ruling families, the al-Nahyan, al-Makhtoum, and al-Qawasim, are non-Najdi and are not tribally linked to the al-Saud, as is the Qatar's ruling family, the al-Thani. Bahrain's al-Khalifah is close to the Utub branch of the Anaza, meaning that Bahrain, at least up to 9/11, was relying on Saudi Arabia for protection. Karasik interviews, UAE cultural officials, April 2005. See also al-Musfir (2001), pp. 316–317.

tems, and other advanced equipment should enable them—even without U.S. direct involvement—to deny Iran the air and sea supremacy it would need to conduct sustained amphibious operations against the Gulf littoral.

Despite improvements in recent years, many Gulf militaries still face problems, particularly due to manpower shortages. Populations in these states are small to begin with, and they often include a high percentage of third-country nationals. Male nationals of military age constitute only a small percentage of the total population, ranging from 12 percent in Qatar and the UAE to 22.3 percent in Saudi Arabia. Moreover, many of these countries face recruiting problems. Military service is not prestigious, and the best potential recruits often pursue other opportunities. As a result, many Gulf states must recruit foreign personnel to meet their force goals. More than half of Qatar's military consists of foreign nationals, and the percentages are also high in Bahrain and the UAE. Most of these foreign personnel come from poorer Muslim states, such as Egypt, Jordan, Pakistan, and Sudan.[96] Foreign contractors also provide crucial technical and maintenance support to the Gulf militaries, since few of these militaries have indigenous support capabilities. The trade-off is that foreign military personnel might not be as reliable or as loyal as nationals. Thus, most regional militaries try to ensure that nationals instead of foreigners staff their elite units; nevertheless, any major engagement would involve other units as well.

The Gulf state forces are not particularly skilled. Regional land forces' capabilities for maneuver warfare are poor. Operational plans have generally been designed for static border defense, so they lack both the equipment and communications assets necessary to go beyond their fixed positions. They also lack effective combined arms and joint capabilities. Moreover, the services do not communicate well with each other, and different elements of single services (e.g., artillery and infantry units) do not coordinate their actions.

The capabilities of Gulf state air forces cannot compensate for the limited numbers and poor skills of their ground forces. Although regional air forces are reasonably skilled at air-to-air operations, they have few air-to-ground capabilities (except for perhaps United Arab Emirates with their F-16 fighters). In general, Gulf state air forces do not train on air-to-ground missions. Their platforms do not possess the most advanced munitions that would enable the destruction or disruption of advancing enemy armored columns. Poor interservice communication within country militaries, as well as among Gulf coalition members, prevents effective land-air coordination. As a result, Gulf air forces could do little to halt a significant invasion. Indeed, despite considerable government investment, the skill level of the Royal Saudi Air Force has declined over the past decade.

---

[96] Some of these militaries are releasing foreign nationals from the military ranks. The key question is, Where do these nationals go and how will they use their expertise in their home or new host countries?

Indeed, the Gulf states' armed forces generally do not train under realistic conditions, although that may have changed to some degree with the Jordanian contingent in Operation Enduring Freedom or the UAE's training of Iraqi security forces. The Gulf militaries tend to spend their procurement dollars on acquiring new and technologically advanced weapons systems instead of developing basic support capabilities; for the most part, they lack the logistics infrastructure to sustain operations for more than a short period of time. Preventive maintenance is not emphasized. Finally, the Gulf militaries suffer from several problems related to the chain of command. Personal relationships, family ties, and political factors often determine key promotion and staffing decisions. This problem is exacerbated when members of the royal family serve in the military, since rank does not always correspond to family status.

Democracy and Reform Programs: The Middle East Partnership Initiative

Finally, U.S. democracy and reform initiatives are extraordinarily active and robust, to encourage reform on the Gulf states' own terms. The administration's primary diplomatic policy and development programmatic tool to support democracy and reform is the Middle East Partnership Initiative (MEPI). MEPI is a presidential initiative that strives to link Arab, U.S., and global private sector businesses, nongovernmental organizations, civil society elements, and governments together to develop innovative policies and programs that support reform in the region. As President George Bush outlined in his November 6, 2003, speech at the National Endowment for Democracy, the United States has adopted "a forward strategy of freedom in the Middle East."[97]

MEPI is structured in four reform areas or pillars. In the economic pillar, MEPI policy and programs support region-wide economic and employment growth driven by private sector expansion and entrepreneurship. In the political pillar, MEPI champions an expanded public space where democratic voices can be heard in the political process, the people have a choice in governance, and there is respect for the rule of law. In the education pillar, MEPI supports education systems that enable students to acquire the knowledge and skills necessary to compete in today's economy and improve the quality of their lives. Finally, in the women's pillar, MEPI works toward economic, political, and educational systems in which women enjoy full and equal opportunities.[98]

Among the hallmark activities being conducted under the auspices of MEPI are Middle East entrepreneurship training in the United States (economic pillar); creation of a Middle East Justice Institute and regional campaign schools for women candidates (political pillar); "partnership schools" that offer alternatives for quality and relevant education for children and serve a models for governments as they build schools in the

---

[97] U.S. Department of State (undated-a).

[98] U.S. Department of State (undated-a).

future (education pillar); and regional micro-enterprise and business internships for women (women's pillar).[99]

On the Arabian Peninsula, the target countries are Bahrain, Kuwait, Qatar, Saudi Arabia, and the United Arab Emirates.[100] MEPI helped to fund judicial reform seminars in Oman and Bahrain and a women's literacy program in Yemen.[101] However, it should be recognized that Bahrain, Qatar, and Jordan have made varying efforts to liberalize their domestic political and economic structures over the past decade. Qatar welcomes the educational and economic components; Saudi Arabia, Oman, and the UAE have shown less interest and tend to view some programs as interference with their own domestic agendas.[102]

Policy Implications and Conclusions

From a policy perspective, the key question in addressing the problem of ungoverned territories on the Arabian Peninsula is how to increase the capacity of the states to extend their reach into these spaces and thereby reduce their availability to terrorist networks. In this regard, there is a raft of U.S. programs, with the Department of State as the lead agency, that represent a low-cost way for the United States to boost state capabilities to tackle both internal threats and transnational border threats. These programs fall under the NADR family of initiatives. The U.S. government has conducted antiterrorism assistance programs with all the states of the Arabian Peninsula. However, in part due to political sensitivities, no state has received Terrorism Interdiction Program support. In addition, no EXBS support has been provided to Kuwait and Bahrain. At present, Yemen is the only country that receives small arms and light weapons disarmament assistance.[103]

There are several areas where the Department of Defense can play a role. One is in joint exercises with Jordan, such as Eager Tiger and Eager Light, that focus on counterterrorism, border security, and expanding Jordan's role as a center for regional cooperation. Another set of exercises, Earnest Leader, brings together the U.S. Third Army and the Royal Saudi Land Forces to practice command and control of coalition operations and foster regional security and peacekeeping.

From the DoD perspective, one area that requires exploration, is how to encourage and enable foreign partners in their fight against violent extremists when their own forces are from the Ministry of Interior and the police—normally the bailiwick of State

---

[99] U.S. Department of State (undated-a).

[100] U.S. Department of State (undated-a).

[101] Sharp (2005), p. CRS-5.

[102] Sharp (2005), pp. CRS-5–6.

[103] Karasik interviews, UAE Security Analysts, Dubai and Abu Dhabi, July 2005.

Department programs—and are not part of engagement programs sponsored by the Department of Defense.

Another area that requires greater attention is long-term support for border and rural surveillance. CENTCOM provides specialized intelligence support via overhead imagery and signals intelligence when necessary. "Area limitation analysis," where activity in remote or rural areas can be part of a larger array of electronic sensor "fences," may be part of this effort. Future military and antiterrorism training for GCC states is likely to include provision for border patrol and mountain warfare training and specialized training for local attack helicopter crews in night operations and strike missions. Outside the GCC, in Yemen and the Caucasus, this form of training has had excellent results.

CHAPTER EIGHT

Case Study: The Sulawesi-Mindanao Arc

Angel Rabasa

The Sulawesi-Mindanao arc—that is, the region comprising the Celebes and Sulu Seas and the land areas bordering on them—constitutes a single geopolitical area that affects the political stability of the larger maritime Southeast Asian region (see Figure 8.1). There is, however, no historical or cultural basis for the separation of the populations around the Sulu Sea among different nations.[1]

The area's borders are porous—with piracy, armed militias, terrorists, separatist groups, and unregulated movement of persons and goods. Within Sulawesi and Mindanao, large areas in Central Sulawesi, in the Philippine provinces of Sulu, Tawi-Tawi, Maguindanao, Lanao del Sur, Lanao del Norte, North and South Cotabato, Sultan Kudarat, and the waters adjacent to these areas meet our criteria for ungoverned territories. In addition, the maritime area between these two islands seems to be a key logistical corridor for the regional terrorist group Jemaah Islamiyah and other extremist groups.[2]

Both Central Sulawesi and the Muslim areas of Mindanao have been historically isolated from the centers of political power in Jakarta and Manila and generally neglected by the central authorities. The Dutch, who ruled the main islands of present-day Indonesia in colonial times, ignored the interior areas of Celebes (Sulawesi) for centuries. Although the Dutch had established a foothold in Makassar, southern Sulawesi, in 1668 and in Palu in 1864, the interior did not come under effective Dutch administration until the beginning of the twentieth century following the inauguration of the Dutch "ethical policy" in the Netherlands East Indies. (The "ethical policy" was designed to promote development, lift the economic and social conditions of the population, and gain the active support of an educated colonial elite.) After the conquest of the region south of Palu in the first decade of the twentieth century, the Dutch began to build the infrastructure to support an agricultural export economy in place of the traditional subsistence economy. They constructed large-scale irrigation projects, introduced the plough, and built a road network in the product-export areas.

---

[1] Rabasa discussion with Dr. Ishak Mastura, Cotabato City, Mindanao, August 12, 2005.

[2] Niksch (2003).

Figure 8.1
The Sulawesi-Mindanao Arc—Political Map

SOURCE: RAND.
RAND *MG561-8.1*

However, plantation agriculture was never introduced, and the region remained economically marginal. In accordance with the precepts of the "ethical policy," the

Dutch set up a school system that offered the possibility of a modern education for the local elite.[3]

Although Mindanao, like Sulawesi, is extraordinarily wealthy in terms of its natural resources, that wealth has brought little benefit to the local inhabitants. The schools are run down, roads are falling apart, and social services are in disarray.[4] Until the middle of the nineteenth century, much of Muslim Mindanao remained outside the jurisdiction of the authorities in Manila. During the period of Spanish colonization, which began with the expedition of Miguel López de Legazpi in 1564, the Spaniards took possession of most of Luzon and the Visayas and converted the lowland population to Christianity. But although Spain eventually established footholds in northern and eastern Mindanao and the Zamboanga peninsula, it failed to establish control over the rest of Mindanao. Until the end of the nineteenth century, the sultanates in Sulu (Jolo) and Maguindanao fought intermittent wars against the Spanish and conducted independent foreign relations with the British and the Dutch. The Sulu sultanate declined after the mid-nineteenth century, when the Spanish began to use steam-powered warships against the Moros, but Sulu was not occupied and made a Spanish protectorate until 1876.

After the Spanish-American War, Mindanao was transferred by Spain to the United States together with the rest of the Philippines. (The Moros protested, to no avail, that since—in their view—their territory was sovereign, Spain had no right to transfer it to a third party.) After the U.S. annexation of the Philippines, the American authorities established direct rule over the south and suppressed Moro resistance. Slavery and polygamy were abolished (at least legally), and public schools, a U.S.-style judicial system, and other reforms were introduced to encourage Muslims to adopt prevailing concepts of modernity.[5]

According to Filipino scholar Patricio Abinales, American military operations in Mindanao in the years after 1905 were preceded by a large-scale campaign to entice settlers from Luzon and the Visayas into the relatively sparsely populated island, with the purpose of creating a new majority that would eventually overwhelm the indigenous population and "civilize" it in the process.[6] Others believe that migration policy of the American authorities in Manila was motivated mainly by economic considerations—the need for labor in the plantation agriculture that was beginning to be introduced to Mindanao. The American authorities acknowledged the unique character of Muslim Mindanao and established a Moro province, separate from the rest of

---

[3] See Weber, Faust, and Kreisel (2002).

[4] Zachary Abuza, private communication, May 2005. The author of this chapter, Angel Rabasa, observed deplorable social conditions during his visit to Cotabato in August 2005. See the discussion of the poverty rate in the Muslim areas of Mindanao later in this chapter.

[5] Rabasa (2003); May (1992).

[6] Abinales (2000).

the Philippines, and a Moro constabulary to pacify the region. The policy of actively encouraging migration to Mindanao began in earnest during the Commonwealth period, when the United States began to devolve authority to Filipino authorities, and accelerated after the proclamation of the republic in 1946. The shifts in the population balance and its effect on land tenure were important underlying causes of the Moro insurgency.[7]

The current Moro insurgency began after President Ferdinand Marcos declared martial law in September 1972 and began attempts to disarm the local population. The insurgency was led initially by the Moro National Liberation Front (MNLF) under the leadership of Nur Misuari, an ethnic Tausug (the MNLF has always been stronger in the Tausug areas of the Sulu archipelago). In 1975 the MNLF entered into protracted negotiations with the Philippine government and was challenged by a Maguindanao-dominated splinter group, which later became the Moro Islamic Liberation Front (MILF), led by Salamat Hashim. In 1996 the government of President Fidel Ramos signed a peace agreement with the MNLF known as the Davao Consensus. The MNLF assumed the governance of the previously established Autonomous Region in Muslim Mindanao, composed of four Muslim-majority provinces—Sulu, Tawi-Tawi, Maguindanao, and Lanao del Sur— and the city of Marawi.[8]

Even before the signing of the 1996 agreement, President Ramos had sounded out the MILF for peace talks. The talks began in February 1997 and resulted in a ceasefire agreement in 1997 and an agreement in principle to recognize the MILF camps in 1998. During the presidency of Ramos's successor, Joseph Estrada, hostilities escalated in violation of the ceasefire, leading to all-out conflict in 2000. Peace talks were resumed after Estrada was deposed in January 2001 and are currently under way.[9]

The Sulawesi-Mindanao Arc as a JI Logistical and Transportation Hub

The Sulawesi-Mindanao arc is a key corridor for the movement of Jemaah Islamiyah personnel. It is no accident that JI placed both the areas of concern in this study, Central Sulawesi and Mindanao, within the same subregional organizational unit, Mantiqi III. This is significant because Mantiqi III serves as a major logistics cell for JI. This regional command is responsible for the procurement of equipment and explosives; more important, it is also responsible for building up relations and creating a network

---

[7]   Vitug and Gloria (2000).

[8]   See Chalk (1997); and McKenna (1998).

[9]   Diaz (2003), pp. 71–83.

of Islamist groups.[10] This network includes al-Qaeda operatives in Southeast Asia and sympathetic groups in the Philippines.[11]

JI operatives and recruits make the journey to safe houses and training camps in the Philippines through Sandakan, in Sabah, Eastern Malaysia. The trip from Sandakan across the Sulu Sea to Mindanao in the southern Philippines takes 12 hours in a wooden tub of a fishing boat with a 270-horsepower diesel engine. In a speedboat with 1,000-horsepower engines, the trip can be made in half the time. The main danger of this trip is kidnapping by pirates, but reportedly there is no shortage of people willing to arrange the trip for a fee of 2,000 Philippine pesos one way, no passport required.[12]

Although since 9/11 the MILF has strenuously denied that it has ever had tactical alliances with al-Qaeda, JI, or the Abu Sayyaf Group, cooperation among elements of all three groups before 9/11 is well documented. Two JI operatives detained in the first wave of arrests in Singapore in December 2001 after the discovery of a JI cell and another two arrested there in August 2002 had been involved in training at MILF camps and fund-raising activities for the MILF.[13] Omar al-Faruq, the senior al-Qaeda operative captured in Indonesia in the summer of 2001, spent time in Camp Abu Bakar, the MILF's main camp in Mindanao.[14]

Prior to 9/11, the coordination of terrorist activities in Southeast Asia could be detected in such developments as the creation of the MILF's Special Operations Group in 1999 with the help of Fathur Rahman al-Ghozi, a JI explosives and demolition expert who participated in numerous terrorist actions in Southeast Asia. Al-Ghozi was responsible for supplying the Laskar Jundullah in Poso with light arms and assault rifles in 1999 and was involved in the August 2000 bombing of the residence of the Philippine ambassador in Jakarta and the December 2000 Rizal day bombings in Manila. Al-Ghozi was arrested in Manila in January 2002, tried, and sentenced to seventeen years in prison. After escaping from prison later that year, he was killed in Mindanao while seeking to avoid recapture.[15]

As was often the case in the networking of Islamic militant groups in the pre-9/11 period, this linkage developed in Afghanistan. The MILF reportedly sent between 500 and 700 fighters to Pakistan and Afghanistan to receive military training and take part in the anti-Soviet jihad. As a result of having its fighters trained by JI instructors in Afghan camps, the MILF incurred an obligation to the JI, which the MILF reciprocated by allowing the JI to open its own training camp within Camp Abu Bakar, the

---

[10] Turnbull (2003).

[11] Abuza (2003a); ICG (2003c), p. 6.

[12] "Home-Grown Terrorism" (2004).

[13] "Web of Terror" (2002).

[14] Ratnesar (2002).

[15] ICG (2003c), p. 6. Also see Abuza (2003b), p. 137.

MILF's main base in Mindanao.[16] Until Camp Abu Bakar was overrun by the Philippine Army in May 2000, the JI operated a separate training facility, Camp Hudaibiyah, which enabled Indonesian and Filipino JI recruits to serve as both trainers and students for a 18-month course in weapons training, explosives handling, tactics, and religious studies. The students also received "jihad exposure" by briefly serving on the front line between the MILF and the Philippine government forces.[17]

After 9/11 and the onset of the U.S.-led global war on terrorism, the MILF leadership began to distance the organization from JI and the global jihadist movement. Philippine authorities say that there is evidence of JI training in MILF camps.[18] The MILF leadership denies these allegations. In an interview with the author, MILF Vice Chairman Ghazali Jaafar said that the government submitted to the MILF the names of JI members alleged to be in MILF territory, but that MILF fighters have not reported the presence of any foreign-speaking men.[19] (See further discussion of alleged MILF-JI links later in this chapter.)

Besides its importance as a logistical and transportation hub for terrorists, the Sulawesi-Mindanao arc is also a theater of jihadist operations. Exploitation of the region's communal conflicts is critical to the recruitment and socialization of JI elements into the group. As the International Crisis Group noted, the JI sent recruits to Poso and Maluku as "easily accessible places where [these recruits] could gain practical combat experience." Recruitment drives were often accompanied by discussions about the jihad in Poso and Maluku and videos showing the killings taking place there. The terrorist-linked Indonesian charity KOMPAK produced and openly distributed "Tragedi Poso Berdarah" ("The Bloody Tragedy in Poso"). This video showed victimized Muslims in Poso unable to defend themselves against a well-armed Christian vigilante group. This type of standard jihadist propaganda was meant to convince local Muslims that fellow Muslims were under attack and that they should support jihadist groups that were purportedly defending them against the aggression of infidels. "Those conflicts," the ICG noted, "served to give concrete meaning to the concept of jihad, a key element of JI's ideology."[20]

---

[16] ICG (2003c), p. 6.

[17] ICG (2004g), pp. 15–17.

[18] Rabasa interview with Armed Forces of the Philippines officials, Camp Aguinaldo, Manila, August 9, 2005.

[19] Rabasa interview with MILF Vice Chairman Ghazali Jaafar, Sultan Kuradat, Maguindanao province, Mindanao, August 12, 2005.

[20] ICG (2002b).

Lack of State Penetration

Central Sulawesi

Not all of Sulawesi or Mindanao is, of course, "ungoverned." There is a reasonable degree of state penetration into society in the Indonesian provinces of South, West, and North Sulawesi and Gorontalo—at least in the major towns and economically significant areas and the road in between. The part of Central Sulawesi that corresponds more closely to our definition of an ungoverned territory is the area around Poso, which was the scene of violent communal conflict from 2000 until 2004 that drew in Indonesian and foreign jihadists. This conflict caused the death of 2,500 people and the displacement of 90,000, who have fled their homes and are now refugees.[21]

The weakness of the state is evident in the amount of violence in Poso after the signing of the Malino I accord, a ten-point bilateral peace agreement between the Muslim and Christian factions brokered by the Indonesian government (a second agreement, Malino II covered Ambon). Of 92 incidents of communal violence in Poso in 2003, including 19 bombings, only nine were solved.[22] The ICG report notes that few arrests were made in the year 2002 as well, in spite of evidence pointing to Mujahidin Kompak as being responsible for violent acts from December 2001 to December 2003.[23] Large numbers of Mujahidin Kompak and Laskar Jihad fighters moved freely in and out of Central Sulawesi, especially after the Bali bombings of October 2002 and the intensified crackdown on Islamic extremists in Java. Laskar Jihad and Mujahidin Kompak elements even fought in Poso City for the control of *poskos* or command posts in certain neighborhoods.[24] That these groups sought refuge in Central Sulawesi shows the lax security in the area and its vulnerability to exploitation by terrorist groups.

Muslim Mindanao

In the Muslim areas of Mindanao, the lack of governance is even more pronounced because of a legacy of longstanding insurgencies, the ineffectiveness of the institutions of the ARMM and the armed presence of the MILF and, to a lesser extent, the Abu Sayyaf Group (ASG). Weak law enforcement and a weak justice system manifest themselves in the privatization of justice. Clan and family feuds, known as *ridos*, are so widespread in Marawi City, the center of the Maranaos, that according to a Manila-based Muslim activist from Marawi, many Maranaos have emigrated from Marawi to escape the ridos.[25] According to a Social Weather Stations survey, 72 percent of ARMM respondents approved of personal retribution to avenge a family member in

---

[21] ICG (2002b).

[22] ICG (2004d), p. 22.

[23] ICG (2004d). For a chronology of communal violence, see Appendix C of the report.

[24] ICG (2004d), p. 14.

[25] Rabasa discussion with Taha Basman, Manila, August 12, 2005.

cases of murder, rape, or injury. This is quite a contrast to the 59 percent of Filipinos outside the ARMM who responded that they disapproved of it.[26] Carmen Abubakar of the University of the Philippines' Institute of Islamic Studies believes that the reason for this is not because Muslims are more prone to violence, but because "the faulty formal justice system in the ARMM leaves people there with hardly any option but to settle serious grievances themselves."[27]

Another manifestation of weak state projection in the Mindanao region is the low level of trust and confidence in the Philippine government. Extreme changes in policy by successive Philippine governments affect the implementation of peace and development initiatives in the region. This makes the people of Mindanao question the sincerity and sustainability of the efforts of the central government in addressing their concerns. The problem of weak state projection concerns not only the weakness of the state but the weakness of the state's interlocutors in Muslim Mindanao as well.[28] Until the August 2005 election in the ARMM, the MNLF was Manila's partner in running the ARMM. (The election resulted in the replacement of MNLF Governor Hussin with the ruling Lakas party's candidate, Datu Zaldy Ampatuan, the son of the governor of Maguindanao Datu Andal Ampatuan, a powerful local figure and ally of President Gloria Macapagal-Arroyo.)

The failure of the MNLF stewardship of the ARMM to bring about any significant improvement in the lives of ordinary people in Muslim Mindanao is well known. According to World Bank figures, the poverty rate in the ARMM actually increased from 62.5 percent in 1997 to 73.9 percent in 2000 (compared to a national rate of 25.1 percent in 1997 and 27.5 percent in 2000). That is, the incidence of poverty in the ARMM is more than double the national rate. In Sulu (Jolo) the poverty rate was an astonishing 92 percent in 2000. (See Table 8.1.)

According to journalists Glenda Gloria and Maritess Vitug:

> On top of the state's ambivalent strategy for peace, stories of corruption, fund real-location, malversation, political maneuvering, clan and family feuds and personal economic gain by MNLF leaders have marred their reputation.[29]

The Moros complain that the weakness of the ARMM was built into its relationship with Manila. For instance, the ARMM is effectively prevented from collecting its own taxes; but even if it were able to collect taxes, the tax base in the ARMM is too small to allow the regional government to fund itself. The ARMM

---

[26] Social Weather Stations (2005a).

[27] Rabasa discussion with Carmen Abubakar, Manila, August 8, 2005.

[28] Dictaan-Bang-oa (2004), p. 161.

[29] Vitug and Gloria (2000).

Table 8.1
Comparative Poverty Rates in the Philippines and the ARMM

Territory	Poverty Incidence		
	1997	2000	% Change
Philippines	25.1	27.5	10
National Capital Region	3.5	5.6	60
ARMM	62.5	73.9	18
Basilan	30.2	63.0	109
Lanao del Sur	40.8	48.1	18
Maguindanao	24.0	36.2	51
Sulu	87.5	92.0	5
Tawi-Tawi	52.1	75.3	45

SOURCE: World Bank (2003).

contributes barely 1 percent of the national GDP and accounts for 0.5 percent of the entire revenue collection of the central government, but takes 2.71 percent of the total central government expenditure.[30] Thus, the ARMM essentially survives on subsidies from Manila, which the central government distributes directly to the 100 or so municipalities in the ARMM, bypassing the regional government.

Lack of Physical Infrastructure

Central Sulawesi

Central Sulawesi's only road linkage with the rest of the island is the Trans-Sulawesi Highway, cut by the Suharto government into the rugged mountain forests of the central part of the island. It links the southern Sulawesi city of Makassar with Manado, in North Sulawesi (see Figure 8.2). According to a recent visitor, "It is at best two lanes, shared by buses, cars, lorries, bicycles, motorcycles, horse carts, ox-carts, cows, dogs, chicken, goats, and children. There are a few small towns that hug the road, but little in these towns was further back than two houses."[31] There is a bus service from the Christian city of Tentena, on Lake Poso in the interior of Central Sulawesi, to the town of Poso, on the west coast of the province, and on to the provincial capital, Palu, on the east coast. The road is in good condition except where it crosses the neck of the northern Sulawesi peninsula. Here, according to travel reports, it is steep, narrow, and dangerous—muddy when it rains and dusty when dry, with plenty of potholes.[32]

---

[30] Data provided by Atty. Suharto Ambolodto, Cotabato City, Mindanao, August 2005.

[31] Zachary Abuza, private communication, May 2005.

[32] "Sulawesi (Palu)" (undated).

Figure 8.2
The Sulawesi-Mindanao Arc—Infrastructure

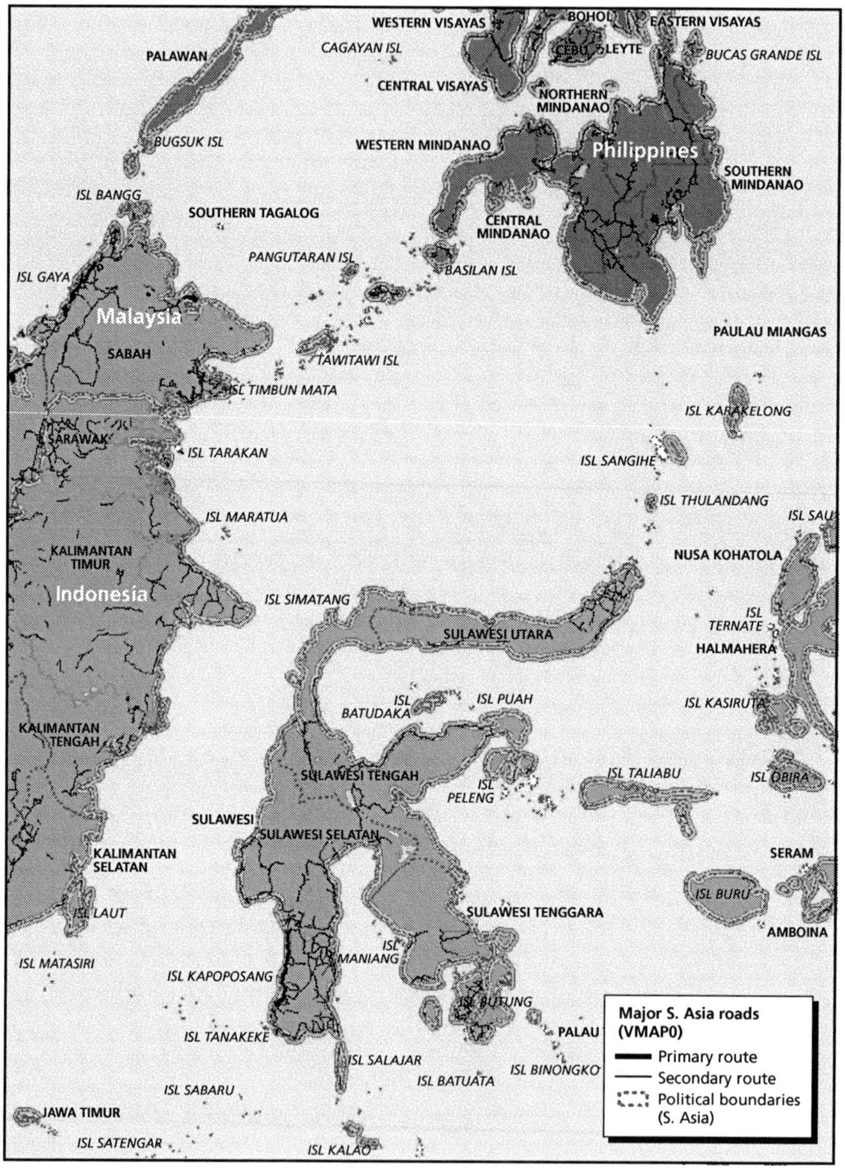

SOURCE: RAND.

RAND *MG561-8.2*

The easiest way to enter Central Sulawesi is by air. There is a small airstrip in Palu that handles daily flights from Makassar and Manado. At one time, Palu was a fairly thriving port for the timber and natural resources from the region. However, deforestation appears to have put an end to the timber trade. Macadamia nuts now seem to be about the only export through Palu. The inter-island ferry stops there roughly every few days.[33]

Muslim Mindanao

As in Sulawesi, the few roads that exist in Muslim Mindanao are small and narrow. There is a national highway, a two-lane paved road that links General Santos with Cotabato City and forks north of Cotabato City to connect it with Davao to the northeast and Marawi to the northwest. The drive between Cotabato City and Davao is generally safe during the day, but the bus line that operates between Davao and Cotabato stops running after 1:00 p.m. The roads into the interior, however, are mostly unpaved, and many are accessible only to four-wheel-drive vehicles.[34]

There are two daily flights between Manila and Cotabato City on Philippine Airlines and other flights on a local airline. The airport accommodates Boeing 737s. It is located in a military zone adjacent to the Philippine Army's 6th Division headquarters and is heavily guarded. South East Asian Airlines, a local airline, has daily flights to Jolo and Tawi-Tawi by way of Zamboanga. The communications infrastructure is weak, but gradually improving. In the past five years, there has been a large expansion in cell phone coverage. In 2000–2001 a cell phone could only be used in the cities. Now almost the entire Davao-Cotabato corridor is covered, as is the General Santos-Cotabato route. There is no coverage from Cotabato to Marawi beyond Parang.[35]

Corruption and the Prevalence of an Informal Economy

Corruption is pervasive in Indonesia and the Philippines. According to Transparency International's Corruption Perception Index 2004, Indonesia ranked 135th and the Philippines 102nd out of 145 countries, with a score of 2.0 and 2.6, respectively (on a scale of 1 to 10, with 1 being "highly corrupt" and 10 "highly clean").[36] In Central Sulawesi, as in other parts of Indonesia, corruption among local bureaucracies is endemic. In 2004, government prosecutors questioned four members of the Donggala and Parigi Moutong regional governments in Palu, Central Sulawesi, amid corruption allegations involving 5.2 billion rupiahs (Rp) of government funds.[37] On May 28, 2005, two explosions at a market in Tentena killed 21 people and injured 74. The bombings were originally thought to have been the work of an Islamist suicide bomber,

---

[33] Abuza, private communication, May 2005.

[34] Rabasa's personal observations and discussions in Cotabato City, Mindanao, August 2005; Abuza, private communication, May 2005.

[35] Abuza, private communication, May 2005.

[36] Transparency International (2004).

[37] Embassy of Indonesia (2005).

but some theorize that they might have been intended to divert attention from the embezzlement by local officials of Rp 2.3 billion ($242,000) in aid for the resettlement of refugees in Poso.[38] In addition, corruption and lawlessness since the fall of Suharto have fueled illegal logging in the province's Lore Lindu National Park.[39]

Addressing deeply rooted problems of corruption, collusion and nepotism (which Indonesians refer to as KKP) has taken central stage in the political discourse in post-Suharto Indonesia. The Indonesian legislature established an Anti-Corruption Commission and passed Law No. 31 on Eradication of Corruption in 1999. To address the problem of backlog cases and allegations of corrupt judges, reforms in the judiciary have ranged from the firing of judges to salary increases, especially for junior judges who make only Rp 1 million a month, not even enough to pay for a plane ticket to Jakarta from a remote province where they may be posted.[40]

Reversing the tide of corruption in Indonesia will likely take a long time because of the low level of income of government officials, the cultural norms that require them to take care of subordinates and relatives, and the resulting need to raise money in unconventional ways. Some Indonesians complain that corruption is more widespread now than under Suharto. According to a 2003 survey commissioned by the Asia Foundation, 69 percent of the respondents thought that government officials were very corrupt (41 percent) or fairly corrupt (28 percent). Bribery appears to be commonplace. More than a third (35 percent) said that they personally knew someone who had to pay a bribe to government or police officers for service or fair treatment. Only 31 percent said they definitely had no contact with someone involved in bribery.[41]

In the case of the Philippines, a 2003–2004 survey revealed that 68 percent of business enterprises had been asked for a bribe in connection with taxes or licenses but only 7 percent had reported the incident. In the same survey, 27 percent of the respondents said they had been asked for a bribe connected with a government transaction, but only 6 percent had reported it. The low percentage of individuals reporting such incidents is a reflection of citizens' lack of trust in government agencies. It is not surprising that the current administration of Gloria Macapagal-Arroyo had a percent net negative public satisfaction level with regard to its performance rating in eradicating graft and corruption. The three agencies cited as having the worst reputation for corruption are the Bureau of Custom, the Bureau of Internal Revenue, and the Department of Public Works and Highways.[42]

---

[38] "14 Detained Over Tentena Bombings" (2005); "Bombing: Theories Abound" (2005).

[39] "Corruption Fuel Epidemic of Illegal Logging in Indonesia" (2002).

[40] "Survey: The Importance of Going Straight" (2004), p. 6.

[41] Meisburger (2003), pp. 150–151.

[42] Social Weather Stations (2005b).

Corruption is reportedly very high in the ARMM. Although billions of pesos have been poured into the ARMM since its inception in 1991, there is very little to show for it. As discussed above, the ARMM remains by far the poorest region of the country. Persistent poverty and lack of economic opportunity—which has resulted in large-scale migration from the Moro areas to other parts of the Philippines—and the poor performance of government institutions has created conditions that fuel separatist sentiment and can be exploited by illegal movements.

Indonesia has one of the largest informal economies in the world and the Philippines is not far behind. During the 1980s and 1990s, the informal sector in Indonesia consistently accounted for more than 60 percent of the total labor force. The growth of the informal sector was particularly high during the 1997–1998 economic crisis. The crash of the modern sector of the economy caused the number of newly unemployed to more than double in the informal sector.[43]

Social and Cultural Resistance

Central Sulawesi

Shifts in ethno-religious balances as the result of internal migration in Indonesia and the Philippines appear to be the common denominator in communal conflict in Sulawesi and Mindanao. In the early part of the twentieth century, Dutch missionaries converted indigenous animist groups in the mountainous interior of what is now Central Sulawesi province to Christianity. The colonial administration envisioned these converts, ethnically identified as Pamona, as allies against the Muslim coastal communities. In the chaotic period after the end of the Japanese occupation, Muslim rebels from South Sulawesi attacked animists and Christians in the interior of Sulawesi. However, well into the republican period, the majority of the population in Central Sulawesi remained Christian, and Pamona leaders exercised partial control over the local bureaucracy.

As in the Moluccas, another theater of communal violence in the post-Suharto period, the ethnic balance in Central Sulawesi began to change with the Suharto government's policy of transmigration—that is, the transfer of population from overpopulated areas of Indonesia, primarily Java and Madura, to the outer islands. Figures for Central Sulawesi are shown in Table 8.2. The population density of the entire Sulawesi-Mindanao arc is shown in Figure 8.3.

---

[43] "Accommodating the Urban Informal Sector" (2003).

Table 8.2
Migration to Central Sulawesi, 1980–2000

Year	Migrants		
	Entered	Left	Net Difference
1980	80,515	17,282	63,233
1990	68,694	28,038	40,656
1995	70,833	28,017	42,816
2000	75,328	30,555	44,773

SOURCE: SP 1980, 1990, 2000 dan Supas 1995
Catatan: Migrasi Resent adalah Migrasi 5 tahun
sebelum dan setelah Sensus Penduduk.

The new roads and settlements established by the central government also attracted a flood of voluntary migrants, especially Muslimsettlers from majority Muslim South Sulawesi. As a result, many Pamona Christians were displaced from their ancestral lands and lost their religious and ethnic majority in the Poso regency (district).[44] According to the 2000 census, the religious composition of Central Sulawesi was 78.4 percent Muslim, 17.2 percent Christian, and the rest belonging to other religions. In Poso, the scene of violent sectarian conflict beginning in 2000, Muslims constituted 55.6 percent; Christians, 40.16 percent.[45]

Muslim Mindanao

A similar dynamic applies in Muslim Mindanao, although social and cultural resistance is much greater on that island than in Sulawesi because the demographic changes took place against a background of historic Moro resistance to Manila. The self-identification of the Muslim population in the southern Philippines as Bangsamoro (the Moro nation) is relatively new in historic terms and emerged as a reaction to outside encroachment on the historic Moro heartland. The Moros are divided into at least 13 distinct ethno-linguistic groups, the most important of which are the Maranao and the closely related Ilano of Lanao del Sur; the Maguindanao of Cotabato and Maguindanao; the Tausug on the island of Jolo (Sulu); the Yakan of Basilan Island; the Samal of Tawi-Tawi and adjacent islands; and the Jama Mapun of Cagayan de Sulu. The Moro languages are not mutually intelligible and Moros communicate with members of other Moro communities in Tagalog, the official language of the Philippines. Nevertheless, there is no question of the strength of the Moro identity. It is a form of "primordial tie" that binds an ethnic and reli-

---

[44] Aragon (2001).

[45] Suryadinata, Arifin, and Ananta (2003), p. 174.

Figure 8.3
The Sulawesi-Mindanao Arc—Population

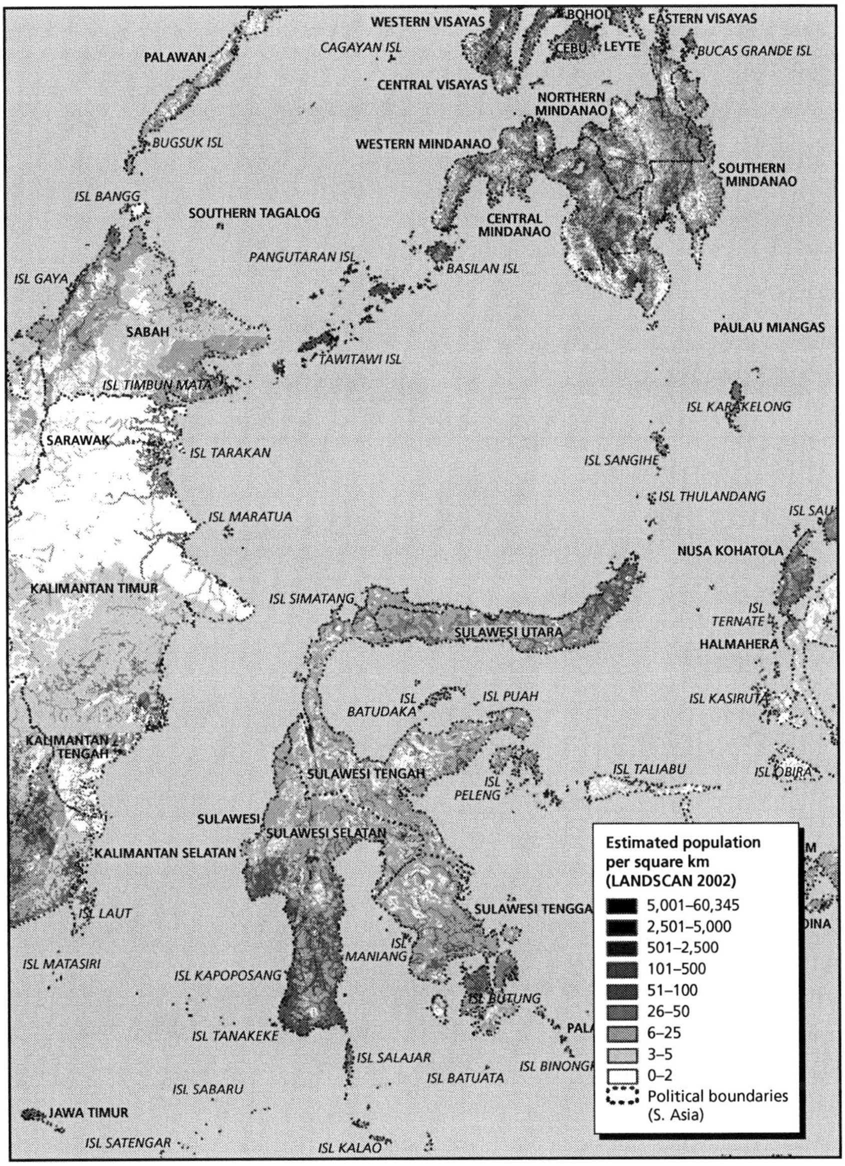

SOURCE: RAND.
RAND MG561-8.3

gious group and can serve to mobilize andunify individuals within the group, especially when their way of life is threatened by political and economic change.[46]

---

[46] Brass (1991).

Transmigration and conflicts over land were key factors in the polarization of ethnic and religious groups and the outbreak of armed conflict in Mindanao. As noted earlier in this chapter, the migration and assimilation polices encouraged by successive Philippine governments altered the ethnic and religious balance in the southern regions: At the end of the nineteenth century, Mindanao and the Sulu archipelago were overwhelmingly Muslim; Muslims make up approximately 17 percent of the population today.[47] In 1903, the Moro Province (Cotabato, Davao, Zamboanga, Lanao, Sulu) had a total population of 395,000: 275,000 Muslims, 40,000 Christians, and 80,000 other non-Christians, spread over 38,888 square miles.[48]

Migration in Mindanao reached its peak soon after World War II. Although many people were wary of migrating to Mindanao because of the widely held view of the island as the "wild country," unfavorable postwar economic conditions and the continued decrease in "man-to-land ratios" elsewhere in the Philippines encouraged many from various parts of Luzon and the Visayas to migrate to Mindanao.[49] From 1946 to 1960, Mindanao's population grew from fewer than 3 million to over 5 million inhabitants, a 7.4 percent annual growth rate that was double the national rate.[50] The resettlement impulse came not only from outside but also from within Mindanao. More than 1.2 million people moved from densely populated to sparsely populated areas within the island, following the opening of roads by either the government or timber companies.[51]

The massive movement of people and the conversion of large parcels of land for industrial use by private companies disenfranchised the Muslim population of Mindanao of both land and resources. The dispossession of Moros from their land resulted from clashing conceptions of land ownership. In the traditional Moro system of landholding known as *pusaca* there was no formal ownership of the land by individuals. The land was held in trust or usufruct and tilled on behalf of a *datu* (member of the Moro nobility) or clan. From the point of view of Manila, however, these were public lands to which titles could be distributed to settlers. Currently, landless tenants constitute 80 percent of the Muslim population of Mindanao.[52]

The population shift also altered the political and social balance in Mindanao. Unlike most other parts of the Philippines, Mindanao did not have large landowners. However, as settlers increased in numbers, so did their economic and political influ-

---

[47] Samuel K. Tan (1995).

[48] *1903 Census of the Philippine Islands*, volume 2. A breakdown of the Christian and non-Christian population in the different cities is at Abinales (2000), p. 191.

[49] Abinales (2000).

[50] Oosterhout (1983).

[51] Krinks (1970).

[52] Dictaan-Bang-oa (2004), p. 154.

ence. The settlers in Cotabato and Maguindanao never really found common ground for long-term peaceful coexistence with the Muslim population, and in Davao linguistic differences were a source of everyday conflict that pitted one migrant group against another—from the electoral arena down to daily encounters.[53]

The issue of migration and settlement in Mindanao provides a clear link between past and present conflicts in Mindanao. Conflicts over land in the 1960s induced settlers to form paramilitary groups; Muslims established their own armed groups to protect their holdings from encroachment by the settlers. These armed groups were the origin of the Moro National Liberation Front.[54] As Arturo Sorogan has said, "If there is a single issue connecting the colonial and immediate post-colonial periods, it is the so-called land problem and its repercussions for . . . stability."[55]

Lack of a Monopoly of Force

A weak state presence, communal conflict in Central Sulawesi, and insurgencies in Mindanao fostered the emergence of alternative power centers. In Mindanao, where the MILF established a para-state with a standing army in the areas that it controls, this alternative structure is much stronger than it is in Sulawesi. In Sulawesi, there is no organized resistance to the state, but the central government has difficulty preventing outbreaks of communal conflict and bringing them quickly under control.

Central Sulawesi

Large-scale violence between the Muslim and Christian communities broke out in Poso, Central Sulawesi, in April 2000. The violence was precipitated, as was the case a year earlier in Ambon, by a trivial incident between members of the two communities. In the first stage of the conflict, attacks by Muslims on Christians culminated in killings and destruction of hundreds of Christian homes. Christians killed hundreds of Muslims in retaliatory attacks. The highland Christian town of Tentena, the stronghold of the Christian fighters, including the notorious Black Bat "ninja raiders," became a de facto mini-state with Christian vigilantes checking cars coming in and out of town.[56] The inability of the military and the police to move rapidly to control the number of fighters from other towns, villages, and islands from entering Poso allowed the violence to expand. According to a Human Rights Watch Report, internal rivalry

---

[53] Abinales (2000), p. 109.

[54] Rabasa discussion with Ishak Mastura, Cotabato City, August 2005.

[55] Sorongan (1955).

[56] "Sulawesi: Actors" (2001).

between the police and the army, coupled with bureaucratic delays, caused the slow response.[57]

There was a resurgence of violence in April 2001, when a local court condemned to death three Christian Black Bat commanders accused of involvement in the violence. In August 2001, the Laskar Jihad, a Java-based extremist group responsible for much of the violence in Ambon, declared jihad in Poso and began to dispatch hundreds of fighters to the district, where the Laskar Mujahidin and another extremist militia, the Laskar Jundullah, were already active. As in Ambon, the arrival of the Laskar Jihad forces decisively tilted the balance against the Christians. The situation stabilized in December 2001, when the national government sent two battalions of soldiers and police (composed predominantly of Christians from North Sulawesi) to the Christian areas. Other troops took over the checkpoints previously manned by Muslim militants.[58]

There are several explanations for the failure of the authorities to respond more quickly and forcefully to the violence. A senior Indonesian security official explained that until they were reinforced at the end of 2001, the security forces were outnumbered by the irregulars and were unable to enforce the law. There were also suggestions that the authorities believed that intervention would only inflame the problem.[59]

Government-sponsored negotiations between the Muslim and Christian camps produced the Malino I and II agreements, in which the two parties undertook to end hostilities in Poso and Ambon, respectively, and to disarm their militias. Although the Jakarta government was careful to avoid giving the appearance of siding with one camp or the other, there were allegations that the security forces took sides in the conflict in Poso. Muslims asserted that the local police and military "turned a blind eye" to the killings of May 2000 while Christians interpreted the pullout of troops in November 2001, leaving them vulnerable, as a tell-tale sign of military collusion with the opposing side. Although the agreement brought an end to large-scale violence in Poso, the security situation remains precarious, with periodic criminal actions and attacks by masked provocateurs. Southeast Asia terrorism expert Zachary Abuza, who visited the region in May 2005, reports that judges, prosecutors, and others involved in the peace process were being systematically killed in an attempt to provoke conflict.[60] It appears, therefore, that only the heavy military and police presence is keeping the lid on a potentially explosive situation.

---

[57] Human Rights Watch (2002), p. 42.

[58] Rabasa (2003), pp. 30–31.

[59] "Sulawesi: Actors" (2001).

[60] Abuza, private communication, May 2005.

Muslim Mindanao

The security situation in Mindanao is very complex. There are two major insurgencies, one waged by the Communist Party of the Philippines/New People's Army (CCP/NPA) and the other by the MILF. As noted above, a cease-fire is currently in effect, and exploratory talks toward a peace agreement between the Philippine government and the MILF are taking place. The JI and remnants of the terrorist-criminal Abu Sayyaf Group are reportedly present, in addition to normal criminal activity.

The Philippine government considers the NPA insurgency to be the country's most pressing security threat because of its nationwide character. According to Philippine authorities, the NPA strength is about 7,000, down from an estimated 28,000 at its peak in the mid-1980s. The NPA is present throughout the Philippine archipelago but is strongest in Samar, in the Visayas. At its height, the NPA has a strong presence in the Compostela Valley in southeastern Mindanao, but its strength there has since declined.[61] Other parts of Mindanao, such as the entire east coast, the Surigao Valley, and the far west, in particular Misamis and Zamboanga del Norte, have a very strong NPA presence and are nearly ungovernable.[62]

According to Philippine military sources, the MILF has an armed strength of 8,000, with other estimates as high as 15,000 or even higher. Its forces are deployed in nine "base commands" throughout western Mindanao. The bulk of the MILF membership comes from the Maguindanao tribe, but Maranaos and Ilanun are also represented, while the MNLF is predominantly Tausug. MILF tactics have taken the form of classic guerrilla warfare, with hit-and-run attacks and ambushes. Generally, the group has not emphasized indiscriminate attacks against civilians and noncombatants, in marked contrast to the ASG, although at times MILF elements have been allegedly involved in bombings, for instance the Davao bombings in 2003.[63]

The MILF leadership is sensitive to the issue of linkages with outside extremists. In 2003, the MILF's longtime leader, Salamat Hashim, renounced terrorism as part of the resumption of a peace process with the Manila government. Since then, according to Philippine military sources, the MILF has refrained from using terror tactics. The MILF's turn to a more flexible approach was accelerated by the accession to the MILF leadership of the organization's military commander, Murad Ebrahim, after Salamat's

---

[61] Rabasa discussions with Armed Forces of the Philippines officials, Camp Aguinaldo, Quezon City, August 9, 2005.

[62] Abuza, private communication, May 2005.

[63] The MILF denies responsibility for the Davao bombing. Nevertheless, as part of the ongoing peace process between the government of the Republic of the Philippines (GRP) and the MILF, the GRP dropped charges against MILF leaders and members implicated in the bombing.

death in July 2003. While Salamat was a religious scholar trained in al-Azhar, Murad is a military man whom some considered to be more pragmatic.[64]

How much control Murad exercises over the organization is a matter of debate. Philippine analysts believe that although Murad enjoys strong support among his fellow Maguindanaos, there are factions within the MILF that may not entirely support his leadership.[65] The JI and the ASG are believed to be trying to exploit this rift.

Increasingly, however, Murad is consolidating his authority within the MILF, as indicated by the overwhelming number of people in attendance at the MILF's first open general assembly on May 29–31, 2005. Both unarmed fighters and civilian supporters of the MILF came in droves to Camp Darapanan, in Sultan Kudarat. The Lanao del Sur delegation registered 4,000 vehicles and a total of 14,000 marshals were deployed. Murad addressed the entire assembly "sounding more like a diplomat than a revolutionary, assured MILF followers that the fight is coming to an end and that peace dividends are near."[66] It is a wise strategy for the MILF leadership to take, given that a 2005 Social Weather Stations poll showed that 89 percent of those in the ARMM favor resolving the Muslim rebel problem through peaceful instead of military means.[67]

The interim guidelines agreed to by the Philippine government and the MILF to implement the Ad Hoc Joint Action Group, the mechanism tasked with isolating criminal and lawless elements found within MILF communities, commits the MILF to cooperate with the Armed Forces of the Philippines (AFP) in arresting terrorists and criminals in MILF camps.[68] Developments in 2005 show that the MILF has stopped providing refuge to the ASG. In July 2005, Murad ordered ASG elements to leave MILF territory.[69] In the latest AFP offensive in Maguindanao, according to Philippine military sources, ASG elements, believed to include ASG leader Khaddafy Janjalani and located in South Opi, Talayan, and Datu Odin Sinsuat in the border between the provinces of Cotabato and Maguindanao, were being pursued by the Philippine military with the active collaboration of the MILF. In order to allow the AFP to go after

---

[64] Andrew Tan (2003), p. 107. Sources close to the MILF argue that Salamat was himself quite pragmatic and that Murad has simply continued Salamat's line.

[65] Including, according to Philippine military sources and political analysts, a faction associated with former leader Salamat.

[66] Vitug (2005).

[67] Social Weather Stations (2005a).

[68] Embassy of the Philippines (2005).

[69] According to Major General Agustin Demaala, commander of the Army's 6th Infantry Division, the MILF asked the Abu Sayyaf to leave in the first week of July 2005. "Abu Sayyaf Kicked out of MILF Turf" (2005).

the ASG, the MILF left its camps in the areas of operations and provided guides to assist the AFP in their search and prevent accidental encounters with MILF troops.[70]

Nevertheless, a continued presence of JI trainers in MILF camps has been reported. As of early 2004, the International Crisis Group reports, based on Indonesian sources, that Indonesians continued to be sent to camps in Mindanao for training in small groups. Some appeared to be JI members; others were members of Darul Islam and other groups.[71] According to a *New York Times* report, about 100 foreign recruits, mostly Indonesians, come for training to Mindanao every year.[72] Philippine authorities have identified by name 29 foreign JI trainers and operatives (although they acknowledge that these names could be aliases). The JI trainers reportedly moved from Mt. Cararao, on the North Cotabato-Lanao del Sur border (because of the presence of international observers who are monitoring the cease-fire between the GRP and the MILF) to Jabal Huda, in North Cotabato, an area with access to Maguindanao and Lanao del Sur.[73] Philippine military intelligence personnel believe that the JI is attempting to work with local MILF commanders but not necessarily with the blessing of the MILF leadership.[74]

The MILF under Murad has sought to distance itself from the global jihadist movement represented in Southeast Asia by JI. It denies the "myth" of JI trainers in MILF camps. However, Zachary Abuza and the International Crisis Group believe that there is a continuing relationship. According to the ICG, it is possible that the MILF leadership is not fully aware of the extent to which individual local commanders have made their own arrangements with JI and other groups. Further, the ICG says that there is growing evidence that Camp Hudaibiyah alumni have used their training not only to revitalize JI ranks at home in Indonesia, but also to carry out terror attacks in the Philippines itself and to breathe new life into the ASG.[75]

There are certainly considerations that could arguably influence the MILF's willingness or ability to move decisively to end these relationships, such as the existence of personal ties between MILF and JI members and the potential usefulness of JI spe-

---

[70] Rabasa discussions with Armed Forces of the Philippines officials, Camp Aguinaldo, Quezon City, August 9, 2005. See also Bonner and Conde (2005).

[71] ICG (2004g), p. 25.

[72] Bonner and Conde (2005).

[73] Rabasa discussions with Armed Forces of the Philippines officials, Camp Aguinaldo, Quezon City, August 9, 2005.

[74] Rabasa discussions with Armed Forces of the Philippines officials, Camp Aguinaldo, Quezon City, August 9, 2005

[75] ICG (2004g), p. 17. MILF sources, however, insist that the group's central military command exercises close supervision and control of subordinate commanders. In a 2005 unpublished manuscript entitled "Structure, Organization and Internal Dynamics of the Moro Islamic Liberation Front," Zachary Abuza, who has made an extensive study of the MILF political and military organization, says there is a significant degree of command and control, considering that the MILF is a guerrilla force.

cialized training to the MILF. The MILF is mindful of the possibility that the peace process may not be successful, and it could hedge its bets by maintaining a residual relationship with JI. The benefits to MILF of a relationship with JI under present circumstances, however, appear to be tenuous, given that the MILF is seeking international respectability and appears to be seriously committed to reaching a peace agreement with the Philippine government.

As the Manila government and the MILF move closer to a peaceful resolution of their conflict, the much smaller Abu Sayyaf Group, which combines terrorism with crime for profit, remains the major Islamist threat to security in Mindanao. The ASG was established in the early 1990s by Abdurajak Janjalani, a Moro veteran of the jihad in Afghanistan, with the support of his brother-in-law, Mohammed Jamal Khalifa. Their goal is to establish an independent theocratic state based on Wahhabi principles in the southern Philippines. After Abdurajak's death in a clash with police on Basilan Island in December 1998, the group lost much of its ideological impetus and appeared to have degenerated into a criminal enterprise disguised in Islamist ideology. The ASG's kidnapping and beheading of American citizens and its earlier association with al-Qaeda made it the principal target of the U.S.-led war on terrorism in the Philippines.

According to Philippine military sources, the ASG has an estimated current strength of about 300 fighters, down considerably from the group's estimated strength of 1,000 during the Sipadan kidnapping incident in April 2000. In the summer of 2005 Khaddafy Janjalani and other Abu Sayyaf leaders left Basilan Island and were believed to be on the main island of Mindanao, on the Cotabato-Maguindanao border, where they were being pursued by Philippine military forces. According an authoritative MILF source, the reason Janjalani and the other ASG leaders left Basilan was that "the people of Basilan, Sulu and Tawi-Tawi don't want them there anymore because of their involvement in kidnappings and other un-Islamic activities." The MILF estimate of ASG numbers is lower than the AFP estimate—only a small band of 20 or so, including the leaders and their security detail.[76]

Another factor contributing to the lack of stability in Mindanao is the higher level of clan and family feuds, or *ridos*, as compared to the rest of the Philippines. According to a survey conducted in December 2004, 28 percent of the acts of violence in the ARMM was due to conflict between families and clans while 20 percent was attributed to conflict between Muslim rebels and the AFP.[77] Another survey in Muslim Mindanao and adjacent areas cited in a study by the Philippines Asia Foundation director Steven Rood shows that 43 percent of conflicts were among families, clans,

---

[76] Rabasa discussion with senior MILF leader, Mindanao, August 11, 2005. According to this source, the fugitive ASG leaders have no future in Maguindanao because there are very few people there who are sympathetic to the ASG.

[77] Social Weather Stations (2005a).

and tribes; 38 percent between Christians and Muslims or between the military and the MILF or the ASG, and 15 percent between landowners and farmers or employers and laborers.[78]

Local police usually do not interfere in these clan and family feuds because they could be killed. Rood notes that clan conflicts tend to get misinterpreted as MILF-military clashes; the military is dragged into these cases when some members of the clan also happen to be rebels. Then the clashes can escalate into full-blown battles. As in the case of other ungoverned territories, such as the Northwest Frontier Province of Pakistan, these feuds are resolved not in the courts but through the payment of "blood money" after the parties swear on the Qur'an not to retaliate. Some communities are trying to take preventative measures. For instance, in Tawi-Tawi the local authorities are setting up rules on how to deal with elopement, so that it does not cause clan wars.[79]

Compromised Sovereignty and Lack of Effective Border Control

Unlike the borders of other ungoverned territories considered elsewhere in this book, the borders of the region studied in this chapter are maritime and have their own special characteristics. Trading routes in the Celebes Sea and the Sulu Sea have been used since time immemorial by travelers moving between what today are Indonesia, Malaysia, and the Philippines. Poorly policed sea borders make the lands bordering on this maritime space, including Sulawesi, Mindanao, and the Malaysian State of Sabah, vulnerable to infiltration by Islamic extremists, as well as by smugglers and common criminals.

At the height of the MNLF insurgency in Mindanao in the 1970s, the MNLF set up training camps at Sandakan, in Malaysia's Sabah state, with the support of the state's chief minister, the late Tun Mustapha bin Datu Harun. (Tun Mustapha was born on the island of Tawi-Tawi in the Sulu archipelago and was Tausug on his mother's side.) The Sabah government's support of the MNLF lasted until Mustapha was eased out by the central government in Kuala Lumpur in 1975. Nevertheless, with its 500,000 (or perhaps more) Philippine migrants out of a total population of 2.2 million, Sabah's demographic makeup and proximity to Mindanao make it a suitable rear area for militants, who can blend into and develop support networks undetected among the large migrant population—the condition that we refer to as invisibility.[80]

Six Indonesians were captured in September 2003 off the coast of Sabah, among them Zulkifli, head of the southern Philippines wakalah of JI, and a significant figure

---

[78] Rood (2005), p. 6.

[79] Rood (2005), p. 6.

[80] For Tun Mustapha's dealings with the MNLF, see Vitug and Gloria (2002).

in the organization.[81] He was allegedly en route to Indonesia to meet with key JI leader Abu Dujana to discuss taking over the leadership of Mantiqui III.[82] Another group, picked up in Semarang, Indonesia, in 2003, reportedly went to the Philippines for a short training course but spent time in Sandakan before and after coming back from the Philippines. There are reports that JI operations leader Zulkarnaen and explosives experts Azahari bin Husin and Dulmatin met on Sebatik Island, south of Sandakan, in March 2003.[83]

Mitigating Factors

Maritime borders are notoriously difficult to control, particularly along the Celebes and Sulu Seas, where the littoral countries for the most part lack the means of patrolling their territorial waters. On the other hand, the archipelagic nature of the region also makes it harder for insurgent and terrorist to transport weapons (which requires hazardous sea voyages) or to establish sanctuaries or supply bases outside their area of operation. The MNLF, for instance, experienced difficulties in obtaining weapons for its struggle after Malaysia shut down its bases in Sabah.[84]

Assessment: The Sulawesi-Mindanao Arc as an Ungoverned Territory

From the above discussion it would seem that despite topographical and cultural similarities, Muslim Mindanao ranks higher on some key indicators of ungovernability than Central Sulawesi, as shown in Table 8.3. Again, the rankings are 1 = low; 2 = medium; and 3 = high. Generally, the higher the ranking, the more ungoverned the territory.

Attributes of the Sulawesi-Mindanao Arc Conducive to the Presence of Terrorist and Insurgent Groups

As noted in the introduction, just because a territory is marked by a degree of ungovernability does not necessarily mean it will emerge as a base for terrorist activity. For

---

[81] The JI is structured into territorial districts known as *mantiqis*, which in turn are subdivided into *wakalah*. It is unclear what level of organization remains after JI's losses since 2003.

[82] According to the International Crisis Group, Zulkifli is linked to a series of arson and bomb attacks in Mindanao in 2002, as well as the Cotabato and Davao airport bombings of 2003. ICG (2004g), p. 19.

[83] "Home-Grown Terrorism" (2004).

[84] Rabasa discussion with Ishak Mastura, Cotabato City, Mindanao, August 12, 2005.

Table 8.3
Indicators of Ungovernability, Sulawesi-Mindanao

Variable	Sulawesi	Mindanao
Lack of state penetration		
Absence of state institutions	2	3
Lack of physical infrastructure	2	2
Social and cultural resistance	1	3
Lack of monopoly of force		
Organized armed groups	2	3
Criminal networks	2	2
Population with access to arms	2	3
Lack of border controls	2	3
External interference	1	1

this to occur, the region in question must have attributes that make it hospitable to insurgent or terrorist groups. The following section takes up these considerations more fully as they apply to the Sulawesi-Mindanao arc. These attributes include adequacy of infrastructure, that is, the existence of an infrastructure that allows terrorist groups to perform basic functions and gain access to targets; sources of income; favorable demographic and social features; and invisibility, the characteristic of the environment that allows terrorists to escape detection by the authorities.

Adequacy of Infrastructure and Operational Access

Although the interior of Central Sulawesi and Muslim Mindanao is difficult to access, there are regular flights to major cities in these regions. Paved roads link these cities to other towns, and, at least in some places there is a communications infrastructure—wireless connectivity, Internet access and satellite coverage—that would make these areas viable centers of operation for militant groups. During a visit to Palu, the capital of Central Sulawesi, Zachary Abuza noted that Palu was the only town in Central Sulawesi that had cellular phone coverage. Two national cellular providers had towers in the town. Abuza thought this was in part the reason that a number of JI members were subsequently arrested in Palu: it was a place with a communications link to the outside world.[85]

Remittances from overseas workers into Indonesia and the Philippines come through both formal and informal channels. A World Bank report showed that, in 2000, 5 percent of total remittances to the Philippines were privately transferred; in the case of Indonesia, 21 percent of total remittances were privately transferred.[86] Remit-

---

[85] Abuza, private communication, May 2005.

[86] El Qorchi, Munzele Maimbo, and Wilson (2000).

tances to Indonesia from 1983 to 1986 amounted to US$551,523,406, with the bulk coming from Saudi Arabia.[87] Filipino workers overseas, on the other hand, remitted US$5.6 billion to the Philippines from January to September 2005.[88] These informal channels can take the form of the alternative and underground hawala system, in which money is transferred without being actually moved.[89] It can be assumed that funding for organizations such as JI comes through similar informal channels, exploiting the same established and trusted method of transferring money that overseas Indonesian and Filipino foreign workers use. A percentage of the JI funds is also believed to be channeled through private couriers.[90]

Sources of Income

JI raises funds through both criminal and noncriminal means. The noncriminal means include written appeals, Internet appeals, and direct fund-raising. For example, Yunnus, a pesantren teacher, asked East Kalimantan employees of oil companies to contribute to the JI.[91] Internet appeals to contribute to the defense of oppressed Muslims conveniently provide a bank account number and phone number.[92] According to the International Crisis Group, a JI funding appeal was timed for the Id ul-Adha:[93] ". . . a JI member wrote to a well known energy drink requesting the donation of funds to buy animals [that will be sacrificed and shared] for families displaced by the Poso conflict." The *Kotak Amal* (charity box) was widely used in Poso fund-raising activities. This box is supposed to provide aid for the humanitarian efforts in Poso, especially for displaced families, yet ICG reports that it has been exploited by the JI as a fund-raising device.[94]

A more blatant and criminal manner by which JI raises funds is through the *fa'i*. The fa'i is the kidnapping and robbing of non-Muslims, which radicals claim is permitted by Islam. According to Sidney Jones,

> The documents were extraordinary in Semarang. They included plans of JI, training manuals, lists of people, plans to basically rob non-Muslims in order to gain

---

[87] Hugo (1995), p. 273.

[88] "OFW Remittances Up 5.1%" (2005).

[89] Jost and Sandhu (2007).

[90] "Terrorist Money Impossible to Stop" (2003).

[91] ICG (2004d), p. 10. *Pesantren* are Indonesian Islamic boarding schools.

[92] ICG (2004d), p. 9.

[93] The Muslim holiday that commemorates the sacrifice Ibrahim (Abraham) was asked to make of his son, Ismail (Ishmael), to show his obedience to God.

[94] ICG (2004d), p. 18.

additional funds for Islamic purposes, i.e. jihad, and some of those plans were extraordinary. There was one doctor who, for example, was targeted and two JI people had already cased his clinic pretending to be patients to try and assess what his movements were.[95]

There are indications that the JI may be running low on cash. The Indonesian State Intelligence Agency (BIN) chief, Syamsir Siregar, suggested that a string of bank and jewelery store robberies in Jakarta and neighboring towns in West Java may have been carried out by militants "trying to raise local funds."[96] Police Commissioner General Makbul Padmanegara stated that a gold store robbery in Yogyakarta in which the storekeeper and his assistant were killed was carried out by members of a gang recruited by JI fugitive Noordin Muhammad Top.[97]

The Abu Sayyaf Group raises its revenue largely through criminal activity. Kidnapping for ransom has been a hallmark of ASG activity. In March 2000, the ASG kidnapped 55 people in Basilan and, one month later, launched the kidnapping of 20 foreigners in the Malaysian diving resort of Sipadan.[98] According to Philippine authorities, in June 2005 the Philippines, in cooperation with Malaysia, foiled another Sipadan-type operation and in the process seized one of two speedboats that the ASG or associated criminal elements were to use in the kidnapping.[99] The Abu Sayyaf Group, of course, is not the only group engaged in kidnappings. In fact, as Steve Rood notes, the high-profile kidnappings by the ASG overshadow a long history of kidnappings in Mindanao whose victims have been primarily members of the Filipino-Chinese community.[100]

As noted in another RAND study, the ASG has carried out numerous pirate attacks off Mindanao and nearby islands, remaining particularly active between Tawi-Tawi, Sulu, Basilan, and the Zamboanga Peninsula.[101] In addition to assaulting commercial carriers, the ASG has also periodically attacked passenger ferries that operate in the Sulu and Celebes Seas. Although these assaults tend to net less money than assaults on cargo containers and fishing trawlers—the ferries are able to carry only a small number of paying customers, most of whom will not be particularly wealthy—the ships themselves tend to offer a highly attractive target of opportunity given their lack of maneuverability, the frequency and regularity of inter-island sailings, and the

---

[95] Four Corners (2003).

[96] "Azahari Death 'May Spark Revenge'" (2005).

[97] "Top Terror Suspect Noordin Behind Gem Shop Heist" (2005).

[98] Abuza (2003b), p. 52.

[99] Rabasa discussions with Armed Forces of the Philippines officials, Camp Aguinaldo, Quezon City, August 9, 2005.

[100] Rood (2005), p. 4.

[101] See "The Abu Sayyaf Group: An Islamic Terrorist-Criminal Group," in Rabasa et al. (2006b).

near total absence of any onboard security.[102] There are no reliable statistics as to how much money the ASG has actually made by engaging in maritime crime. However, most commentators believe it to be substantial.[103]

According to Philippine military sources, the CCP/NPA runs large marijuana plantations and derives much of its revenue from marijuana trafficked to urban areas. The group also produces hashish oil that is exported to Europe through syndicates in metropolitan Manila; one small vial reportedly commands a price of 15,000 pesos (US$273).

There is no evidence that the MILF is involved in drug trafficking, which it considers un-Islamic. The group is alleged to have been engaged in extorting money from legitimate businesses and kidnappings.[104] Sources sympathetic to the organization, however, attribute these activities to so-called "lost commands," rogue elements not under central leadership.[105] The main sources of income for the MILF appear to be contributions by sympathizers and, according to Philippine authorities, the *zakat* (a charitable donation made by Muslims as a religious obligation) and funds diverted from nongovernmental organizations.[106]

Favorable Demographic and Social Characteristics

As noted above, the regions bordering the Celebes and Sulu Sea is home to a multitude of extremist religious, ethnic and criminal entities, many of which have proven susceptible or vulnerable to outside co-option. The JI focused its initial recruitment in Palu on young out-of-school thugs. According to the ICG, "Those most eager to sign up as mujahidin were youths whose families had been directly affected but who also had a history of violence—thus, the preponderance of young gang members."[107] An ICG interview conducted in September 2003 noted that the Tanah Rutnuh area of

---

[102] Chalk (2002).

[103] This perspective on the ASG was expressed to Chalk in various meetings and interviews in the Philippines, London (International Maritime Bureau/IMB) and Singapore between 2000 and 2003. It is unclear how the escape of ASG leaders from the Sulu archipelago to the Mindanao mainland in 2005 has changed the situation.

[104] Abuza (2003b), p. 96.

[105] One of these sources, a Muslim religious scholar in Manila, notes that while the MILF leadership, particularly the late chairman Salamat Hashim, strongly disapproved of criminal activities for religious reasons, the MILF central command's inability to adequately pay and meet the materials needs of its fighters may have forced some local commanders to seek supplementary sources of income.

[106] Rabasa discussions with Armed Forces of the Philippines officials, Camp Aguinaldo, Quezon City, August 9, 2005.

[107] ICG (2004d), p. 8.

Poso, now a "stronghold of Muslim militants, used to be known as a gathering place of thieves and gang members."[108]

It is not surprising that most of those arrested had a history of membership in a street gang. Some students of terrorism refer to such recruits as misfits or drifters.[109] The ICG report refers to them as "situational mujahidin." These young people are induced by economic and social circumstances to join jihadist groups. The same report showed that these young people have at best a junior high education, although most have attended only elementary school.[110] Some were recruited through the network of radical pesantren, which also provided entrée into local communities. The pesantren in Palu for instance, admitted students from the Poso branch displaced by the conflict.[111]

In Mindanao, acceptance of JI members among the Moro communities in the period before 9/11 was more a matter of pragmatism than of genuine affinity. The mainstream Moro insurgencies, the MNLF, and later the MILF, always viewed their struggle as confined to the Moro homeland in the southern Philippines, even if they were willing to form tactical alliances with foreign partners. After 9/11, for instance, the MILF's late leader, Salamat Hashim, stated that the fight between the United States and the Taliban was not the Moros' business.

Invisibility

With vast tracts of inhospitable terrain and areas that are effectively outside the central government's purview (particularly in Mindanao), Sulawesi and Mindanao offer conditions of invisibility that allow terrorist to stay hidden from national law enforcement and counterterrorism agencies and their international partners. JI terrorists, who are largely Indonesians, can blend in well in Central Sulawesi where, as noted earlier, there has been a fair amount of migration from other parts of Indonesia. But in the Philippines, they can be given away by their language, since it would be unusual for Indonesians to speak fluent Tagalog or one of the Moro languages. As a Philippine official said in an interview, "they can pass unnoticed as long as they keep their mouth shut." This condition of invisibility depends, of course, on the toleration of the local population and could become quite precarious if the authorities are able to secure local cooperation.

---

[108]ICG interview, September 2003.

[109]Nesser (2005).

[110]ICG (2004d), p. 8.

[111]ICG (2004d), p. 8.

Assessment of the Conduciveness of the Sulawesi-Mindanao Arc to a Terrorist Presence

Table 8.4 summarizes the indicators of conduciveness of the Sulawesi-Mindanao arc to a terrorist presence. The values are 1 = low, 2 = medium; and 3 = high. As with the indicators of ungovernability, Mindanao ranks higher than Sulawesi on some key indicators, which would explain why JI has attempted to use Mindanao as a rear area for its operations in Indonesia.

Table 8.4
Indicators of Conduciveness to Terrorist Presence, Sulawesi-Mindanao

Variable	Sulawesi	Mindanao
Adequacy of infrastructure		
Communications	1	2
Financial infrastructure	2	2
Transportation	2	2
Operational access	1	2
Sources of income	2	2
Favorable demographics	2	3
Presence of extremist groups	2	3
Supporting social norms	2	3
Preexisting state of violence	2	3
Criminal syndicates	2	2
Invisibility	3	3

U.S. Policies and Programs

Soon after Operation Enduring Freedom in Afghanistan, the United States considered Southeast Asia to be the "second front" in the war on terrorism. This reflected the perceived high level of the terrorist threat in Southeast Asia—in December 2001, 13 members of a JI cell were arrested in Singapore and the group had well-developed plans to bomb the American and Israeli embassies, the Australian and British high commissions, and U.S. business and military targets in Singapore. Although the major JI terrorist attacks in Southeast Asia since 9/11 have, in fact, taken place in Indonesia (in Jakarta and Bali), Mindanao has been the focus of the U.S.-led war on terrorism in Southeast Asia. This is because Mindanao and its surrounding waters, with their vast swaths of ungoverned territory, offered shelter to Islamist extremists, particularly the notorious Abu Sayyaf Group (which had kidnapped two Americans and murdered a third) and also because the government of Philippine President Macapagal-Arroyo was willing to enlist unreservedly in the global war on terrorism.

Manila has allowed U.S. overflights of Philippine airspace and use of airfields in support of Operation Enduring Freedom. The United States, in turn, increased security assistance to the Philippines to levels not seen since the withdrawal of U.S. bases in 1992, from $2 million in FMF in FY02 to a sustained level of $19.0 million or more in FY02 and subsequent years, as shown in Table 8.5.

In addition, the United States allocated $10 million in drawdown authority to the Philippines (i.e., authority to transfer defense equipment and services) to re-equip, transport, and train the Philippine military, and transferred significant amounts in excess defense articles (EDA): one C-130B, two Point Class cutters, 5 UH-1H helicopters, and 15,000 M-16 rifles worth $37.5 million in FY02; 33 two-ton cargo trucks, three UH-1H helicopters, one Cyclone-class ship, and another 15,000 M16 rifles worth $24.81 million in FY03; and 20 UH-1H Huey helicopters worth $18.60 million in FY04. Other assistance programs include two separate counterterrorism assistance programs: the Counterterrorism Fellowship Program, funded by the Department of Defense, and a program directed at the police, funded by the Department of State and other U.S. government agencies.

Relevant to the counterterrorism campaign in the southern Philippines, the United States and the Philippines began a series of annual Balikatan combined military exercises in 2001. About 160 U.S. Special Forces personnel, including Navy SEALS, Army Green Berets, Marines with special operations capabilities, and 6th Air Force Special Operations Squadron (SOS) personnel, provided training, advice, and technical support to the AFP in counterterrorism operations against the Abu Sayyaf Group. The U.S. personnel accompanying Philippine troops on patrol were armed and authorized

Table 8.5
U.S. Security Assistance to the Philippines,
FY01–FY06 (millions of U.S. dollars)

Year	FMF	FMF CT[a]	PDA[b]	IMET
FY01	2.0			1.4
FY02	19.0	25.0	10.0	2.0
FY03	44.87[c]	30.0	10.0	2.4
FY04	19.88	15.0	10.0	2.7
FY05	29.76			3.0
FY06[d]	25.0			2.9

[a] Emergency Supplemental FMF grants to improve counterterrorism capabilities.
[b] Presidential Drawdown Authority.
[c] Includes $25 million in Supplemental FMF for engineering spares.
[d] FY06 request.

to fire in self-defense. These forces provided critical counterterrorism skills and capabilities to the AFP in its fight against the ASG in Basilan and Jolo.[112]

With regard to AFP capability-building, it is important to mention the Philippine Defense Reform Program, the defense planning process that is being implemented with the assistance of U.S. experts. The priority is to improve internal security, with special focus on combating terrorism, assisting national development, and responding to disasters, man-made or natural. The Philippine Ministry of Defense (MOD) is looking across doctrine, force structure, training, and equipment to redirect defense planning in accordance with MCAPS (Multi-Year Capabilities Planning System), a plan with an 18-year horizon divided into three-year segments. The MCAPS has two subsystems: one medium-term that is an enhanced version of the U.S. Planning, Programming and Budgeting System; and one long-term, which is based on best practices in the United States, the UK, Singapore, Australia, and New Zealand. This effort is constrained, of course, by resources. The MOD has asked the president for an add-on of 5 billion pesos (P) a year (US$100 million) for the next six years, rising to P10 billion/year for the following six years, and P20 billion/year for the final six years of the plan.[113]

The United States and Indonesia have gone a long way in deepening counterterrorism cooperation since 9/11, although political barriers on both sides have prevented the full normalization of their security relationship. Given Indonesia's status as the world's largest Muslim majority country and its geostrategic importance, the U.S. administration made it a policy priority after 9/11 to resume military cooperation with Indonesia, which had been interrupted after the violence on East Timor in 1999. After President Megawati Sukarnoputri's visit to Washington on September 19, 2001, barely a week after the 9/11 attacks, the United States also agreed to a significant expansion of military relations, including an annual Indonesia-U.S. strategic dialogue and the transfer of nonlethal military articles through the Direct Commercial Sales program (the definition of nonlethal items, however, did not extend to spares parts, even safety of flight equipment for the Indonesian Air Force's F-16s). There has also been robust cooperation in counterterrorism between Indonesia and the United States.

In 2005, following a further development in U.S.-Indonesia relations as the result of Indonesia's third free presidential election (and the first direct presidential election) since the fall of Suharto, which brought to office retired General Susilo Bambang Yudhoyono, and the U.S. and international response to the tsunami of December 2004, the United States took important steps to normalize its security relationship with Indonesia. In early 2005, the United States restored full IMET for Indonesia ($600,000 in FY05 and $800,000 requested for FY06), and reinstated FMS sales of nonlethal items,

---

[112] The Philippine Constitution prohibits foreign combat forces on Philippine soil without congressional authorization.

[113] Rabasa discussions with Under Secretary of Defense Antonio Santos and with U.S. advisors to the MOD, Manila, September 2005.

nonlethal safety-of-use spare parts for lethal end-items, and defense services related to nonlethal defense items. The FY06 Foreign Operations Appropriations bill passed by the U.S. House of Representatives in June 2005 included no restrictions on FMF or IMET for Indonesia. The Senate bill, however, restricted FMF to the Indonesian navy and included a certification requirement for other uses of FMF. In November 2005, the United States lifted the embargo on the transfer of lethal military equipment to Indonesia.

On the Indonesian side, the Indonesians have taken important strides to address concerns in certain U.S. circles about human rights, civilian control of the military, and transparency in military budgeting. The peace agreement signed by the Indonesian government with the Acehnese separatists in Helsinki in August 2005 put an end to nearly 30 years of conflict in Aceh. Papua remains a source of bilateral friction. Indonesians across the political spectrum are sensitive to periodic moves in the U.S. Congress to link Papua to U.S. security assistance. The Indonesians are also moving forward with military reform. Beginning in May 2005, a program has been put in place to centralize all the procurement through the civilian-controlled MOD.

Deficiencies in Partner Country Capabilities

The Philippines. The Philippines' focus on internal defense means a downgrading of its conventional capabilities. The ancient F-5s that were the mainstay of the Philippine air force have been mothballed and the fighter base downgraded from a wing to a group. Helicopters will now be the priority of the air force. The air force has limited night vision/flight, air insertion, and evacuation capabilities, which it acquired as the result of U.S. training. There are some small aircraft for maritime surveillance, OV-10s and others, but with limited capabilities—they have only visual means of surveillance. There are plans to fund some land-based radar systems and the AFP is looking to use fast boats for a response capability. The Philippine navy cannot venture into the high seas because its platforms have deteriorated.[114]

Aside from the maritime patrol aircraft, Philippine air force procurement priorities are largely related to the counterinsurgency mission. These include additional C-130s (the air force has a requirement for nine; currently there are two in the inventory) and 120 utility helicopters (preferably Blackhawks) for mobility; attack helicopters (the air force prefers Cobras); and trainer aircraft (the Filipinos have expressed an interest in decommissioned U.S. Navy Trojans). After 2010, assuming a reduction in the internal threat, the AFP foresee a shift to the external defense mission.[115]

Indonesia. As in the case of the Philippines, lack of resources is a major obstacle to military reform and to the military's ability to perform its responsibilities effectively.

---

[114] Interview with Under Secretary of Defense Antonio Santos, Camp Aguinaldo, Manila, August 9, 2005.

[115] Interview with Lt. Gen. Reyes, Commander, Philippine Air Force, Villamor AFB, Pasay City, December 2, 2005.

According to Minister of Defense Juwono Sudarsono, the defense budget is below 50 percent of the minimum required. Seventy percent of the budget goes for personnel, maintenance, and operations and only 30 percent for capital development. The lowest ranks of enlisted personnel are paid the equivalent of US$45–55 a month; with other allowances their compensation goes up to US$100. A similar pattern exists in the police. Inadequate pay interferes with professionalization and creates the temptation to engage in corruption.[116]

Of direct consequence for the Indonesian government's ability to address the problem of ungoverned territories (both land and maritime) within the archipelago is the woeful state of Indonesia's naval and air transport capabilities. Only between one half and one third of the current fleet of 120 ships (including 57 patrol boats) is seaworthy. The rest of the ships are either in maintenance or inoperable.[117] The Indonesians also find it difficult to integrate air and naval assets in maritime patrols because of the readiness problem of its air force. According to the then Air Force Chief of Staff (and current Indonesian Armed Forces Commander), General Djoko Suyanto, only 30 percent of the aircraft in the Indonesian Air Force inventory are operational. The major requirements are for components and spare parts. Many of these items, e.g., engines, avionics, compressors, etc., had been sent for maintenance to the United States, Korea, Singapore, Malaysia, and Brazil, but had not been returned to Indonesia because of the U.S. embargo.[118] As of this writing, in December 2005, Indonesian authorities are in the process of reviewing the condition of the military equipment that was stranded overseas due to the U.S. embargo but can now be returned to Indonesia.

Policy Implications and Recommendations

The typology of ungoverned territories developed in the introduction to this study breaks down ungoverned territories into three classes, depending on whether the predominant form is contested, incomplete, or abdicated governance. Each, of course, has different policy implications. Mindanao is clearly a case of contested governance because the principal obstacle to the extension of central government control over this region is the armed opposition of locally based organizations, the most representative of which is the MILF.

Cases of contested governance present more complex policy issues because—even where the national government being challenged for control of a territory is a U.S. ally, as in the case of the Philippines—U.S. policy needs to take into account the impli-

---

[116] Rabasa discussions with Minister of Defense Juwono Sudarsono, Jakarta, August 4, 2005.

[117] Percival (2005), pp. 28–29.

[118] Rabasa discussion with Indonesian Air Force Chief of Staff Air Marshal Djoko Suyanto, Indonesian Air Force Headquarters, Jakarta, August 3, 2005.

cations of U.S. involvement, direct or indirect, in what is essentially a local conflict. Part of the calculus involves an assessment of the strength and representativeness of the group challenging the central government; its links, if any, to global terrorism; the effectiveness of the national government's policies; and the desired outcomes from a U.S. policy perspective. In the case of Mindanao, U.S. and Philippine interests are best served by promoting a negotiated settlement that both protects the territorial integrity of the Philippines and meets legitimate grievances of the Moros and that discourages linkages between the MILF and the global jihadist movement.

Of course, this does not preclude assistance to improve governance in general, as well as the intelligence and military capabilities of the Philippines, as described above. In fact, this assistance is critical in order to enable the Manila government to cope with multiple internal security threats, including regional manifestations of global terrorism, and to prevent the expansion of existing ungoverned spaces. To the United States' credit, its policy has distinguished between the JI and the remnants of the Abu Sayyaf Group, against whom U.S. military assistance has been targeted, and the MILF, which has been enlisted in support of the AFP against the ASG within MILF territory.

In the case of Indonesia, the lack of a state presence in regions such as Central Sulawesi is due to abdicated or incomplete governance. Although there is still a low-level insurgency in Papua, the peace agreement in Aceh has hopefully brought to an end a significant insurgency. Nevertheless, implementation of the Aceh peace agreement could run into some rough patches and it would behoove the United States to lend active support to the coming stages in the peace process in Aceh.

With the conflict in Aceh out of the way and consolidation of democratic control of the military proceeding, the United States has a demonstrable interest in helping the Indonesian government reduce the scope of ungoverned territories within the archipelago. Since there is a critical need for mobility, the U.S. Air Force in particular has a role in lending its expertise in air special operations (as it has done in the Philippines) and in the air transport sector.

CHAPTER NINE

Case Study: The East Africa Corridor

Peter Chalk

The eastern corridor of Africa is attracting growing attention among Western security officials as an area of potential interest to al-Qaeda and affiliated elements.[1] Not only are several states in this region unable to exercise control over their territory—Somalia being a graphic case in point--but Islamists with established links to the international jihadist movement are known to have both operated in and passed through this part of Africa. This chapter examines the extent to which certain areas in southeast Africa can be considered ungoverned territories and delineates attributes that might make them conducive to the presence of terrorist groups. The analysis covers a broad swathe of geopolitical space that extends from Sudan and Somalia in the north, through Kenya and Tanzania, to Zimbabwe and Mozambique in the south.

To be sure, much of the ungovernability associated with southeast Africa reflects contemporary problems stemming from poor leadership, rampant corruption, socio-economic mismanagement, and manipulation of ethno-religious differences. That said, the foundations of weak statehood were laid back in the late nineteenth century when Africa became the object of competition by European powers seeking to extend their own global influence while simultaneously checking that of their competitors. Popularly depicted as "the scramble for Africa," this frantic process of territorial conquest involved the formation of colonial outposts that took no account of extant topographical, natural, or population characteristics. Not surprisingly, the entities that emerged typically lumped together all sorts of ethnic, religious, and commercial groups into artificially conceived administrative zones.

Confronted with this complex mosaic, imperial officials made little attempt to foster a viable sense of national identification and cohesion.[2] By contrast, control was elicited primarily through the co-option and subsidization of local powerholders—including tribal leaders, clerical spokesmen, and clan elders—leaving successor politi-

---

[1] Chalk discussions with British intelligence officials, London, January 2005. See also Behn (2005).

[2] Migdal (1988), p. 141.

cal units that possessed neither a consistent framework of social control nor a robust system of infrastructural power.[3]

Following independence, the governments of the newly liberated states in Africa typically adopted two means to consolidate their authority and overcome the lack of wider civic penetration. First, they vigorously upheld the sanctity of their inherited boundaries, forcefully rejecting claims for post-colonial self-determination (on the rationale that this would lead to an unstoppable process of territorial fragmentation). Second, most sought to provide "the good life" only to those segments of society that were deemed instrumental in supporting their rule (such as a particular clan or tribe). What resulted was the creation of a whole series of so-called "quasi-states"—territories that possessed the trappings of sovereignty (a flag, membership in the United Nations, internationally recognized frontiers, overseas diplomatic representation) but that lacked functional utility (in terms of providing basic goods and services) or legitimacy.[4] In varying degrees, this situation continues to hold sway throughout much of the southeast African corridor.

Lack of State Penetration of Society

State penetration is limited or completely lacking in several parts of East Africa. The most chronic situation of ungovernability is in Somalia. The Transitional Federal Government (TFG), a coalition of various political factions, businessmen, and warlords based in the town of Baidoa, bears the closest resemblance to a central government. The TFG, however, does not control military forces and, as a result, cannot practically claim to control any territory.[5] In June 2006, the Union of Islamic Courts, an Islamist coalition, gained control of Mogadishu after defeating the Alliance for the Restoration of Peace and Counter-Terrorism, a collection of warlords and power brokers. The Islamic Courts garnered a degree of support among the population for bringing some semblance of order—along with strict enforcement of Islamic laws and norms—in areas under their control.[6] Other parts of Somalia and surrounding areas exhibit a variety of degrees of order and effectiveness of government institutions. Northern Somalia, the "Republic of Somaliland," is quite peaceful, and its capital, Hargeisa, is a safe place

---

[3] Kal Holsti, "Weak States, Strong States and War," unpublished working document supplied to Peter Chalk, p. 5.

[4] Robert Jackson has written extensively on this interpretation of post-independence statehood in Africa. See, in particular, Jackson (1982, 1987, 1995); and Jackson and Rosberg (1982). Other useful references include Buzan (1991); Job (1992); Holsti (1995); Mazrui (1995); and Zartman (1995).

[5] Jane's Information Group (2007).

[6] Some of the Union of Islamic Courts leaders reportedly have been associated with al-Qaeda. See the section of this chapter entitled "Presence of Organized Armed Groups."

to visit. Puntland is not as stable, but its authorities have managed to set up a rudimentary administration.[7]

Somali territorial control takes on somewhat more of a coherent picture when viewed as a clan-based society. The majority of the Islamic Courts in Mogadishu are associated with the Hawiye clan, which dominates the capital. In the far north of the country, the Isaaq dominate the semiautonomous region of Somaliland, which local leaders are eventually hoping will emerge as a fully independent state. To the east of this area and situated on the Horn of Africa is Puntland, which, again, functions as a relatively viable territorial space existing under the collective control of the Harti, Sool, and Sanaag clans.[8]

Similarly in Sudan, territorial control is a fluid term. The central government is able to exert some influence throughout the country. Yet only three areas are under the undisputed control of the central government: (1) Khartoum State; (2) the oil producing states in the south; and (3) and the city of Port Sudan. Technically, a government of national unity has controlled the (Arab) north and (Christian) south of the country since the signing of the peace agreement in January 2005, which ended the 20-year-old insurgency of the Sudanese People's Liberation Movement/Army (SPLM/A).[9] In reality, however, the country remains split along a north-south ethno-religious divide and continues to confront the possible specter of a full-scale southern secession—particularly following the untimely death in July 2005 of John Garang, the SPLA leader and Sudan's vice-president (a position that he attained as part of the peace agreement).

Central control is especially weak in Sudan's western Darfur province. The region, which is roughly the size of Spain (500,000 square kilometers), has been wracked by an ongoing civil conflict since 2003 that pits Khartoum-backed irregulars known as "Janjaweed" against local Muslim groups opposed to the government's policy of "Arabizing" the area. Two organizations currently stand at the forefront of this struggle: the Sudan Liberation Movement (SLM) and the Justice and Equality Movement (JEM).[10] The situation is more complex than a government/rebels polarity, with some rebel movements forging links with factions in Khartoum. For instance, the JEM has been linked to Hassan al-Turabi, the leading ideologue in Sudan's former Islamist government.[11]

A new territorial challenge has emerged in the east in the form of militias that operate along the Red Sea coast from the semiautonomous Hameshkoreb region on

---

[7] Dr. William Reno, review of manuscript.

[8] For further details see Menkhaus (2004). At the time of writing in the summer of 2005, Somaliland and Puntland were the only entities in Somalia that come close to exhibiting the functional capacities of a state.

[9] The accords provided for an interim government of national unity and guaranteed that a referendum on secession for the south (if desired) would be held in 2010. See Hoge (2005).

[10] Jane's Information Group (2004b).

[11] Dr. William Reno, review of manuscript. The JEM was accused by the Bashir government of participating in an plot masterminded by al-Turabi.

the Eritrean border. In June 2005, a coalition of forces drawn from the Beja Congress, an armed militia of Beja tribesmen that has been fighting the Khartoum government since the early 1990s, and Rashaida tribe's Free Lions attacked government forces and temporarily captured the coastal city of Tokar, some 200 kilometers south of Port Sudan.[12] The government was rattled, since the rebellion threatened the flow of oil, which is exported through Port Sudan at a rate of 300,000 barrels a day.[13]

Although the anarchy in Somalia and parts of Sudan is not replicated in other east African countries, state penetration and control are minimal in numerous areas. East African borders (both land and maritime) are especially porous, reflecting a general inability of central governments to police the outer reaches of their territorial jurisdictions (as discussed later in this chapter). This is especially true of the Kenyan frontier with Somalia, but it is also the case with Kenya's southern coastal belt as well as in Mozambique to the north of Beira.[14] In Tanzania, the semiautonomous island of Zanzibar runs largely according to its own Islamic norms and precepts despite coming under the authority of Chama Cha Mapundzi (CCM),[15] the same party in power on the mainland. Arguably more important is the influence of the opposition Civic United Front (CUF), which retains considerable popular support and which has repeatedly balked at the central authority of Dar es Salaam on account of its perceived corruption and insensitivity to legitimate Muslim needs.[16] Finally in Mozambique, the government's capacity to exert its authority beyond the capital and major commercial centers is questionable, particularly in the country's western provinces, which continue to be subject to widespread banditry.[17]

The lack of state penetration is also manifest in the lack of acceptance of or adherence to formal institutional practices and laws, both by local officials and the population at large. Law and order, such as there is, in Somalia's southern provinces is ad hoc, reflecting the idiosyncratic exercise of Islamic jurisprudence. In the towns of Borama, Luuq, Jowhar, Beled Weyn, and Merka, for instance, local polities do little more than simply keep the peace via the Sharia Court.[18] The exceptions are Somaliland and Puntland, where the regional authorities provide enough security and space to at

---

[12] Jane's Information Group (2005a).

[13] "Enemies Everywhere" (2005).

[14] Chalk interview, southern and East Africa analysts, Control Risks Group, London, January 2005.

[15] The CCM came to power in 1995 following Zanzibar's first ever multiparty elections. It was returned to power in 2000 amid widespread claims of voter irregularity and central government interference aimed at ensuring a CUF loss.

[16] Chalk interview, British officials, High Commission of the United Kingdom, Dar es Salaam, September 2003.

[17] Chalk interview, southern and East Africa analysts, Control Risks Group, London, January 2005.

[18] Menkhaus (2004). It should be noted that some polities do offer some basic services, such as operating piped water systems, regulating marketplaces, and collecting taxes.

least allow NGOs and small businesses to operate and establish themselves as viable enterprises.[19]

Corruption is rife throughout the region, remaining particularly serious in both Kenya and Zimbabwe. In the former case, a full two-thirds of the country's judiciary was purged in 2004 during an anticorruption drive enacted under U.S. pressure through the Department for Justice and Constitutional Affairs.[20] Although the current President, Mwai Kibaki, has pledged to build on this effort and fully clean out the bureaucracy, graft, bribe taking and kickbacks continue to be prevalent at all levels of the civil service and law enforcement community.[21] The severity of the problem resulted in the United States canceling a $2.5 million anticorruption aid package in February 2005, with Washington charging that Nairobi was demonstrating neither the will nor the capacity to tackle the issue in a meaningful fashion.[22]

In Zimbabwe, corruption within the police and security forces is so blatant that the central government is no longer considered capable, or indeed willing, of guaranteeing fundamental public goods such as order and personal safety.[23] More seriously, senior members of the ruling ZANU-PF party are widely believed to be deeply involved in illegal currency deals and company takeovers that have had an utterly detrimental effect on the national economy.[24] While an Anti-Corruption and Anti-Monopoly Ministry has been established, its effect has been marginal largely because those responsible for running the new ministry use it more to protect their own interests than as a concerted instrument for ensuring clean administrative conduct and practices.[25]

On a popular level, the pervasiveness of corruption has alienated large sections of the citizenry, with many no longer willing to buy into systems that are considered dysfunctional and rapacious. Tax avoidance has become pervasive, as have underground economic enterprises and more generalized organized crime. The resort to these activities, which many consider the only means of survival, has led to the development of

---

[19] Jane's Information Group (2007).

[20] Chalk interview, British officials, High Commission of the United Kingdom, Nairobi, February 2004.

[21] Two anticorruption laws have been introduced in Kenya as part of this effort: (1) The Anti-Corruption and Economic Crimes Act; and (2) The Public Officers Ethics Act. The former established anticorruption courts and an anticorruption commission; the latter makes it a prerequisite for public officials (civil servants, police, judges, local bureaucrats) to declare their wealth on appointment. Although these acts represent a positive development on paper, it is not apparent to what extent either initiative will be vigorously enforced. Chalk interview, British officials, High Commission of the United Kingdom, Nairobi, February 2004.

[22] Lacey (2005a).

[23] Rotberg (2002), p. 136. At the time of writing, the average bribe to have an arrest expunged in Zimbabwe was $300.

[24] ZANU-PK stands for Zimbabwe African National Union–Patriotic Front.

[25] ICG (2004f), pp. 6–7.

parallel structures that directly impinge on the state's formal institutions. As Robert Rotberg notes with respect to Zimbabwe: "Public order has broken down. . . . Political institutions have ceased to function fully. . . . Even though the [country] remains intact, the [regime's] legitimacy is now seriously challenged."[26]

Limited state penetration is also apparent in the inability of many southeast African states to provide basic social, health, and educational services. For example, in Somalia, the TFG has no control over any of Somalia's ports, airports, or roads and thus is unable to collect taxes or customs revenues.[27] Because the TFG has no revenue, it is unable to fund the social infrastructure normally associated with a functioning central government. Mogadishu does not even have a functioning police force, let alone a national school system or health infrastructure.[28] Indeed, much of the social infrastructure (i.e., health and education) that exists in Somalia is funded by Islamic charities and, to a lesser extent, by Western NGOs. For example, the largest orphanage in Mogadishu was funded by the Saudi-based al-Haramayn Foundation until it was forced to suspend operations because of the involvement of several of its branches in the funding of terrorist activities.[29]

In southern Sudan, as a result of civil strife and government neglect, social infrastructure is almost nonexistent. Adult literacy is 24 percent. Over 70 percent of the south's population has no access to clean water, and infant mortality hovers around 15 percent.[30] The situation is not much better in the Darfur region and the east, despite the absence of conflict until 2003. According to the Global Internally Displaced Persons (IDP) project, the "coverage of the existing water supply facilities remains very low in [these areas]." Primary education enrollment in the east is around 50 percent; in Darfur itself, only 33 percent of the population has access to clean water. The central government's neglect of areas outside Khartoum is most apparent when Khartoum's statistics are juxtaposed against the rest of the country. In the greater Khartoum region, over 80 percent of children are enrolled in school, 87 percent of the population has access to clean water, and adult literacy is over 75 percent.[31]

In Zimbabwe, the provision of basic social, health, and education services has become increasingly tenuous over the past several years. Chronic shortages of everything from fuel and electricity to staple foodstuffs occur on an almost daily basis as a result of economic mismanagement, asset stripping, and fast-track land reform, while the operation of schools and hospitals has been severely crippled by the emigra-

---

[26] Rotberg (2002), p. 136.

[27] Jane's Information Group (2007).

[28] Jane's Information Group (2007).

[29] ICG (2005a).

[30] See Internal Displacement Monitoring Centre (undated).

[31] Internal Displacement Monitoring Centre (undated).

tion of trained teachers and medical professionals. The country's population is as poor today as it was in 1970, with an astounding 70 percent living below the poverty line.[32] Indeed, Zimbabwe, which during the 1980s and 1990s was considered one of Africa's more promising post-independence success stories, was ranked 147th out of 174 states in the United Nations Development Program (UNDP) 2004 Human Development Report.[33]

Finally, in Tanzania and Kenya, as in Somalia, the infrastructure void has been filled by Islamist charitable organizations based in the Middle East, particularly Saudi Arabia, that play a pivotal role in underwriting the construction of gas stations, mosques, schools, and hospitals. In both countries, large sections of the local Muslim population now clearly interpret their interests as dependent on outside benefactors.[34]

Lack of a Monopoly of Force

Organized Armed Groups

Various alternative centers of power exist across the East Africa corridor. Especially evident are the aforementioned warlords in Somalia, who run competing fiefdoms and behave as laws unto themselves. This is particularly true of Mogadishu, the base of the late infamous warlord Mohammed Farah Aideed and the scene of endemic fractious clan warfare that continues to divide the city's shattered administrative, economic, and communications infrastructure.[35] Elsewhere private "entrepreneurialism," enforced through the barrel of a gun, has engendered a dangerous and capricious mercantilist spirit throughout much of the country, ripping the underlying social fabric that is so essential for any functioning polity.

In Sudan, the primary threat to the government's authority historically came in the South from the Sudan People's Liberation Movement, an amalgamation of the Dinka and Nuer people.[36] As noted, this threat has been neutralized, at least temporarily, as the result of the peace agreement between the government and the SPLM and the formation of a national unity government. In the Darfur region, however, a brutal campaign by the government-backed Janjaweed irregulars against the local population and resistance on the part of the Sudan Liberation Movement/Army (SLM/A), a union of three non-Arab peoples—the Fur, Masalit, and Zaghawa—have left much

---

[32] ICG (2004i), p. 2.

[33] See United Nations (2004).

[34] Chalk interview, southern and East Africa analysts, Control Risks Group, London, January 2005.

[35] Rotberg (2002), pp. 133–134.

[36] Jane's Information Group (2004b).

of Darfur in a state of anarchy.[37] On the Red Sea coast, as noted before, a coalition of rebel groups has emerged as a new threat that could rapidly escalate, particularly if reports that eastern rebels are receiving support from Eritrea turn out to be true.[38]

The Khartoum government also faces a political challenge from the Asmara-based National Democratic Alliance, an umbrella group representing all the northern opposition political parties and, to varying degrees, the armed rebel movements of Darfur and the east.[39] The most important figure in this disparate coalition is the enigmatic Hassan al-Turabi, whom President Bashir released from prison in December 2004. (Al-Turabi's connections to rebels in Darfur complicate Western campaigns against government-sponsored violence in the region.)

Islamic radicals and nonreligious militias also constitute a residual problem. With regard to the former, there are three groups of current concern. First, the al-Qaeda cell that perpetrated the 1998 U.S. embassy bombings in Tanzania and Kenya as well as the 2002 attacks against Israeli targets in Kenya, still appears to be based in Somalia.[40] Second, al-Itihaad al-Islaami (AIAI), a violent Islamist group linked to al-Qaeda whose aim is to establish an Islamic fundamentalist state in Somalia.[41] Although the group has primarily operated in and around the Horn of Africa, it is now believed to have established a foothold in Kenya and Tanzania. In the latter country, one alleged associate organization known as Simba wa Mungu (literally God's Lion) has been implicated in armed takeovers of several moderate mosques over the last two years. According to Gorill Husby, a journalist specializing in Islamist-African affairs, the group is moving to step up the scale of its violent activities in the capital, Dar es Salaam.[42] Finally, an independent Islamist network apparently has emerged in Mogadishu. This loose network of individuals was allegedly responsible for the recent attacks against Westerners in Somalia, including the October 2003 assaults against two British aid workers. Aden Hashi 'Ayro, the leader, is Afghan-trained and said to have ties to both al-Qaeda and the AIAI.[43]

Further south, the activities of nonreligious militias are cause for concern. In Zimbabwe, the idiosyncratic actions of so-called war veterans constitute a daily threat in the country's hinterlands. Although originally (and conspicuously) used by President Mugabe to harass members of the opposition and seize white-owned farms as part

---

[37] Jane's Information Group (2004b).

[38] Jane's Information Group (2005a).

[39] Jane's Information Group (2004b).

[40] ICG (2005a).

[41] It should be noted that most of the AIAI's operational cells are believed to have been driven underground in the wake of the U.S. designation of the organization as a terrorist entity in December 2001 and Ethiopian military offensives during late 2002. See ICG (2005a).

[42] See Husby (2003), pp. 30–31.

[43] ICG (2005a).

of a supposed program of land reform and redistribution, these radicals have developed into a quasi–youth militia (known as the Green Bombers) that increasingly appears more concerned with its own empowerment than the predilections of the central government.[44] In Mozambique, ex-RENAMO guerrillas hold sway over the country's vast western provinces, an area that, in many ways, has yet to be consolidated under the authority of the Maputo government.[45]

Criminal Networks

A variety of criminal networks exists along the southeast African corridor. At sea, pirates and profiteers are active along large stretches of the Somali, Kenyan, and Tanzanian coastlines. Especially prominent are gangs in the Gulf of Aden and waters to the immediate south of the Horn of Africa, which, combined, constitute one of the most piracy-prone regions of the continent (generally only superseded by attacks off Nigeria). The syndicates are well armed, usually operate within a predetermined and mutually agreed sphere of influence, and engage in everything from looting and ransacking to more sophisticated hostage taking and hijackings.[46]

West African crime groups have also cemented a strong presence in the region. Predominantly run by expatriates from Nigeria, Liberia, and Ghana, these organizations, which collectively have several thousand members, engage in a broad spectrum of criminal activities, including credit card theft, identity forgery, advanced fee fraud (otherwise known as 419 scams),[47] and the trafficking of guns, animal parts (ivory and rhino horns), people, narcotics (primarily heroin, cocaine, crack, ecstasy, and cannabis shipped to South Africa)[48] and gems (mainly "blood" diamonds smuggled out of conflict zones in Sierra Leone, the Democratic Republic of the Congo, and Angola). These endeavors have grown markedly in scale and scope, in line with the general opening

---

[44] Chalk interview, southern and East Africa analysts, Control Risks Group, London, January 2005. See also ICG (2004i), p. 5.

[45] Chalk interview, southern and East Africa analysts, Control Risks Group, London, January 2005. RENAMO (*Resistencia Nacional Mocambicana*) was established in 1976 by Rhodesian security forces to operate against the Zimbabwe African People's Union (ZAPU) and ZANU guerrillas based in Mozambique. RENAMO and the ruling party in Mozambique, FRELIMO, eventually signed a peace agreement on October 4, 1992.

[46] Chalk interview with a maritime terrorism expert, The HART Group, London, May 2001. See also Chalk (2000b), p. 49; and Chalk (2001), pp. 44–45.

[47] This form of criminality essentially entails the creation of bogus business proposals (generally relating to the use of third parties, often outside Africa, to access and reinvest assets held in Nigeria) that promise substantial rewards for participating. Once the prospective "client" agrees to become involved in the scheme, various requests for prepayments are made to cover necessary fixed and/or overhead costs such as legal fees or taxes. Securing these and subsequent monies is the point of the scam, although in a number of cases victims have also provided full details of their bank accounts, which have then been unceremoniously emptied. See Shaw (2002), pp. 300–304; and Chalk (2003b), pp. 32–42.

[48] Although South Africa remains the principal market for the continent's drug trade, it also acts as an important transshipment hub for consignments to Southeast Asia, South America, North America, and Western Europe.

up of South Africa—the main market for most regional illegal enterprises—and the increasingly faltering economic and political situation in West Africa.[49] While syndicates avoid openly explicit shows of force, most are armed and ready to engage in violence to protect lucrative sales turfs, eliminate rivals, and intimidate members of the law enforcement community who may be moving to curtail their activities.

Population with Access to Arms

Feeding the coercive options and capabilities of these various militia and criminal entities, as well as the population at large, is a ready supply of weapons. Demand for arms and access to them is especially high in Somalia, reflecting the chronic chaos that besets much of the country. Most munitions originate from stocks left over from the Cold War. However, it is also known that sizable consignments have been shipped to the country from South Asia and the Middle East—either directly or through Eritrea— including, allegedly, the explosives and missiles used in the Mombassa attacks of 2002 (discussed below).[50] In Kenya, a budding underground trade in weapons has emerged both as a result of the spillover effects of neighboring civil wars fought in the Great Lakes Regions of Uganda, Sudan, the Democratic Republic of the Congo, Rwanda, and Burundi and of Nairobi's inability to monitor its Indian Ocean coastline, a principal conduit for munitions trafficked from the Arabian Peninsula and the Horn of Africa.[51] As with Somalia, ineffective post-conflict disarmament has left sizable arms dumps and caches in Mozambique, which are both driving internal procurement and feeding proliferation to Zimbabwe.[52]

Quite apart from availability, many of the weapons in East Africa are extraordinarily cheap, which has helped to open up a large buyer's market. An AK47 can currently be purchased for around $100 in Kenya, while in Zimbabwe there have been reports of assault rifles being exchanged for as little as $14 along the border with Mozambique.[53] Moreover, the existence of pliant, shady regional arms brokerage firms and dealerships, some of which have been directly tied to the international acquisition

---

[49] For further details see Shaw (2002); Chalk (2003b); and Hubschle (2004).

[50] Chalk interview, British officials, High Commission of the United Kingdom, Nairobi, February 2004. See also Hubschle (2004). Particularly prominent in this regard are weapons originating in Yemen and Pakistan, most of which have been smuggled via unregulated routes that are sustained by tribal links and religious sympathies and that parallel historical trade links between South Asia and the Horn of Africa.

[51] A small vessel can travel from Mogadishu to Kenya in approximately three days; a modern ship can do the same trip in less than 12 hours. See Lacey and Filkins (2002).

[52] For good overviews of the historical dynamics driving the trade in light weapons throughout southern Africa, see Smith, Batchelor, and Potgieter (1996); Smith (1997); Smith and Vines (1997); Honwana and Lamb (1998); and Vines (1998).

[53] Chalk interview, southern and East Africa analysts, Control Risks Group, London, February 2004. See also Chalk (2000c), p. 11.

efforts of insurgent and designated terrorist organizations,[54] ensures that weapons can be readily purchased in bulk quantities if so desired.

Two major initiatives have been undertaken to curb the proliferation of small arms in the general southeast African region: (1) The Nairobi Declaration, which aims to control the movement of light weapons in Kenya, Tanzania, Ethiopia and Burundi; and (2) The Regional Secretariat for Small Arms Proliferation, the mandate of which theoretically extends to all of East Africa. Neither has, as yet, however managed to make a concerted dent in the trade, largely because of the difficulty of tracking and intercepting covert consignments.

Lack of Border Controls

As noted above, many of the borders in the eastern corridor are porous and subject to little if any control. A number of land crossings are highly informal or unpoliced. This is especially true of the rugged Kenyan-Somali frontier, which cuts across some 424 miles of dense forests and savannah to the shores of the Indian Ocean,[55] but it also pertains to Mozambique's northern border with Tanzania as well as to sections of the country's northwestern boundary with Zimbabwe,[56] both of which remain devoid of infrastructure such as paved roads.[57]

Coastal surveillance is equally lacking across much of the region. Somali waters fall under the control of militias and pirates while aging or inoperable equipment and a lack of funds have divested both Kenya and Tanzania of the ability to undertake regular maritime patrols.[58] In the latter case, problems are significantly multiplied by the existence of an "archipelagic border" in waters around Zanzibar. Not only does the island greatly expand the area of territory that the Dar es Salaam government needs to

---

[54] A particularly glaring case in point concerns Zimbabwe Defense Industries (ZDI), which in 1997 was complicit in redirecting a major shipment of mortar bombs, initially ordered and paid for by the Sri Lankan government, to the Liberation Tigers of Tamil Eelam (LTTE). For further details see Winchester (1998); and Chalk (2000a).

[55] Kenyan border police routinely claim they lack the resources and tools to comprehensively monitor the border with Somalia or combat the illicit crossings of criminals, nomadic farmers, and suspected terrorists.

[56] It should be noted that, although this part of the border is largely unregulated, it remains a hazardous crossing on account of the large number of land mines that are still buried along the frontier (originally planted by Rhodesian security forces to deter ZAPU and ZANU guerrilla incursions).

[57] Chalk interview, southern and East Africa analysts, Control Risks Group, London, January 2005. See also Hubschle (2004).

[58] Chalk interviews with a maritime terrorism expert, The HART Group, London, May 2001; and southern and East Africa analysts, Control Risks Group, London, February 2004.

monitor in the Indian Ocean, it also provides a relatively easy back-door channel for entry to the mainland.[59]

In Sudan, the Jebel Kurush mountain range in the northeast, which runs parallel to the Red Sea, is perfect for smuggling drops—drugs, weapons, and fighters—and for insurgent excursions into Jeddah and other parts of Saudi Arabia.[60] Indeed, in 2004, al-Qaeda apparently set up multiple refugee and terrorist training camps in the area for these very reasons.[61] According to western diplomats in Saudi Arabia,

> There is significant traffic from these camps to the peninsula [Saudi Arabia] across the Red Sea . . . there is no real Sudanese government or army control over the mountains. The terrorists slip through the cracks, up into the hills where they can train, rest and build up the spirit of jihad. With things hot over here [Saudi Arabia] they can get organized over there [Sudan].[62]

Security at major airports in East Africa is also weak. Computerized networks for registering entry and exit are either rudimentary or nonexistent In Mozambique, for instance, all records are hardcopy; no country has a system in place for an integrated terrorist or criminal watch list. In contrast, immigration officials at Nairobi airport have the equipment to machine-read passports.[63]

Compounding the situation is pervasive corruption among law enforcement, customs, and immigration officials. In the words of one local commentator remarking on the situation in Tanzania/Zanzibar: "You can get almost anything into the country because the police can be so easily bought off."[64]

The attributes of ungovernability discussed above are summarized in Table 9.1. Indicators are graded according to the following scale: high = 3; medium = 2; and low = 1. As might be expected, the situation is worst in Sudan and Somalia and least severe in Kenya and Tanzania (which by the standards of the region are relatively functioning states). Although Mozambique has managed to exert a degree of governance over its territory since the end of the country's civil war, the central administration in Maputo has yet to establish a true monopoly of force and continues to suffer from weak border control. By contrast, although the Mugabe regime's physical presence is fairly

---

[59] Once an individual arrives on Zanzibar, he or she is not required to undergo any additional checks in Tanzania because travel is considered domestic. Immigration procedures only take place in Zanzibar, although they are highly perfunctory in nature. Chalk's observations, Tanzania and Zanzibar, September 2003.

[60] Darling (2005).

[61] Ulph (2004).

[62] McElroy (2005).

[63] As recently verified by William Rosenau in his review of the manuscript.

[64] Chalk interview, State University of Zanzibar, September 2003.

Table 9.1
Indicators of Ungovernability, East Africa

Variable	Somalia	Sudan	Kenya	Tanzania	Mozambique	Zimbabwe
Lack of state penetration						
Absence of state institutions	3	2	2	2	2	1
Lack of physical infrastructure	3	2	1	1	2	2
Social/cultural resistance	3	3	1	2	1	3
Lack of monopoly of force	3	3	1	1	2	1
Armed groups	3	3	1	1	1	1
Criminal networks	3	2	2	1	2	2
Population with access to arms	3	3	1	1	2	1
Lack of border controls	3	3	2	2	2	1

strong throughout Zimbabwe, it has little legitimacy and is increasingly failing to provide even the most basic of services to its population.

Adequacy of Infrastructure

Financial Infrastructure
Internationally connected banks equipped with modern ATMs are scattered throughout major cities in Tanzania (except Stone Town, the capital of Zanzibar), Kenya,
and Mozambique, allowing ready access to funds deposited in overseas accounts.[65]
Moreover, because many of these facilities exist in the absence of strong regulatory
controls, they have developed an international reputation as highly attractive hubs
through which to launder "dirty" money.[66] Informally, there is a thriving underground
foreign exchange market in Zimbabwe. Fueled by the country's massive inflation rate
and the nonconvertibility of the Zimbabwe dollar, this nonofficial remittance system
affords the opportunity to procure large amounts of local currency for the minimum
cost; while the Zimbabwean dollar ostensibly trades at Z$56 for US$1.0 (July 2005
rate), illegal brokers may offer rates as high as Z$20,000.[67]

Sudan's banks are also relatively advanced for the developing world and until
recently maintained correspondent relationships with Western financial institutions.
According to the central government, terrorist groups are banned from banking in the

---

[65] While there are also branches of well-known financial institutions in Zimbabwe (Barclays and Standard Chartered both retain offices in the country), their use for procuring funds located in international accounts is limited
given the country's abysmally low foreign exchange rates.

[66] Hubschle (2004). This is particularly true of Mozambique, which has long been regarded as a haven for money
laundering in the Indian Ocean area. As Hubschle remarks, "[Maputo] alone has 36 exchange bureaux and 12
banks, which begs the question whether there is enough business for everyone."

[67] See Rotberg, (2002), p. 135; Cornwell (2003); and ICG (2004i), pp. 2–5. Zimbabwe currently has the highest
inflation rates of any country in the world.

country. It should be noted, however, that Khartoum's definition of terrorist groups is somewhat less restrictive than it is elsewhere. According to an unofficial report by a Dutch defense analyst, soon after 9/11, bin Laden and the Taliban transferred large sums of money (primarily in the form of gold and gemstones) to the Sudan, probably to be deposited in Islamic banks.[68]

Transportation and Communications

Kenya, Tanzania, Zimbabwe, and Mozambique are serviced by a functioning road, train, bus, ferry, and air network that provides relatively easy travel (by African standards) within and between the four countries. Even Sudan has the semblance of a working surface transportation system, consisting of 1,900 kilometers of paved and gravel roads as well as a highway that runs from the oil-producing southern regions to the Port of Sudan.[69] Kenyan Airlines and, to a decreasing extent, Air Zimbabwe are still among the most reliable on the continent, and each offers direct routes to major regional capitals as well as to central hubs in Western Europe, such as London and Amsterdam.[70] In addition to public modes of movement, it is possible to hire four-wheel-drive vehicles and standard cars in Kenya, Tanzania, and Zimbabwe.[71]

Communications are further facilitated by the wide availability of cell phones and Internet cafes. Coverage and accessibility is fairly extensive, and prices are generally cheap. Subscriber Identity Module (SIM) cards in Kenya and Tanzania can be purchased for around US$10; charges for Internet access and email accounts run from an average of 10 cents a minute in Nairobi to 3–4 cents a minute in Maputo.[72]

As one might expect, physical infrastructure is least developed in Somalia. There are few paved roads in the country and no train service. Even there, however, a range of options exists for internal and external travel. Limited bus service connects major settlements in Somaliland, while Daallo Airlines offer connections from Djibouti to Hargeisa and other towns in Somaliland, Mogadishu, and Addis Ababa, and flies direct routes to London, Paris, and Dubai. It is also possible to fly nonstop to Mogadishu from Addis Ababa on Ethiopian Airlines. Wireless networks also cover most major towns and rates for standard international calls made from the country are the cheapest in Africa. Indeed, a recent ICG report characterized Somalia's relevance to terrorism as follows:

---

[68] "Islam, Jihadism and Terrorism in Sudan" (2004).

[69] NationMaster.com (2005).

[70] Air Zimbabwe increasingly has to cancel flights because of a shortage of jet fuel and spare parts, reflecting the deepening economic crisis that is currently afflicting the country.

[71] Chalk's observations during fieldwork in the region, 2003–2004. Again, the rental and purchase of vehicles in Zimbabwe now has to take account of frequent fuel shortages.

[72] Chalk's observations during fieldwork in the region, 2003–2004.

Somalia is an excellent location for short-term transshipment and transit operations. . . . Its natural beach ports and long coast allows easy and undetected smuggling of people and material . . . its innumerable dirt landing strips also allow
access by small aircraft. Local partners in such short-term operations are easily
contracted for the right price . . . al-Qaeda and other groups have used Somalia in
the past and will likely continue to do so.[73]

Operational Access

East Africa's physical infrastructure is operationally relevant because it can be used to
mount strikes against venues both within the region and in nearby states. There are
numerous targets of opportunities across this part of Africa, particularly in Kenya and
Tanzania—diplomatic missions, Western-owned banks and businesses, hotels and restaurants catering to foreign tourists, international schools, and foreign aid offices.

Zimbabwe and Mozambique also provide a useful base from which to mount
forays into the Republic of South Africa (RSA). Although the Thabo Mbeki government is not a major supporter of Washington's global war on terror, the country does
reflect the general U.S. preference for liberal democracy and remains part and parcel
of the global capitalist system that the international jihadist movement so vehemently
opposes. As with Kenya and Tanzania, the RSA also offers a target-rich environment
with numerous facilities symbolic of Western cultural and economic influence.[74]

These facts have clearly not been lost on al-Qaeda and its affiliates. In 1998, the
group conspicuously exploited regional transportation, communication, and financial
networks to facilitate preparations for the terrorist attacks against the U.S. embassies
in Nairobi and Dar es Salaam.[75] Between 1996 and 1998, bin Laden placed more than
50 satellite calls to the strike team in Kenya, supporting its activities through monies
wired directly to two Girocredit and Greenland Bank accounts opened in the respective capital cities.[76] Investigations of the 2002 bombing of the Israeli-owned Paradise
Hotel in Mombassa, as well as the simultaneous attempt to shoot down an Arkia
Boeing 757 charter jet as it took off from the city en route to Tel Aviv, show that both
attacks were facilitated by the terrorists' ability to access reliable transport and financial
platforms. Preparation for the attacks incorporated explosives and missiles smuggled
from Yemen, planning meetings in six Kenyan towns (Nairobi, Siyu, Mombasa, Nyali,

---

[73] ICG (2005a).

[74] Holt (2004a).

[75] For a good account of the background planning for these attacks, see Bergin (2001), Chapter 6.

[76] Kaplan and Lovgren (1998), pp. 30–32; Hirschkorn (2001); *United States of America v Usama Bin Laden et al.*
(2001), pp. 1184–1185.

Kikambala, and Lamu) and three external countries (Somalia, Yemen, and Tanzania) mostly arranged via coded cell phones, and the electronic transfer of some $100,000 in funding.[77]

Besides these documented cases, there are claims that bin Laden has sought to establish Zimbabwe as a logistical "way station" to help coordinate attacks against Western interests in South Africa, including a series of alleged "spectaculars" that were reputedly planned for mid-2004.[78] According to one report, Ayman al-Zawihri, al-Qaeda's second in command, traveled to Zimbabwe on at least two occasions specifically to institute arrangements for coordinating the activities of an East Africa Islamic network that would connect cadres from the Persian Gulf to Cape Town.[79]

Sources of Income

There is pervasive organized criminal activity along the southeast African corridor, ranging from drug trafficking to identity theft, advanced fee fraud scams, and gem smuggling. As noted above, Nigerian, Ghanaian, and Liberian syndicates control most of these enterprises, establishing a particularly strong stranglehold over 419 scams and the illicit narcotics trade.[80] While this monopoly obviously limits the potential income-producing opportunities for independent players, al-Qaeda does appear to have made inroads in at least one area: smuggling gems.[81]

Revelations of links between bin Laden's network and the illicit African diamond trade first emerged late in 2002 following a yearlong investigation into jihadist terrorist financing. According to European law enforcement and intelligence officials, al-Qaeda made a conscious decision to convert its assets into less traceable commodities after the United States moved to freeze its finances in response to the East Africa embassy bombings. Diamonds were deemed to be a particularly useful medium in this regard, both because they represented a highly concentrated form of wealth that retains its value and because of the opaqueness that characterizes the trade in these gems, which

---

[77] U.S. Department of Homeland Security (2004).

[78] "Gujarat Raid for Qaeda" (2004); Holt (2004a, 2004b); Johnson and Diamond (2004); Wines (2004). Attack venues were alleged to have included the Johannesburg stock exchange, the national parliament, various waterfront attractions in Cape Town, the *Queen Elizabeth II* while it was docked at the port of Durban, and the Sheraton Hotel and U.S. Embassy in Pretoria.

[79] See Johnson (2004), p. 1.

[80] The 419 scams are thought to earn West African crime groups upward of $250 million a year from American victims alone. See Chalk (2003b), p. 32.

[81] There is also evidence to suggest that al-Qaeda has moved into identity fraud; however, it would appear that the group's interest in this trade has more to do with availing the international movement of personnel (South African passports, for instance, allow visa-free travel to many African and European countries) than as a form of revenue per se.

makes them far less susceptible to seizure or forfeiture. In the eight months prior to 9/11, it is estimated that al-Qaeda acquired between $30 and $50 million in diamonds procured from Sierra Leone, the vast bulk of which were purchased in deals involving the Revolutionary United Front (RUF)[82] brokered through intermediaries based in Liberia and Burkina Faso.[83] As Douglas Farah of the *Washington Post* remarked: "[The investigation] offers the clearest picture yet of al-Qaida's secretive business operations in West Africa and an elaborate plot that began in 1998 to hide substantial terrorist assets in diamonds."[84]

It is not known to what extent al-Qaeda has benefited from illicit gem trading in southeast Africa. However, regional commentators do believe the group has sought to replicate the success of the Sierra Leone model by purchasing rough-cut stones procured from Angola and the Democratic Republic of the Congo.[85] There have also been allegations directly linking al-Qaeda to Zimbabwe through the sale of so-called blood diamonds, many of which were reportedly obtained during the course of Harare's forcible intervention into the Congolese civil war. As R. W. Johnson noted:

> One also has to remember that Zimbabwean military involvement in the Democratic Republic of the Congo had given Mugabe and the top Zanu-PF elite control over several diamond mines there, including a joint venture with Al Shanfari's Oryx Group in the Senga Senga Mine. According to a confidential study prepared by Kroll Associates in 2002, "Al Shanfari and Oryx launder diamonds for several Lebanese traders linked to al-Qaeda." Thus here too there was a direct—and profitable—relationship between Mugabe and al-Qaeda.[86]

Besides conflict diamonds, there is at least circumstantial evidence that al-Qaeda has established control over a sizable proportion of the trade in tanzanite—an extremely rare gemstone that is only found in a 13-kilometer-square patch of graphite rock in northern Tanzania. Prior to his murder in Pakistan, *Wall Street Journal* reporter Daniel Pearl undertook an extensive investigation into jihadist involvement in the tanzanite trade, concluding that Muslim extremists loyal to the al-Qaeda network were key players in smuggling stones out of Tanzania to free-trade havens such as Dubai and Hong Kong via two main front companies—Tanzanite King and Black Giant. The same investigation revealed that the Taqwa mosque in Mererani doubled as an open-air tanzanite trading space in which Abdulhakim Mulla, one of the country's main brokers,

---

[82] The RUF, a proxy of then Liberian President Charles Taylor, was at the forefront of the conflict in Sierra Leone, becoming infamous for amputating body parts of its victims as well as forcibly exploiting men, women, and children to extract diamonds from mines under its control.

[83] Jones (2003); "Washington Revisits Africa's Strategic Importance" (2004); Amnesty International (2005).

[84] Farah (2002).

[85] Chalk interviews, Associated Press journalists, Nairobi, February 2004.

[86] Johnson (2004).

would act as a middleman arranging deals for the transfer of stones between extracting mining companies and al-Qaeda sympathizers, who then used the gems to transfer terrorist funds around the world.[87]

Finally, given the scale of profits that can be made from the sale of cocaine and heroin, the possibility that al-Qaeda has established mutually beneficial links with drug syndicates operating in East Africa cannot be discounted. Although there is no definitive evidence to support that this has actually occurred, jihadists connected with bin Laden's network have shown little compunction in working with narco-gangs in other parts of the world, including Afghanistan, Uzbekistan, Tajikistan, and Russia. There is no reason that affiliates would not see similar advantages in Africa; indeed, there has been speculation that the 2002 attacks in Mombassa were financed, at least in part, by profits procured from the lucrative Kenyan drug market.[88]

Favorable Demographic and Social Characteristics

Demographic and social characteristics conducive to a terrorist presence are not uniform through the East Africa corridor. There are certainly pockets of disenfranchised and radicalized Muslims whom outside demagogues could use and lever in support of their own agendas. In Kenya, Muslims are actively opposed to the introduction of antiterrorism legislation (which is seen as discriminatory) and the limited constitutional role of Islamic "qadi" courts (which deal with specific issues pertaining to marriage, divorce and inheritance).[89] Discontent has been further fueled by poverty, unemployment, and the continued refusal of the authorities to register the Islamic Party of Kenya, the country's main organized Muslim group, as a recognized political entity.[90]

In Tanzania, antigovernment sentiment among Muslims is being driven by concern over protecting the rights and traditions of the country's Muslim population.[91] Repeated crackdowns by the authorities on outward manifestations of Muslim religious identity have bolstered perceptions of discrimination and persecution, fueling a

---

[87] Block and Pearl (2001); Maharaj (2002); "For a Few Dollars More" (2003); Hubschle (2004).

[88] "The Drugs Connection in the Terror Hunt at Coast" (2002); Hubschle (2004).

[89] Christians in Kenya are actively opposed to any extension of qadi courts and have, in fact, been pushing to eliminate all references to Islam in the country's constitution.

[90] Chalk interviews, southern and East Africa analysts, Control Risks Group, London, January 2004; and British officials and AP journalists, Nairobi, February 2004.

[91] Muslims currently constitute about 45 percent of the population, about the same proportion as Christians. Hindus make up the remainder.

growing mind-set among Muslims that is increasingly opposed to the prevailing political and socioeconomic status quo.[92]

Sudan's ethnic composition makes it easier for terrorists to blend into society, largely because nearly 40 percent of the population is of Arab descent.[93] Moreover, although Sudanese President Bashir, under pressure from the United States, expelled bin Laden in 1996, there still remains a degree of sympathy in the country for the broad aims of al-Qaeda. This has been evident in the context of the Iraqi insurgency, where Afghan-trained Sudanese have participated in the fighting against U.S. and coalition forces.[94]

Throughout Somalia, Kenya, Tanzania, and Zanzibar, many Muslims are also clearly opposed to the broad tenets of U.S. foreign policy. In Mombassa, one highly influential publication, *Sauti Ya Haki* ("Voice of Reason") has been especially instrumental in mobilizing Muslim opposition to contemporary American global imperatives, which are denigrated as a thinly veiled attempt to consolidate Western power in key geopolitical and economic regions of the world.[95]

Underscoring these various factors is a strong Arab influence that reflects long-established historic, cultural, and trade links between the East Africa coast and the Arabian Peninsula. Several commentators have tied this coreligious identity to outbursts of communal violence, including attacks against symbols of secularism, moderation, and so-called Western decadence. U.S. officials have speculated that Islamists working directly with al-Qaeda, or at least on its behalf, have sought to exploit the Arab presence in this part of the continent to establish a regional jihadist network for both logistical and operational purposes.[96]

While it would be imprudent to dismiss these concerns out of hand, the overall susceptibility of southeast African Islamic communities to external militant agendas may be less obvious than might appear on the surface. Three considerations are worth bearing in mind in this regard. First, the Kenyan Muslim population remains divided along sectarian, cultural, ethnic, and tribal lines. There are two main Muslim conglomerations—one in the northeast (most of whom are ethnic Somalis) and one

---

[92] Chalk interviews, British and Canadian officials, High Commission of the United Kingdom and the Canadian Embassy, Dar es Salaam, September 2003.

[93] According to official population statistics, indigenous Africans constitute 52 percent of the population; Arabs, 39 percent; Beja, 6 percent; foreigners, 2 percent; and others, 1 percent. Arabic is the official language. See *CIA World Factbook* (2005).

[94] Ulph (2004); Schmitt (2005).

[95] Chalk interview, U.S. official, Nairobi, February 2004.

[96] Chalk interviews, southern and East Africa analysts, Control Risks Group, London, January 2004; and U.S. official, Nairobi, February 2004. The United States has linked several suspected mid-level al-Qaeda commanders to East Africa, including Khalfan Ghailani, Fazul Abdullah Mohammed, Fahid Mohammed Ally Mslan, Mustafa Mohammed Fadhil, and Shiekh Ahmed Salim Swedan, all of whom are on the FBI's most wanted list of international terrorists.

along the southern coast (the bulk of whom retain ties with the Middle East). They do not speak with the same voice; for the most part, the northerners have suffered the most in terms of poverty, with many viewing the southern Arabs as exploitative and only interested in amassing wealth.[97] This lack of unity has arguably served to dilute the rhetoric of outside demagogues by preventing a focused message from being concentrated on a single community.

Second, the vast majority of Muslims in Kenya and Tanzania (including those in Zanzibar, who are often portrayed as the gatekeepers of an extremist backdoor to the continent) are opposed to Wahhabism. This is due both to the strict fundamentalist tenor of the sect as well as its intolerance to other religious beliefs.[98] The former runs counter to the modernist and capitalist orientation of east African Muslims; the latter is an anathema in a region that is strongly oriented toward communal intermixing, irrespective of faith or religious denomination. In Zanzibar, for instance, it is common practice for Muslims and Christians to live in the same neighborhood, to work together, and to attend each others' family ceremonies and celebrations. As one senior academic at the University of Zanzibar notes:

> Christian-Muslim relations are very good. . . . There are very few old Christian families on the island, many of whom readily adopt Islamic culture and dress. . . . There are no separate communities for Christians and Muslims. If you go to a Christian funeral, often more Muslims turn up.[99]

Invisibility

As noted at the outset of this chapter, Western governments have increasingly begun to focus on the East Africa corridor as an area of potential interest to al-Qaeda and its affiliates. This is especially true of Somalia, Sudan, Kenya, and Tanzania, which have been in the spotlight of U.S. counterterrorism concern since 1998, the year of the embassy bombings in Nairobi and Dar es Salaam. Attention on these countries was further sharpened following the 2002 attacks in Mombassa (which were directly tied to al-Qaeda) and has been further heightened with the July 21, 2005, failed bombing attempts in London carried out by individuals of east African descent.[100] According to U.S. and British officials, the Horn of Africa now features as a regular and increasingly

---

[97] Chalk interviews, British officials, High Commission of the United Kingdom, Nairobi, February 2004.

[98] Chalk interviews, local muftis, Zanzibar; and British official, High Commission of the United Kingdom, Da-es-Salaam, September 2004.

[99] Chalk interview, State University of Zanzibar, September 23, 2003.

[100]See, for instance, Lacey (2005b).

central component of their respective risk-vulnerability assessments.[101] As a result, both Washington and London have moved to provide targeted counterterrorism assistance to governments in the region, most of which presently revolves around two main programs: the U.S.-led East Africa Counter-Terrorism Initiative (EACTI) and the British sponsored Counter-Terrorism Assistance Program (CTAP). (We discuss the specific components of these initiatives in the section on U.S. and Western policies and programs.) These initiatives have played an important role in offsetting the type of territorial obscurity that al-Qaeda exploited so effectively in Afghanistan and Sudan during the 1990s. That said, the true visibility of the wider east African corridor remains questionable in several respects. To begin with, very little attention has been given to either Zimbabwe or Mozambique in terms of the war on terrorism. The lack of attention to the former could prove especially problematic given its relatively sophisticated transport, finance, and communications network and proximity to potential attack venues in Kenya, Tanzania, and South Africa.[102] As Johnson observes:

> From al-Qaeda's point of view Zimbabwe would have . . . many advantages. Once an atrocity on the scale of September 11 took place the US would clearly scan the Muslim world for possible al-Qaeda hideouts. Sudan and Afghanistan were clearly already potential targets, as were African countries with large Muslim populations. But Zimbabwe was not in that category—and it also ha[s], as most African countries don't, the modern communications and banking facilities al-Qaeda needed. It was also conveniently close to Nairobi, Durban and Cape Town—three centers where Bin Laden [allegedly] already had links.[103]

There is also some reason to believe that East Africa has been sidelined in importance by West Africa vis-à-vis the war on terror. The latter subregion remains in the spotlight of U.S. security calculations, largely because of majority Muslim populations in such states as Chad, Niger, Mali, and Mauritania—fringe elements of which U.S. intelligence analysts fear are already being co-opted or at least swayed by outside jihadists.[104] Moreover, there is a concern that al-Qaeda is possibly positioning itself to target the energy infrastructure in Nigeria (where Islam is the faith of roughly 63 million people), not least because the country accounts for a substantial volume of Ameri-

---

[101] Chalk interviews, British officials, High Commission of the United Kingdom, Nairobi; and Dar es Salaam, 2003 and 2004.

[102] It is conceivable that Zimbabwe could also prove an attractive alternative base from which to travel to more distant locations, such as London, Amsterdam (both of which are serviced by daily nonstop flights), New York, and Perth (each of which can be reached via Johannesburg). These corridors, at least in the short run, could conceivably prove to be more attractive for infiltrating operatives into Europe, North America, and Australia, largely because Zimbabwe has no major identifiable link with the Muslim world and has yet to be recognized as a significant operational al-Qaeda hub. See Holt (2004b).

[103] Johnson (2004), p. 4.

[104] Chalk interview, U.S. official, Nairobi, February 2004. See also Reeve (2004), p. 7.

can non–Middle Eastern oil imports.[105] The relative weight of these considerations is reflected in a U.S.–West African counterterrorism assistance package known as the Trans-Sahara Counter-Terrorism Initiative (TSCTI) that, at the time of writing, was being funded at a level 25 percent higher than that of EACTI.[106]

Somalia presents additional difficulties. Although the United States is clearly concerned about the country's potential to act as an al-Qaeda hub, Washington currently has virtually no established human resources in this part of the continent—the vast bulk of Western presence is confined to European Union (EU) and United Nations (UN) aid groups. The paucity of U.S. intelligence assets in Somalia has inevitably translated into an intelligence picture that is unintegrated, sporadic at best, and wholly ignorant of prevailing conditions on the ground at worst.[107]

In sum, the region as a whole continues to have relevance as an area of general terrorism invisibility. When one considers the limited operational space al-Qaeda and its affiliates have had to deal with and adjust to in the post-9/11 era, such an attribute could prove to have particular weight in decisions pertaining to al-Qaeda's future logistical basing and attack options.

Summary of East Africa's Conduciveness to Terrorism

Table 9.2 summarizes the conduciveness of East Africa to a terrorist presence. Indicators are graded according to the following scale: 1 = low; 2 = medium; and 3 = high. The significance of the table is that the two countries shown to be the most devoid of a functioning system of government—Sudan and Somalia—are also the least attractive in terms of supporting militant extremist activities. This correlates with the general notion that weak states, rather than failed or failing states, are most likely to harbor a terrorist presence. This is particularly true of those states that are not in the current international security spotlight or that are characterized by favorable demographics.

U.S. and Western Policies and Programs

Cognizant of the region's potential for terrorism, the United States has established a military presence in the Horn of Africa and, together with its coalition partners, has

---

[105] Nigeria currently accounts for 15 percent of U.S. oil imports; this proportion is set to rise to as much as 25 percent over the next decade. See Chalk (2004), pp. 414, 427, footnote 47.

[106] See Koch (2004), pp. 30–31; McElroy (2004); and "The Quiet US Front in the War on Terrorism" (2004). The TSCTI was formerly known as the Pan Sahelian Initiative. It currently includes Chad, Senegal, Niger, and Mauritania, and may be further expanded to embrace Morocco, Tunisia, and Libya.

[107] Chalk interviews, southern and East Africa analysts, Control Risks Group, London, January 2005.

Table 9.2
Indicators of Conduciveness to Terrorist Presence, East Africa

Variable	Somalia	Sudan	Kenya	Tanzania	Mozambique	Zimbabwe
Adequacy of infrastructure						
Financial infrastructure	1	2	3	3	2	2
Transportation and communications	1	1	3	3	2	2
Operational access	2	2	3	3	2	2
Sources of income	2	1	2	2	2	2
Favorable demographics	2	2	1	1	1	1
Invisibility	2	2	1	1	3	3

enacted directed counterterrorist assistance programs in that part of the continent. The U.S. military presence in East Africa is centered in Djibouti, the headquarters of the Combined Joint Task Force—Horn of Africa (CJTF-HOA), whose mission is detecting, disrupting, and defeating transnational terrorism across the Horn of Africa in conjunction with coalition partners. As part of this mission, the unit is heavily involved in civic action, from providing medical treatment in villages in Ethiopia and polio vaccination in Djibouti to renovating schools in Yemen. As of August 2005, CJTF-HOA comprised about 1,600 personnel, including 275 employees of Kellogg, Brown and Root, who provided combat service support; 400 soldiers—active-duty, reserve, and National Guard; and 65 aircrew and maintainers from the New York Air National Guard's 102nd Rescue Squadron, who serve in the 449th Expeditionary Rescue Squadron.[108]

Counterterrorism assistance efforts revolve around two main U.S. initiatives and a British program: the U.S.-led EACTI (modeled on the TSCTI—see Chapter 10), the Global Peace Operations Initiative, and the British-sponsored CTAP. Both U.S. programs are funded by the Department of State and managed by the U.S. European Command.

The EACTI was inaugurated by the United States in 2004. It seeks to bolster the security of the east African region by channeling funds into several key areas: (1) military training for border and coastal surveillance; (2) programs designed to strengthen the control of the movement of people and goods; (3) aviation security capacity-building; (4) assistance for regional efforts to counter terrorism financing; and (5) police training. The operation of EACTI falls under the U.S. Central Command and complements a Combined Planning Group consisting of 21 foreign advisors that has been set up to assess and refine Washington's counterterrorism efforts in the Greater Middle East and the Horn of Africa.[109]

---

[108]"Combined Joint Task Force—Horn of Africa" (undated).

[109]Pope (2004).

The Global Peace Operations Initiative is a U.S. initiative announced at the G8 Summit in Sea Island, Georgia, in June 2004. The initiative focuses on training and equipping African peacekeeping and constabulary forces, in combination with G8 nations. The United States plans to contribute approximately $660 million over five years toward the initiative. The "Action Plan for Expanding Global Capacity for Peace Support Operations" announced at the G-8 summit includes the following:

- Train and equip a total of 75,000 peacekeepers worldwide by 2010, including 10 African battalions.
- Establish G-8 expert-level meetings to serve as a clearinghouse for exchanging information on individual efforts to enhance African peace support operations capabilities.
- Conduct periodic exercises and provide training to ensure that the peacekeepers maintain their skills.
- Enhance the institutional capacity of African regional and subregional organizations to plan for and conduct peace operations.
- Develop transportation and logistics support arrangement to help countries deploy and support their forces.
- Increase contributions to the training of stability police units, which are used to establish order and deal with lawlessness during peace missions by supporting existing centers and promoting an Italian initiative to establish an international center of excellence for doctrine and training of stability police units.[110]

The UK's Counter-Terrorism Assistance Program aims to showcase Kenya as an example of an African country that can be given directed foreign aid to help formulate and integrate a viable counterterrorism strategy. Several specific programs are already under way as part of this effort. They include

- security upgrades around hotels and restaurants, particularly those popular with foreign tourists
- installation of perimeter defenses at Mombassa and Nairobi airports, including the construction of towers to defeat surface-to-air missiles[111]
- counterterrorist training, focusing on rapid response tactics for the General Services Unit (a mobile paramilitary force that is primarily responsible for dealing

---

[110] Degrasse, Dickson, and Dziedzic (2004); Citizens for Global Solutions, "Global Peace Operations Initiative" (2006).

[111] A dedicated Aviation Security Liaison Officer is to be dispatched to ensure that upgrades in airport security are maintained and integrated with developments that are taking place in the wider east African region.

with serious threats to civil disorder) as well as specialized forensics and scene-of-the-crime skills[112]
- legal and organizational reform, focusing on an effective framework of anti–money-laundering legislation, an overhaul of the Public Office of Prosecutions, the automation of data held at the Criminal Records Office, and the development of a National Police Leadership faculty.[113]

Is East Africa an Attractive Prospect for Terrorists?

As in the case of other regions in this study, the East Africa corridor confronts a number of serious governance challenges. Borders—both land and sea—are porous and subject to little formal control and surveillance. Corruption is endemic throughout the region, alienating large numbers of citizens, who in many cases are no longer willing to accept systems that they regard as dysfunctional and rapacious. Central governments bring to bear only varying degrees of control over their sovereign jurisdictions, a situation that is reflected in the existence of thriving parallel economies, pervasive criminality, and the routine inability of state security and law enforcement structures to decisively exercise a monopoly over coercive violence.

These considerations take on added salience when one considers that, in several respects, East Africa retains a relatively high degree of attractiveness for terrorist activities. A functioning transportation and communication infrastructure is in place; countries such as Kenya, Tanzania, and Zimbabwe offer operational access to targets both domestically as well as regionally (specifically in South Africa); a range of highly lucrative income-producing opportunities is available (notably in the drug trade and gem-smuggling); and there are sectors of the population that share an affinity with extremist groups.

Deficiencies in Partner Country Capabilities

The confluence of ungovernability and functional utility for terrorism in East Africa has fostered an environment that is highly hospitable to militant extremism in many ways—both logistically and in terms of viable attack options. However, joint counterterrorist structures and policies in the region remain nascent or have yet to be developed. The reasons for this lack of progress are complex and multifaceted, although most relate to one or more of the following considerations: the highly personalized nature of governance and politics that generally holds throughout Africa, which has both hindered the development of institutionalized forms of cooperation and made these efforts contingent on the nature of individual relationships; differing perceptions

---

[112] As part of this effort, London is looking into the feasibility of establishing a permanent secondee from the Metropolitan Police to help with counterterrorist investigations and to identify areas where British support would be most effective and instrumental with regards national counterterror law enforcement and intelligence.

[113] Chalk interview, British official, High Commission of the United Kingdom, Nairobi, February 2004.

of terrorism and of the threat that it poses; the use by some states of proxy substate actors to undermine and destabilize bordering states; and a general absence of integrated national counterterrorist structures through which to channel and direct wider regional responses.[114]

Policy Implications and Recommendations

The counterterrorism assistance programs described in the preceding section, if sustained and backed up with appropriate reform at the national level, could help to lay the groundwork for a more robust regime of counterterrorism collaboration in East Africa. To be truly effective, however, the focus of assistance should be extended to include countries such as Mozambique, which constitutes a central component of the wider eastern corridor of ungovernability. While this is also true of Zimbabwe, furnishing support to that country is difficult to contemplate or justify at this point, given the increasingly erratic and destructive policies of the Mugabe regime.

In addition, counterterrorism assistance should ideally be accompanied by the provision of "soft" aid that is aimed at fostering institutional state development and civil society. Regional experts have repeatedly emphasized the importance of this type of external support in U.S. congressional hearings devoted to Africa and the war on terrorism. Among the measures proposed that are relevant to the problems of ungovernability identified in our study are the following: augment human capital; root out corruption; avail two-way trade; dampen sectarian divisions and promote peaceful interethnic coexistence; increase debt relief; and promote socioeconomic management capacity.[115]

The overall aim should be to build sustained national resilience that is intolerant of, and effective against, terrorist and associated extremist designs. This can only occur if hard security initiatives are linked with a broader array of policies designed to promote political, social, and economic stability. Without such a two-track approach, there is little chance that counterterrorist modalities will take root or provide the basis for the effective mitigation of threats to peace and normalcy.

---

[114] These contributory factors are present in North and West Africa. See Chalk (2005).

[115] See, for instance, "Africa and the War on Global Terrorism" (2001). Commenting on the general salience of these prescriptive modalities, Susan Rice, former Assistant Secretary of State for African Affairs, concluded:

> In short, we will have to pay the price . . . to lift the peoples of Africa and other underdeveloped regions out of poverty and hopelessness. If we do not, we will reap the harvest of a disaffected generation's hostility and growing anti-[Westernism], from the Middle East to Central and South Asia and, indeed, to Africa.

CHAPTER TEN

Case Study: West Africa

Kevin A. O'Brien and Theodore Karasik

Introduction

This chapter discusses the region between the Sahara and pan-Sahel and the Gulf of Guinea, the western half of a zone of conflict and known terrorist activity stretching to the east and southeast. West Africa is becoming more important to the West, not just in "hard security" terms, such as in the war on terrorism, but also in terms of other security considerations, such as fuel and resource security—all of which makes it of ever-increasing relevance to the outside world. This chapter provides, first, a brief overview of West Africa, focusing on geopolitical issues, including previous and ongoing Western interventions. Then, using this study's analytical framework of ungovernability and conduciveness to terrorism, it discusses and evaluates West Africa's suitability—or lack thereof—for potential terrorist activities, including both support and operational functions. The chapter concludes with an assessment of the overall implications of West Africa to U.S. and Western interests.

For the purposes of this study, we will consider the major countries of Sierra Leone, Liberia, and the regional hegemon, Nigeria, in greatest depth. Additional countries of interest across the region include the other West African states (Benin, Togo, Ghana, Cote d'Ivoire, Niger, Guinea (Conakry), Guinea-Bissau, The Gambia, Senegal, Mauritania, and Burkina Faso), the states of the Sahel-Sahara zone (Chad and Mali), and the countries on the Gulf of Guinea (Equatorial Guinea and Cameroon) (see Figure 10.1).

Each country has different characteristics, and each characteristic has a deep effect on the domestic, regional, and international stances of the country, as well as on the way that other countries or international bodies deal with it. Many of the countries suffer from serious problems of governance, corruption, and trafficking (in virtually anything), making them potential prospects for terrorist presence as well.

Figure 10.1
West Africa—Political Map

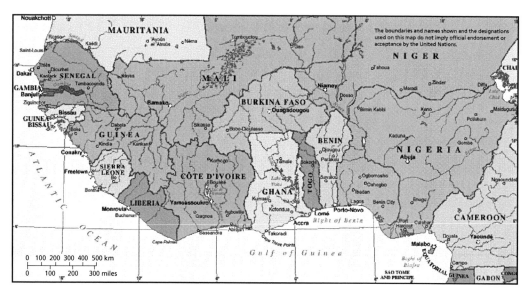

SOURCE: United Nations, Department of Peacekeeping Operations, Cartographic Section, Map No. 4242, February 2005, www.un.org/Depts/Cartographic/map/profile/westafrica.pdf.
RAND MG561-10.1

Overview of West Africa

West Africa is a vast region, covering 5 million square kilometers—roughly the size of the continental United States—on the world's poorest and most unstable continent.[1] Above and around it, the Sahara and pan-Sahel regions span a vast space that includes some of the least populated areas on the planet (see Figures 10.2 and 10.3), alongside some of the loosest government control to be found.[2] The topography of this vast region varies—from the bone-dry desert of the Sahara, to the semi-arid terrain of the Sahel, through the limited savannah and bush reaching west and south, to the far more lush jungles and equatorial forests of West Africa.

___

[1]   "West Africa," Wikipedia (2005).

[2]   The Sahara is the world's largest desert at approximately 3,500,000 square miles (9,065,000 square kilometers). It extends more than 3,000 miles (4,830 kilometers), from the Atlantic Ocean to the Red Sea. The Sahara stretches south around 1,200 miles (1,930 kilometers) to the Sahel, a steppe across west and central Africa that forms its southern border. The Sahara includes most of Western Sahara, Mauritania, Algeria, Niger, Libya, and Egypt, the southern portions of Morocco and Tunisia, and the northern portions of Senegal, Mali, Chad, and Sudan. The Sahel is the semiarid region of Africa between the Sahara to the north and the savannas to the south. It extends from Senegal, in the west, through Mauritania, Mali, Burkina Faso, Niger, northern Nigeria, Sudan, to Ethiopia in the east.

Figure 10.2
West Africa—Population Density

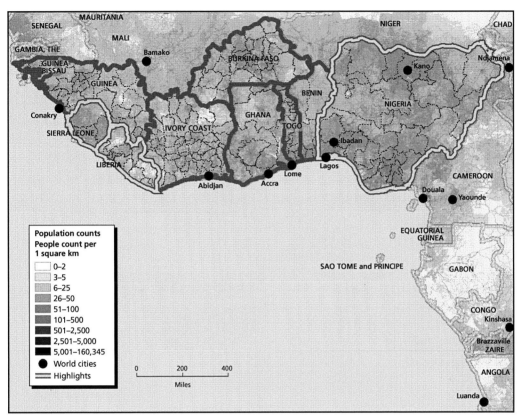

SOURCE: RAND.
RAND *MG561-10.2*

A major trading area for centuries, particularly with the Berbers and Arabs of North Africa, West Africa became the hub of the slave trade (both intra-African and Western) following exploitation by the Portuguese in the mid-15th century and subsequently by the British and the French. Throughout the early colonial period, West Africa was the source of most of the West's slaves, either brought out of West African client-states or using those client-states to generate far more slaves from the interior. It was also the period in which West Africa's natural resources, including precious minerals, fruits, woods, and other commodities, were first commercialized by the West. The slave trade was abolished by the British in the early part of the nineteenth century. And together with the rest of the European colonial empires, most of the West African colo-

Figure 10.3
West Africa—Population (in thousands)

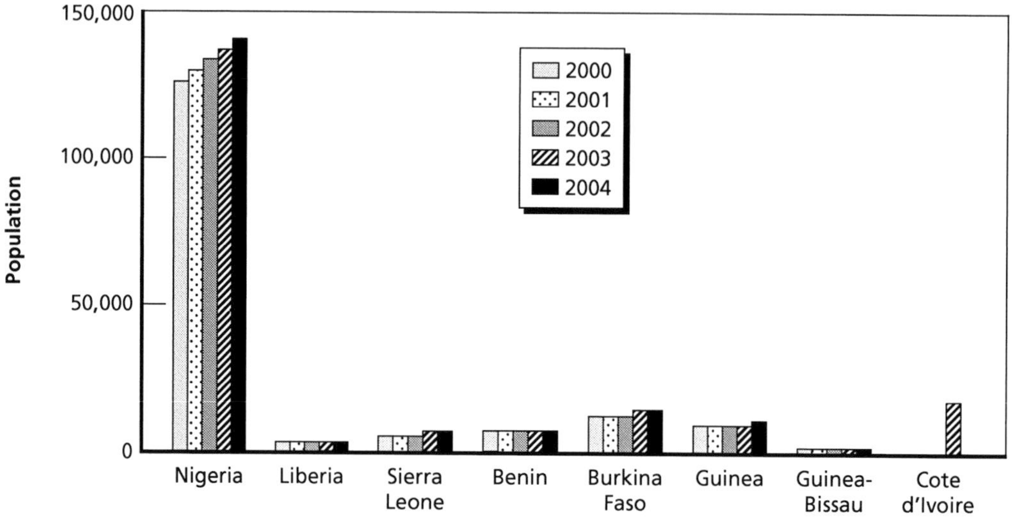

SOURCE: *CIA World Factbook* (2005).

RAND *MG561-10.3*

nies (all the current west African states except Liberia, which remained independent since its founding) attained their independence in the 1950s and 1960s.[3]

West Africa as an Ungoverned Territory

Unlike most of the other regions covered in this study, few countries in West Africa can profess to have a fully established system of governance (whether political, ethnosocial, infrastructural, or otherwise) over the territories that they comprise. Indeed, every country in one form or another, having emerged from a colonial legacy, represents that old adage about borders being merely lines on a map that bear little resemblance to traditional boundaries and divisions, tribal settlement patterns, or other more natural means toward the establishment and division of political entities such as states. There are exceptions, of course. Ghana and Senegal appear to have fairly capable government administrations, even in small towns and rural areas, and anyone who has visited Guinea can see the surprising extent of government control outside the capital.[4]

For this reason, the region has always had some of the least-defined boundaries in the world. Trade, population flows, and other movements across the region con-

---

[3]   Major decolonization occurred, respectively, on the following dates: Sierra Leone (1961), Cote d'Ivoire (1960), Ghana (1957), Burkina Faso (1960), Guinea (1958), and Nigeria (1960).

[4]   Dr. William Reno, review of manuscript.

tinue to take little account of the political borders that divide these countries. Thus, in many senses, the whole region suffers from whatever instability or blight that any one country in the region suffers from; it could be said that when one country or warlord sneezes, all others catch cold to some degree.

What is striking about West Africa—once again, with some exceptions—is the tempo and intensity of the conflicts that have engulfed the region for such a long period. Since decolonization, most of these countries have witnessed ongoing cycles of violence in one form or another. This appears to reflect the trend across much of Africa, but there are some differences. The first is that West Africa was generally not as affected as every other region of Africa by great-power competition during the Cold War; however, this did not prevent the region from stumbling into corruption and instability. Second, rather than fighting for liberation from colonial or white-minority rule, as was the case in other parts of Africa, the governmental structures of many West African countries, such as they were, were being decimated by domestic warlordism, as well as by the interference visited on them by other countries or warlords in the region.[5]

Lack of State Penetration of Society[6]

Historically, West Africa has come to be seen as one of the most chaotic regions of the world—in terms of the plight its populations, the instability caused by intra- and interstate conflict, the crime and corruption that appear to grip its populations and governments, and the sheer lack of development found in most of the countries of the region. It is a region in which external interventions have occurred in almost every country time and again.

Nigeria is an exception. Not only the region's hegemon, but also Africa's most populous country with a wealth in oil and natural gas, Nigeria has developed more than other countries in the region and has been able to project military power outside its borders in the context of multilateral peacemaking operations.[7] Following nearly 16 years of military rule, Nigeria adopted a new constitution in 1999 and completed a peaceful transition to civilian government. The country's leading concerns are to rebuild the economy, institutionalize democracy, and defuse long-standing ethnic and religious tensions.

---

[5] Except for Guinea-Bissau.

[6] Unless otherwise noted, all facts and figures derive from the *CIA World Factbook* (2005).

[7] The capital-intensive oil sector provides 20 percent of GDP, 95 percent of foreign exchange earnings, and about 65 percent of budgetary revenues: See *CIA World Factbook* (2005), "Nigeria." In the 1990s, through its leadership of the Economic Community of West African States (ECOWAS) and its military arm, the Economic Community of West African States Monitoring Group (ECOMOG), Nigeria dominated the region—intervening in civil wars in both Liberia and Sierra Leone a number of times.

To support these endeavors, Nigeria appears to have functional state institutions, certainly when compared with other countries in West Africa and many across Africa more generally (although, as discussed elsewhere in this book, there are certainly pockets of ungovernability). As a starting point, Nigeria's security forces enforce the government's writ. At present, Nigeria has some 152,000 personnel in the national police force and an additional 95,000 personnel in other security forces. Each of Nigeria's 36 states and the federal capital territory is run by a state Commissioner of Police; these states are then grouped into 12 zones, each under an Assistant Inspector General. Nigeria currently has a ratio of police officers to population that approximates those found in South Africa and the United Kingdom.[8] (These ratios, however, do not tell the whole story; as in the cases of the North Caucasus and Guatemala, the police are highly corrupt and have been accused of collusion with criminal elements.)

Two countries in the region, Liberia and Sierra Leone, have generated sufficient internal violence and anarchy to warrant external intervention. Nine-five percent of Liberia's population is composed of members of indigenous tribes (including Kpelle, Bassa, Gio, Kru, Grebo, Mano, Krahn, Gola, Gbandi, Loma, Kissi, Vai, Dei, Bella, Mandingo, and Mende), with the remainder composed of Americo-Liberians (descendents of former American slaves) (2.5 percent), and Congo people (descendants of former slaves in the Caribbean) (2.5 percent).[9] Over the past two decades, Liberia has witnessed years of civil war: first, a rebellion by warlord Charles Taylor and later a rebellion against Taylor's leadership after he had taken over the country.[10]

Until 2001, Liberia had not been thought of as a potential haven for Islamist extremist terrorists, but subsequent investigations into possible linkages between Sierra Leone's "conflict diamonds" and al-Qaeda resulted in serious accusations that Taylor had conspired to assist al-Qaeda operatives, including its chief financier, to obtain readily transportable currency, in the form of diamonds, in the months leading up to September 2001.[11]

In Liberia, only 20 percent of the population speaks English; the others speak an additional 20 languages, which correspond to distinct ethnic groups.[12] As a result, the effective level of governance is the local or tribal level, with the chief overseeing local affairs. Directly related to this situation is the virtual nonexistence of a public security

---

[8]   Human Rights Watch (2005b).

[9]   Nationmaster.com (2005), "Liberia: People." Nationmaster.com draws its statistical data from the *CIA World Factbook* and other globally acknowledged key sources of data.

[10]   Taylor was originally an antigovernment warlord in Liberia who became Liberia's president for a brief period in the late 1990s before being indicted for war crimes in the aftermath of Sierra Leone's civil war. As of the time of writing in the fall of 2005, he had moved to Nigeria where he was granted political asylum, while allegedly continuing to interfere in the internal affairs of Liberia.

[11]   This is documented and discussed in Rabasa et al. (2006b).

[12]   Nationmaster.com (2005), "Liberia: Language."

element in Liberian society for many years. The United Nations Mission in Liberia (UNMIL), established in September 2003, is considered the de facto rule of law in Liberia, with 1,070 international police personnel.[13]

In neighboring Sierra Leone, the 12-year civil war (1989–2001) resulted in major displacements of more than half of its 4.5 million people by the time of the 2001 peace accord.[14] Since the end of the civil war, order in Sierra Leone has been enforced by the United Nations Mission in Sierra Leone (UNAMSIL). At the time of the UN peace-keepers' deployment in 1999, the government of President Tejman Kabbah had little control over its territory. In 2000, President Kabbah requested additional assistance from the UN and Britain. UNAMSIL expanded its peacekeeping force from 8,000 to 13,000 through September 2000, with the UK sending an additional 1,500 elite troops to secure Freetown and its airport. At the time its training began (September 2001), the Sierra Leone army had expanded to 8,500 troops with a small air wing and some 200 navy personnel; however, the Sierra Leone police remains the weakest link in the security sector, with shortfalls in personnel, training, and resources.[15]

Adequacy of Infrastructure

While Nigeria's infrastructure is relatively good compared with the rest of West Africa, it is still problematic (see Figure 10.4). For example, Nigeria has more than 60,000 kilometers of paved highways (30.9 percent of all roads) or approximately one kilometer of paved road for every four square kilometers of territory, compared with Liberia's 657 kilometers of paved roads (approximately one kilometer of paved highway per 160 square kilometers of territory) and Sierra Leone's 904 kilometers of paved roads (approximately one kilometer of paved road per 80 square kilometers of territory).[16] In Liberia, UNMIL reports major deterioration on all highways because of heavy rains and lack of maintenance.[17] In June–July 2003, officers of the Sierra Leone Roads Authority reported through the District Recovery Committees on the condition of 5,830 kilometers of roads throughout the country. More than one-third of roads were indicated as "bad sections," with an average road damage index of 3.055 on a scale of 1 (very good) to 4 (bad). In addition, many roads are usable only in the dry season.

Although most of Nigeria's state capitals and large towns are accessible by paved roads, poor maintenance and heavy traffic have combined to degrade a significant amount of this network, resulting in many "paved" roads being closer

---

[13] Dukuly (2005).

[14] "Sierra Leone Security Information" (2007).

[15] "Sierra Leone Security Information" (2007); ICG (2003e).

[16] Nationmaster.com (2005), "Liberia: Transportation."

[17] Nationmaster.com (2005), "Liberia: Transportation."

Figure 10.4
West Africa—Infrastructure

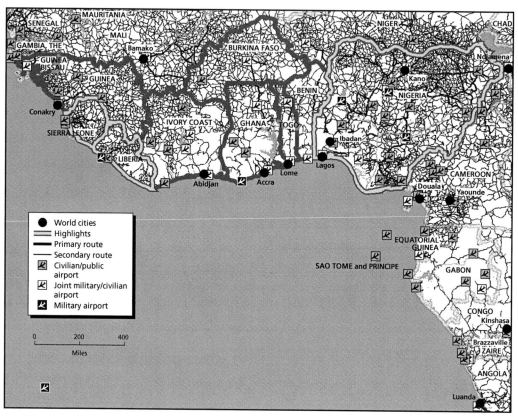

SOURCE: RAND.
RAND *MG561-10.4*

to gravel. The maintenance and upkeep of roads, even in cities, is hugely problematic; this is especially in light of fluctuations in world oil prices, each of which has a large impact on Nigeria's GDP and thereby on the government's resources.[18] On these roads, public transportation remains unstable and often dangerous, according to warnings from Western representatives. Nigeria also has approximately 3,557 kilometers of railway, all of which are reportedly unreliable. This compares to just 490 kilometers of railway in Liberia, much of which was destroyed or sold off during the civil war (see Figure 10.5).[19] Finally, Nigeria has 70 airports, almost half of which have paved runways. This

---

[18] Most paved roads in Nigeria are in poor condition. Lack of maintenance makes much of the established infrastructure unusable at times.

[19] In 1989, all three Liberian rail systems were owned and operated by foreign steel and financial interests in conjunction with the Liberian government. One of these, the Lamco Railroad, closed in 1989 after iron ore production ceased; the other two were shut down by the civil war. Large sections of the rail lines have been dismantled,

compares with two airports with paved runways in Liberia and only one airport with a paved runway and two heliports in Sierra Leone.

In terms of its public and private communications, Nigeria is similarly ahead in West Africa (see Figure 10.6). Its telecommunication system provides one main telephone line for every 156 people. This is being supplemented—even supplanted—by mobile telephony, with now one mobile phone for every 42 people; like the road networks, however, Nigeria's telecommunications networks are also suffering from poor maintenance, and major expansion is required.[20] In Liberia, there are currently just over two phone lines per 1,000 people, with 6,700 lines.[21] In contrast, in Sierra Leone, there are more than 24,000 main lines in use and more than 67,000 mobile phones; however, the main lines are notoriously unreliable, one of the main reasons pushing the mobile telephony network.[22] See Figure 10.7 for the number of mobile phone users in West Africa.

Figure 10.5
Road and Rail Networks in West Africa, 1992–2002

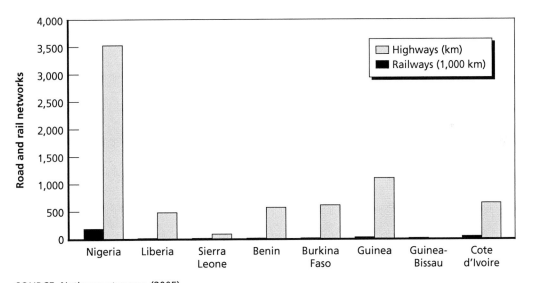

SOURCE: Nationmaster.com (2005).
RAND *MG561-10.5*

---

and as of 2001, approximately 60 kilometers of railroad track were exported for scrap. Nationmaster.com (2005), "Liberia: Transportation."

[20] Total number of main telephone lines in use: 853,111; total number of mobile telephones in use: 3,149,500.

[21] Nationmaster.com (2005), "Liberia: Media."

[22] *CIA World Factbook* (2005), "Sierra Leone."

Figure 10.6
Main-Line Telephony in West Africa

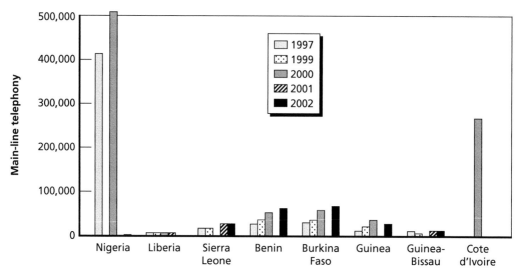

SOURCES: *CIA World Factbook* (2005); Nationmaster.com (2005).
RAND *MG561-10.6*

Figure 10.7
Mobile Phone Users in West Africa

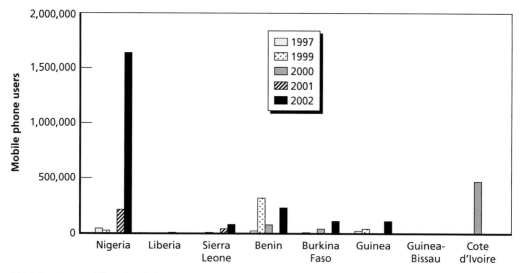

SOURCE: *CIA World Factbook* (2005).
RAND *MG561-10.7*

In a similar manner, Internet usage, while extremely low in most West African countries compared to the developed world (or even other more developed African countries, such as South Africa) is small but growing. Nigeria, as with all else, dominates with 420,000 users (as of 2002), yet this constitutes only .03 percent of Nigeria's population, compared with Senegal, where Internet usage stands at over 2 percent of the overall population. The country with the highest per capita use of the Internet in West Africa is, somewhat surprisingly, Togo, at almost 4 percent. Yet Sierra Leone has the fastest rising Internet use rate over the past few years, with Cote d'Ivoire, Guinea, and Benin close behind. Coupled with mobile-phone use—another key "new technology" for Africa that is greatly increasing connectivity in a continent where historical communications have been sparse—these same countries are demonstrating the greatest leaps forward.

Effects of the HIV/AIDS Epidemic in West Africa

Perhaps the most important factor that must be taken into account in assessing any sub-Saharan African country is HIV/AIDS and the devastating effect it could have (and already has, although infection rates in West Africa are generally lower than other parts of Africa—see Figure 10.8) on governance and stability. Sub-Saharan Africa has just over 10 percent of the world's population, but is home to more than 60 percent of all people living with HIV.[23] In this sense, as Jonathan Stevenson notes clearly, "there is a clear connection between a high incidence of HIV/AIDS and regional insecurity,"[24] which, frankly, does not even begin to outline the central importance that confronting this devastating epidemic will likely have on the ability of most African states to govern themselves. In any consideration of the potential for West African territories to become more, rather than less, "ungoverned," the effects of HIV/AIDS must be at the forefront.

In West Africa, overall HIV prevalence is lowest in the Sahel countries and highest in Côte d'Ivoire, Burkina Faso, and Nigeria.[25] The latter has the third-largest number of people living with HIV in the world (after South Africa and India), with commercial sex being the main driver of the epidemic.[26]

---

[23] Approximately 25.4 million people in Sub-Saharan Africa are infected by HIV—an average infection rate per country of 7.4 percent. Swaziland and Botswana are the worst of these per capita, with around 38 percent infection levels, while South Africa is the worst numerically, with 5.3 million (21.5 percent of the population) living with HIV-AIDS—followed by Nigeria with 3.6 million infected (5.4 percent of the population): *CIA World Factbook* (2005); "Rank Order HIV/AIDS: People living with HIV/AIDS; and "Field Listing HIV/AIDS: Adult prevalence rate."

[24] Jonathan Stevenson (2003–04), p. 162. For more substantive analysis of this issue, see O'Brien (2005, 2006); Singer (2002); and Elbe (2003).

[25] In West Africa, Guinea-Bissau has the highest infection level at 10 percent, followed by Cote d'Ivoire at 7 percent.

[26] UNAIDS (2004).

Figure 10.8
West African HIV/AIDS Infection Rates (Compared with Other African Countries)

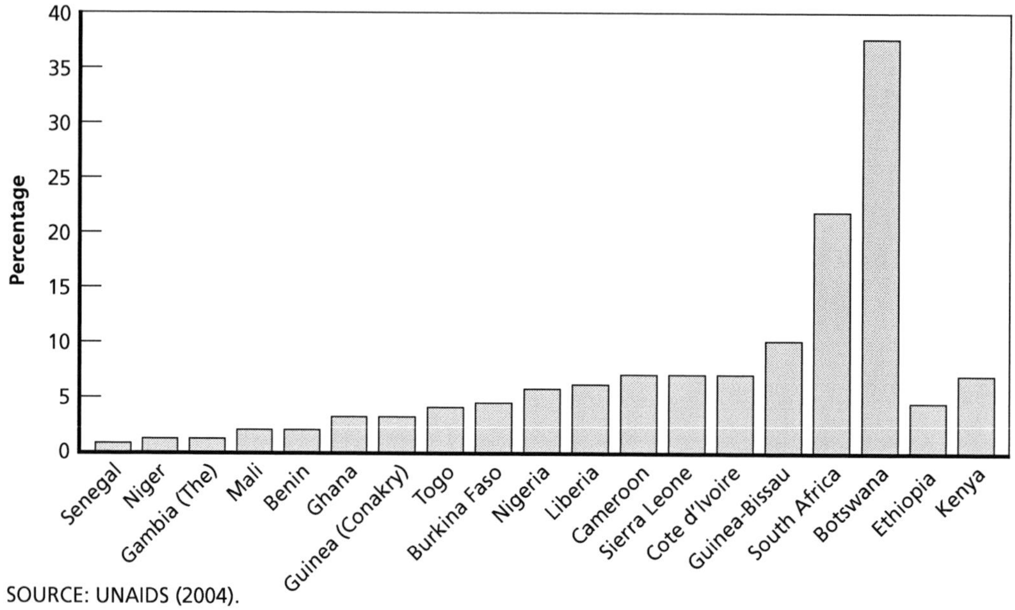

SOURCE: UNAIDS (2004).

RAND *MG561-10.8*

Nigeria has just passed the 5 percent HIV/AIDS infection-rate threshold, with 3.6 million people, or 5.4 percent of the population, infected as of 2003. Above this rate, infection levels climb rapidly to pandemic levels; this could lead to deteriorations in the governance structures across the country as the pandemic worsens, if other countries' patterns are replicated.[27] To stem this health threat, the Nigerian government is able to spend 4.7 percent of GDP on health care. Although this appears to be a significant amount, it equaled just $19 per capita as of 2002.[28]

In Liberia, the HIV/AIDS infection rate is 5.9 percent; in 2002, the government was spending around 2.1 percent of GDP or $4 per capita on health care. In the same year, Sierra Leone's government spent 2.9 percent of GDP, or $6 per capita, with the HIV/AIDS infection rates at an estimated 7 percent.[29] The African Development Bank has provided funding for the rehabilitation of three main referral hospitals in Freetown. Sierra Leone's social services network, largely destroyed by the civil war, is now being rebuilt through a Child Protection Technical Committee established in every district, which liaises with the Sierra Leone police (which may not mean much, given the weakness of the police).

---

[27] *CIA World Factbook* (2005), "Nigeria."

[28] World Health Organization (2005), "Nigeria."

[29] World Health Organization (2005), "Sierra Leone."

Formal and Informal Economies

In many developing countries, a significant informal or "shadow" economy exists, which is a result of the underdevelopment of the national economy and an avenue by which members of these societies can maintain financial activities out of the government's sight. The concern that such economies are being used by terrorists in West Africa arises from the possibility that al-Qaeda, in the months and years before 9/11, traded upon well-established Hezbollah networks in Sierra Leone to use "conflict diamonds" to launder money, as well as to create easily transportable funds in the form of diamonds and other precious minerals. Informal economies could be used to transfer or exchange funds illicitly, to fund terrorist support activities out of the government's view, and to move both funds and people across porous borders and regions.

In Nigeria, the government has been called "organized crime."[30] Whether or not it is intentional, the Nigerian government has created an ideal environment for the propagation of organized crime. Nigeria is well known for its criminal economy—much of it based on organized crime groups that exploit naïve (and greedy) individuals abroad through what are known as "419 scams."[31] There has also been an increasing use of government stationary and seals in crime and scams, increasing concerns over seemingly ever-developing levels of "official" corruption. Indeed, criminal networks are largely incorporated into the government itself on a national level, as well as locally with regional and tribal systems. However, the broader problem is that Nigeria's government, like all others in the region, has not yet been able to get a firm grip on this informal economy, ensure that tax revenues are collected, and—crucial from the standpoint of counterterrorism—ensure government oversight of all economic activity.

Most Nigerians earn their income in the informal economy. In Nigeria it is estimated that overall untaxed revenues amount to between 40 and 45 percent of the total economy. This low level is due not only to the activities of the population to hide revenue and financial activities from the government but also to the weak fiscal capacity of the state and local governments. These revenues are further weakened by the volume of traffic in illegal drugs, arms, and people that enters Nigeria (primarily from Benin and the port of Cotonou). Indeed, in many ways, this illegal traffic, which has come to form a significant portion of Nigeria's shadow economy, depends on the lawlessness and poor governance in the countries surrounding Nigeria.[32] With the election

---

[30] According to Dr. William Chambliss, a professor in the sociology department of George Washington University, Washington D.C., "The government was, and is, organized crime." For example, the U.S. embassy is perpetually inundated with requests from Americans who have been defrauded by Nigerians.

[31] "419" is the line in the Nigerian Criminal Code to which this offense relates. These scams attempt to obtain funds from individuals abroad by promising them that untold wealth is simply waiting for them "on account of someone's death" or a corrupt or embezzlement activity if the contactee would only send them a good-faith commitment.

[32] See Offoaro (2005).

of President Olusegun Obasanjo in 1999, the Nigerian government has begun to take steps to scale back the existing high levels of corruption.[33]

The economies of the rest of West Africa are similar to Nigeria's. In Liberia, where unemployment is as high as 82 percent, there is no countrywide tax structure, and little economic activity takes place on the record.[34] Few taxes are collected via trade or tariffs. The gray market is simply massive, with most dealings being conducted off the record. During and since the civil war, especially across areas of the country controlled by Charles Taylor, Liberia became a major center for criminal enterprise. It has become the transshipment point for Southeast and Southwest Asian heroin, as well as South American cocaine, for the European and U.S. markets; it is a significant center for arms dealing, money laundering, and illegal diamond trading, which has greatly expanded of late, with little or no Ministry of Mines presence in any of the key diamond-mining areas. The overall illegal trade is conservatively valued at around US$350,000 per month.[35] Overall estimates of the illegal lumber trade range from US$75,000 to US$100,000 per month (but this only counts those trucks noted entering Monrovia). A number of routes support illegal transactions from Liberia into Sierra Leone, Guinea, and Cote d'Ivoire. Timber and diamonds particularly have passed illegally between Liberia and Sierra Leone, funding armed militias.[36] While UNMIL has increased the levels of regulation and control previously found on these areas, this remains a fraction of what is required.

In Sierra Leone, historically (and even before the civil war began in 1989) the economy was generally informal. By the mid-1980s, most of the economy had been forced underground and was being controlled by a small group of Lebanese businessmen.[37] Funds were diverted en masse from the banking system because dealers needed to hold large cash balances to finance under-the-counter activities, leading to a severe shortage of domestic currency. Government regulation of commodities markets tightened from 1971 to 1990; subsidies on imported rice and petroleum products increased with domestic inflation, further discouraging domestic production and inducing smuggling of imports to neighboring countries.[38] Diamonds, agricultural products, and gold were

---

[33] According to one report, the Nigerian government rarely realizes more than 10 percent of its collectable taxes in the country, and one half of that 10 percent is lost to diversion to private accounts, embiezzlement, and mismanagement. Bakre (2005).

[34] Infoplease (2005), "Liberia."

[35] Global Witness (2005).

[36] Dr. William Reno, in his review of the manuscript, says there has been considerable progress in Sierra Leone in marketing diamonds through official channels.

[37] Sierra Leone has long had a sizable Lebanese population that constitutes a significant (and now indigenous) portion of Sierra Leonean society. The Lebanese have traditionally controlled much of the banking and diamond industry, and they have also provided a conduit for Hezbollah's presence in Sierra Leone. See Rabasa et al. (2006b).

[38] Davies (2001).

all smuggled through Liberia and Guinea along with these imports. Between 1991 and 2000, GDP in Sierra Leone had a negative average annual growth rate of –8 percent.

This informal economy has slowly been brought under better control since 2001. The ratio of tax revenues to GDP has been steadily increasing since the late 1990s and is viewed as a major key to post-conflict stability. With 21,979 million Leones (US$2.6 million) in direct taxes and 37,660 million (US$4.38 million) in indirect taxes collected in 1999, the ratio has increased annually over the past five years.[39] Part of this success has been due to the government's moves to recognize this large parallel market to some degree (including even listing parallel-market currency exchange rates on its official government Web site!) and its attempt to develop the formal and informal economies in tandem.[40] However, in one particular area, great efforts are under way to restrict the size of the gray market, which in the late 1990s was responsible for the majority of diamond exports from the country.

Social and Cultural Resistance

Nigeria's underlying reality is the massive multiethnicity of the country, with more than 250 ethnicities.[41] There is no majority ethnic or linguistic group: major minority groups include the Yoruba (19 percent), Hausa (18 percent), Ibo (17 percent), Fulani (8 percent), Ibibio (3 percent), Tiv (2 percent), Anang (1 percent), and Ebira (1 percent).[42] More than 515 languages are spoken across Nigeria, with Edo, Efik, Adamawa, Fulfulde, Hausa, Idoma, Igbo, Yerwa Knauri, Yoruba, and English recognized as official languages.[43] In addition to this complicated ethnic mix, Nigeria also suffers ethnoreligious tensions between the peoples of the north—dominated by the Muslim Hausa tribe, who largely constitute the ruling elite of the country, and the peoples of the south, dominated by the Yoruba tribe.[44] This is largely a legacy of colonial rule, when Nigeria's British colonizers encouraged rivalry between the Muslim north and the Christian south. As a result, the majority of Christian missionary schools were built in the south, which remains the better-educated industrial hub today. Southerners control business in both the north and the south. In contrast, the north is associated with the military, producing a military elite prone to coups.[45] This has also contributed

---

[39] Government of Sierra Leone (2001).

[40] Government of Sierra Leone (2001).

[41] *CIA World Factbook* (2005), "Nigeria."

[42] MOST Ethno-Net Africa Database (2004), "Nigeria."

[43] MOST Ethno-Net Africa Database (2004), "Nigeria."

[44] The Yorubas are evenly divided among Christians and Muslims, with about 20 percent still practicing the traditional Yoruba religion.

[45] Racial rioting in May of 2004 resulted in hundreds of casualties. Between 1999 and 2001, over 60 people were killed by civil unrest in Nigeria.

to sometimes bloody conflicts between the central government and the marginalized minorities of the Niger River Delta.[46]

Of 133 million Nigerians, about half are Muslims, approximately 40 percent are Christians, and the remainder profess indigenous beliefs.[47] In the past four years, 12 states of the north have adopted Islamic law.[48] There have also been recent religious clashes, including an uprising by a group called Al-Sunna wal Jamma in Kanamma and Geidam, small towns in Yobe State in northeast Nigeria near the Niger border.[49] Nigeria also has severe problems in the oil-rich Niger Delta (which have continued through 2006), where official neglect, poverty, dislocations, and environmental degradation caused by energy projects are aggravating unrest across the region.

Concerns have also been raised regarding the activities of certain Islamic preachers, many with suspected links to foreign terrorist organizations (both in other parts of Africa and abroad), which the government feared were radicalizing Muslims in northern Nigeria. Immediately after 9/11, several Afghan and Pakistani preachers were arrested and deported because, according to the authorities, they could not give satisfactory explanations of their mission in Nigeria; this followed the 2000 arrest and deportation to the United States of Mohammed Suleiman al-Nalfi, wanted in connection with the 1993 bombing of the World Trade Center. Nigeria is also concerned that it was mentioned along with Jordan, Morocco, and Saudi Arabia on a tape purportedly released by bin Laden as a country where Muslims needed to be liberated.

Recent incidents, such as the Al-Sunna wal Jamma uprising mentioned above, have generated growing concerns over the fertility of the region for violent Islamist extremism.[50] Although Nigerian troops quickly crushed the uprising, as many as 1,000 followers may still be operating in the area, potentially with the support of foreign radical Islamist groups. In some ways, this rise in Islamic extremism in the north could make Nigeria attractive to international jihadist groups; however, it is another question entirely as to whether local extremists would see their place within the al-Qaeda–inspired global jihadist movement or whether they would remained focused on local concerns.[51]

---

[46] Institute for Strategic Studies (Pretoria), "Nigeria Security Information" (undated).

[47] CIA World Factbook (2005), "Nigeria."

[48] In an attempt to assuage Christian minorities in the north, officials insist that *sharia* will be applied exclusively to Muslims living in the 12 states.

[49] The group allegedly wanted to establish a "Taliban-style government" in northern Nigeria. See IRINnews.org (2004).

[50] IRINnews.org (2004).

[51] Greenberg (2004).

Lack of Monopoly of Force

At the sociopolitical level, the armed forces in Nigeria seem to have grown "coup weary," with the political landscape not conducive to further successful installations of military governments; it is more likely that ethnic, religious, or regional tensions will persist on an intermittent basis, with the dissolution of a federal Nigeria as a remote possibility.[52]

A variety of secessionist forces are active in Nigeria, for instance, the Yoruba separatist Oodua People's Congress; Ijaw Egbesu in the Niger Delta; the Bakassi Boys in the southeast; and the Arewa People's Congress in the north.[53] Across the country and outside these more organized groups, there are innumerable gangs and crime rings. Social unrest, religious and ethnic strife, and crime affect many parts of Nigeria, and many foreigners living in Nigeria, as well as visitors, report widespread muggings. Nigerian and expatriate oil workers are regularly kidnapped in an attempt to extort cash from foreign operators.

This is directly related to another problem that Nigeria cannot seem to overcome: the growing success of criminal syndicates and criminal violence. Crime is on the upswing; in one period between August 2002 and May 2003, over 270 civilians and 84 policemen were killed in Lagos alone. Bands of armed vigilantes have moved in to occupy the vacuum left in the wake of ineffective law enforcement in many parts of the country. As a result, militia-like vigilantes identify those they believe to be criminals, and attack or execute them.[54] This situation is not helped by public distrust of Nigeria's law enforcement structures. Perceived corruption within Nigeria's police force, alongside a history of criminal organizations infiltrating or overwhelming local law enforcement, has left the population with little trust of authorities and reliant on private justice via families or clans and regional strong men.[55]

In Liberia, a new criminal justice system is being implemented slowly, after years of conflict and autocracy. At present, because of a severe lack of regulation and a culture of impunity, crime is endemic and incalculable; since the tenuous peace that has followed the end of the civil war, demobilized fighters have added to the crime rate in rural areas, while security forces and corrupt officials undermine the legitimacy of the government. Indeed, soldiers and police, who are rarely paid and have little loyalty to the regime,[56] are a significant threat to stability. Both Liberian and international stakeholders in the Liberian peace process are unanimous that the Armed Forces of Liberia

---

[52] Institute for Strategic Studies (Pretoria), "Nigeria Security Information" (undated).

[53] Institute for Strategic Studies (Pretoria), "Nigeria Security Information" (undated).

[54] Olukoya (2003).

[55] "Nigeria Police Force," Globalsecurity.org.

[56] On June 15, 2005, Liberian soldiers blockaded the Ministry of Defence to protest the withholding of their wages (West, 2005).

(AFL) must be restructured and trained to reflect geographic and ethnic balances, to submit to civil authority, and to respect human rights.[57]

Partly as a result of the lack of public security services in Liberia and partly also because of the direct involvement in criminal activities of many of those same police, Liberia has long been both a nexus and a haven for international crime. Under Charles Taylor's patronage, international arms dealers worked alongside alleged al-Qaeda operatives, Israeli and South African mercenaries, Hezbollah diamond merchants, and Russian and Balkan organized crime figures.[58] Ineffective arms embargos and regulations have left a large percentage of the population heavily armed; for example, a UN arms-for-cash deal provided many fighters with $75 in exchange for weapons; but because an AK-47 costs much less than $75, such activities may actually have increased the arms flow to Liberia.[59]

In Sierra Leone, although the civil war may be over and the RUF rebels and "sobels" ("soldiers-by-day, rebels-by-night") defeated and dispersed, criminality remains high.[60] Corruption is a significant issue among underpaid government employees. Across the whole of Sierra Leone today, confidence in the government remains low. For this reason, Sierra Leone's population, to varying extents, relies on informal structures of governance rather than the national authorities. The disarmament of excombatants ended in January 2002, though weapons remain in the country, especially in the provinces, where they are nearly impossible to trace.[61]

Even so, the weaponry in private hands does not represent opposition to the government. Indeed, since the ending of the civil war, the trend in Sierra Leone has been to reintegrate into society groups established during the civil war. There appears to be a recognition that the country has much to achieve collectively, and that it must rebuild and stabilize rather than concern itself with past conflicts.[62]

---

[57] "Liberia: AFL Goes Amok Again!" (2005). The roughly 9,000 AFL forces recruited during the war years from 1989 to 2003 are expected to begin demobilizing shortly. See Human Rights Watch (2005c).

[58] Farah (2004a).

[59] Doyle (2004).

[60] On May 15, 2001, a deal was signed in Freetown between the government and Sierra Leone's RUF rebels agreeing to an immediate cessation of hostilities and the deployment of UNAMSIL peacekeepers into the former RUF territory as a prelude to disarmament. The RUF were forced into the deal as a result of the British presence and because of the opposition of the Guinean army. As of September 2001, 60,000 former combatants had been disarmed under the August 14, 2001, UN-administered Disarmament, Demobilization and Reintegration process; however, while the RUF have lost their command structure and their political party struggles to keep offices and members, and the reintegration program is near completion, many excombatants have yet to complete training programs, and even with assistance many are finding jobs scarce and believe that the government should be doing more. Institute for Strategic Studies (Pretoria), "Sierra Leone Security Information" (undated).

[61] ICG (2003e).

[62] O'Brien interviews, Sierra Leone (Freetown) May 2005. The only external concern most Sierra Leoneans had was over continued interference by Charles Taylor of Liberia in their internal affairs; otherwise, many Sierra

Lack of Border Controls

Nigeria has 4,049 kilometers of border to protect, and its customs and border control police are thought to be the most corrupt sector of government. As a result, currency, arms, drugs, and people are all trafficked across its borders.[63] This lack of border controls also results in a readily accessible trade in small arms and light weapons. The density of arms among the civilian population increases with proximity to the Niger Delta region, where the populace is especially disenfranchised. In Liberia, border control is virtually nonexistent. This condition provided former Liberian warlord Charles Taylor with the conduits he required to support rebel activities and interfere in the affairs of neighboring countries. Most recently, the Ivorian government accused Liberia of supporting rebels.[64] Arms and other illicit goods move with little restriction across the border from Sierra Leone to Liberia, as well as north and west to Burkina Faso and Guinea-Bissau. As late as January 2004, the Sierra Leone army was deployed to prevent Liberian militias from moving weapons into the country.

External Interference

West Africa's states witnessed a multitude of external interventions over the 1990s.[65] The first major intervention was carried out by the Nigerian-led ECOMOG. This was a peacemaking intervention into Liberia in an attempt to stabilize that country, and then further into Sierra Leone and Guinea when the Liberian civil war spilled over into these countries. ECOMOG was authorized by the United Nations to undertake regional peacekeeping activities at a time when the international powers did not plan or wish to intervene in these regional conflicts in Africa. The ECOMOG mission to Liberia lasted from 1990 to 1998, when a peace deal was signed in Monrovia. The mission was initially composed of some 4,000 troops, mostly from Nigeria but also from Ghana, Guinea, Sierra Leone, and Gambia. Following the May 1997 coup in Sierra Leone, ECOMOG was also authorized by the UN Security Council to intervene there, which took place following the withdrawal of the private military company Executive Outcomes. ECOMOG also intervened in Guinea-Bissau after armed conflict between the president and a rebel military chief, and in Guinea-Conakry to halt

---

Leoneans expressed the desire to be recolonized by the British, who were now providing much of the security and reform to their society.

[63] The human trafficking industry comes to Nigeria via the Sahara. Prostitutes are then shipped to Europe, often via Italy.

[64] Nationmaster.com (2005), "Liberia: Transport."

[65] See Reno (1997) for a full exploration of the links between the wars in West Africa, specifically Sierra Leone, and strategic minerals.

weapons and guerrilla infiltration around Sierra Leone and Liberia at the times of their peace settlements.[66]

The worst result of the spillover of the Liberian civil war into other West African states—particularly Sierra Leone and Guinea—was the creation of the RUF, an unbelievably brutal group of criminal youths and rebel Sierra Leonean soldiers who terrorized Sierra Leonean society for almost a decade while attempting to take control of its rich diamond fields. Led by Foday Sankoh, the RUF was the creation of Charles Taylor, who was responsible for so much of West Africa's instability over the course of the 1990s.[67]

The RUF was not the only scourge to strike Sierra Leone. From the establishment of its first democratic government in 1989, Sierra Leone fell into civil war that was fed not only by the RUF but also a range of other actors—some military officers staging coups, others antigovernment rebels. A major part of this civil war was over control of the diamond regions of Sierra Leone, a prize not only for domestic rebels like the RUF but also for external players such as Taylor. Ultimately, this competition became intertwined with allegations that al-Qaeda was involved in the diamond trade.

In 1995, outside commercial firms wishing to exploit Sierra Leone's mineral resources—especially diamonds—began to import their own security because the Freetown government could not provide it. The best known of these was the South African private military company Executive Outcomes (EO). By mid-1995, EO had intervened in the civil war, acting not just to protect commercial interests inside the country but also to confront and destroy the rebel alliance confronting the Freetown government (including the RUF and rebel military elements). For the first time in years, Sierra Leone had a degree of stability and security that even allowed for the first democratic elections to take place in 1996.

With EO's withdrawal following these elections, the country descended into chaos once again despite the presence of UNAMSIL. In 1999 and 2000, several hundred UNAMSIL peacekeepers were taken hostage by a splinter group from the RUF. In response, the UK government dispatched troops to free the UN hostages. This accomplished, Britain reestablished a form of neocolonial tutelage over Sierra Leone's security sector by means of the International Military Assistance Training Team (IMATT), the purpose of which was to give the new Sierra Leone government a professional military dedicated to public security. As of the time of writing in 2005, this approach appeared to be succeeding in stabilizing the country.[68]

---

[66] A quick overview of ECOMOG may be found at "Profile: ECOMOG" (2004). For a full study of ECOMOG, see Magyar (1998); and Adebajo (2002).

[67] See Rabasa et al. (2006b).

[68] This was confirmed through O'Brien's research and interviews in Sierra Leone in May 2005, where the author discussed the security situation, the allegations of al-Qaeda involvement in Sierra Leone, and other related matters with members of the British and American missions to Sierra Leone, IMATT leaders, officials with the Special Court for Sierra Leone and Sierra Leonean government officials.

The UK was not the only Western power to intervene in West Africa's conflicts, however. In August 2003, the U.S. Marines were sent to the coast of Liberia, with some actually landing in the capital, Monrovia, to assist Economic Community Of West African States (ECOWAS) forces already deployed there. Similarly, France has intervened a number of times over the past decades to stabilize Cote d'Ivoire, such as the intervention there in the aftermath of the 2002 coup. Today, threats to the region's stability, such as the attempted coup in Equatorial Guinea in the spring of 2004, instability in Cote d'Ivoire, and continued uncertainly about Charles Taylor's influence and intentions, have the potential to prompt further interventions.

The various attributes of ungovernability discussed above are summarized in Table 10.1. Indicators are graded according to the following scale: high = 3; medium = 2; and low = 1. As might be expected, the situation is dire in almost every country: Lack of border controls ranks a uniform 3 across the board. Nigeria is in a somewhat better position than most of the other regional states, scoring 2 on absence of state institutions and lack of a monopoly of force.

Conduciveness to Terrorist Presence

Adequacy of Infrastructure

Nigeria may be one of the most advanced countries in West Africa, but its infrastructure remains underdeveloped, especially in such key areas as electricity and transportation and communications networks. Although mobile telephone use is on the rise, with one mobile phone for every 42 people, the infrastructure needed to support these units is very thin—there is a lack of breadth and depth in the market at the same time as the telecommunications networks are suffering from poor maintenance. The same can be said of Liberia, where phone lines and Internet connections are scarce. In contrast, as noted in our discussion earlier in the report, Sierra Leone has a larger network—24,000 main telephone lines in use, compared to 6,700 main lines in Liberia—and more than 67,000 mobile telephones, but the main lines are notoriously unreliable (which is why mobile phone use is on the rise).

Another strong consideration is whether the region's financial infrastructure is sufficiently developed or robust enough to support terrorist interests. Nigeria has a substantial banking system, but more than 40 percent of transactions occur in the parallel economy; newspapers carry a daily exchange rate for currency on the legitimate market, as well as on this parallel market. Most people subsist on unreported income. This gray economy could be very attractive to terrorists looking to keep their transactions hidden from public scrutiny. In Liberia, however, the total lack of a

Table 10.1
Indicators of Ungovernability, West Africa

Variable	Benin	Ghana	Guinea	Togo	Burkina Faso	Nigeria	Liberia	Sierra Leone	Cote d'Ivoire	Guinea-Bissau
Lack of state penetration										
Absence of state institutions	2	2	2	2	3	2	3	3	2	3
Lack of physical infrastructure	3	3	3	3	3	2	3	3	3	3
Social/cultural resistance	2	2	2	2	3	2	3	2	3	3
Lack of monopoly of force										
Illegal armed groups	1	1	1	1	2	3	3	3	2	2
Criminal networks	2	2	2	2	3	3	3	3	3	3
Population with access to arms	3	3	3	3	3	3	3	3	3	3
Lack of border controls	3	3	3	3	3	3	3	3	3	3
External interference	2	2	3	2	3	2	3	3	3	3

well-developed financial system limits the country's utility in this regard.[69] In Sierra Leone, although the parallel market is large enough to have been historically able to mask a large trade in diamonds (which the Kimberley Process, an international certification scheme, is now moving to bring under control and oversight), little capital moves through the country, similarly limiting its attractiveness as an illicit financial hub.

Sources of Income

The region's wealth in extractive resources, such as minerals, precious stones, oil, and lumber (much of which is diverted into the informal economy), provides an ample source of income for warlords and other nonstate actors across the region. In Nigeria, an estimated 40 to 45 percent of national income is derived from the parallel market and goes unrecorded, opening the door for illicit industries and exchanges. In Liberia, however, the situation has long been far more dire. Lack of UN control over resource-rich regions has lead to increased levels of organized and unaccounted-for logging and diamond mining by excombatants and their former commanders, as well as by the businessmen who organize them.[70] In an attempt to bring this activity to a halt, the Liberian Forestry Initiative has been introduced to end the exploitation of the logging industry.[71] The situation in Sierra Leone, on the other hand, is between that of Nigeria and Liberia. Around 60 percent of the country relies on subsistence agriculture, and the new government is having growing success tapping into the diamond industry, which constitutes an increasingly large percentage of the national GDP.

Favorable Demographics

It may appear that the significant Muslim populations of West African countries could provide a ready pool of recruits for radical Islamic groups. However, there are few indications that even the existing ethno-religious conflicts that exist—primarily in Nigeria—have been of utility for recruitment into the global jihadist movement. The countries of West Africa include some of the poorest countries in the world; however, very few known al-Qaeda or affiliated jihadists (captured or killed since al-Qaeda came to the general attention of the international community with the bombings of the U.S. embassies in Kenya and Tanzania in 1998) have come from West Africa, compared to a notable number of militants from North and East Africa. This is an indication that West African militants may be interested not in the global Islamic struggle but in their local causes.

Therefore, if one were to use the potential for co-option of local populations by international jihadists as a metric to assess involvement in the global jihad, West Africa

---

[69] Nationmaster.com (2005), "Liberia: Crime."

[70] Global Witness Limited (2005).

[71] Global Witness Limited (2005).

would not have a high score. This is not to say that there has not been a known or sus-pected al-Qaeda (or related) presence in some of these countries or examples of radical Islamic violence against other population groups. (Table 10.2 shows the Muslim popu-lation of West Africa in each country). A greater danger, however, is that many of these countries have a cohort of young people who have grown up knowing only violence or have fought in the region's numerous civil wars over the past 15 to 20 years, and may be willing to take part in another violent struggle, for largely personal or criminal reasons, regardless of the cause.

In Nigeria, the prolonged lack of governance in many parts of the country has precipitated a form of gang rule as the social norm. This level of failed governance is nothing, however, compared with Liberia's, where the long civil war has left little gov-ernment control and little rule of law, and where excombatants, criminal gangs, terror-

Table 10.2
Muslim Populations of West Africa,
by Percentage of Overall Population

Country	Population (000s)		
	Muslim	Total	% Muslim
Senegal	10,500	11,126	94
Mali	11,000	12,291	90
Niger	10,500	11,665	90
The Gambia	1,430	1,593	90
Guinea (Conakry)	8,000	9,467	85
Sierra Leone	3,600	6,017	60
Burkina Faso	7,600	13,925	55
Nigeria	64,000	128,771	50
Cote d'Ivoire	6,700	17,298	39
Guinea-Bissau	538	1,416	38
Benin	1,492	7,460	20
Cameroon	3,300	16,380	20
Liberia	696	3,482	20
Ghana	3,400	21,029	16
Togo	778	5,681	13.7
TOTAL	133,534	267,601	50

SOURCES: U.S. Department of State (2004d); "Islam by Country," Wikipedia.

NOTE: Does not include the 3.1 million Muslims of Mauritania (99.9 percent of its population) or the 5.3 million Muslims of Chad (54 percent of its population), the two other countries that, with the above countries, make up the Sahel–West Africa zone of interest to this study.

ists, smugglers, pirates, and other criminals come together or regroup in preparation for further illegal activity. These conditions can produce an opening for international terrorist groups. Indeed, Al-Qaeda operative Mustafa Mohamed Fadhil, a Middle Eastern businessman who visited Taylor frequently, has been on the FBI's list of most wanted terrorists and was indicted in the Southern District of New York in connection with the 1998 U.S. embassy bombings.[72]

Liberia also demonstrates another key problem of many West African states—unemployed soldiers, many of whom will often turn to petty crime and corruption to make a living. To alleviate this problem, newly emerging governments have—with Western assistance—introduced vocational training schemes for former combatants. In Liberia, more than 1,000 excombatants graduated from the Monrovia Vocational Training Centre in May 2005. Such people are vulnerable to financial inducements by terrorist organizations, especially in situations where corruption and apathy in law enforcement lead to officials turning a blind eye to terrorist co-option. In principle, similar conditions could exist in Sierra Leone, but the extensive intervention there since 2000 means that the remnants of criminal soldiery from the civil war have by and large been culled. Overall societal violence, as a trend, is decreasing, although much criminal violence remains, particularly outside Freetown.

Thus, the degree to which terrorists may take root in West African societies and succeed in recruiting members for the wider global jihad varies greatly. It must be said that West Africans are generally far more concerned about rebuilding their own countries and sustaining a living than about joining the wider jihad. While this finding may not hold true for all West Africans, a balanced assessment would find it to be true for the vast majority of citizens, with the major danger being the possibility of exploiting the population through corruption and bribery by terrorists.

Invisibility

Although there appears to be a relatively small possibility that al-Qaeda or affiliated groups could generate significant support in the countries of West Africa, this does not necessarily mean that terrorist operatives could not find the means to support their operations in these countries—quite the opposite. With loose borders between states, loose controls within states, and an extensive gray economy that supports all kinds of illegal activity, terrorists could find West Africa a very conducive environment as a sanctuary and base for operations. Recruits could potentially be generated relatively easily across West Africa through economic inducements. Those communal conflicts that do exist, primarily in Nigeria, could be exploited to stir up further conflict.

In all the above senses, West Africa provides a high degree of invisibility for terrorists without governments being aware of their presence, let alone being able to do

---

[72] *United States of America v. Usama bin Laden et al.* (2001).

much against them.[73] Even in countries whose urban centers are relatively small—Monrovia, Liberia's capital, for example, has only 962,000 inhabitants—blending in is not impossible where the existence of criminal networks is widely accepted.[74] Similarly, at least for the time being, the general disorder within Sierra Leone could be conducive to terrorist invisibility.

Summary of West Africa's Conduciveness to Terrorism

Table 10.3 summarizes the conduciveness of West Africa to a terrorist presence. Indicators are graded according to the following scale: 3 = high; 2 = medium; and 1 = low. As noted in the narrative, the conduciveness of the countries of the region is generally low with regard to adequacy of infrastructure and operational access, uneven across different countries with regard to sources of income, and high on favorable demographics and invisibility.

U.S. Policies and Programs

This section is divided into three parts: (1) the U.S. global defense posture for West Africa; (2) partner country capability deficiencies and security cooperation tools available to address threats unique to West Africa; and (3) democracy and reform programs.

U.S. Global Defense Posture Implications for West Africa

At present, the areas of highest concern to the United States and its allies in Africa are North Africa (particularly Algeria and Morocco), the Sahara-Sahel region (southern Algeria, Chad, Niger, Mali, and Mauritania), and the Horn of Africa (Ethiopia, Eritrea, and Somalia). Within the wider security assistance field, the United States supports a number of key initiatives in partnership with African countries. These include the long-running African Crisis Response Initiative (ACRI), launched in 1997 to bolster African peacekeeping capabilities. From 1997 to 2002, ACRI funded cooperative training initiatives with Senegal, Uganda, Malawi, Mali, Ghana, Côte d'Ivoire, and

---

[73] This could be the case in several senses: First, in Nigeria, the 12 Muslim states in the north could provide an ideal harbor for terrorist activities—pointing to the potential for Islamic terrorists to find this "invisibility" within Muslim communities in West Africa. Second, the extremely low levels of governance and sovereignty across West Africa point to the opportunity for terrorists simply to hide out in these societies. What militates against the second is that, outside the major (capital) cities, most societies remain so tribally centered that strangers or "outsiders" would presumably by easily identified and reported by local leaders; inside major cities, their presence would be noticed relatively quickly by the citizenry and security forces—especially in those countries with slowly growing governance. Both these scenarios, therefore, further militate against this likelihood.

[74] Nationmaster.com (2005), "Liberia: Geography."

Table 10.3
Indicators of Conduciveness to Terrorist Presence, West Africa

Variable	Benin	Ghana	Guinea	Togo	Burkina Faso	Nigeria	Liberia	Sierra Leone	Cote d'Ivoire	Guinea-Bissau
Adequacy of infrastructure										
Financial infrastructure	2	2	1	2	1	1	2	2	2	1
Transportation and communications	2	2	1	2	1	2	1	1	1	1
Operational access	1	1	2	1	2	3	2	2	2	2
Sources of income	1	1	1	1	1	3	3	3	2	1
Favorable demographics	2	2	3	2	3	3	3	3	3	3
Invisibility	3	3	3	3	3	2	3	2	3	3

Benin. ACRI has provided training and nonlethal equipment to almost 6,000 peace-keepers from seven African militaries. The Africa Contingency Operations Training Assistance (ACOTA) was set up in 2002 to take the place of ACRI. ACOTA includes training in light infantry tactics and small unit tactics to enhance the ability of African troops to conduct peacekeeping operations in hostile environments.[75] Both programs come under the IMET programs in Africa.[76] The United States also supports other IMET programs across the continent, especially in East and southern Africa.

Other initiatives, especially in West Africa, include the African Coastal Security Program, which provides equipment and training for coastal surveillance; the Gulf of Guinea Guard Program; and the Africa Fuel Hubs Initiative, launched in 1999 by EUCOM's Joint Petroleum Office and the Defense Energy Support Center to determine where and what parts of the African coastal regions could support logistics and fuel storage. To combat terrorism, U.S. military forces have a semipermanent assistance mission in the Sahara-Sahel region (see below).

The United States is currently deeply concerned about the potential for ungoverned territories, such as those of West Africa, to become terrorist sanctuaries. The major U.S. counterterrorism initiatives in West Africa recently have centered on two contiguous programs:

1. The Pan-Sahel Initiative (PSI) was a U.S. State Department–funded program designed to enhance border capabilities throughout the region against arms smuggling, drug trafficking, and the movement of transnational terrorists. It provided U.S. Army Special Forces to assist the militaries of Mali, Mauritania, Niger, and Chad. The PSI helped train and equip at least one rapid-reaction company, about 150 soldiers, in each of the four Saharan states. The program was primarily designed to "get ahead of the problem," anticipating future possible terrorist developments in the region, rather than reacting to events and developments once they had occurred. Despite its successes, PSI was constrained from its inception by limited funding and a limited focus.[77]

2. The Trans-Sahara Counter-Terrorism Initiative (TSCTI) builds on the PSI. Completed in early 2004, it now includes Algeria, Morocco, Tunisia, Senegal,

---

[75] "U.S. Support to African Capacity for Peace Operations: The ACOTA Program" (2005).

[76] See U.S. Department of State (2000). The United States contributes to UN peacekeeping operations in Africa and elsewhere through a program entitled Contributions to International Peacekeeping Activities (CIPA). Funds for CIPA are appropriated in the legislation that funds the Departments of Commerce, Justice, and State, rather than in the Foreign Operations appropriation, which governs foreign assistance. CIPA for Africa increased significantly in FY2002 because of U.S. support for UN peacekeeping in Sierra Leone and the Democratic Republic of the Congo. Stabilization in Sierra Leone has brought a subsequent reduction in the program. These programs usually run well under $1 million per country, although Senegal is slated for $1 million under the FY2004 request and South Africa would receive $1.6 million. Overall, IMET would rise from $11.1 million to $12.5 million under the FY2004 request.

[77] Koch (2004), pp. 30–31; "Pan Sahel Initiative (PSI)" (undated).

Ghana, and Nigeria (with Libya possibly to follow later if relations improve). TSCTI is funded at a higher level than PSI was ($30–60 million in FY05, then up to $100 million each succeeding year until 2011), and will increase assistance with detection of, and response to, the migration of asymmetric threats throughout the region. The initiative will also help those nations maintain security by building their capacity to prevent conflict at its inception, all the while helping these states become more self-reliant.[78]

In June 2005, the TSCTI was launched through Exercise FLINTLOCK, a planned Joint Combined Exchange Training–type biennial exercise in which 1,000 U.S. military personnel, alongside more than 3,000 personnel from Algeria, Senegal, Mauritania, Mali, Niger, and Chad, cooperated in an antiterrorist operation training activity designed to halt the flow of illicit weapons, goods, and human trafficking in the region and to prevent terrorists from establishing sanctuaries in remote areas.[79] U.S. special operations forces taught military tactics critical for enhancing regional security and stability, including airborne operations, small-unit tactics, security operations, land navigation, marksmanship, medical skills, human rights training, and land warfare. Finally, this exercise helped participating nations to plan and execute command, control, and communications systems in support of future combined humanitarian, peacekeeping, and disaster relief operations.[80]

Deficiencies in Partner-Country Capabilities

One of the major challenges confronting U.S. and Western partners in seeking a larger West African role in counterterrorism is the lack of capabilities of West African military and security services. West African militaries for the most part lack adequate funding, training, and logistics.[81] There are also political obstacles to cooperation.[82] For example, Benin's failure thus far to sign an Article 98 agreement with the United

---

[78] Knights (2005b), p. 26; Pope (2005). The United States has also recently launched a parallel programme in East Africa—the East Africa Counterterrorism Initiative (EACTI), which has committed $100 million for assistance and training for counterterrorism initiatives in six countries in the Horn of Africa: Djibouti, Eritrea, Ethiopia, Tanzania, Uganda, and Kenya. See Greenberg and Cain (2005).

[79] FLINTLOCK exercises and cadres, like JCETs, must first satisfy U.S. special operations forces training requirements and use DoD funds to conduct the training event. The U.S. European Command (USEUCOM) and Special Operations Command Europe (SOCEUR) determine FLINTLOCK locations. See "Flintlock" (2005).

[80] Garamone (2005); "Trans-Sahara Counterterrorism Initiative (TSCTI)" (2005). For a more realistic narrative on just how successful these efforts are, though, see Tyson (2005).

[81] Denning (2004).

[82] Herbst (2004).

States has prevented the reinstatement of an IMET program.[83] All forms of U.S. military assistance to Equatorial Guinea, except for participation on a case-by-case basis in the Africa Center for Strategic Studies (ACSS) activities and at Gulf of Guinea conferences, are suspended because of the Equatorial Guinea government's poor human rights record and lack of progress on democratic reform.

The ACSS supports democratic governance by offering senior African civilian and military leaders a practical program in civil-military relations, national security strategy, and defense economics. ACSS participation also helps build and maintain long-term, continuing interaction with and amongst participants, and supports additional research, seminars, conferences, and other exchange activities.[84]

Few, if any, African nations have the technical and logistics capacities to protect and monitor their territories and borders; the militaries of many of the Sahel nations—for example Niger, Chad, and Mali—have no aircraft available for patrolling the Sahara, making it almost impossible to control a space the size of Europe. The institutions that African countries do have to conduct counterterrorist initiatives are severely underresourced. As Jonathan Stevenson points out,

> Until now, such institutions have largely been geared towards suppressing domestic terrorist threats, tribal unrest or separatist insurgencies rather than transnational Islamic threats . . . while many sub-Saharan governments are apt to be enthusiastic counterterrorism partners, they face the daunting task of re-orienting their counterterrorism apparatuses towards a new kind of threat . . . [their] security institutions are simply too undermanned, ill-equipped and inexperienced to combat terrorist activity effectively.[85]

Stevenson further warns that, in many of these states, the "inhabitants may be susceptible to the material rewards that well-funded non-state actors could provide them"—a warning that applies equally to the government employees of these countries as much as to average citizens.

The United States and other Western countries cannot assume that Sub-Saharan African countries are equipped and capable of conducting the robust antiterrorist actions that the West may wish of them. These include not just military and law enforcement actions but also actions to combat the organized criminal elements of terrorism, along with defeating terrorists' recruiting and logistics and support activities. If the United States and the West want to see these countries become bulwarks against

---

[83] An Article 98 agreement is a bilateral agreement by which a signatory pledges not to seek prosecution of U.S. citizens in the International Criminal Court. U.S. law prohibits military assistance to countries that have not signed an Article 98 agreement.

[84] Africa Center for Strategic Studies (undated).

[85] Stevenson (2003–2004), pp. 157–158.

Islamic extremist violence and terrorism, a much stronger level of assistance and direct involvement would be required.

A final consideration is that U.S. programs have to take into consideration the health dynamics of West African militaries because HIV-AIDS runs rampant in parts of West Africa.[86] An example of U.S. efforts to mitigate the effects of the HIV/AIDS epidemic is the HIV/AIDS Education and Awareness Program, carried out under the auspices of the U.S. Defense Attaché Office (DAO), Guinea. The program is funded by the Department of Defense and managed by the DAO's implementing partner, Population Services International. During its first 14 months, this program has resulted in the development of the Guinean Armed Forces' first HIV/AIDS policy. It has also trained peer educators, promoted condom distribution and use, and initiated construction of the military's first voluntary counseling and testing facility.[87]

Democracy Programs

USAID has a robust set of programs for West Africa. The mandate of the West Africa Regional Program (WARP) is to tackle long-term development issues that are inherently regional in nature. Thus WARP works closely with the other USAID missions in the region, U.S. embassies in countries where USAID does not have a mission, and the region's leading intergovernmental organizations, such as ECOWAS, the Permanent Interstate Committee for Drought Control in the Sahel (CILSS), and the West African Economic and Monetary Union (WAEMU), to implement a program that benefits Benin, Burkina Faso, Cameroon, Cape Verde, Chad, Cote d'Ivoire, The Gambia, Ghana, Guinea, Guinea-Bissau, Liberia, Mali, Mauritania, Niger, Nigeria, Senegal, Sierra Leone, Togo, and (most recently) Sao Tome and Principe.

The four program areas WARP is concerned with are (1) fostering regional economic integration and trade; (2) increasing the adoption of effective policies and approaches to reproductive health, child survival, and HIV/AIDS; (3) enhancing the capacity to achieve regional food security, improved management of natural resources, and agricultural growth; and (4) improving the conditions for peace and stability in West Africa. Continued funding from the Presidential Initiative for Trade for African Development and Enterprise will be used to expand the range of goods traded within the region and exported to the United States under the African Growth and Opportunity Act and to propagate the principles of the World Trade Organization. Further funding from the Presidential Initiative to End Hunger in Africa will be used to implement the new regional market information system that will supply timely agricultural pricing information to farmers and traders. USAID will promote the development of biotechnology policies and regulations as a means of raising agricultural productivity and rural incomes. The three key regional intergovernmental institutions—ECOWAS,

---

[86] "Deadly Connections (2004); Garrett (2005).

[87] U.S. Department of State (2005b).

CILSS, and WAEMU—have all demonstrated their commitment to working collaboratively on biotechnology. USAID addressed the anticipated reappearance of locusts in 2005 with targeted training and the provision of essential equipment to the affected countries.[88]

Policy Implications and Conclusions

The United States has a number of strong interests in West Africa resulting in an increasing level of engagement in the region. Traditionally, West Africa, and the continent at large, has elicited little direct interest from the United States except as it generates humanitarian crises and presents problems to be solved. Now, however, Africa looks likely to take a greater and more central place in U.S. foreign policy and defense priorities. This strategic shift is due to four major factors.

First, as the United States seeks to reduce its dependence of Middle East oil, West Africa's strategic oil reserves are increasingly important to future U.S. and Western requirements. From northern Angola through Gabon and Cameroon to Sao Tome and Nigeria, West Africa provides one of the most important sources of energy outside the Middle East.

Second, concerns have continued to grow about the presence of Islamist terrorists in Africa, manifested in the increased number of terrorist attacks staged from Mombassa to Casablanca. However, a positive aspect has been the development of cooperative counterterrorist activities with the predominantly Muslim countries in the region. Guinea, for instance, agreed to allow the destruction of its entire stockpiles of man-portable air defense weapons (MANPADS) and antipersonnel mines under a U.S. Department of State–funded Small Arms/Light Weapons Destruction Program in October–November 2003.[89]

Third, the "traditional" challenges presented by Africa—those of a continent requiring constant support and upkeep—have been seriously enhanced by the AIDS epidemic and the consequent cascading impact it has had on governance. Although AIDS epidemic in not full-blown in West Africa outside of Nigeria, it has the potential not only to undermine the very fabric of West African states, but also to contribute to mass displacements of populations and an overall increase in instability and insecurity across the continent.

Fourth, both in response to these challenges and because of the geographic proximity of some parts of Africa to the Middle East, the United States has begun to develop a greater focus on Africa. U.S. military leaders, such as General James Jones, U.S. Marine Corps, who was the Supreme Allied Commander Europe (SACEUR) until 2006, stated in May 2004, ". . . the [U.S. Navy] carrier groups of the future and

---

[88] See USAID (2005a).

[89] See Center for Arms Control and Non-Proliferation (2004); and U.S. Department of State (2005b).

the expeditionary strike groups may not spend six months in the Mediterranean but I bet they will spend half the time going down the west coast of Africa."[90]

For more than a year, EUCOM has spoken openly about developing a permanent presence in West Africa similar to the CJTF-HOA, which has been in place since November 2002.[91] Such clear expressions of both concern and intention are indicative of the growing U.S. interest and presence in West Africa. In February 2007, the president directed the establishment of a U.S. Africa Command (AFRICOM) with headquarters on the African continent. The establishment of the new command represents the U.S. government's recognition of Africa's strategic importance and commitment to building partnership capacity in African states.

---

[90] Knights (2005b), pp. 24–25.

[91] The CJTF-HOA's area of operations covers the total airspace and land areas of Djibouti, Ethiopia, Eritrea, Kenya, Somalia, Sudan, and Yemen. Schofield (2004), p. 46. See also Mills (2004).

CHAPTER ELEVEN

Case Study: The North Caucasus

Jennifer Moroney and Theodore Karasik

Introduction

The National Intelligence Council's (NIC's) 2004 report, *Mapping the Global Future,* discussed future hot spots of instability extensively. The North Caucasus was highlighted as a critical region that will remain a source of endemic tension and conflict.[1] In the universe of ungoverned territories around the world, the North Caucasus is certainly worth studying because this highly heterogeneous region lies at a critical juncture between European and Asian civilizations, has a high level of corruption, and serves as a transit route for the smuggling of illegal commodities and weapons. According to the NIC report, "lagging economies, ethnic affiliations, intense religious convictions, and youth bulges will align to create a 'perfect storm' for internal conflict." The governing capacity of states will determine whether and to what extent conflicts will occur. Those states, such as Russia, that are unable to both satisfy the expectations of their people and resolve internal disputes are likely to encounter the most severe and frequent outbreaks of violence.[2]

This chapter is organized as follows. First, we provide a brief overview of the North Caucasus, specifically focused on geopolitical and ethnic issues. Second, we present more extensive discussion and evaluation on the North Caucasus relative to the study's variables and indicators of ungovernability, which include (1) state penetration of society; (2) lack of state monopoly of force; (3) lack of control over borders; and (4) external interference. Next, we discuss the North Caucasus relative to the study's indicators of conduciveness to terrorism. Finally, we present a detailed discussion of the overall implications of the North Caucasus security situation for U.S. interests.

---

[1] National Intelligence Council (2004), p. 54.

[2] National Intelligence Council (2004), p. 97.

Overview of the North Caucasus Region

The entire Caucasus region—primarily the North Caucasus, situated between the Caspian and Black Seas—is a hub of intense economic and political problems. These problems concern Russia and neighboring states but have largely escaped the attention of the rest of the world, with the exception of violence and terrorism emanating from the war in Chechnya.[3]

Two overarching themes are repeated in the academic and policy literature on the North Caucasus republics: (1) the lack of attention, including coherent policy for the North Caucasus from Moscow, and (2) the absence of a solution to the question of the status of Chechnya. The greatest security challenge in the North Caucasus, at least as far as Russia is concerned, is the Chechen Republic, which does not recognize Russian national laws and which, by its very existence, threatens the sovereignty and integrity of the Russian Federation. Radical Chechen separatists seek to establish an independent Islamic state, stretching from Georgia to the Caspian Sea, known as the "Great Imamate."[4] Were such a state to be created, its authorities would control a key portion of the greater Caspian region, including oil and gas transit lines.[5]

An aggressive Saudi version of Wahhabism began spreading in the North Caucasus in the late 1980s.[6] It was particularly strong in Dagestan but also gained a foothold in the north of Azerbaijan. Wahhabism was especially attractive to the younger portion of society, whose new converts were eager to serve Islam.[7] There are also newer Islamic trends in Chechnya that are a result of foreign influences that include Wahhabism (referred to as "Vakhabsim" in Chechnya). "Vakhabsim" first appeared in Chechnya around 1991 and has been a conduit for enlisting foreign fighters, including veterans of the Afghanistan war.[8] After 1999, Wahhabism became the main ideological tool for recruiting new fighters in Chechnya. Many of the newer recruits have tended to be young—by some reports, as many as one-third are teenagers between ages 15 and 17. These younger fighters grew up in an environment of pervasive warfare and criminal activity. This has resulted in a disconnect between the generations of fighters, with older combatants tending to believe they are fighting a war for Chechen independence and adhering to traditional Islam (here, Sufi Islam), and younger fighters perceiv-

---

[3]   Kulikov (1999).

[4]   Kulikov (1999).

[5]   It should be noted that the current Chechen administrative head Alu Alkhanov has extensive financial interests including a chain of gas stations in Chechnya and Dagestan. See Fuller (2005).

[6]   We are using the term "Wahhabism" here because Russian authorities frequently use this term even to describe dissidents who may not be "Wahhabist" at all.

[7]   "Dagestan Incursions" (1999).

[8]   Akhmadov et al. (2001).

ing a completely different fight—between the Muslim and Christian worlds.[9] Wahhabis view Chechnya as the logical origin of a Muslim state. Dagestan, Karachayevo-Cherkessiya, Kabardino-Balkariya, North Ossetia, and Ingushetiya would all be included in the unified Muslim state advocated by the Chechen separatists.

For Russian leadership, terrorism has come to be associated with Chechnya and more broadly, with the North Caucasus. In 2000, President Putin expressed concern about a movement to create a caliphate that would include the greater Middle East, Central Asia, the North Caucasus, and the lower and middle Volga regions. He also spoke about a larger arc of instability stretching from Northern Africa across the Balkans, to the Middle East, the Caucasus, Central Asia, and on to Southeast Asia. Putin wanted the West to accept this theory and, thus, his methods in dealing with Chechnya. But the Russian military's indiscriminate tactics diminished its credibility in the international community.

After the USS *Cole* attack and 9/11, there was a short-lived rapprochement between the United States and Russia on Chechnya, characterized by a toning down of the Bush administration's criticisms of Russia's tactics in the North Caucasus. Europeans remained staunchly critical of tactics used in Chechnya. European proposals for a cease-fire, withdrawal of troops from the region, and peace negotiations were not taken seriously by Moscow.

On the whole, Putin has been losing points with the international community over Chechnya. Even with the Moscow theater and Beslan school tragedies, at which the international community expressed outrage, the response tactics used by the Russian military were seen as clumsy, causing the death of many innocent civilians. The conundrum currently facing Moscow prohibits an effective solution to the problem; thus, the entire North Caucasus region is likely to remain an ungoverned—or perhaps in this case an undergoverned—territory for the foreseeable future. We discuss these points in detail in the following section, which focuses specifically on the indicators of ungovernability in this problematic region within the Russian Federation.

The North Caucasus as an Ungoverned Territory

The factors causing the conflicts are historical, ethno-national, economic, religious, and cultural. Some are new; others, including warrior societies and mythmaking based on violence, have become deeply rooted over time.[10] The causes underlying this potentially explosive situation are multifaceted and hinder the central authorities from gaining control over the region. Certainly, the Russian government has made mistakes that negatively affected social and economic development in the region. The defeat of the

---

[9] Iskandryian (2002).

[10] Grant (2005).

rebels on the battlefield clearly did not make Russia safe from terrorism—quite the contrary. According to analyst Dmitri Trenin, because terrorism is a tactic employed by the weaker of the two sides, Russia's military dominance is being offset by asymmetrical strikes.[11]

Moscow has not been able to develop a consistent policy toward the region, let alone serve as a broker in the various conflicts. According to Russia's former Minister of the Interior, General Anatoliy Kulikov, Moscow has oscillated between using military force and tolerating extreme nationalism. However, Moscow's current destructive processes are due not necessarily to policy mistakes but rather to Russia's own domestic economic and political weakness. Russia's weakened condition is the reason that certain forces in the republics of the North Caucasus seek wealthier, influential patrons outside Russia's borders to help in what Kulikov describes as a struggle for national self-determination.[12]

A low level of citizen compliance with existing laws is reflected in the electoral process, taxation issues, law enforcement and judicial issues, and corruption and crime in the North Caucasus region. First, the legitimacy of elections in the region has been called into question by international and regional observers. State Duma members "representing" the various regions are usually selected by Moscow.[13] Fair elections are rare, and there has been no international election watchdog since the OSCE closed its monitoring office in the North Caucasus in 2003.[14]

In 1999, the Communist Party consistently had the largest share of the votes in the North Caucasus. However, during the March 2004 presidential election, Putin was overwhelmingly supported, especially in Dagestan (94.6 percent), Ingushetiya (98 percent), and Karbardino-Balkariya (98 percent).[15]

Second, many North Caucasus communities do not pay taxes to Moscow. Local parliaments enact laws granting special taxation status to mountain peoples to protect local community rights. Table 11.1 presents figures on social expenditures in the North Caucasus region in 1998.

Third, law enforcement is dysfunctional and the judicial system is not impartial. In the North Caucasus, torture of suspects is often condoned. Ill-treatment of prisoners and detainees and police misconduct is widespread particularly in Chechnya.[16] Local governments discriminate against religious, ethnic, and national minorities. Extra-

---

[11] Danilov et al. (2005), p. 106.

[12] Kulikov (1999).

[13] See, for instance, Zoller (1999).

[14] "Izvestiya Interview with OSCE Chairman-in-Office Dr. Dimitrij Rupel" (2005).

[15] "The Russian Federation" (2005).

[16] Amnesty International (2002).

Table 11.1
Distribution of Direct Federal Expenditures Among the Regions in 1998

Republic	Direct Expenditures	Government Expenditures	Expenditures on Education	Expenditures on Public Health	Social Expenditures
Dagestan	291	41	53	4.0	13.1
Ingushetiya	613	29	18	2.8	362.5
Kabardino-Balkariya	528	36	60	6.8	113.3
Karachayevo-Cherkessiya	516	78	74	6.8	64.9
North Ossetiya	731	75	105	5.8	328.3
Chechnya[a]	—	—	—	—	—

SOURCE: Lavrov and Makushkin (2001), Table A.4.

NOTE: Expenditures are in rubles per capita.

[a] Expenditures for Chechnya are included with Ingushetiya.

judicial activity includes arbitrary executions and torture. The North Caucasus does not have well-functioning central authorities that try to invoke the rule of law. Rather, the majority of the police forces are on the payroll of criminal groups. Without a strong judicial system and a police force to enforce the rule of law, citizen compliance is a moot point.[17] The events of October 2005 in Kabardino-Balkariya point to other dimensions of the relation of political grievances and Islam: The Nalchik police chief's precipitous attack on young men in the city whom he believed were what he called "Wahhabis" seems to have aligned clan communities to protect new independent mosques, particularly north and east of the city. The episode highlights the problem of inadequate central control over incompetent local officials.[18]

In the Shali district of Chechnya, Russian Special Forces facilities are present, and several thousand troops deployed to the region. However, providing security is not their focus; as elsewhere in the former Soviet Union, citizens often calculate that the best way to protect themselves is to bribe the police. The local police territorial forces generally stick to the foothills of the mountains. In Shali, there are only 20 policemen for every 20,000 people—and they have no means of transportation. In other sections of Shali district, the police-to-citizens ratio is similar, and in some sections, the police exist on paper only.[19]

---

[17] The *Kadyrovtsy* criminal group is particularly worth watching and could become a police force with the ability to impose some order. The Kadyrovtsy are officially part of a special regiment named after Ramzan Kadyrov's late father, Akhmad Kadyrov, and total about 1,250 men. Unofficially, they number 2,500; 86 people from among the Kadyrovtsy are on Russia's federal wanted list. See Human Rights Violations in Chechnya (2005).

[18] Dr. William Reno, review of manuscript.

[19] Moroney discussion with Professor Mikhail Alexseev, University of San Diego, March 14, 2005.

Fourth, violent crime is rife and kidnapping is on the rise.[20] There is a lack of accountability by Russian officials. Local officials and criminals often bribe law enforcement forces, and crimes committed by security forces in North Caucasus are not investigated. According to the official crime statistics, however, crime rates in the North Caucasus are lower than average crime rates across Russia, though other expert data on crime tells a different story. Crime rates are by and large highest in Karachayevo-Cherkessiya, North Ossetia, and Kabardino-Balkariya.[21] Crimes in the North Caucasus related to theft, hooliganism, the economic sphere, and the illegal narcotics trade ranked highest. In 2003, the largest theft problems were in Kabardino-Balkariya and Dagestan. Links between crime and the narcotics trade were strongest in Dagestan, Kabardino-Balkariya, and North Ossetia.[22]

Surveys of law-enforcement officers and judges in Krasnodar Krai conducted by the Saratov Center in 2003[23] showed the following:

- 22 percent think that crime groups actively operate in the region
- 16 percent suggest that there are large criminal organizations dealing with all kinds of criminal activity, including commission and financing of terrorist acts
- 15 percent speak of communities of criminal leaders who decide common organization questions (i.e., distribution of influence spheres, etc.)
- 64 percent consider the territory of the krai to be controlled by "thieves in law," "positioners," or "lookers," i.e., criminalized authorities.

Overall, ethnicity, clans, and tribes determine the level of citizen compliance with the central authorities. In Dagestan, the political structure of the djamaat, or village community, has subsumed Dagestani clans and other kinship structures for centuries. This tradition is one of the reasons why Dagestan's current political system has successfully embraced more than 20 ethnic groups; indeed, the drafters of the Dagestani constitution obviously went to extraordinary lengths to ensure ethnic balance in the new government.[24] By contrast, Chechen society lacks a tradition of an authoritative, overarching political structure. It is traditionally organized around a complex, seven-level kinship structure, in which the taip, or clan, is the preeminent organization.[25] North Caucasus ethnic breakdown by region is shown in Table 11.2 and Figure 11.1.

---

[20] International Helsinki for Human Rights (2004).

[21] *Regiony Rossii* (2004), Table 8.1.

[22] *Regiony Rossii* (2004), Table 8.2.

[23] Saratov Center for the Study of Organized Crime and Corruption (2003).

[24] "Dagestan Incursions" (1999).

[25] Ware (2003), p. 167.

Table 11.2
North Caucasus Ethnic Breakdown, by Region

Region	Population (2005 estimate)	Ethnic Breakdown
Dagestan	2,100,000	28% Avars, 16% Dargins, 13% Kumyks, 11% Lezgins, 9% Russians
Ingushetiya	315,000	Mainly Ingushetians but also communities of Russians and Chechens
Kabardino-Balkariya	750,000	49% Kabardinians, 32% Russians, 9% Balkarians
Karachayevo-Cherkessiya	500,200	31% Karachai, 9% Cherkessians, 42% Russians
North Ossetia	660,000	53% Ossetian, 32% Russians and Ukrainians

SOURCE: Jane's Information Group, "Russia and the CIS" (2005).

Physical Infrastructure

The major road and rail lines in the North Caucasus end around the great Caucasus ridge. This pattern closely follows the old Caucasus lines from the 1700s. Major cities are served by standard Soviet transportation and communications infrastructure, but in smaller towns the condition of the infrastructure is far worse. Between cities and towns, roads are rugged, uneven, and narrow, and full of potholes and shaky bridges. Snow is only cleared in select places.[26] Tables 11.3 and 11.4 present statistics on paved roads and rail lines.

Table 11.3
Paved Roads in the North Caucasus

Republic	No. of Kilometers
Dagestan	7,385
Chechnya	3,057
Ingushetiya	816
Kabardino-Balkariya	2,918
Karachayevo-Cherkessiya	1,889
North Ossetiya	2,288

SOURCE: Europa World Plus (2005).

---

[26] Moroney discussion with Professor John Colarusso, Caucasus specialist, McMaster University, January 25, 2005.

Figure 11.1
Ethnolinguistic Groups in the Caucasus Region, 1995

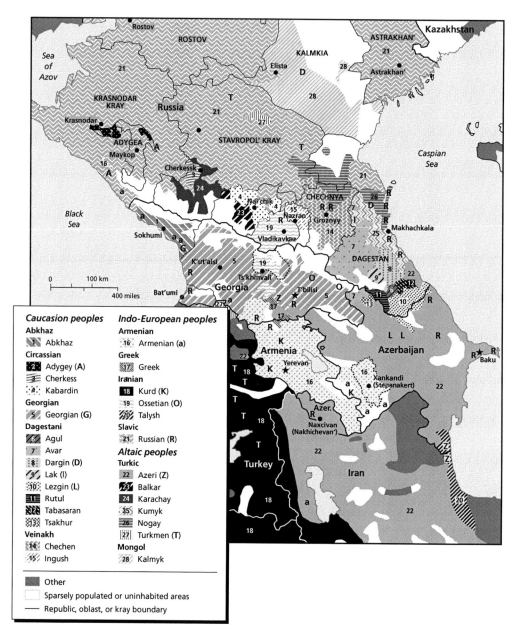

SOURCE: Central Intelligence Agency, http://www.lib.utexas.edu/maps/commonwealth/
ethnocaucasus.jpg.

RAND *MG561-11.1*

Figure 11.2
North Caucasus—Population Density

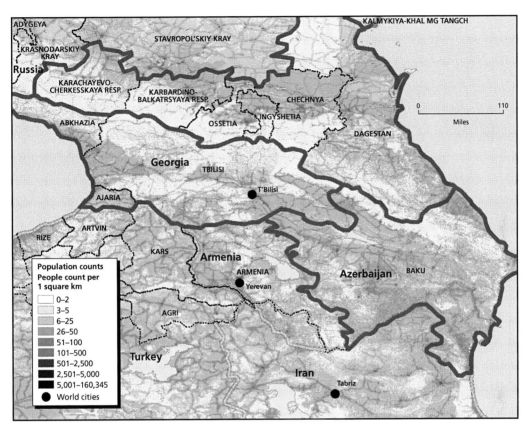

SOURCE: RAND.
RAND *MG561-11.2*

Table 11.4
Railways in the North Caucasus, 2000

Republic	No. of Kilometers
Dagestan	516
Chechnya	304
Ingushetiya	39
Kabardino-Balkariya	133
Karachayevo-Cherkessiya	51
North Ossetiya	144

Figure 11.3
North Caucasus—Infrastructure

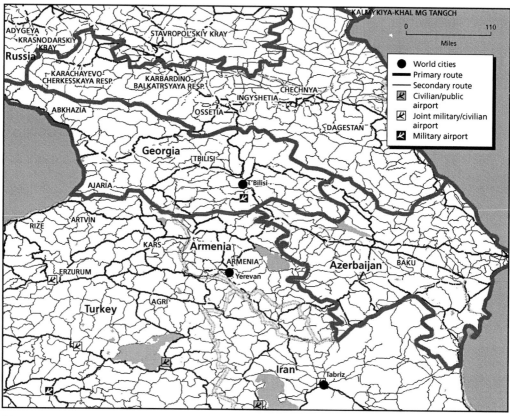

SOURCE: RAND.
RAND *MG561-11.3*

Public transportation in the region is not reliable. Buses are found only in the cities, so citizens who can afford it tend to hire cars to travel between towns. As shown in Table 11.5, compared to the rest of Russia, public transport by bus in the North Caucasus is minimal. Similarly, compared to the rest of Russia, the number of people who travel by public railway in the North Caucasus is also very low, as shown in Table 11.6.

Cell phones are available with a major contract awarded for a Global System for Mobile Communications (GSM) in 2001, but cell phone use in the North Caucasus is almost nonexistent compared to the rest of Russia (see Table 11.7).[27]

---

[27] Moroney discussion with Professor John Colarusso in 2005. See also *Cellular News* (undated).

Table 11.5
Passenger Transport by Public Bus (in millions of persons)

Republic	1990	1995	1996	1997	1998	1999	2000	2001	2002	2003
Russian Federation	28,626.1	22,817.1	23,185.0	23,664.7	23,102.8	22,882.5	22,032.7	20,883.1	19,619.5	17,897.6
Southern Federal District	3,039.9	1,970.0	2,015.5	2,219.9	2,063.2	1,826.7	1,738.3	1,504.0	1,378.8	1258.0
Dagestan	147.7	74.7	80.5	83.9	71.3	58.1	74.1	60.5	65.2	65.1
Ingushetiya	91.2	8.4	9.5	10.6	11.5	15.9	17.6	16.3	13.2	15.3
Kabardino-Balkariya	158.6	117.9	111.1	83.5	98.5	91.8	73.4	71.3	69.3	69.7
Karachayevo-Cherkessiya	—	10.1	13.0	15.3	13.1	11.5	12.0	14.0	14.1	13.7
North Ossetiya	80.0	94.2	89.2	81.8	71.5	63.5	60.5	76.1	76.8	69.8
Chechnya	91.2	—[a]	—	—	—	—	—	—	—	18.4

SOURCE: *Regiony Rossii* (2004), Table 16.5.
[a] The drop in transport is related to warfare and collapse of the transit system.

Table 11.6
Passenger Transport by Public Railway (in thousands of persons)

Republic	Year													
	1990	1995	1996	1997	1998	1999	2000	2001	2002	2003
Russian Federation	3,142,512	1,832,971	1,417,672	1,599,604	1,471,306	1,337,509	1,418,780	1,305,873	1,270,679	1,303,534
Southern Federal District	130,231	95,762	79,637	83,141	69,035	67,193	68,360	62,403	57,097	53,001
Dagestan	2,233	3,106	2,594	2,110	1,174	850	895	865	605	610
Ingushetiya (includes Chechnya)[a]	1,723	2	—[b]	—	8	48	90	70	61	62
Kabardino-Balkariya	843	805	777	944	564	333	400	349	297	319
Karachayevo-Cherkessiya	142	67	59	86	70	69	59	43	32	32
North Ossetiya	1,618	1,638	1,510	1,698	775	595	641	598	643	672
Chechnya (includes Ingushetiya)[a]	1,723	511	727	408	251	71	62	101	123	121

SOURCE: *Regiony Rossii* (2004), Table 16.4.
[a] Chechnya and Ingushetiya were one entity in the early 1990s and then split later into two units.
[b] The drop in transport is related to warfare and collapse of the transit system.

Table 11.7
Number of Cellular, Data Transmission, and Telematic Communication Service Subscribers

Republic	No. of Recorded Susbscriptions for Cellular Service (000s)						No. of Recorded Susbscriptions to Install Service for Data Transmission and Telematic Communcation (000s)		
	1999	2000	2001	2002	2003		2001	2002	2003
Russian Federation	1,370.6	3,263.2	7,750.5	17,508.8	35,603.5		1,176.9	2,259.8	4,357.6
Southern Federal District	74.0	205.2	693.8	1,976.4	4,638.3		131.7	233.0	288.2
Dagestan	—	—	—	0.1	38.3		2.1	3.6	5.1
Ingushetiya	0.5	0.5	—	—	—		—	—	—
Kabardino-Balkariya	1.0	1.8	4.0	17.2	65.9		0.2	0.2	4.5
Karachayevo-Cherkessiya	0.5	1.0	1.3	1.0	0.6		0.2	0.3	0.6
North Ossetiya	0.6	3.7	10.1	20.1	30.6		0.4	0.5	0.7
Chechnya	—	—	—	—	—		—	—	—

SOURCE: *Regiony Rossii, 2004*, Table 17.4.

Prevalence of the Informal or Shadow Economy

Approximately 55 percent of the total North Caucasus economy is unofficial.[28] In Chechnya and Dagestan, the underground economy is heavily augmented by profits from oil and gas transactions. Three groups sustain the shadow economy in the North Caucasus: (1) the Russian military; (2) rebel forces who transport illegal energy supplies in collusion with the Russian military on these ventures; and (3) the Kadyrovtsy, a well-armed security force appointed by President Putin, which runs run a large portion of the illegal oil businesses.[29] In Dagestan, illegal caviar poaching is big business; 1,500 people are arrested per year and many others escape detection.[30] In North Ossetiya and Ingushetiya, illegal vodka selling and smuggling are prevalent. Throughout the North Caucasus, caviar, bottled water from Georgia, and other commodities with a high tax in the official economy are smuggled by gangs belonging to criminal networks.[31] Figure 11.4 shows the smuggling routes in the Caucasus.

Official statistics on drug trafficking and the smuggling routes depicted in Figure 11.4 indicate moderate problems through the North Caucasus. In 2003, Russian customs registered 24 seizures of illegal drugs (3.3 percent of the Russian total), 11 seizures of illegal psychotropic medicines (3.7 percent of the Russian total), and 3 seizures of illegal chemicals from the South Caucasus (6.7 percent of the Russian total). From January to September 2004, the Southern Customs Office initiated 189 criminal cases for smuggling (10.2 percent of the Russian total).

A 2003 study on smuggling published by the Transatlantic Crime and Corruption Center focusing on the Caucasus (North Ossetia, South Ossetia, and Abkhazia), could not find evidence of large-scale organized smuggling. Most of the smuggling involves individuals and small groups. A considerable portion of smuggled goods consists of food and consumer goods. The remaining portion includes oil products, drugs, and weapons.

Poverty in the North Caucasus is one and one-half to two times higher than the average for Russia. The hardest hit area is Ingushetiya, followed by Dagestan and Karachayevo-Cherkessiya. This dire economic situation tends to attract poor, unem-

---

[28] Statistics are very difficult to locate, as might be expected.

[29] Moroney discussion with Professor Mikhail Alexseev, University of San Diego, March 14, 2005.

[30] U.S. Department of the Interior (2004).

[31] Moroney discussion with Professor John Colarusso, 2005. The Russian government banned this activity in April 2006.

Figure 11.4
Smuggling Routes in the Caucasus

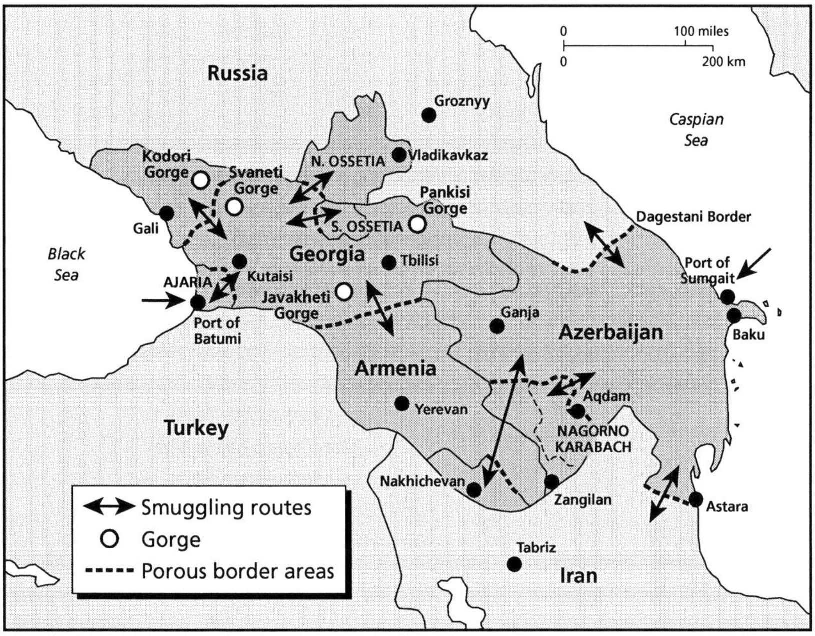

SOURCE: *Jane's Intelligence Review*, November 2003.
RAND *MG561-11.4*

ployed Muslim youth to extremist ideas.[32] The leader of the Azeris in Dagestan, Said Qurbanov, states, "People here consider war in the North Caucasus, including in Chechnya and Dagestan, to be a commercial activity. They like trading in weapons with the Russians."[33] Dagestan has the lowest monthly income in the North Caucasus, averaging only $17 a month, which helps to attract rebels. Making matters worse, the Dagestan birthrate is double that of the rest of the North Caucasus.[34]

Funds brought into the North Caucasus are usually carried in bags. Banks are distrusted because people perceive them as run by outside gangsters (except those run by their own trusted gangsters who guarantee that funds reach the intended recipients). Fuel, in some cases, is a black market commodity. People tend to buy fuel from

---

[32] Briefing Notes on Islam, Society, and Politics" (2002), p. 6.

[33] "Dagestan in the Run-Up to an Islamic Revolution" (2004).

[34] "Russia's Caucasian Nightmare" (1999).

individuals selling it on the street corner. Trade is bazaar-style, with sellers and buyers bartering for goods and services.[35]

Social and Cultural Resistance to State Penetration

Foreign Islamist groups have supported the resurgence of Islam in the North Caucasus since the fall of the Soviet Union. Outside funding grew dramatically during the First Chechen War (1994–1996). There were strong socioeconomic reasons for this resurgence. The ruin of Chechen economic and political structures and widespread disillusionment with reforms fostered calls for an Islamic alterative that would reinstate traditional Islamic standards and social justice and bring security and stability. Although the radical Islamic population in Chechnya is a minority, fluctuating between 10 and 25 percent according to some sources, it has represented an organized force that brought foreign financial support into an economically devastated region.[36] (An associated phenomenon is mass outmigration to Russian cities.) The resurgence of Islam in Chechnya appears to have been more a political phenomenon than strictly a rebirth of Islamic beliefs following suppression under Soviet rule. In fact, Islam in Chechnya may have been less entrenched prior to the war than it was in many other parts of the former Soviet Union.[37]

There is some evidence to suggest that Islam emerged as an alternative ideology, from an initial call to ethno-nationalist goals of state independence to the idea of an Islamic state. Islam became important to the struggle in Chechnya only after the West would not support Chechen demands for independence, at which point Chechen President Dudayev began to look to the Muslim world for support.[38]

However, conflict does not need to begin with religious goals to become a religious war. The goals, composition, and ideology of the parties are likely to evolve through protracted conflict. In Chechnya, what started as a fight for independence was transformed by the need for international support and the ambitions of foreign Islamic groups. As an ideology of the weaker combatant, Islam was a powerful mechanism for enlisting the support of a broader international Muslim community. The weakness of the Chechen state as an outcome of the First Chechen War served as an invitation for foreign radical Islamic elements to establish Chechnya as a base of operations to expand their influence among the Chechen factions.[39] In this sense, the First

---

[35] Moroney discussion with Professor John Colarusso, 2005. Although there are legitimate banks in the North Caucasus, terrorists and their sympathizers do not use these banks because federal authorities may seize their assets.

[36] Malashenko (2001).

[37] Walker (1998).

[38] Walker (1998).

[39] Lafraniere (2003). The post-1996 power struggle within the separatist camp was also a factor.

Chechen War facilitated the radicalization of Islam in the North Caucasus.[40] Religion also played a major role in the Second Chechen War, which started in 1999 and is still going on. This is attributable to the shifting dynamics of Islam within Chechnya and the composition of the Chechen fighters.

Chechens use Islam as a tool for identifying, preserving, and unifying the cultural community. Citizens identify with smaller religious groups rather than a nationwide Russian Federation Muslim community. Newer Islamic trends in Chechnya and Dagestan are a result of foreign influences that include Wahhabism. What is interesting about radical Islam in Chechnya is the newness of its introduction and the fact that Sufi Islam has penetrated the social structures for years.[41] Sufism in Chechnya has historically been anti-Russian, but although most Chechens follow Sufi practices, they tend to identify with smaller religious groups rather than with a nationwide Muslim community. The historic locus of Chechen social life stems from tribal allegiances and religious influences, which have simultaneously served to unite and divide Chechens. The Sufism that developed in Chechnya is unique and reflects the strong influences of clan-based social values and norms.[42]

Dagestan has the largest concentration of mosques in the North Caucasus, and the largest number of higher Islamic learning institutions.[43] For this reason, it is a key region in the Caucasus for Islam, including the radical Wahhabi variant. Buynaksk, Kazbek, Khasavyurt, and Botlikh have the largest concentrations of Wahhabis in Dagestan. Extremist religious figures in these cities organize mass meetings and distribute leaflets encouraging believers to join the Dagestan army, to abolish all Russian laws, and to set up their own laws based on the Qu'ran.[44]

Resistance to state penetration of society in the North Caucasus is generated by social as well as religious factors. New power relationships have developed, with local potentates or "princes" exercising authority and ensuring food supplies and the safety of citizens. The princes, however, do not have direct authority by virtue of their social status. The newly emerging power structure is being interpreted in traditional ways, making it more difficult for Moscow to intervene or have much political influence. Citizens seek assistance from powerholders outside any formal mandates they hold. They also expect easy access to these individuals and to be able to freely express their concerns.[45] Comparatively new economic elites have also emerged. Some of the newly rich have joined the establishment, mostly by marrying into the traditional elite. The

---

[40] *The Time of the South* (2002).

[41] Hill (2004).

[42] Akhmadov et al. (2001).

[43] "Briefing Notes on Islam, Society, and Politics" (2002), p. 6.

[44] Blandy (1998).

[45] Moroney discussion with Professor John Colarusso, 2005.

Kabardinian and Balkarian elite is characterized by mixed marriages between Kabardinians and Balkars, high authority positions, and mutual aid. It has played an important role in preventing and relaxing tensions in the region.

In spite of the obvious contrast between the mountains and the plains, people living in the mountains and in the low-lying areas have for the most part based their relationships on traditional rules and mechanisms of mutual and nonconflictual land use. A good example of such a mechanism is *transhumance,* the seasonal movement of livestock to regions with different climates (e.g. high mountains and plains). Thanks to the transhumance system, mountain peoples have winter pastures on the plains, whereas peoples living in the plains have summer pastures in the mountains. Insofar as livestock breeding is the main source of subsistence for rural people, nonconfrontational relations were and still are vitally important. The system of arable land distribution is also mutually profitable when mountain collective farms (now cooperatives), which have a lack of arable land, get small plots of fertile land in the plains. Such plots are important for surviving mountain farms. This system of the land distribution contributes to maintaining the balance between Kabardinians and Balkars.

Two processes undercut Moscow's influence in the North Caucasus: separation and unification. In the twin republics of Karbardino-Balkaria and Karachaevo-Cherkessia serious tensions have developed between the two major ethnic groups that were arbitrarily grouped together in Soviet times. Small ethnic groups, such as Abazins and Nogais, claim the right to territorial autonomy. There is a parallel movement to unite ethnically close peoples, e.g., within a Greater Circassia, which would embrace Kabardino, Kabardino-Balkariya Cherkessia, Adyghea, Abkhazia, and the lands claimed by the Abazin and the Shapsug. The federal authorities have been resisting both processes, since any change of existing borders would inevitably open a Pandora's box of ethnic conflict.

The Don and Kuban Cossacks constitute an indigenous ethnic group. Their leaders insist on their groups' distinct identity within the Russian ethnos. The radicals among the Cossacks call for the restoration of the semiautonomous Territory of the Don Host, abolished by the Bolsheviks. Much of that territory coincides with the current Rostov region, but parts of it are in the neighboring Voronezh region and across the border in Ukraine (Luhansk and Donetsk regions). Terek Cossacks have long been demanding the return of two districts that were included into the Chechen-Ingush republic in 1957. When the Russian federal forces in the course of an "antiterrorist operation" in Chechnya overran those districts, ideas were put forth about a possible partition of the republic, giving its northern third to the Cossacks. Other Cossack groups raised territorial claims to parts of North Ossetia, Kabardino-Balkaria, and Dagestan.

At their peak in the 1990s, the Cossacks and their allies among Russian nationalists accused the Russian government of inaction and cowardice and insisted on more proactive policies or, failing that, threatened to take the law into their own hands.

However, despite their loud claims and resolute and warlike appearance, the Cossacks have been unable to organize themselves, either within Chechnya or on its periphery, even to repel frequent Chechen incursions. In the rest of southern Russia, their leaders have been more interested in lucrative business practices than in politics.

In addition to the regions discussed above, political instability in the republic of Karachayevo-Cherkessiya hinders Moscow's influence, but the regional authorities there have managed to mitigate the problem somewhat. For example, in November 2004, when angry demonstrators took over the government palace in Cherkessk, Dmitry Kozak, Russian President Vladimir Putin's envoy to the Southern Federal District, met with 50 antigovernment activists who had occupied the office of President Mustafa Batdyev. The protestors said that they would not leave the office until they saw Batdyev sign his own letter of resignation.[46] Kozak, probably under instructions from the Kremlin, stated that he was categorically against this solution since "We cannot set a precedent." Kozak's statement revealed the federal government's strategy: to keep Batdyev in his seat by any means, because his resignation would set a dangerous example for other regions where people are not satisfied with local authorities and have no legal means of redress.[47]

Lack of a Monopoly of Force

Presence of Organized Armed Groups

The state's authority in the North Caucasus is contested by numerous armed factions, most of which are Chechens who, while seeking independence from the Russian Federation, are also engaged in criminal acts and in battles over turf with other factions. (Some of these groups are listed in Table 11.8.) The ability of the Russian military to operate is hampered by a number of factors, including language. There are hardly any Chechen speakers in the Russian military. Chechens use Chechen for field communications, thereby limiting the ability of Russian military forces to understand their conversations.[48]

Violence spills over through murder-for-hire and revenge killings throughout Russia. Dagestan is attractive to Chechen criminal networks because of its Caspian Sea coastline and the potential for profit from Caspian oil and gas transport, illegal caviar transport, and other smuggling activities. There is a high level of collu-

---

[46] Smirnov (2004).

[47] On November 11, 2004, when the government restored its control over the center of Cherkessk, the republic's capital, the authorities launched their counterattack. About 3,000 policemen and troops were brought to Cherkessk from neighboring Stavropol region. Smirnov (2004).

[48] Karasik interviews with Armed Forces Medical Intelligence Center), 2003–2004.

Table 11.8
Armed Groups in the North Caucasus

Republic	Group
Dagestan	Riyad us-Saliheyn Martyrs' Brigade Al-Qaeda Dagestan Liberation Army Sword of Islam
Kabardino-Balkariya	Riyad us-Saliheyn Martyrs' Brigade
Chechnya	Black Widows Islamic International Peacekeeping Brigade (IIPB) Movsar Baryayev Gang Riyad us-Saliheyn Martyrs' Brigade Special Purpose Islamic Regiment (SPIR) Sword of Islam

SOURCE: MIPT Terrorism Knowledge Base (2005).

sion between the armed groups and the state's security services. Russian troops frequently interact with Chechen rebels by buying or selling weapons, food, and alcohol.[49]

The Chechen diaspora plays an important role in sustaining Chechen resistance to Moscow. In addition to the majority of Chechens who live in Chechnya and other parts of the North Caucasus, there are large Chechen communities outside the territory of the Russian Federation. The number of Chechens in diaspora communities breaks down approximately as follows: Turkey (100,000), Jordan (8,000), Egypt (5,000), Syria (4,000), and Iraq (2,500). Kailani also notes that there are significant numbers of Chechens living in the countries of the South Caucasus. Some analysts estimate that one million Chechens live in Georgia and one million in Armenia, although these figures are unreliable.[50] In the wake of the October 2002 seizure of a Moscow theater, Russia asked Turkey to shut down Chechen foundations located within its territory, saying the rebels were in contact with them during the theater siege. Moscow also charged that Chechen charities in Turkey finance the rebels. About 25,000 Chechens live in Istanbul and western Turkey, and up to 5 million Turks trace their roots to the Caucasus region.[51]

A large contingent from the Chechen rebel force led by the late Shamil Basayev and his deputy, Amir Khattab (a Saudi with probable ties to al-Qaeda), invaded Dagestan in August 1999.[52] Despite the failure of this venture and the redeployment of Russian troops to Chechnya in 2000, Basayev did not stop his attempts to move the war eastward beyond the Chechen borders. Basayev initiated a careful, slow process of

---

[49] See, for instance, Akhmadov (2005); Politkovskaya and Crowfoot (2001). For statistics on homicides and attempted murders in the North Caucasus, see *Prestupnost' i pravoporiadok v Rossii* (2003), Table 13.5.

[50] Kailani (2002).

[51] Pro-Chechen rebels have carried out hijackings and hostage takings in Turkey, including an April 2001 siege at an Istanbul hotel in which 120 people were held captive for 12 hours before rebels surrendered and released the hostages unharmed. See "Chechens in Theater Raid Linked to Turkish Foundations" (2002).

[52] Nabi (2003).

preparing Dagestan for guerrilla warfare. The hundreds of militants from Dagestan who had joined Basayev's group in the mid-1990s made this process much easier to organize.[53] Basayev was killed in an explosion on July 9, 2006.

Foreign jihadists also played an important role in Basayev's movement. A prominent associate was the Jordanian extremist Abu Havs. Known also as Amzhet, he was born in Jordan and is believed to have Saudi citizenship. Havs arrived in Chechnya in 1995 during the first war with Russia and was an instructor at a terrorist camp. As a weapons procurement expert, Federal Security Service (FSB) officials believe that Havs helped Basayev organize the Beslan siege, in which 331 hostages, mostly children, were killed.[54] FSB reports also claim that Havs is a main link between the Arab world and Chechen rebels, and may have links to al-Qaeda. At the height of the second war with Russia, Havs sought refuge in the Pankisi gorge region, where he set up training camps.

In 2002 a group called Jennet ("heaven" in Arabic) made its appearance in Dagestan. Rasul Maksharipov, a Dagestani who had fought with Basayev in 1999, headed the group. Jennet's principal objective was to eliminate senior police and FSB officers in Dagestan. More then 30 police and FSB officers were killed in Dagestan in 2004. Dagestan's Police Department for the Struggle against Extremism and Criminal Terrorism has lost 29 officers in recent years.[55] The insurgents managed to assassinate such important figures as Colonel Khamil Etinbekov, who played a key role in FSB operations in Dagestan; Akhberdilav Akilov, who headed the Department for the Struggle Against Extremism and Criminal Terrorism; and Magomed Gusaev, the republic's Minister of National Policy, Information, and External Relations.[56]

The rebels made Makhachkala, Dagestan's capital, the center of their activities. Nearby Tarki-Tau Mountain, which is covered with thick forests, became an ideal hideout. After each operation in the capital, Jennet members fled to the mountains on the western outskirts of the city.[57] In late 2004, Jennet was transformed into a much larger organization called Sharia Jamaat, Arabic for "sharia community."[58]

---

[53] Smirnov (2005a).

[54] According to the same report, the FSB said that the explosives used in Beslan were prepared by one of Havs' closest associates.

[55] *Kommersant*, January 17, 2004.

[56] *Rossiiskaya gazeta*, June 24, 2004; Smirnov (2005a).

[57] Smirnov (2005a).

[58] On December 27 and 30, 2004, the rebels assassinated two police colonels in Makhachkala. One of them was the warden of the local prison camp and the other headed the Operations Department of Dagestan's Ministry of Interior Affairs. Sharia published a statement on the Kavkazcenter Web site on January 2, 2005, proclaiming that the organization had killed FSB and police officers for their "lawless actions against Muslims in Dagestan." The statement blamed "Russian death squads" for the kidnapping and murder of civilians in the Republic." See Smirnov (2005a); Kavkazcenter, January 2, 2005; and *Kavkazky Uzel*, January 14, 2005.

Some analysts have estimated that there are numerous training camps and approximately 1,500 fighters in the North Caucasus region. The camps and the pathways leading to them are all mined. Tall corn shields the houses, which allows for covered passage out of the house and into the forest to the camps.[59] One of the main al-Qaeda lieutenants in the Chechnya-Georgia region is a Jordanian known as Abu Atiyya. In addition to overseeing the deployment of militants to training camps, he is thought to play a key role in reassigning trained personnel to terror networks, including setting up sleeper cells in Azerbaijan and Turkey.[60]

The Chechen conflict appears to be entering a potentially more extreme and polarized stage with the killing of Chechen president Maskhadov in March 2005. Although the Russian media trumpeted Maskhadov's death as a victory, it clearly deprived the rebel movement of its moderate counterbalance to Islamic extremism. A British political consultant who knew Maskhadov well described his death as a tragic loss for the Chechen people because the rebel leader was willing to engage in talks with Moscow to find a peaceful solution.[61] Maskhadov's replacement was the little-known Abdul Khalim Sadulaev. Sharia Jamaat declared him to be the new "Amir" of the Caucasus and of all Muslims of Russia.[62] In June 2006, the Mujahideen Shura Council of Chechnya announced Sadulaev's death in a confrontation with Russian forces as "martyrdom."[63]

Insurgents in Dagestan and Karbardino-Balkaria continued their campaign after Maskhadov's death. On March 10, 2005, Yarmuk, an insurgent group in Kabardino-Balkaria, released a statement announcing their readiness to conduct military operations in the spring and summer. The statement called upon "all Muslims of Kabardino-Balkaria who work in local law-enforcement agencies" to leave their jobs and warned traffic policemen against stopping cars carrying rebels. Yarmuk warned tourists, hunters, and foresters not to go to the mountains because "they would be regarded as spies if found near the rebels' bases."[64]

Military units from Russia's North Caucasus Military District in Krasnodar Krai have allegedly supported special-task police units from Kabardino-Balkaria to attempt to quell this threat, specifically to detect suspicious persons and search for illegal firearms. The possible connection between Yarmuk and so-called Wahhabi groups is par-

---

[59] Moroney discussion with Professor Mikhail Alexseev, University of San Diego, March 14, 2005.

[60] "A Poisonous Plot" (2005).

[61] Franchetti (2005).

[62] *Moskovsky komsomolets*, March 10, 2005.

[63] SITE Institute (2006).

[64] Smirnov (2005b).

ticularly worrisome. The strength of the Yarmuk force is not well documented, but some reports estimate it to have 200 fighters.[65]

Presence of Organized Crime Networks

The NIC report mentions Russia (although not specifically the North Caucasus) as a region where organized crime is likely to thrive in the next 15 years, and where there might be some direct connections to terrorist organizations (even if only temporary). The rationale is that Russia is a resource-rich state undergoing significant political and economic transformation, making it vulnerable to criminal and terrorist behavior.

There is a strong criminal element in the North Caucasus. The head of the Russian Interior Ministry Department for Combating Organized Crime and Terrorism, Nikolay Ovchinnikov, stated that approximately 100 criminal groups, with a core membership of 3,500 to 4,000, are currently operating in Russia. "Most criminal fraternities operate in the Central, Siberian, Volga, and Southern federal districts. Criminal fraternities are actively seeking to extend their influence abroad and to establish transnational links.[66]

Criminal groups dominate the "personal protection" services for foreigners and some Caucasians. The potential for Westerners being kidnapped is very high. These protective networks operate outside the law, and in most cases law enforcement authorities are directly or indirectly involved with them. The Caucasus diaspora in New Jersey is allegedly tied into this network; however, this appears to be more a matter of traditional honor, with status accruing to the protectors in hope of rewards offered at some future time.[67]

In the North Caucasus, the relationship between terrorists and organized criminals is likely to remain primarily a matter of business. Criminals are businessmen first and foremost. Most do not have terrorist goals, but rather concentrate on making money through illegal trade of highly taxed commodities. Terrorists turn to organized crime groups when they need something specific, such as forged documents, smuggled weapons, etc., but organized crime groups are not likely to form permanent alliances with terrorist networks. For one thing, the possible negative ramifications of being linked to a terrorist group hinder long-term cooperation.[68]

Population with Access to Weapons

The possession of small arms is a tradition in the North Caucasus. In Chechnya, people age 12 and above are likely to be armed; many have automatic weapons, specifically Kalashnikovs. Caravans with weapons transit the region regularly from Russia and

---

[65] Smirnov (2005b); Wilhelmsen (2005).

[66] See *Organized Crime News* (2005).

[67] Moroney discussion with Professor John Colarusso, 2005.

[68] National Intelligence Council (2004), p. 96.

Turkey via Azerbaijan and Abkhazia to Dagestan and Chechnya. Firepower is growing in Chechnya, in particular, with rebels gaining access to sophisticated MANPADs and rocket-propelled grenades.[69]

Lack of Border Controls

There is no concept of "border security" according to Western standards in the North Caucasus region. The Chechen-Dagestani border is particularly problematic. Vans filled with weapons pass easily with a small bribe across this border. In regions to the south, the border controls are even looser, although the transit is not as prevalent to the south.

It is not possible to block and regulate all the roads connecting Dagestan and Chechnya. Consequently, Chechen fighters have been able to penetrate Dagestan easily by avoiding or bypassing known checkpoints. According to one source, caravans with weapons from Azerbaijan regularly move through Dagestan to Chechnya. A large number of roads are incomplete and passable only with four-wheel drive vehicles or horses. At night, the border checkpoints are wide open.[70] Guarding remote border areas on a consistent basis is simply beyond the capabilities of the authorities, who are unable to sustain outposts in harsh terrain over a prolonged period.

Armed raids are a regular occurrence in North Caucasus border regions. Chechen armed raids are done by *bandformirovaniya* (Chechen bandits). Activities include kidnapping, robbery, and theft of cattle and agricultural equipment. Citizens in the border regions in particular are forced to defend themselves because both Russian and Chechen authorities are powerless (or unmotivated) to provide security to the population.

External Interference

A characteristic of some, though not all, ungoverned territories is external interference that prevents or diminishes a state's ability to control its territory. In the case of the North Caucasus, the central authorities—namely, Moscow—cannot be considered external in the traditional state-to-state sense. However, direct projection of authority from Moscow is viewed as "external" interference by the North Caucasus peoples because they reside in autonomous republics within the Russian Federation. Moscow exerts control over the domestic political and economic space, preventing effective governance at the regional and local levels. This interference is direct, intentional, and

---

[69] Peters et al. (2006).

[70] Blandy (1998).

justified, according to Moscow, because of the need to quell terrorist and criminal activities in the republics.

Some questions relating to the degree of Moscow's influence in the North Caucasus, particularly with regard to the state of governance in the region, are the following:

- How much influence does Moscow have on the internal activities of the North Caucasus republics?
- Do any other external actors directly influence the region? To what extent do external actors exacerbate or, alternatively, mitigate problems in the region?
- Is external involvement a cause or symptom of the problem?

On the first question, Moscow's influence in the North Caucasus is uneven. Militarily, Russia has several thousand soldiers deployed to the region; unfortunately, these forces are not a source of security for the North Caucasus peoples. Many of the soldiers are involved in criminal activities and networks that bring greater instability to the region. Moscow attempts to influence the direction of the regional governing authorities in the North Caucasus republics by applying political and economic pressure.[71] Economically, North Caucasus trade is primarily domestically directed, and Moscow has economic leverage in the following areas: energy, social benefits, and trade throughout the region.

Among the other "external" factors aside from Moscow, the influence of the North Caucasus diaspora, as discussed above, is worth noting. The diaspora's links with Turkey and Jordan are particularly strong, and the American diaspora seems to have direct contacts with Karbardino-Balkaria. The connections between the peoples of the North Caucasus and the diaspora are not exclusive and are often interrupted. The Circassians raise funds for displaced persons in Ingushetiya and Chechnya, but it is not clear how much of those resources reach the intended recipients. In any case, the locals tend to blame the Russians for any diversion of funds, even when the local criminal networks may really be at fault.[72]

On the question of the ability of external actors to affect the situation, for better or worse, it is hard to identify areas where Moscow's involvement has actually improved conditions. Moscow has been unable to significantly improve the economies of the North Caucasus republics and, as discussed earlier, Russian security services deployed to the region do not actually contribute to security.

External involvement in the North Caucasus is both a cause and symptom of the problem. The so-called "power vertical" (efforts by Moscow to impose its will on region) has the potential to aggravate strife among sectors of the Caucasian popula-

---

[71] See, for example, the role of the presidential envoys in Fuller and Corwin (2004); and Trenin (2005).

[72] Moroney discussion with Professor John Colarusso, 2005.

tions. The closing of prospects for a negotiated settlement of the Chechen conflict and the rise of Islamic fundamentalist movements in the region, along with extremely poor economic conditions, ensure that conditions are likely to become more violent in Chechnya and progressively more unstable in the other republics.

Assessment of Ungovernability

The North Caucasus manifests high levels of ungovernability across all the indicators. Penetration of the society by state institutions is very low. About half the economy is informal. Crime and corruption are rife, law enforcement is dysfunctional, and there is a lack of effective border control. Terrorist groups are active in Chechnya and Dagestan and able to stage attacks in other North Caucasus republics—even in the Russian heartland. Table 11.9 provides values for indicators of ungovernability in the North Caucasus republics. The indicators are as follows: 1 = low, 2 = medium, and 3 = high. Thus, a value of 3 would indicate a high level of ungovernability.

Table 11.9
Indicators of Ungovernability, North Caucasus

Variable	Dagestan	Ingushetiya	Kabardino- Balkariya	Karachayevo- Cherkessiya	North Ossetiya	Chechnya
Lack of state penetration						
Absence of state institutions	3	2	2	2	2	3
Lack of physical infrastructure	3	3	3	3	3	3
Social/cultural resistance	3	2	2	1	2	3
Lack of monopoly of force						
Illegal armed groups	3	2	2	1	2	3
Criminal networks	3	3	3	2	3	3
Population with access to arms	3	2	2	2	2	3
Lack of border controls	3	3	3	3	3	3
External interference	3	3	3	2	3	3

Conduciveness to Terrorist Presence

Adequacy of Infrastructure

Until a Georgian security crackdown in 2003, Georgia's Pankisi Gorge was a lawless haven for guerrillas, drug dealers, and kidnappers. Al-Qaeda camps in the area specialized in training recruits in the use of explosives and in basic chemical terror, including the poisoning of water and food supplies.[73] Georgian security sources say the al-Qaeda

---

[73] Murphy (2004).

operatives in the Pankisi region who moved out in the middle of 2003 included Middle Eastern "chemists" skilled in poisons. U.S. authorities subsequently arrested many of them when Georgians thwarted poison attacks against American citizens and installations in other parts of the Caucasus and Central Asia.[74]

Georgian antiterror operations in the Pankisi Gorge forced the main lines of communication to move back to the North Caucasus region. Supplies are transported via helicopter (Yak-18), plane, truck, mule, or horse from Azerbaijan and the Russian Federation parts of the North Caucasus. Some of these supplies, such as pharmaceuticals, later diverted back onto the black market, are frequently purchased, cut, and repackaged. Food and water are also prepositioned in various locations months in advance.[75] Mountain brooks can also be used for water supplies. Foods such as boiled meat and flatbread can also be procured from local farmers, cooked by sympathetic villagers, or until recently, brought up from Georgia.[76]

Chechens have also established elaborate networks to help them recuperate after battle. After fighting, Chechens commute on their own accord to rest and eat. Medical aid is provided to Chechen rebels in northern Georgia, Azerbaijan, East Kazakhstan, and Turkey through networks of apartments as well as clinics and hospitals staffed by sympathizers. In the latter example, Chechen fighters pose as refugees in order to rest up and receive aid from local health agencies. It is rumored that the system for rest and medical treatment has been operating for "a long time" in Azerbaijan and Kazakhstan.[77]

Operational Access

The North Caucasus is not only a theater of operations for rebel and jihadist forces but also a platform for operations beyond the Caucasus region—giving them what we refer to as operational access. The Chechens and the jamaats have been able to organize, train, and equip freely and conduct numerous terrorist attacks, most notably the September 2004 Beslan attack.[78] Doctrine and lessons learned are shared in rest areas and in the rear areas of the battlefield in both urban and rural settings. In the last two mass hostage-taking cases—Beslan and the Dubrovka Theater in October 2002—the Chechens relied on a Russian counterattack, which caused heavy civilian casualties

---

[74] Henley (2004).

[75] Prepositioned foods include canned or smoked meats, mutton, cornmeal, potatoes, noodles, wild onions, bags of rice, and sunflower seeds.

[76] Karasik interviews with Armed Forces Medical Intelligence Center (AFMIC), 2003–2004.

[77] Karasik interviews with AFMIC, 2003–2004.

[78] Chechens train cadres to draw schematics, take video of buildings and security personnel, and raise funds for operations. Battle-hardened veterans of the first Chechen war are planners while those from the second war are foot soldiers and ISR specialists for subsequent hostage seizures. Shamil Basayev was the key planner in all events; he recruited Chechen cell leaders to lead varying groups of suicide attack teams (30–210 individuals). Karasik interviews with AFMIC, 2003–2004.

and confusion, to gain support for their cause. Of late, their operations are part of a wider plan to ignite a war throughout the North Caucasus.[79]

Favorable Demographic and Social Factors

Caucasian terrorists and rebels take advantage of widespread anti-Russian sentiment among many of the region's peoples. Chechens employ the historical concept of *nabag*, in which Chechen raiders would seize Russian hostages to press for greater autonomy from tsarist rule. History is a strong motivator for today's Chechen cause to establish an Islamic state in the North Caucasus free of Russian rule.[80] When threatened by outside forces, Chechens have traditionally used intertribal fusion to confront the invader. It is a part of their lore that they unite together to fight against empires.[81] This phenomenon is known as the *taip* system and it feeds a very deep sense of community and the instinctive will to fight "infidels."[82] Many field commanders can trace their roots to such a structure.[83] Finally, the older generation continues on the whole to trust the Spiritual Board of Muslims, which is close to the authorities. The younger generation is increasingly turning to the less obedient unofficial Muslim leaders.[84]

Finally, the political proclivities of the North Caucasus peoples fall between support for Russia on the one hand and anti-Russian sentiment on the other. As violence by Chechen and other jamaats escalates against Russian officialdom and non-Muslims, economic conditions deteriorate, and governmental capabilities to govern effectively evaporate, anti-Russian sentiment grows stronger among affected ethnic groups in the various republics. In other words, Russia's failed attempt at counterinsurgency operations is breeding a whole new wave of anti-government hatred.

---

[79] Chechen rebels frequently conduct operations against health agencies to resupply their medical stocks. Growing reports of Chechen raids on hospitals or clinics may signal that the local black market is void of necessary goods and services. The Chechen network of clandestine hospitals and clinics includes many that are quite sophisticated. Karasik discussions with AFMIC, 2001–2004.

[80] Ram (1999).

[81] See, for example, Akhmadov et al. (2000); Williams (2003).

[82] Chechen clan structures are known as *taip*. The members are identified by their descent from a common ancestor twelve generations removed. A taip constitutes two to three villages of 400 to 600 people each. Each taip has a Council of Elders, economic interests, rules, and regulations. Simultaneously, each taip is grouped into cross-cutting tribal units called *tukhum* that possess unique dialects, taboos, and tribute systems. A particular taip might supply 600 fighters. These groups are broken down into units of 150 and further subdivided into squads of about 20 for combat operations that work one-week shifts, one after the other. See Arquilla and Karasik (1999).

[83] Akhmadov et al. (2000).

[84] For instance, the unofficial emir of Muslims of Kabardino-Balkaria, Mussa Mukhozhev, who heads 40 Islamic communities across the republic, which number more than 10,000 followers. Tlisova (2004).

Populations Vulnerable to Co-Option and Intimidation

Groups in the North Caucasus are vulnerable to co-option and intimidation by the Chechen militants. People in Kabardino-Balkariya are afraid that Islamic militants will target their republic, which has seen growing turbulence since 2004. Classes in kindergartens, schools, and colleges have been disrupted because parents keep their children at home. Public agitation has been intense since an article appeared on the popular Internet site Kavkazweb entitled "End of the World: How Chechen separatists are planning to destroy Kabardino-Balkariya and Karachayevo-Cherkessiya."[85] Ethnic divisions are growing, and people are taking notice of who belongs to an Islamic group and who does not.

Invisibility

Many recruits to the Chechen cause look like ethnic Russians and are able to enter Moscow unnoticed to carry out terrorist attacks.[86] Chechen militants observe and take note of roadblocks and videotaped facilities before they launch an attack. They have posed as Russian mercenaries (*kontrakniki*) and as "Cargo 200" personnel to get through sentry posts. "Cargo 200" is a moniker for Russian military and internal security forces transporting war dead in coffins; much of their supplies are in the coffins.[87] In July 2004, several of the Beslan attackers posed as construction workers to learn the interior layout of the school and scope out sniper positions and potential booby trap locations. For the Beslan attack, the terrorists used trucks with "Office of the Russian Prosecutor General" markings to get through roadblocks to the school.[88]

Assessment of Conduciveness to Terrorism

Table 11.10 summarizes the values that we have assigned to the indicators identified as conducive to the presence of terrorist groups. Values are 1 = low; 2 = medium; and 3 = high.

---

[85] Tlisova (2004).

[86] Cherkessians with criminal/terrorist intentions are difficult to identify. They are ethnically mixed through intermarriage, have blonde/red hair and thus appear Russian. Discussion with Professor John Colarusso, 2005.

[87] Buse et al. (2004).

[88] Buse et al. (2004).

Table 11.10
Indicators of Conduciveness to Terrorist Presence, North Caucasus

Variable	Dagestan	Ingushetiya	Kabardino-Balkariya	Karachayevo-Cherkessiya	North Ossetiya	Chechnya
Adequacy of infrastructure						
Financial infrastructure	1	1	1	1	1	1
Transportation and communications	1	1	1	1	1	1
Operational access	3	3	3	2	3	3
Sources of income	3	2	2	2	2	3
Favorable demographics	3	2	2	2	2	3
Invisibility	3	2	2	2	2	3

Trends in the North Caucasus and Implications for U.S. Interests

The revival of Muslim identity in regions such as the North Caucasus will create a framework for the spread of radical ideology outside the Middle East. Further destabilization of the North Caucasus has the potential to spill over to adjacent regions where U.S. political and military interests are more clear-cut. The Caucasus and Central Asia are areas of growing concern because of the number of potentially failing states and regions, the rise of Islamic extremism, and the region's role as a transit zone in the Caspian Sea energy corridor.[89]

Russia's Weakening Hold

Russia's hold over the Eurasia republics is weakening. The Rose Revolution in Georgia, the Orange Revolution in Ukraine, and the Tulip Revolution in Kyrgyzstan are testament to this fact. Perceived setbacks in Ukraine and Georgia are likely to lead President Putin to redouble his efforts to defend Russian interests abroad, especially Russia's internal interests in the North Caucasus republics, while balancing cooperation with the West.

President Putin has resorted to the old "power vertical" concept, in which power flows from the president to local authorities.[90] He remarked to President Bush during their February 2005 summit in Slovakia that the Russian people had a history with tsars and were accustomed to the government playing a strong role in their lives.[91] The downside of the power vertical is that it could lead to the eventual erosion of the entire political system. If power is concentrated at the center and the center falters, the whole edifice could come down. As Dmitri Trenin has noted,

> Should the President's [Putin's] popularity dip, should the backroom succession process run into difficulties, or should the next president lack credibility with the electorate, the political system will either crumble or have to be replaced by some sort of a dictatorship.[92]

Moscow is concerned that separatism inside Russia and radical Islamic movements beyond its borders might threaten stability in the North Caucasus. As we have discussed, Chechen extremists have increasingly turned to terrorism. With Maskhadov's death, it is reasonable to predict that rebels will carry out attacks against civilian or military targets elsewhere in Russia in 2005. According to one source, the role, attitudes, and actions of the *siloviki*—the ex-KGB officers that Putin has placed in posi-

---

[89] National Intelligence Council (2004), p. 117.

[90] Danilov et al. (2005), pp. 108–109, 111.

[91] "Bush Presses Putin on Democracy" (2005).

[92] Danilov et al. (2005), p. 112.

tions of authority throughout the Russian government including the republics—may be critical determinants of the course Moscow will pursue in the year ahead.[93]

President Putin is clearly trying to portray Chechen separatism and the security situation in the North Caucasus through the prism of 9/11 and terror rather than as a nationalist movement. At the same time, the leadership in the North Caucasus republics, in particular the rebel Chechen leadership, has made critical mistakes, particularly in its toleration of terrorism. For example, one of Basayev's former associates, Chechen rebel fugitive Ilyas Akhmadov, recently stated that "with Beslan, Basayev cast a death sentence on all of Chechnya and any hope of a negotiated settlement. He has dug our national grave and foolishly played right into Putin's hands".[94]

The fierce competition between the center and the periphery that has been brewing and the strong possibility of more violence in coming months is likely to keep the North Caucasus, and particularly Chechnya, as an important facet of U.S.-Russia relations. However, with the United States waging a war of its own in Iraq and engaged in a broader war on terrorism in which it needs Russian support, it is difficult for the U.S. government to chastise the Russians about their policies in the North Caucasus. The ability of the United States to influence developments in a region that is, after all, part of the Russian Federation, is limited. Still, a larger U.S. political and military presence in nearby South Caucasus could potentially have beneficial effects on stability on the North Caucasus regions, for example, in terms of improved border security capabilities.

Russia's Security Sector Reform Relative to the North Caucasus

Despite an improving economy, Russia continues to face endemic challenges related to its post-Soviet military decline.[95] According to U.S. defense analysts, Russia is seeking to portray itself as a great power and has made some improvements to its armed forces, but has not addressed difficult domestic problems that will limit the scale and scope of its military recovery. Russian conventional forces have improved from their mid-1990s low point, but they still have a long way to go. Large-scale procurement has been delayed until after 2010, and defense spending is still below requirements.[96]

The wars in the North Caucasus have taken their toll on the Russian military. Moscow's struggle with the Chechen insurgency continues with no end in sight and is likely to worsen in the next few months. Although Moscow is employing more pro-Russian Chechen security forces against the insurgents, the war severely strains Russian ground forces. Concerns over spreading violence has led to new security initiatives

---

[93] Goss (2005).

[94] Brzezinski (2005).

[95] Russia's gross national product averaged 6.7 percent growth over the past five years, mostly from increased energy prices and consumer demand.

[96] Jacoby (2005).

and a stronger hand in the region, justified by the crackdown on terrorism within the Russian Federation.

President Putin declared that dealing with the terrorist threat in Russia is the primary task of the FSB; however, reform of the military and security services in Russia as a whole has not been a priority for the administration. Corruption in the Russian law enforcement and border security agencies has allowed terrorists and would-be terrorists to move around the Russian Federation relatively freely. For instance, in August 2004 suicide bombers bribed their way onto aircraft that they later destroyed mid-flight. Investigations into the Moscow apartment building and theater attacks, the Beslan school seizure, and other attacks have been less than satisfying to the Russian population, and court cases for accused terrorists have been few and far between. Killing them, as opposed to bringing them to justice, seems to be the preferred Russian approach. Within the Russian armed forces, there is a desperate need for strict discipline, a higher quality of professional soldiers, and improved training and equipment.

To be fair, however, some reforms within the security agencies have taken place in recent years. For example, in an effort to improve border security, more-stringent procedures have been put into play regarding identification checks, which are seen to some degree as an attempt to encourage the European Union to ease visa requirements for Russian nationals. In 2000, Putin adopted a policy of "Chechenization." Realizing that only Chechens could rule Chechnya, he thus rejected the ideas of appointing military governors-general to preside over the North Caucasus republics. Moreover, in 2004, in an effort to reach out to the Muslim community, a Muslim was appointed as head of the Interior Troops (which are responsible for Chechnya). But overall, it seems that little thought has been given to how Russian actions contribute to the rise of violence in the region. Moreover, insufficient consideration has been given to how the lack of reforms within the security services, the military in particular, have contributed to the spread of violence.

Opportunities for Productive U.S.-Russian Relations

Despite all the problems associated with U.S.-Russia relations currently, some developments, should they occur, could potentially spur more positive bilateral relations. The conditions under which Russia and the United States might see eye to eye on Chechnya as a source of organized terrorism include

- overall strengthening of the jihadist movement in the North Caucasus
- a radical Chechen attack on an American target directly in Europe or Eurasia
- a WMD attack or attempted attack on the United States or U.S. interests that could be traced to Chechen terrorists.

If any of the above occurs, any U.S. administration would have to revisit the issue of the role of Chechen groups in the global jihadist movement. Are they local fighters or should they be included in the front rank of the movement led by al-Qaeda? Before the 9/11 attacks, President George W. Bush criticized Russia's human rights record in Chechnya, although the president expressed his personal fondness for Putin. There has been some drop of criticism about the Chechen issue in the wake of the Beslan school seizure.[97] Nevertheless, questions remain: Is the apparent Russian strategy of solving the Chechen conflict by force (including the decapitation of the moderate Chechen leadership) counterproductive in the long term? And what could be the appropriate U.S. policy response?

Opportunities for cooperation with the West in the fight against terrorism include expanded cooperation with the United States; closer cooperation with NATO/EUROCORPS forces in Afghanistan; improved border security to curtail the transit of terrorists, weapons, and drugs; and cooperation with the EU and the OSCE in the area of conflict resolution. Modernization of Russia's governmental structures, the strengthening of its economy and civil society, and the avoidance of a backslide into authoritarian rule are necessary steps in the right direction.

U.S. Assistance to the Region

As of 2005, the U.S. combatant commands are working to create regional strategies for their security cooperation efforts throughout the world. The OSD Security Cooperation Strategy and the combatant commands' Theater Security Cooperation Strategies guide the regional strategies. The North Caucasus region is technically within the sphere of EUCOM; however, because the North Caucasus republics are part of the Russian Federation, there is no regional strategy. All assistance to this region goes though Moscow. Nevertheless, EUCOM is in the process of developing a strategy for the Black Sea region called the Black Sea Initiative (BSI), and, together with CENTCOM, EUCOM is also developing a strategy for the Caspian region. Both regional strategies are targeted at territories adjacent to the North Caucasus.

Although the United States does not provide any direct assistance to the republics of the North Caucasus, support provided to adjacent states has the potential to indirectly improve the security situation in the North Caucasus. For example, through the Georgia Train and Equip Program (GTEP), the United States has trained Georgian soldiers to improve Georgia's border security and counterinsurgency capabilities to root out terrorism in the Pankisi Gorge region.

U.S. Special Forces stood up the DoD–sponsored GTEP program during the summer of 2002 and provided battalion-level staff training in addition to training the first battalion of infantry soldiers—about 2,600 soldiers in total. U.S. Marines took over responsibility for the program in December 2002 and trained three battalion-sized light infantry units and one company-sized mechanized unit. Although GTEP ended in 2004, future training events between the U.S. military and Georgian armed forces

---

[97] Tully (2003).

will continue to take place, such as mobile training teams to train additional forces. Military equipment transferred included uniform items, small arms and ammunition, communications gear, training gear, medical gear, fuel, and construction materiel, at a total cost of $64 million over three years.[98] U.S. defense officials have reported that GTEP may have pushed some fighters into Ingushetiya and Dagestan.[99]

Aside from GTEP and its follow-on efforts, EUCOM's Black Sea Initiative and Caspian regional strategies, once developed and executed, have the potential to have a positive impact on the North Caucasus. For example, both programs have a strong focus on Caspian and Black Seas maritime security and aim to train maritime forces of the littoral countries in the identification, search, and seizure of illegal persons or substances.

Implications for U.S. Global Defense Posture

The U.S. strategy of supporting the development of expeditionary capabilities to problematic regions is likely to include a continuation of U.S. military presence in Eurasia. Russia, however, remains wary of such plans. A more permanent U.S. military presence in what Russia sees as its area of influence goes beyond the original understanding that limited U.S. military presence to operations in Afghanistan. In other words, once Operation Enduring Freedom and the mission of the International Security Assistance Force (ISAF) in Afghanistan are completed, U.S. troops are supposedly required to leave, pending a new agreement with the host nations, including consultations with Russia.

Not only does the Global Defense Posture strategy imply problems in bilateral relations with Russia, it also has the potential to draw U.S. forces into regional conflicts in close proximity to the North Caucasus, where they would otherwise not be involved. If U.S. interests were directly threatened, there would be a greater possibility of political or military action, and with that action would come complications with Moscow.

---

[98] "U.S. Ambassador Thanks Marines, GTEP Cadre" (2004).

[99] Moroney interviews with OSD/Joint Staff officials, April 2005.

CHAPTER TWELVE

Case Study: The Colombia-Venezuela Border

Steven Boraz

Introduction

The 1,400-mile-long border separating Colombia and Venezuela is lengthy and diverse. Neither Bogotá nor Caracas have paid sufficient attention to the region, which suffers from extreme poverty and a three-sided armed conflict involving Colombian government forces, Marxist insurgents of the Revolutionary Armed Forces of Colombia (FARC) and the smaller National Liberation Army (ELN), and the groups constituting the United Self Defense Forces of Colombia (AUC).[1] These organizations vie for control of the drug trade in the region and use the porous border to support their illicit transactions, to obtain arms, and to provide safe haven from Colombian forces.

This chapter is organized in four parts. First, it provides a historical context of the border region. The second and third parts examine the factors that make the region "ungoverned" and conducive to the presence of illegal armed groups, based on criteria developed in the introduction to this study. Finally, we derive the implications of the analysis for U.S. strategy toward the region.

Colombia and Venezuela emerged as separate entities in 1830 following the breakup of South American liberator Simon Bolivar's Gran Colombia. In both countries, central authority was contested throughout the nineteenth century. Civil wars were frequent, and the central government's authority was effectively confined to the major political and economic centers. Border areas were generally ignored by the governments in Bogotá and Caracas unless they offered some tangible economic advantage. The discovery of oil in the Gulf of Maracaibo in Venezuela at the turn of the twentieth century accelerated the movement toward state consolidation in that country, which (except for a ten-month period in 1948) took the form of military dictator-

---

[1] The terms "illegal armed groups" or "armed groups" will be used throughout this chapter to denote all three of these groups. The term "insurgent groups" will be used to denote the ELN and the FARC. Many refer to the AUC as the paramilitaries or simply "paras," although we consider the term inappropriate because it denotes a government security force with some military training and equipment, e.g., the Italian Carabinieri or Turkish Jandarma. It should be noted that in the last few years the Bolivarian Liberation Forces (FBL), a group of radical supporters of President Chávez estimated to have 5,000 members, have been increasing their operations and attempts at control portions of territory on the Venezuelan side of the border.

ships until the beginning of the democratic era in 1958. A third period, involving a return to authoritarian rule, appears to have been inaugurated with the consolidation of President Hugo Chávez's populist-authoritarian regime. Oil revenues and, for the most part, stable central governments throughout most of the twentieth century have meant that the Venezuelan state was able to establish a more substantial presence on the border than was the case on the Colombian side.

Colombia's political development followed a different pattern. In Colombia, the nineteenth century was punctuated by civil wars involving liberal and conservatives. After the end of the War of the Thousand Days in 1902, the country settled into a pattern of elections, but intense partisan rivalries generated significant levels of violence. In the ten-year period known as "La Violencia" that began in 1948, more than 200,000 people were killed in politically motivated fighting and massacres. Although the National Front formally put an end to the conflict between liberals and conservatives in 1958, violence in the countryside continued. Marxist guerrilla groups, primarily the FARC and the ELN, emerged from communist self-defense groups operating during La Violencia. Since the mid-1960s, both groups have had a military presence throughout large areas of Colombia, particularly along the country's borders with Panama, Venezuela, and Ecuador.

The ability of these groups, particularly the FARC, to challenge the central government increased significantly in the 1980s and 1990s, as revenue from the drug trade, kidnapping, and extortion enabled them to expand their military capabilities—so much that in the mid-1990s the FARC was able to defeat Colombian government forces in set-piece battles and actually overran some Colombian military bases. President Andrés Pastrana's government (1998–2002) attempted to come to terms with the FARC. The negotiation process involved giving the FARC a 42,000-square-kilometer territory in central Colombia known as the *Despeje,* or cleared area.[2] As a 2001 RAND report predicted, this process failed miserably because the FARC was then able to arm its forces and build and consolidate significant portions of the drug trade.[3] The Pastrana government ended the talks in February 2002, abrogated the agreement for the Despeje, and attempted to assert control in the area through military operations that continue today.

The third party to the Colombian conflict, the AUC, traces its roots to northwestern and central Colombia in the mid-1980s as an anti-kidnapping force with close ties to landowners, cattle ranchers, and drug cartels. It was formally organized under the titular leadership of Carlos Castaño, now presumed dead. (The brothers Fidel and Carlos Castaño established the group to avenge the kidnapping and murder of their

---

[2]   The Despeje is most often referred to as a demilitarized zone, but that is a misnomer because it implies that no armed actors were operating in the area. While the Colombian government did not maintain a military presence within the zone, the FARC most certainly did.

[3]   See Rabasa and Chalk (2001).

father by the FARC. Carlos Castaño became the AUC leader after Fidel's death in an encounter with the FARC in 1996.) The AUC challenges the FARC and ELN for control of the country where coca can be grown and has become a key player in the drug trade. The central government began peace talks with the AUC in 2002; the talks continue today and many AUC combatants have been demobilized.

In many parts of the country, the FARC and AUC (the ELN is increasingly unable to exert authority) operate as the de facto government—collecting taxes, dictating social norms, and controlling agriculture production (chiefly coca). The conflict has increased in intensity since the central government began a military campaign known as Plan Patriota to gain control of the former Despeje and launched other operations throughout the country.

Fighting in the border regions is not just between the illegal armed groups and the government but also among the groups themselves, as they vie for control of drug-processing centers and transit routes that are used to smuggle drugs, weapons, and gasoline to support their respective agendas. Over 100,000 persons have died in the past 25 years as the result of the conflict, and as many as 3.5 million have been internally displaced.[4] All Colombia's neighbors have been affected, but the impact on Venezuela, where many of the displaced Colombians have fled, including an estimated 130,000 near the border, is particularly acute. Kidnapping, extortion, and violence there are on the rise.[5]

Colombia and Venezuela are each other's third-largest trading partners,[6] but the two governments have had an uneasy relationship for many years, stemming from border disputes and concern about the other's intentions.[7] Tensions are higher today because Colombia has not been able to control its border areas, and Venezuelan President Chávez has provided at least tacit and probably material support to the Colombian rebels and has recently embarked on a major arms buildup.[8] This friction, combined with Chávez's hard-line anti-U.S. stance and Bogotá's close coordination with Washington in fighting the drug trade and the insurgency in Colombia, has raised the risk of conflict along the border.

---

[4] Estimates of the number of people displaced by the conflict vary widely. They often do not account for people who return to their villages or those who have moved voluntarily to seek their fortune in the illegal drug industry.

[5] ICG (2004b), p. 15.

[6] After the United States and the European Union.

[7] The two countries have an active dispute over the delimitation of the submarine seabed in the Gulf of Venezuela and its potential for petroleum reserves.

[8] In late 2004 and early 2005, Venezuela signed deals with Russia to purchase 100,000 Kalashnikov-style assault rifles and at least ten helicopters. In 2005, Venezuela also signed a deal with Spain to purchase ten transport aircraft and eight patrol boats.

The Colombia-Venezuela Border as an Ungoverned Territory

The Colombia-Venezuela border region exhibits high levels on most indices of ungovernability, as summarized in Table 12.1. The four variables used are lack of state penetration, lack of monopoly on the use of force, lack of border controls, and external interference. Some of these variables, in turn, are broken down into a number of indicators. The scores are 3 = high; 2 = medium; and 1 = low. Thus, a high score on absence of state institutions indicates a low or nonexistent state presence in the region.

Table 12.1
Indicators of Ungovernability,
Colombia-Venezuela Border

Variable	Score
Lack of state penetration	
Absence of state institutions	3
Lack of physical infrastructure	3
Social and cultural resistance	1
Lack of monopoly of force	
Organized armed groups	3
Criminal networks	3
Population with access to arms	3
Lack of border controls	3
External interference	2

Lack of State Penetration

The border region that includes the Colombian departments of La Guajira, César, Norte de Santander, Arauca, Vichada, and Guainía and the Venezuelan states (equivalents of departments or provinces) of Zulia, Táchira, Apure, and Amazonas (see Figure 12.1) exhibits many of the factors that characterize ungoverned territories.

Apart from the main border towns of Cúcuta (Norte de Santander) and San Cristóbal (Táchira), which host most cross-border trade and where the main highway connecting Bogotá and Caracas runs, "most areas are poor, underdeveloped, underpopulated, inaccessible by road and abandoned by the central state."[9]

Colombia, in particular, has great difficulty in creating a secure environment in many parts of the country.[10] In 2004, Colombia had more than 20,000 murders (a

---

[9]   ICG (2004b), p. 10.

[10]   See Ann C. Mason's excellent article (Mason, 2005).

Figure 12.1
Colombia-Venezuela Border Region

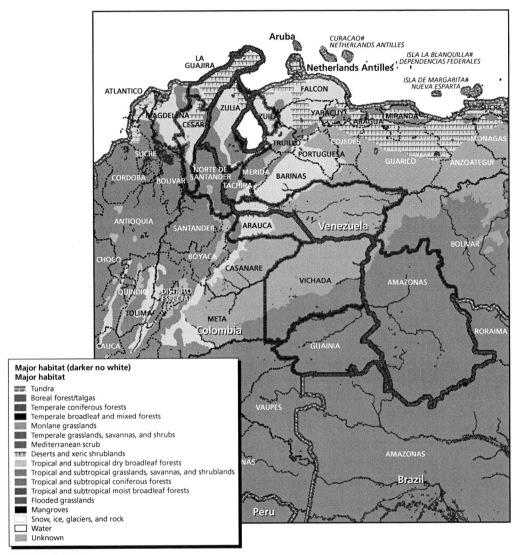

SOURCE: RAND.
RAND *MG561-12.1*

rate of 44.7 per 100,000), 250 massacres,[11] and by far the highest kidnapping rate in
the world, with one person kidnapped every six hours (although the overall trend is
improving under the Álvaro Uribe administration). The situation is particularly severe
in the six border departments, where the overall rates of homicide, kidnapping, armed

---

[11] A massacre in Colombia is technically defined as the homicide of three or more persons in a single event.

conflicts, and attacks against government institutions exceed the national average.[12] The state has only recently increased its presence with the deployment of thousands of military personnel as part of Plan Patriota and increased operations throughout the country, including some in the border departments.[13] The government was able to meet its goal of establishing a presence in each of the country's 1,098 municipalities (equivalent to counties in the United States) in 2004; just three years before, nearly 200 lacked any central presence.

Still, government presence is largely limited to the immediate areas around population centers. All the illegal armed groups attempt to control or influence local governments through threats and intimidation of local officials. One method is to influence local elections. Current and former officials are recognized by the United Nations High Commissioner for Refugees (UNHCR) as having refugee status because of the numerous threats and acts of violence carried out against them. In 2002, 246 mayors were forced to govern their municipalities from Bogotá because of the violence. While most have returned to their municipalities, many cannot venture out of their fortified municipal buildings. In 2004, three sitting mayors and 11 former mayors were killed, six fled the country, and more than 30 former mayors have applied for asylum outside the country. Even when a mayor is able to perform his functions, the illegal armed groups attempt to control municipal spending or levy "taxes" on municipal budgets.[14]

The AUC, in particular, has gained political strength through co-option and violence in the northern border departments of La Guajira, César, and Norte de Santander. For example, the mayors of two departmental capitals, Cúcuta (Norte de Santander) and Riohacha (La Guajira), were arrested last year for alleged ties to AUC. The chief prosecutor in Cúcuta is on the run, after claims that she was an AUC collaborator. Leftist mayors have been executed. The AUC's influence is felt throughout the country as well. Former AUC leader Salvatore Mancuso has claimed that the AUC controls 30 percent of the Colombian Congress.[15]

Beyond security issues, the lack of state presence, combined with crippling poverty, has left populations vulnerable to illegal groups. The Colombian Department of Statistics estimates that 50–60 percent of the population in La Guajira and Norte de Santander; 61-70 percent in César; and an unknown number in Arauca, Vichada, and

---

[12] See Republic of Colombia (2005).

[13] For a superior account of Operations in Arauca province see Robinson (forthcoming). For a detailed current account of each of the military division's activities, see Fundación Seguridad y Democracia (2005).

[14] UNHCR (2005), p. 28; "World News Quick Take" (2004).

[15] See Forero (2004); ICG (2004b), p. 6; and "Politics, Drugs and the Gun" (2005). While this claim might be exaggerated, there is a group of rural legislators who openly support the AUC in varying degrees and who played a significant role in the July 2004 appearance before Congress of three AUC leaders. Even the government itself has admitted that while it has a demobilization program for armed combatants (see the section on the AUC below), there is no policy for dismantling more-complex paramilitary economic, political, and social structures. U.S. Office on Colombia (2004–2005), p. 4.

Guainía live below the poverty line. All of Colombia's population has been affected by the violence and lack of government presence. Even where there is state presence, the effectiveness of state agencies is hampered by interservice rivalry and poor coordination and information-sharing. At a graduation ceremony of Administrative and Security Department (DAS)[16] agents in October 2002, President Uribe noted, "paucity, lack of coordination in government information and, what can be even worse, rivalry between the agencies responsible for collecting and managing this information and intelligence, has been mentioned over and over again as the first and foremost flaw of our public security system."[17]

Corruption and the poorly functioning judicial system make matters worse in Colombia. Colombia ranks 60th out of 146 countries in Transparency International's (TI) Corruption Perceptions index. TI has noted that the public prosecutions office, a body created in 1991 to fight impunity and corruption, was "mired in its worst ever crisis, facing allegations of corruption and of infiltration by paramilitary soldiers and drug traffickers."[18] The Colombian branch of TI notes that 143 of 146 state entities surveyed were at medium or high risk of corruption including the police (medium), the military (medium), and prosecutor's office (high).[19] The judicial system functions poorly, and all actors in it—from judges to victims—face serious risks from illegal armed groups and criminal networks.[20]

State penetration is only slightly better on the Venezuelan side of the border and far from perfect.[21] Venezuelan Army and National Guard troops have been operating in *Teatros de Operaciones* (theaters of operation) since the mid-1990s, with theaters 1 and 2 based in Guasdualito, Apure and La Fría, Táchira, respectively. An additional two theaters were supposedly established in December 2004 in municipalities in Zulia and Táchira, though few specifics are available.[22] Despite the presence of Venezuelan forces in the area, they are limited in their ability to establish control. In January 2005, General Oswaldo Bracho, the commander of Teatro de Operacion 1, lamented his

---

[16] DAS is often referred to as the Colombian equivalent of the CIA; however, its functions encompass activities carried out in the United States by the FBI, the Secret Service, and the former Immigration and Naturalization Service.

[17] Quoted in McDermott (2003).

[18] Transparency International (2005), pp. 133–135.

[19] See *Transparencia Por Colombia*, pp. 10–13.

[20] UNHCR (2005).

[21] Human rights organizations estimate that 76 percent of human rights violations are caused by regional and municipal police. See ICG (2004b), p. 14.

[22] The *Teatros de Operaciones,* created under Venezuelan law and combining military (central government forces) and National Guard (state forces), place an area under military rule. Boraz interviews at U.S. Southern Command (USSOUTHCOM) April 22, 2005. Also see "Venezuela refuerza su frontera con Colombia" (2004); and Delgado (2005).

inability to control the FARC, AUC, or FBL operating in the region because of his limited ability to conduct any maneuver operations. He went on to delineate many other significant problems, including the following:

> Limited ground transport capability; little accessibility and [the] critical state of the area; little willingness of the population to collaborate in intelligence efforts; significant logistic and financial support obtained through drug trafficking, smuggling, and extortion that allows [the illegal groups] to have any amount of money to buy consciences [and] weapons; few job opportunities in the border strip, which gives the population an incentive to get connected with the illegal activities conducted by those subversive groups; proven ineffectiveness of the few bodies of administrative police that operate in all of the area; little presence of the national, state, and municipal powers; and open willingness of the authorities of the public power to accept bribes. . . .[23]

Further south in Amazonas Department, across from the FARC strongholds in Guainía and Vichada, the Venezuelan military bases a 4,000-strong army brigade in Puerto Ayacucho, a city of 150,000; however, their maneuver ability is probably limited.[24]

As pointed out by General Bracho, Venezuela also suffers from security coordination problems. Each municipality has its own police force under command of the elected provincial governor, whereas the central government controls the military, National Guard, the national intelligence service (DISIP) and the police forensic corps (CICPC).[25] This disjointed police and intelligence system contributes to Venezuela's governance problems, especially in the border regions.

Lack of Physical Infrastructure

Numerous municipalities in the border region remain isolated by poor infrastructure. Only 15 percent of rural dwellers have access to telephone services, 62 percent to potable water, and 32 percent to sewage treatment services. Nationally, approximately 6 percent of Colombians are Internet users and 5 percent have access to mobile phones, with the majority of users living in urban areas. In the border regions, the Colombian infrastructure also suffers from regular guerrilla attacks. Colombia did establish an "energy and road" plan to limit attacks, and it has succeeded in reducing sabotage by 44 percent in 2004, including on the Cano Limon-Covenas oil pipeline that runs

---

[23] Alcala (2005).

[24] ICG (2004b), p. 5.

[25] ICG (2004b), p. 14. The National Guard, an active branch of the military, has powers to arrest and is largely responsible for public order, guarding the exterior of key government installations and prisons, conducting counternarcotics operations, monitoring borders, and providing law enforcement in remote areas. The interior and justice ministry controls the CICPC, which conducts most criminal investigations, and the DISIP, which collects intelligence and is responsible for investigating corruption, subversion, and arms trafficking.

through the border departments.[26] Nonetheless, these attacks on infrastructure continue to have a huge impact on the communities in the region, which are sometimes left isolated and without electricity or running water.[27]

Four major road-crossing points connect Colombia and Venezuela: Riohacha–Maracaibo, Cúcuta–San Cristóbal, Arauca–El Amparo, and Puerto Carreño–Puerto Paez (see Figure 12.2). In addition, the populace uses the Arauca, Meta, Guaviare, and Guainía rivers as transportation routes between the two countries (primarily for black market traffic).

Social and Cultural Resistance

The Colombian border region is home to many of the more than 80 indigenous groups that live in Colombia and some of the autonomous regions that they were granted under the 1991 Constitution. The most prominent in the region are the nearly 100,000 Wayuu people in La Guajira, about 10,000 Sikuani in Arauca and Vichada, and about 10,000 Arnauco in César (see Figure 12.3).[28] With alarming frequency, the indigenous populations are the victims of intense fighting in Colombia. Occasionally, however, they are part of it; the Wayuu people, who are well armed, are heavily involved in the contraband trade.[29]

Tax collection is another good example of social resistance. Colombia's ability to collect taxes from its citizens is woefully low. World Bank, IMF, and Colombian experts note that tax evasion is a huge problem in Colombia. In fact, less than 37 percent of the eligible populace pays income taxes and about 28 percent of Colombians feel tax evasion is justified. Land taxes, which are administered by municipal authorities under the Colombian constitution, "are practically ignored by landowners—as local governments are often either too weak to exert coercive power over local elite interests, or are subject to subornation by illegal armed groups."[30]

---

[26] The pipeline is jointly owned by the Colombian Government and U.S. Occidental Petroleum Company. It pumps crude from northeast Arauca Department through Norte de Santander, Cesar, and Magdalena Departments to the Caribbean coast lifting terminal at Covenas.

[27] See *CIA World Factbook* (2005); UNHCR (2005), pp. 18–19; and USAID (2005b).

[28] According to 1993 census figures; Colombia is currently in the process of completing a new census.

[29] ICG (2004b), p. 6.

[30] Quoted in Sweig (2003). Sweig's statement notes that only 740,000 Colombians pay income taxes out of an economically active population of 20 million. The numbers used here are based on the Colombian government's target of 2 million, which excludes a high number of those exempt from taxes. The World Bank indicates that the taxable population is closer to 8 million, though they find "some scope to the lower threshold" of 2 million. See World Bank (2005a), pp. 91–93.

Figure 12.2
Colombia-Venezuela Border—Roads

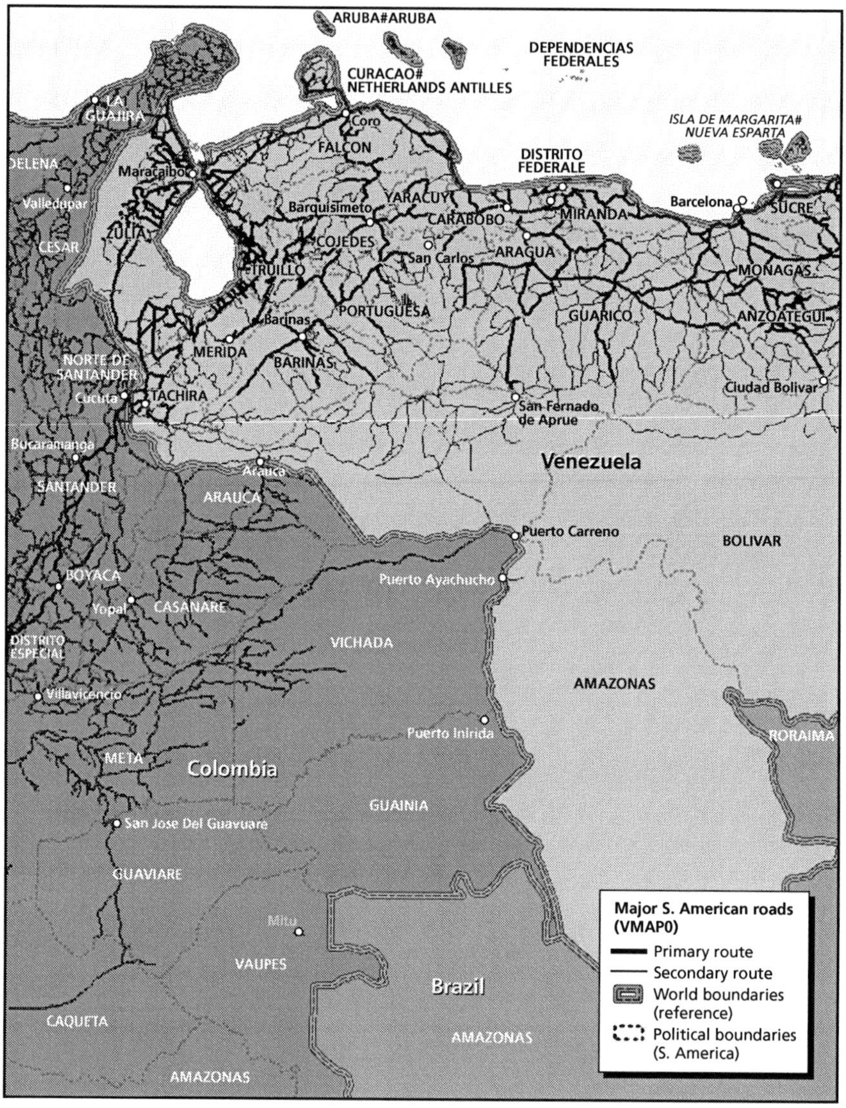

SOURCE: RAND.
RAND MG561-12.2

Lack of Monopoly of Force

Organized Armed Groups[31]

As previously noted, there are three primary illegal armed groups in Colombia, the FARC, the ELN, and the AUC.

---

[31] For description and analysis of the armed groups, see Rabasa and Chalk (2001).

Figure 12.3
Colombia-Venezuela Border—Population

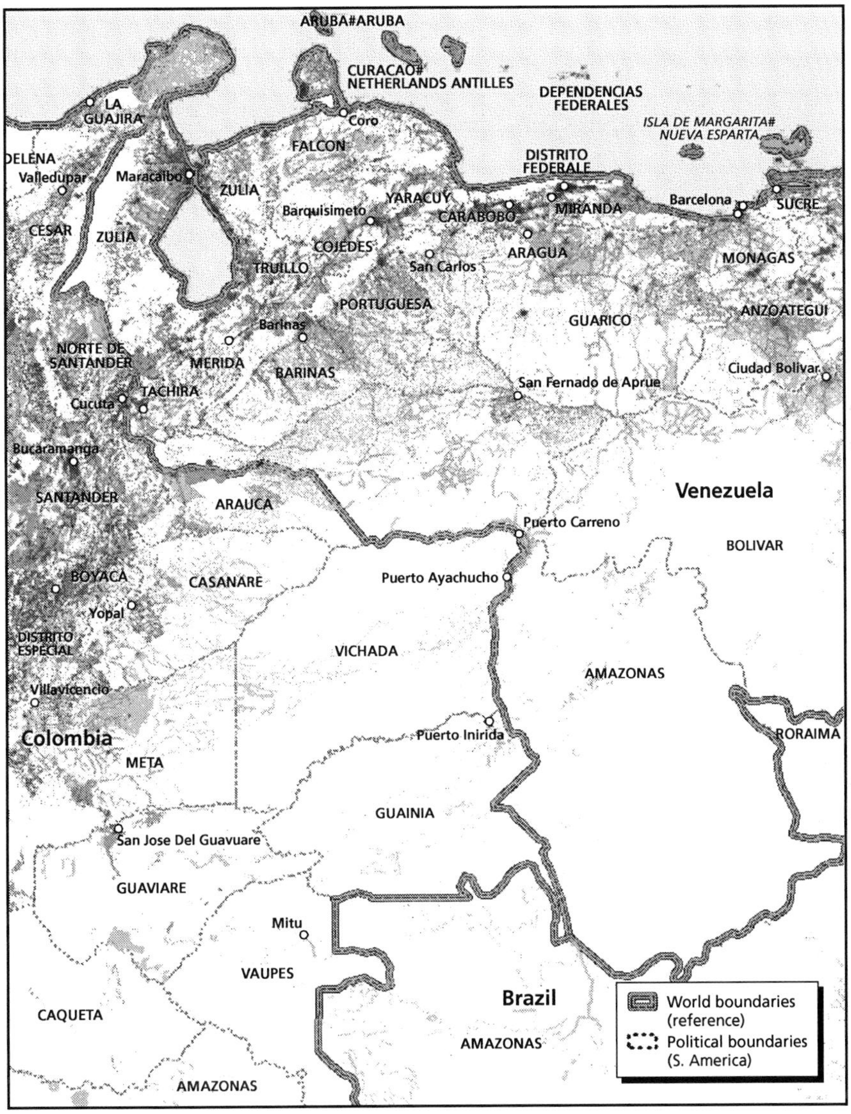

SOURCE: RAND.
RAND *MG561-12.3*

The FARC, established in 1964, is a Marxist (originally Moscow-line) group that follows a Maoist strategy of protracted people's war with the long-term aim of over-throwing the Colombian government and establishing a Marxist state in Colombia. The FARC has been led since its inception 40 years ago by the legendary Manuel Marulanda Vélez (alias Tirofio or Sure Shot), although key strategic decisions are made within a FARC secretariat composed of a cadre of senior FARC leaders. It has an estimated fighting force of 12,000–15,000 organized into seven regional "blocs" across the country. The blocs are further subdivided into fronts in specific regions. Some units are "mobile" in that they are not tied to a specific region and are typically well equipped and better trained; they patrol larger swaths of the countryside. The FARC gained control of significant amounts of territory in the mid- to late 1990s in large part because of increased revenues from the drug trade and the establishment of the Despeje—which, while it lasted, served as the hub of a network of logistical and operational corridors that the FARC had established throughout the country. While the FARC has urban militias and sympathizers, its areas of influence are primarily rural.[32]

The ELN, founded in 1965 by graduates of the University of Santander, combined Cuban revolutionary theory with liberation theology. The ELN has approximately 3,500 fighters, with most of its strength in the northeastern departments of Santander, Norte de Santander, as well as in the coastal department of Bolívar and in the department of Antioquia. It operates in the oil region of northeastern Colombia, attacking the oil infrastructure and deriving income from the oil companies by extortion. The ELN has been reduced in stature over the past ten years because of military losses to Colombian forces, the FARC, and the AUC, and its limited involvement in the drug trade. In early 2004, the ELN initiated negotiations with the government for a peace process. Mexico agreed to mediate, but the ELN backed out of the process, rejecting Mexico as the mediator.[33]

FARC pressure on landowners led the latter to seek out a new partner in illegal self-defense groups. The creation of the Death to Kidnappers (Muerte a Secuestradores) in 1981 and the Self-Defense Forces in the Middle Magdalena Valley paved the way for the establishment of the AUC.[34] The AUC, numbering approximately 10,000–12,000,[35] has succeeded in displacing the FARC from key coca-growing areas by destroying the FARC infrastructure in these areas, a process that usually involves the ruthless killing of suspected FARC sympathizers. The AUC and the central government agreed in December 2002 to a cease-fire and demobilization, which was to be completed by the end of 2005. In July 2005 the Colombian congress passed the Ley de Paz y Justicia (Justice and Peace Law), which established incentives to facilitate the demobilization of the AUC. In some areas of the country, demobilization has taken place, but the AUC is far from unified. AUC organizer Carlos Castaño was probably assassinated in April 2004, and since then other AUC commanders have also been killed. Indeed, not all AUC groups have committed to demobilization, and those who

---

[32] Boraz interviews, U.S. Southern Command (USSOUTHCOM), Miami, Florida, April 22, 2005.

[33] See Rabasa and Chalk (2001), pp. 30–31; ICG (2002a), p. 4; ICG (2004b).

[34] See ICG (2003b), pp. 6–7.

[35] At the start of the peace process, the AUC claimed at least 20,000 fighters.

have demobilized are seemingly still involved in extortion in areas where they once were operating.[36]

In addition to the three primary groups, the People's Liberation Army (EPL) has some active members in the border region, although many of its forces demobilized in a 1990 peace settlement with the government. Since the Colombian military captured its leader, Francisco Caraballo, and other senior leadership in 1994, it has had little influence.[37]

All the illegal armed groups maintain a significant presence and influence on the Colombian side of the border, as depicted below in Figure 12.4 and Table 12.2. The groups also maintain a presence on the Venezuelan side as well, as we describe later in this chapter.

Criminal Networks

Criminal networks pervade the Colombian landscape but are particularly prominent in the border regions. (Crime statistics in the Colombian border departments are given in Table 12.3.) These groups exist to traffic drugs, weapons, and gasoline; to launder money; to extort money; and more. The illegal armed groups all act as criminal networks and are in league with others to profit from various illicit activities to support their war efforts. All of them, particularly the FARC and AUC, have links to organized drug trafficking organizations. In fact, according to the ICG, "the armed groups became increasingly involved [in the drug trade], to the point where they are now present in all coca cultivation areas in the country and monopolize the buying and selling of coca paste in the territories they control."[38]

An interesting phenomenon in Colombia is the emergence of "baby" cartels—the networks that emerged following the Colombian government's dismantling of the infamous Cali and Medellín cartels in the early 1990s. Since the disappearance of the large cartels, between 200 and 400 small organizations have emerged with thousands of members all over the world working in support of the drug trade.[39]

Population with Access to Arms

Legal and illegal arms are abundant in Colombia, with estimates ranging between four and ten million—a number that at the high end translates to one weapon for every 4.5 people in the country.[40] These arms range from handheld pistols, to high-powered

---

[36] Boraz interviews, U.S. Southern Command (USSOUTHCOM), Miami, Florida, April 22, 2005. See also ICG (2004c); "Politics, Drugs and the Gun" (2005); and UNHCR (2005), pp. 9–11.

[37] Rabasa and Chalk (2001), pp. 32–33.

[38] ICG (2005c), p. 4.

[39] It would be an exaggeration to call these groups "networks" because the majority are essentially small family-run businesses. ICG (2005c), p. 11. Also see Cirino, Elizondo, and Ward (2004), p. 20.

[40] Alvarado (2003), p. 12. Also see "From Chaos to Coherence?" (2004).

Figure 12.4
Illegal Armed Group Presence on the Colombia-Venezuela Border

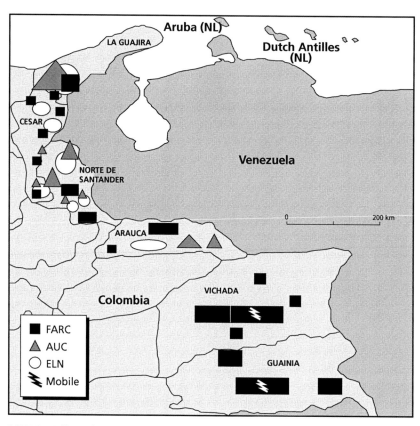

SOURCE: Office of the Vice-President Colombia, Observatorio de Derechos Humanos.
RAND MG561-12.4

rifles, to MANPADs.[41] The most comprehensive study on the subject is Cragin and Hoffman (2003), in which the authors discuss the users, sources, and trafficking pattern of small arms in Colombia. Users include the illegal armed groups, criminals and their organizations, as well as private citizens. Access to these arms is available through all Colombia's porous borders, air and water routes, and from internal sources as well.[42] The internal demand for arms drives a significant legal, gray, and black market.

---

[41] There are numerous reports of the FARC having MANPADs. One highly regarded example is from the UN's *Small Arms Survey* (2004) entitled "Big Issue, Big Problem? MANPADS," p. 88.

[42] Cragin and Hoffman (2003), p. xvii, note that 75 percent of small arms in Colombia come from external sources. During their study, the Despeje was still in effect and the authors noted that 50 percent of all small arms flown into Colombia arrived in the Despeje or on clandestine airstrips in Guainía and Vichada departments.

Table 12.2
Illegal Armed Groups Operating in the Colombian Border Region

Department	Armed Group	Bloc or Front Name
Arauca	AUC	Vencedores de Arauca; Bloque Oriental de Arauca[a]
	FARC	10th Front
	ELN	Quadrilla Domingo Laín
César	AUC	Autodefensas Campesinas del Sur de César; Bloque Central Bolívar
	FARC	19th, 20th, 33rd, 41st, 59th, and Héroes y Mártires de San Rosa
	ELN	6th of December; José Manuel Martínez Quiroz; Camilo Torres
Guainía	FARC	16th Front; Marquetelia Mobile Column[a]
La Guajira	AUC	Frente de Contrainsurgencia Wayuu
	FARC	59th Front
	ELN	Luciano Ariza Front; Gustavo Palmerzano Front
Norte de Santander	AUC	No specified names
	FARC	33rd and 46th fronts
	ELN	Carlos Cacua Guerrero; Juan Fernando Porras; Efraín Pabón Pabón
Vichada	FARC	16th, 39th, Marquetalia Mobile Front;[a] Hernando González Acosta Column;[a] Reynal Méndez Column[a]

SOURCE: Office of the Vice-President Colombia, Observatorio de Derechos Humanos (2005).

[a] Indicates the illegal armed group is a "mobile" group.

Table 12.3
Crime and Drug Trade Statistics in the Colombian Border Region

Department	Homicide Rate per 100,000 (2004)	Kidnappings (2003)	Coca Cultivation in Hectares (2003)	Opium Cultivation in Hectares (2003)	Laboratories Destroyed (2003)
Arauca	144.6	48	539 (–76%)		350
César	52.8	186	negligible	651 (43%)	—-
La Guajira	87.2	90	275 (–22%)	249 (?)	—-
Guainía	2	2	726 (–3%)		0
Norte de Santander	61.4	11	4,471 (–44%)		114
Vichada	15.5	—	3,818 (–22%)		32

SOURCES: Colombia Coca Cultivation Survey, Office of the Vice-President Colombia, *Observatorio de Derechos Humanos* (2005); *Fundación Seguridad y Democracia* (2005).

NOTE: Numbers in parentheses indicate percentage change from previous year.

According to Cragin and Hoffman, the general trend of arms procurement is that small quantities of arms trickle in through more than 100 different smuggling routes in neighboring countries, including 21 from Venezuela; yet there is ample evidence that the illegal groups have significant weapons caches.[43] In addition to the small arms mentioned above, the illegal armed groups, especially the FARC, have become experts at using explosives, mines, and gas-cylinder mortars, techniques the FARC possibly improved upon through their contacts with the Provisional Irish Republican Army.[44] It is clear that access to arms is readily available in Colombia, and the illegal groups have sufficient weapons to challenge the state.

Lack of Border Controls

The frontier is difficult to monitor, and both countries acknowledge the relative ease with which irregulars can cross their shared border.[45] The porous border leads to significant opportunities for the illegal armed groups and criminal networks to smuggle weapons, drugs, and other contraband. Colombia's borders are not secure at all and Bogotá's focus is clearly in prosecuting the ongoing war against the illegal armed groups and the drug trade. In the case of Venezuela, the State Department notes:

> Venezuela continued in 2004 to be unwilling or unable to assert control over its 1,400-mile border with Colombia. Consequently, [the FARC, ELN and AUC] continued to regard Venezuelan territory near the border as a safe area to conduct cross-border incursions, transship arms and drugs, rest, and secure logistical supplies, as well as to commit kidnappings and extortion for profit.[46]

Venezuela did increase border security and temporarily shut the legal border crossings in January 2005 following an incident in which a senior FARC official, Ricardo Granda, was abducted in Caracas by bounty hunters and transported to Colombia. Additionally, Venezuela has between 20,000 and 30,000 troops operating in the Teatros de Operaciones that are designed to support border security—although, as pointed out above, their capability is limited. The Venezuelan reaction suggests that the Chávez

---

[43] The Colombian government has acknowledged at least 98 routes, and Cragin and Hoffman highlighted at least three additional routes (p. 18, pp. 47–50). The most recent arms cache was discovered in May 2005 in Caqueta province and included more than 500,000 rounds of ammunition, as well as grenades and other explosives. See "Colombia Makes 'Record Arms Haul'" (2005).

[44] These are mortars that use oxygen cylinders to increase their range and lethality. With respect to mines, the FARC have become experts at drawing Colombian military forces into ambushes that force them to traverse minefields and have used an iterative process to hone the technique. Boraz interviews, U.S. Southern Command (USSOUTHCOM), Miami, Florida, April 22, 2005.

[45] Sanchez (2005).

[46] U.S. Department of State (2004b), p. 86.

government has some ability to enforce border controls more vigorously if it chooses.[47] On a positive note, the two countries do have a "verification commission," which is a bilateral instrument used to facilitate investigations of security incidents along the border. Unfortunately, the commission has rarely been used by the two countries to deal with both military and illegal armed group activities in the border region.

Generally, the border can be subdivided into three sections that support various licit and illicit activities (which will be further documented in the subsequent portion of this chapter on income-producing activities). These sections are in the north (La Guajira and César departments in Colombia and Zulia state in Venezuela), where the main transportation artery is the road connecting Riohacha, Colombia, to Maracaibo, Venezuela; a central/mountain section that connects Cúcuta and Arauca, Colombia, with San Cristóbal and El Amparo, Venezuela; and a southern section with the main crossing point at Puerto Carreño, Colombia/Puerto Paez, Venezuela.

In the northern section, the Wayuus, who live on both sides of the border and take advantage of dual citizenship, transport all sorts of contraband across the border. Their primary market is in gasoline where they profit from a significant price difference.[48] The Wayuus, however, have lost some of their contraband business to the AUC who have made serious inroads in the region and on several occasions have had armed clashes with the Wayuus. The north is also home to important drug and gun smuggling routes where traffickers take advantage of port access in both countries and of Lake Maracaibo, where drug cartels, some associated with the AUC, are said to have purchased large amounts of land to facilitate movement of their product. There is also arms trafficking via ports on the Gulf of Venezuela into the city of Maicao, Colombia. According to a Colombian military commander in Riohacha, the border is literally impossible to control without air support.[49]

The central section of the border presents the best transportation routes for legal and illegal trade. Cúcuta, the most active border trading town, is the primary route used by migrants to flee the fighting and probably hosts a great deal of illegal activity as well. After significant violence in the town over the past several years, the AUC is now believed to control most of the illegal routes now, transporting chemical drug precursors and arms, and laundering money. However, other areas of Norte de Santander and Arauca facilitate at least the smuggling of small arms.[50] The southern portion of the border also presents known entry points for arms and export points for drugs from the

[47] The border was only reopened after a meeting between the two presidents and the protestations of the governor of Guajira and the citizens in the area, who were substantially affected by the closure. See "Presidente Colombia visita frontera con Venezuela en medio de crisis" (2005); and Sanchez (2005).

[48] In July 2004, gasoline was $.02 a liter in Venezuela and $.46 a liter in Colombia. See Ceasar (2004).

[49] See ICG (2004b), p. 6. Also see Cragin and Hoffman (2003), p. 33; and ICG (2004c), p. 4.

[50] As Cragin and Hoffman (2003, p. 33) point out, "much of the border is swampland, making the entry points fairly amorphous, a problem that is particularly acute in Venezuela's Táchira Department."

jungle regions in Guainía and Vichada, across from Venezuela's Amazonas province, where the FARC is very influential.[51]

External Interference

While Venezuela does not have troops stationed in Colombia proper,[52] President Chávez has ignored FARC and ELN cross-border activity and tolerates their camps within Venezuela, which are used to support logistics, training, care for their wounded, recruiting and propaganda. Chávez is ideologically close to these groups—his V Republic Movement is part of the Sao Paolo Forum, a Cuban-inspired international organization of Latin American radical groups, together with the FARC and the ELN—and he has refused to call them terrorists.

Colombian insurgent groups operate on both sides of the frontier. They have received support from Venezuelan forces, and numerous sources have documented as much.[53] In January 2005, Colombian President Uribe sent Chávez tape recordings documenting activity of the FARC and ELN on the Venezuelan side of the border and the complicity of Venezuelan forces in these actions. In one case, the head of the FARC's 33rd front was literally welcomed with open arms by Venezuelan military members at a meeting in 2000 allegedly coordinated by Venezuelan General Rafael Román Betancur, who was then head of Teatro de Operaciones 2. Other information revealed that both ELN and FARC forces were allowed to transport supplies across the border and received safe passage in order to collect extortion money in exchange for bribes. All the illegal armed groups trade cocaine for weapons with the Venezuelan military and National Guard at the going rate of one kilo of cocaine for one automatic rifle.[54]

Additionally, information from a Venezuelan intelligence report entitled "Presence of Colombian Subversive Organizations in the Venezuelan Border Area" documents FARC, ELN, and EPL presence in Venezuela. According to the report, these groups operate to influence Venezuelan politics, look for logistical and intelligence support, infiltrate state financial institutions, recruit, create popular militias or networks in urban and marginalized areas, promote antimilitary and antistate rhetoric, run kidnapping and extortion rings, establish linkages with other terrorists in urban

---

[51] ICG (2004b), p. 5.

[52] Venezuelan forces occasionally cross the Colombian border to prosecute engagements with illegal groups, and the border has been the scene of numerous armed incidents over the years. Boraz interviews, USSOUTHCOM, Miami, Florida, April 22, 2005.

[53] These reports include "Relaciones peligrosas" (2002); Linda Robinson (2003), pp. 20–22; Cirino, Elizondo, and Ward (2004), pp. 30, 37; Fundación Seguridad y Democracia (2004), p. 5; ICG, (2004b); "Ex guerrilleros acusan a la GN (2005); and Varase (2005).

[54] See "Relaciones peligrosas" (2002); "Ex guerrilleros acusan a la GN" (2005); and Varase (2005).

centers, and increase drug cultivation.[55] And although the Venezuelan intelligence report did not explicitly mention the AUC or the FBL, those groups certainly have a presence in the border region. Table 12.4 summarizes the locations of insurgent groups in Venezuela.

Since the middle of 2004, there appears to have been a potential shift in Venezuelan toleration of activities by illegal Colombian groups. Seventeen FARC combatants captured after a June 2004 firefight along the border were deported to Colombia; Venezuela arrested a high-ranking FARC official in February 2005, extraditing him to Colombia in April; and the Venezuelan National Guard killed two and injured nine in a firefight with the FARC in March 2005.[56]

Table 12.4
Insurgent Groups' Areas of Operations in Venezuela

Insurgent Group	Venezuelan States	Fronts or Blocs
ELN	Apure, Barinas, Mérida, Táchira, Zulia	Domingo Laín Sáenz, Efraín Pabón Pabón, Juan Fernando Porras Martínez, Claudia Isabel Escobar Jerez, Carlos Armando Cagua Guerrero, José Martínez Quiroz y Camilo Torres Restrepo
FARC	Amazonas, Apure, Barinas, Mérida, Táchira, Zulia,	Fronts 10, 16, 20, 21, 33, 41, and 45
EPL	Táchira, Zulia	Libardo Moro Toro, Ernesto Rojas, Virgilio Ernesto
AUC	Zulia	Unknown

SOURCES: *Quinto Día*, January 21–28, 2005; *El Universal*, January 28, 2005.

Mitigating Factors

The situation in Colombian, although severe, is not as dire as it might appear. A number of factors have helped to ameliorate the situation. First, new operational and tactical approaches on the part of the Colombian military since 1998 have produced improved performance, especially an increased tempo of counterinsurgency actions. The closing of the Despeje in February 2002 deprived the FARC of its main sanctuary and disrupted critical logistics and troop mobility corridors. The election of President Uribe, who ran a campaign promising the eradication of the illegal armed groups, with more than 53 percent of the vote on the first run of the ballot (a rarity in Colombia), signaled

---

[55] Varase (2005).

[56] "Dos GN heridos durante enfrentamientos en la frontera" (2004); "Venezuela deporta hacia Colombia 17 personas (2004), p. 3; "Farc y Eln combaten en frontera venezolana" (2005); "Policía confirma que detenido en Venezuela la semana pasada" (2005); "Tribunal Supremo de Venezuela" (2005).

the emergence of a consensus around the need to mobilize the resources of the state and society against the armed groups. Uribe promulgated his Defense and Democratic and Security Policy, a detailed plan for consolidating state control, protecting the population, eliminating the drug business in Colombia, maintaining a dissuasive capability against insurgent forces, and promoting efficiency, transparency, and accountability in government.[57] Finally, the United States changed its policy, which had previously limited the use of U.S.-provided equipment to antidrug operations, freeing it up for use for counterinsurgency operations.

The Colombian government's efforts to reassert control over the country began in force in mid-2003, with the launching of Plan Patriota. Colombian government forces began by securing the region in and around Bogotá, where the effort has largely been seen as successful.[58] Defense spending increased 30 percent from 2001 to 2004, overall troop strength was increased by more than 80,000 troops, and thousands were operating in the field against the illegal armed groups. The government has succeeded in establishing a presence in every one of Colombia's municipalities and garnered successes against the FARC—reducing FARC mobility corridors, causing FARC desertion rates to go up by one-third, and shrinking the organization's overall strength from 18,000 to 12,000.[59] Other security indicators were very positive in 2004 compared with just two years before: homicides were down by 30 percent; massacres, by 61 percent; kidnapping, by 51 percent; overall terrorist attacks, by 56 percent; and the number of internally displaced persons, by 41 percent. These numbers reflect the lowest level of violence in Colombia since 1989.[60]

The Uribe administration has also focused on fiscal reform policies, including the restructuring of Colombia's tax system. Colombia adopted a new tax structure in 2002, which included a value added tax (VAT), and a one-time wealth tax in which it collected more than $800 million.[61] In December 2003, Colombia's congress approved increases in the wealth tax and the financial transaction tax. However, in December 2004, the Uribe administration withdrew his third tax reform proposal because of strong congressional opposition, despite months of negotiations. Overall, the results

---

[57] See *Política de Defensa y Seguridad Democrática* (2003).

[58] Securing Bogotá was both important and symbolic because the FARC had set off bombs and fired mortars near the inauguration site and the Colombian Congress building on the day of Uribe's inauguration.

[59] The Colombian government assesses the size to be 12,000. Other analysts believe FARC strength to be closer to 15,000.

[60] Noriega (2005).

[61] The "security tax" was a one-time payment of 1.2 percent of liquid assets worth more than US$50,000. See ICG (2002c). Also see U.S. Department of State (2005c).

of tax reform and collection have been impressive: Colombia has boosted tax revenues from around 12 percent of GDP in 2000 to 20.3 percent in 2004.[62]

Bogotá has not resorted exclusively to violence. As mentioned previously, the Colombian government and the AUC are implementing a demobilization agreement. The government has also pursued peace talks with the ELN.[63] There are some problems facing the state with this process. Some NGOs and members of the U.S. Congress have derided the Justice and Peace Law as too lenient on the paramilitaries. Critics claim that the law does not adequately account for gross violations of human rights, fails to dismantle the AUC structures, and does not affect the assets of the AUC members who have amassed considerable wealth from the drug trade. On a visit to Colombia in April 2005, Secretary of State Condoleezza Rice hoped a law would be enacted "that will effectively dismantle illegal armed groups, bring justice and reparation to victims, and punish those guilty of major crimes and atrocities."[64] In addition, most of the demobilized troops lack skills, and the $156-per-month stipend the state gives for an 18-month period hardly seems substantial to keep these ex-fighters away from crime.[65] Still, however imperfect, this process is far better than the alternative, in which the AUC forces are in the field challenging the central authority.

Backed by U.S. aid, Colombia has established 38 justice offices that help to provide access to the Colombian justice system for poor Colombians. As of May 2005, these institutions had handled nearly three million cases. In addition, there are 35 oral trial courtrooms and thousands of new lawyers, judges, and public defenders who are building a system designed to reduce impunity, provide transparency, and accelerate the traditionally slow judicial process.[66]

Despite this progress, the FARC was able to launch successful attacks against military and civilian targets in 2005 in Norte de Santander, Cundinamarca, Cauca, and Arauca departments, inflicting the worst losses on the military under the Uribe administration. Since the start of 2005, at least 120 soldiers and civilians have been killed in FARC attacks. In February 2005, Raul Reyes, the FARC's second-in-command, said the spate of attacks was "only the start of what is coming," though it is yet to be seen if this is rhetoric or, in fact, a counteroffensive strategy on the part of the FARC.[67]

---

[62] The constitutional court has also intervened in Colombia's fiscal policy, striking down a portion of the VAT provisions from 2002. See IMF (2005a), pp. 4, 8; and IMF (2005b), p. 5.

[63] See ICG (2005b).

[64] See U.S. Department of State (2005d).

[65] Of those demobilized, 12.5 percent are illiterate, 50 percent have no more than a fifth-grade education, and 88 percent own no possessions whatsoever. See Van Dongen (2005).

[66] Farrar (2005a).

[67] See, for example, Molinski (2005); and Webb-Vidal (2005).

Attributes of the Colombia-Venezuela Border Conducive to the Presence of Insurgent Groups

The border area exhibits some important aspects that may be conducive to the presence of insurgents and other illegal armed groups, and could afford opportunities to international extremist and terrorist organizations (see Table 12.5). The scores are 3 = high; 2 = medium; and 1 = low.

Adequacy of Infrastructure and Operational Access

As noted in the above section on infrastructure, the border regions do not have sophisticated communications architectures, banking networks, or transportation hubs. However, they are not entirely without technology, especially in the northern and central regions, particularly in Venezuela. Maracaibo, Venezuela's second-largest city, is a major oil shipment location and terrorists can gain access to the Caribbean from ports on Lake Maracaibo. Internet cafes also exist in major cities such as San Cristóbal, Maracaibo, and Valencia.[68] Colombia's north includes "special customs zones," which offer tax-free incentives for trade in a variety of goods in Maicao, Uribia, and Manaure (all in La Guajira Department).[69] Cúcuta in Colombia and Maracaibo, Valencia, and Puerto Ayacucho in Venezuela all have international airports.

Table 12.5
Indicators of Conduciveness to Terrorist Presence, Colombia-Venezuela Border

Variable	Score
Adequacy of infrastructure	
Communications	2
Financial infrastructure	1
Transportation	1
Operational access	2
Favorable demographics	
Presence of extremist groups	3
Supporting social norms	1
Preexisting state of violence	3
Informal social networks	1
Criminal syndicates	3
Sources of income	3
Invisibility	2

---

[68] LatinWorld.com, Cybercafés in the Latin World (undated).

[69] See "Special Trade Regimes in Colombia" (undated).

The illegal armed groups have had years to develop routes to support their activities, and they are able to generate literally billions of dollars in illicit transactions.
Existing infrastructure, such as the Pan-American Highway and developed ports on
both the Caribbean Sea and the Pacific Ocean, provide significant opportunities for
terrorists, insurgents, and criminal networks to move materiel. All the groups are adept
at information operations and each maintains a Web site—several, in the case of the
AUC.

Illegal combatants and criminal syndicates have historically been able to use
waterways and roadways to attack municipal centers and government forces and have
easy access to larger cities within Colombia and Venezuela where U.S. interests could
be attacked. On a worrisome note, the Chávez government has liberally provided identity cards to people from a variety of countries, primarily Colombia, but also such
Middle East nations as Syria, Egypt, Pakistan, and Lebanon. Some of these identity
cards have been used to obtain Venezuelan passports and even American visas.[70]

Income-Producing Activities

Perhaps more than any other region discussed in this book, illegal groups are capable of
producing substantial income in the Colombian environment. Revenues from the drug
trade, kidnapping, extortion, arms trafficking, and gasoline smuggling are as high as
$5 billion annually, although not all this is tied specifically to the border region.[71]

The Drug Trade

Colombia produces nearly 80 percent of world's cocaine and provides an estimated one
half of the U.S. supply of heroin. In 2004, potential cocaine production was estimated
at 460 metric tons and potential heroin production at 7.8 metric tons. Revenue in the
drug trade, estimated to be between $1.5 and $2.5 billion annually, can be raised at
three stages: cultivation, processing, and trafficking. The FARC, AUC, and the ELN
all have stakes in the business, though the ELN's is limited. The United Nations estimates that "out of 189 municipalities where coca cultivation has been detected, guerrilla groups" (without specifying which ones) "may be found in 162 and paramilitaries in 86." Official sources also consider the FARC to be present in 90 percent of the
poppy-growing regions, although it frequently must confront AUC in these areas.[72]

FARC involvement in the drug trade is chiefly at the cultivation level. FARC
commanders are said to lend farmers money to plant coca. They then buy all the coca
base, which is sold to selected drug cartels. The FARC provides protection for labora-

---

[70] Robinson (2003).

[71] See *Colombia: Country Profile* (2004), p. 11.

[72] See UNODC (2004), p. 39; ICG (2005c), pp. 3, 11; and U.S. Department of State (2005c).

tories at the processing level, has increasingly developed its own laboratories, and has tried to become more involved at the higher-profit trafficking level. The FARC also generates revenue from its tax, or *gramaje,*[73] on protection and services to drug producers and smugglers. FARC fronts involved in the drug trade in the border region include the 19th and 59th fronts operating in the Sierra Nevada de Santa Marta and the 41st in the Serranía of Perija in La Guajira and César Departments; the 33rd front in the Catatumbo region in Norte del Santander; the 10th, 28th, and 45th fronts in Arauca; the 39th front in Vichada; the 1st and 16th operating in Guanía; and mobile brigades that operate throughout the region. Depending on the source, estimates note that the FARC derives half of its income from the drug trade, estimated at between $150 and $500 million a year.[74] A very thorough International Crisis Group report estimated the funds gained from the drug trade by the FARC and the AUC to be about $100 million each, still quite a substantial sum.[75]

The AUC has deep historical links to drug cartels and is believed to be more involved at each stage of the drug trade than is the FARC. The U.S. ambassador to Colombia has stated that the AUC controls up to 40 percent of the drug trade in Colombia. The AUC likely runs its own refining facilities and has built up an international drug-trafficking network. Like the FARC, the AUC has a presence throughout most of the drug-growing areas in the border region and consistently challenges the FARC for control of the cultivation fields, laboratories, and trafficking routes. The Heroes del Tayrona operate in the Sierra Nevada de Santa Marta; Bloque Gabarra and Bloque Catatumbo, in the Catatumbo region; and the Autodefensas del Meta y Vichada, in Vichada and northern Meta. AUC leaders also have sought alliances in La Guajira to gain control over ports in Portete and Bahia Honda. The AUC draws an estimated 70 percent of its total financing, an estimated $190 million, from the drug trade.[76]

There has been drug trafficking in Venezuela for years; however, it now appears that some of the efforts in Colombia are pushing the trade to the east. During 2004, there was an increase in illicit cultivation in the Serranía del Perijá, and drug cartels have begun to position themselves more permanently on the Venezuelan side of the border.[77]

Even U.S. forces are not immune to the lure of illicit enrichment through the drug trade. The most recent case, in 2005, involved five soldiers' attempt to smuggle

---

[73] The FARC maintain a precise schedule of fees for production; protection of laboratories and coca and poppy fields; airfield security; and cocaine shipments—be they by land, air, or water.

[74] See Rabasa and Chalk (2001), p. 32; and ICG (2005c), p. 19.

[75] See ICG (2005c), p. 19.

[76] The 70 percent figure comes from a statement in 2000 by then-AUC leader Carlos Castaño. ICG (2005c), pp. 1, 13–15, 19.

[77] "Observatorio de Seguridad Suramericano" (2004), p. 5.

about 35 pounds of cocaine into the United States. The most infamous occurred in 2000 when the wife of the military group commander was arrested for attempting to send $700,000 worth of heroin to New York and the commander himself was sentenced to five months in prison because he knew of his wife's attempts to launder money and run drugs.[78]

Other Sources of Income

Each of the illegal armed groups, as well as other criminal organizations, also fills its coffers through kidnapping, extortion, and trafficking in contraband, chiefly arms and gasoline. Colombia remains the kidnapping capital of the world, accounting for 1,441 registered kidnappings in 2004, a significant decrease from levels seen in 2003 (2,000) and 2002 (2,986). Kidnapping generated an estimated $230 million in 2000,[79] and while the numbers are down significantly, this activity still generates a significant amount of income. Although some attribute most kidnappings to the FARC and ELN, the Colombia-based think tank Fundación Seguridad & Democracia asserts that the illegal armed groups were responsible for fewer than half of the kidnappings (FARC 21 percent, AUC 10 percent, ELN 10 percent), although 27 percent could not be attributed to any group. This is an indication that other criminal organizations are becoming more involved in the activity. The ELN, which generates as much as 60 percent of its revenues from kidnapping and has suffered significant losses to government forces and the AUC over the last few years, can attribute its weakened position to a more than seven-fold decline in its share of kidnappings from 2001 to 2004.[80]

Extortion has also been lucrative, netting an estimated $300 million a year. Each of the armed groups participates in this activity, which target the oil industry and municipal governments.[81] As operations against kidnapping have improved, the levels of extortion are reportedly rising.

Both kidnapping and extortion have spilled over to Venezuela. In Táchira, there were 50 kidnappings between January and August 2004, whereas 50 occurred in 2003, 41 in 2002, and 23 in 2001. Also, in oil-rich Zulia, 108 people were kidnapped between 2001 and mid-2004. Most of this can be attributed to the FARC, ELN, and a rise in overall criminal activity, although some of the kidnappings have been attributed to the FBL.

Smuggling gasoline, which is an important ingredient in cocaine processing, is also a lucrative business, netting between $75 and $90 million per year; upward of 60,000 barrels per day enter the Colombian market illegally. According to the former

---

[78] "U.S. Soldiers Arrested for Colombian Cocaine Plot" (2005).

[79] See Pax Christi-International (Netherlands) (2001), Section 2.9.

[80] The ELN kidnapped about 1,000 people in 2001; these numbers were down to about 140 in 2004. See Fundación Seguridad y Democracia (2004), pp. 6, 55.

[81] Pax Christi-International (Netherlands) (2001), Section 2.9.

head of the Colombian armed forces, the AUC is responsible for 98 percent of the theft but FARC and other actors play a role as well.[82]

Favorable Demographics

Components of the variable we refer to as favorable demographics include the presence of extremist groups, a preexisting state of violence, and the existence of criminal networks are clearly evident in the frontier and have already been explored in this chapter. In this section, we will touch on the issue of supportive social norms and investigate the presence of foreign extremist groups in the region.

Supportive Social Norms

The AUC, ELN, and FARC are not popular organizations in Colombia: a Gallup poll conducted in September 2001 noted unfavorable views of 83 percent for the AUC and 91 percent for the ELN and FARC. That said, 8 percent of the populace viewed the AUC favorably and 2 percent viewed the ELN and FARC favorably.[83] Those numbers translate to about 3.6 million supporters for the AUC and about 900,000 each for the ELN and FARC. Clearly, the consensus is against these organizations, but there is also a base of support that has helped sustain the FARC and ELN for 40 years and elements of the AUC for nearly 25.

In Venezuela, President Chávez and his circle have clearly expressed an affinity with revolutionary groups and have sought to align Venezuela with nations hostile to the United States, including Libya, Iran, China, and especially Cuba. Chávez has cancelled numerous military-to-military training activities with the United States and recently ended a 35-year-old military assistance program. His tacit approval of FARC and ELN camps within Venezuela may bode well for other international terrorists, some of whom are already operating in Venezuela (see below). The FBL and the People's Army in Arms (EPA) are operating in Venezuela now. Both groups are supposedly designed to help repel what Chávez has claimed to be an impending U.S. invasion. For his part, Chávez has denied supporting either of these organizations, though many question whether he is providing at least tacit support for them[84]

Presence of Foreign Extremist Groups

Aside from the FARC, ELN, and AUC, there are international terrorist organizations that receive at least funding and material support from the border region. Hamas and Lebanese Hezbollah receive some support from backers in the sizable Muslim popu-

---

[82] "Observatorio de Seguridad Suramericano" (2004), p. 5; ICG (2005c), p. 14; Castro (undated).

[83] Gallup results available in *Fuerzas Militares de cara al Siglo XXI* (1998–2001), p. 43.

[84] See "Guerrilla venezolana antiyanqui" (2005); and Toothaker (2005).

lations in the area and in Maicao, Colombia, and Margarita Island and Maracaibo, Venezuela. Maicao, in La Guajira, is home to about 8,000 persons of Arab origin out of a total population of about 58,000. This population is of Lebanese, Syrian, and Palestinian origin. Originally most were Christians, but in recent decades there has been an influx of Muslims, both Sunnis and Shi'ites. Arabs are believed to control 70 percent of the commerce in the special duty-free city and reportedly send 10–30 percent of their profits to Hezbollah, utilizing banks in Maracaibo or Panama. Hezbollah also has established arms trafficking and money-laundering networks in Maicao. These groups reportedly also have ties to Colombian drug cartels. An Egyptian terrorist with possible ties to al-Qaeda, Muhammad Ubayd Abd-al-Al, was suspected of hiding out in Maicao in the late 1990s. The State Department's list of terrorists promulgated after 9/11 included the names of three individuals who lived in Maicao, and one Maicao-based family was suspected of being financially involved in the 1993 World Trade Center bombing.[85]

Banks in Maracaibo (and elsewhere in Zulia state) are important centers for laundering funds for narcotics traffickers in Colombia and terrorist groups. These activities have raised the concern of Venezuelan and Interpol authorities.[86] Margarita Island, a duty-free zone off the northern coast of Venezuela with a sizable Muslim population, is home to radical groups as well. Venezuelan authorities have broken up radical cells, arrested several individuals with terrorist ties on the island, and investigated ties to money-laundering operations based there. Additionally, support cells for Hamas and Hezbollah, which raise money for their parent organizations in the Middle East, are all present on Margarita Island.[87]

Elsewhere in Venezuela, U.S. officials asked about Hakim Mamad al Diab Fatah, a Venezuelan who had been deported from the United States in 2002, and his possible links to September 11 hijackers. Sheik Ibrahim bin Abdul Aziz runs a radical mosque in Caracas. One of the mosque's officials was arrested in London in February 2003 for carrying a grenade on a Caracas–London flight.[88]

Invisibility

Invisibility manifests itself at two levels: the attention to a particular region by the intelligence and counterterrorist agencies of the United States and other major powers, and the ability to blend in with populations and to remain outside the purview of the

---

[85] See Castillo (2001); and *A Global Overview of Narcotics-Funded Terrorist And Other Extremist Groups* (2002), pp. 44–45, 49.

[86] *A Global Overview* (2002).

[87] Robinson (2003).

[88] Robinson (2003).

security services. With regard to the first criterion, Colombia does not rank high on the U.S. agenda in the global war on terrorism, which is focused on al-Qaeda and the global jihadist movement. On the other hand, the activities of extremist groups in the region have not slipped under the radar of policymakers in the United States and Colombia. President Uribe has made security his number-one priority, and he is expending significant political and economic capital to combat the insurgency and the drug trade. The United States has provided over $4.0 billion in aid to Colombia since 2000, making Colombia the third-highest recipient of U.S. assistance behind Israel and Egypt. The 2006 aid request is for approximately $550 million.

With regard to the second aspect of invisibility, the FARC, AUC, and ELN all have the means and ability to blend in with the Colombian populace because they are themselves Colombian. Their ability to use intimidation, bribery, and their knowledge of areas in which they have been operating for years or decades allows them to evade government forces. The fact that the all the groups, especially the FARC and ELN, seem to be able to operate in Venezuela gives them an increased measure of security. With respect to Islamic terrorist organizations, Muslim communities in Venezuela and Colombia, as noted above, offer the opportunity to disguise their presence. Venezuelan President Chávez's anti-U.S. orientation, long-standing ties to Middle East extremists, and interest in strategic alliances with radical states such as Iran may afford Middle East extremist and terrorist organizations space to operate in Venezuela.

U.S. Policy and Programs

As noted above, Colombia receives a significant amount of aid (see Table 12.6) from the United States, which supports a plethora of programs designed to strengthen democracy; support Colombia's fight against the FARC, ELN, and AUC; fight drug trafficking and the organizations that take part in it; promote the rule of law and human rights; and foster development and address humanitarian needs. The majority of that funding is under the Andean Counterdrug Initiative (ACI) umbrella which provides $152 million for alternative development, humanitarian assistance, judicial reform, and institution building, along with $311 million for narcotics interdiction and eradication programs that include training and operational support for the air activities of the army and national police. IMET provides significant training for the Colombian military that emphasizes human rights and democratic control. FMF funds are designed to help Colombia extend its authority throughout the country and provide a wide variety of assistance for training, supplies, repair parts, maintenance, infrastructure, and specialized equipment such as night-vision goggles and communications gear. FMF supports all manner of Colombia's military, be they operating in Plan Patriota, protecting the Cano Limon-Covenas oil pipeline, or interdicting drugs and illegal groups on the water or in the air. Nonproliferation, anti-terrorism, demining, and related programs (NADR), Anti-

Table 12.6
U.S. Aid to Colombia (in thousands of U.S. dollars)

Account	FY 2004 Actual	FY 2005 Estimate	FY 2006 Request
ACI	473,900	462,767	463,000
FMF	98,450	99,200	90,000
IMET	1,676	1,700	1,700
NADR-ATA	—	3,920	3,920
NADR-SALW	—	200	200

SOURCE: Congressional Budget Justification for FY06 Foreign
Operations, p. 507.

Terrorist Assistance, and Small Arms and Light Weapon (SA/LW) programs assist in stopping the trafficking of illicit arms across Colombian borders, the destruction of small arms, and the continued implementation of an Anti-Kidnapping Initiative (AKI) that supports the Colombian government's military and police anti-kidnapping units, the Unified Action Groups for Personal Liberty (GAULA).[89]

The implications for U.S. policy regarding Colombia's plight are well known and generally understood within policy circles. The United States has provided significant support to Plan Colombia, the Pastrana administration's six-year roadmap developed in 1999 for strengthening democracy, combating the narcotics industry and those involved in it, pursuing economic growth and development, and promoting a peace process with the illegal groups.[90] President Uribe's administration fully endorsed Plan Colombia on taking office and furthered many of its principles through his own Democratic Security Policy. Plan Colombia is due to expire in 2005 and, while it may not be renewed in name, its broad goals will be continued. The overall view of Plan Colombia within the U.S. administration is that it has been a success, given the positive indicators of security implementation, the reduced coca crop, and the increase in drug interdiction. At a May 2005 hearing before the House International Relations Committee entitled "Plan Colombia: Major Successes and New Challenges," several government witnesses, who were accompanied by Colombian officials, extolled the successes made in Colombia since the initiation of the plan in 1999. Unfortunately, no witnesses were invited to offer an alternative view, despite the myriad organizations with expertise in the Colombia situation.[91]

Had critics been able to attend, they would have pointed to four significant issues regarding U.S. support to Colombia: First, funding has been skewed significantly

---

[89] See U.S. Department of State (2005e), pp. 507–510.

[90] Though many claim that the United States had far too large a role in the development of the plan.

[91] The witnesses included members of Congress, the Office of National Drug Control Policy (ONDCP), the State Department, USAID, and the Department of Homeland Security.

toward military solutions. Second, the overall impact on the U.S. drug trade has been insignificant because there has been virtually no change in the price, purity, and availability of cocaine in U.S. markets.[92] Third, Colombian security forces are still major human rights abusers. Fourth, the counternarcotics programs in Colombia have actually had negative consequences for the civilian population and for the promotion of democracy in general.[93]

Those who bring these points up are correct in doing so; however, the overall impact of U.S. support to Plan Colombia and stability in the region in general is helping Colombia regain control of its borders. Even the Colombian economy has been improving. Most important, Colombia's democracy could be called "resurgent" in that it is no longer in the sort of danger it was in earlier this decade, due in large part to U.S. support. In short, U.S. backing of Colombia has been largely successful and should continue at high levels to support democracy; combat drugs, terrorism, and corruption; and support a wide array of development programs to combat some of the underlying causes of the insurgency. But funding must be adjusted appropriately to address some of the root causes of insurgency and spent more wisely with regard to drug interdiction.

Policy Implications and Recommendations

Recommendations for the U.S. Government

Continued support for Colombia should be based on needed reform throughout all government entities, especially with regard to the rule of law, transparency and respect for human rights, and the critical need to support development.

As pointed out previously, some criticize the inadequate balance between military and developmental aid. The United States often responds to this criticism by pointing out that its military aid primarily supports high-end equipment. The United States would do well to carry out a careful analysis of its spending priorities to determine the levels of both effectiveness and efficiency at achieving policy goals. This analysis can then provide the basis for striking the right balance between security and development.

Improving government efficiency and coordination has been perhaps the top issue in the Uribe administration, and U.S. policies should support every effort to increase

---

[92] ONDCP's National Drug Threat Assessment for 2005 notes: "Key indicators of domestic cocaine availability show stable or slightly *increased* availability in drug markets throughout the country despite interagency estimates that indicate sharp decreases in the amount of cocaine transported toward the United States from South America in 2003"(emphasis added). See U.S. Department of Justice (2005), p. 1.

[93] It should be noted that during their testimony policymakers did mention the need to produce better development opportunities. They discussed issues regarding human rights abuses by the Colombian military and the reasons why cocaine price and purity have not changed in the United States.

transparency, work to continue the progress made in the judicial system, and ensure that those organizations involved in the fight against drugs and insurgents have the tools to coordinate their efforts. Too much evidence exists that this is not the case regarding the Colombian military and intelligence organizations.[94] It is a positive indicator that the Uribe administration is well aware of the problem, and a great deal of support should be provided for improving coordination of information and operations throughout the government.

And although the justice system is improving, there is still a long way to go in addressing impunity. Colombia must be able to show that it is willing and able to hold accountable those who commit violations of human rights. Policymakers already have the necessary legal apparatus to condition aid based on Colombia's pursuit of human rights abusers.

This is especially true regarding the paramilitaries and the current peace processes because it will set the precedent for any future negotiations with the ELN and the FARC. Extradition to the United States has been a substantial roadblock to the dialogue, and Washington should strongly consider dropping extradition requests in exchange for other, more important concessions. Rather, our efforts should ensure that these paramilitary armies are off the field, that a Colombian solution regarding accountability for atrocities committed consistent with internationally acceptable conventions is developed, that illegal groups provide information which results in further dismantling of their organizations and ties to drug traffickers, that their status as noncombatants is verifiable, and that their assets are seized. U.S. policy should also ensure that reintegration programs provide opportunities for former fighters so that they do not return to the battlefield or simply join the ranks of the drug traffickers. This process will lay the groundwork for future peace initiatives. It is hugely important in establishing credibility for the government and will sow the seeds of reconciliation throughout the country.

Economically, there is little doubt that many of the underlying causes that lend support to insurgencies—poverty, marginalization, a lack of infrastructure—need to be addressed. The Colombian government is likely on the right path in a macroeconomic sense, but it must provide much greater opportunities for rural and indigenous populations, and U.S aid should support these efforts. A restructuring of the tax system and tax administration would also be a worthwhile effort for Colombia, and U.S. policy should encourage this. The United States should also help Colombia develop strict asset forfeiture laws that could help finance military operations, alternative development, and land reform. As eradication efforts continue, Colombia must be able to provide alternative development and offer resettlement of populations when necessary. Finally, Bogotá also needs to consider the effect that stopping the drug trade may have on the Colombian economy and develop appropriate mitigating strategies.

---

[94] The most definitive work on the subject is Villamizar (2004).

The United States should strongly reconsider its aerial spraying campaign. While recent testimony indicated overall coca cultivation had been reduced by 33 percent, from almost 170,000 hectares in 2001 to about 114,000 at the end of 2004, it would be more accurate to note that the estimated coca crop was 122,500 hectares at the end of 1999 when the spraying program as part of Plan Colombia began in earnest.[95] Since then, a total of 564,500 hectares have been sprayed with the overall net reduction of only about 8,000 hectares, greater than a 70:1 ratio of required spraying to reduction in potential coca cultivation.[96] Even at the high end, this means that it required the spraying of 470,500 hectares to yield a reduction of only 56,000 hectares, greater than an 8:1 ratio.

Thus, our analysis questions whether the results of the aerial eradication program justify the significant expenditures. Further, most evidence shows that those who grow plants have already devised ways to circumvent the spraying. They replant quickly, clean the plants after they have been sprayed, or simply relocated to national parks, where spraying is not allowed. The Catatumbo region in Norte de Santander is one of the more prominent cases in point.[97] In the case of the crop growers, much more activity needs to take place on the ground to remove coca and replace it with other crops. Governors and representatives from the chief coca-growing departments in Colombia met in May 2005 to promote their support for manual eradication. They emphasized that manual eradication does not harm the environment nor create displacement of people who are forced to move when spraying kills their legal crops.[98] In fact, just as in a conventional war, an air campaign is insufficient to permanently roll back the enemy.

A comprehensive regional border strategy needs to be developed that will help Panama, Brazil, Peru, and especially Ecuador and Venezuela combat drug trafficking, organized crime, and the spillover effects from the illegal armed groups. This should include information-sharing and required technical equipment to more accurately assess and combat cross-border illicit activity. Altthough some of this occurs already, greater emphasis should be placed—particularly with regard to border security—on involving Colombia's neighbors in an approach that is as multilateral as possible.

While this book is not designed specifically to look at the issues of drug consumption in the United States, we would be remiss if we did not at least mention that pro-

---

[95] Government Accounting Office (2003), p. 3; Farrar (2005a). A hectare is 2.47 acres.

[96] Spraying was conducted on 42,000 hectares in 1999, 47,000 in 2000, 84,250 in 2001, 122,695 in 2002, 127,000 in 2003 and 136,555 in 2004. See the Colombia section of the South American portion of U.S. Department of State (2005c).

[97] The Colombian congress is currently debating lifting the ban on spraying in national parks.

[98] The governors were from Meta, Putumayo, Arauca, and Amazonas. Delegations from Guainía, Caquetá, Casanare, Vaupés, and Vichada also participated. See "Gobernadores apoyan" (2005).

grams designed to reduce demand here in the United States are just as critical as those that concern eradication and interdiction.

Finally, the United States has great deal of opportunity to work with Canada, the EU, the UN, the World Bank, the IMF, and myriad NGOs to help Colombia achieve a long-lasting peace, reduce poverty, honor human rights, and improve its democratic institutions and practices. There is little doubt that a secure, democratic Colombia, free from insurgency, criminal networks, and drug trafficking, can only have a positive impact on regional stability and on U.S. security.

Recommendations for the Defense Department and the U.S. Air Force

The Colombian military is engaged in combat on a daily basis and has been in the field fighting an offensive war since Plan Patriota began in earnest. Prior to that, Colombian forces have had significant combat experience for upward of 40 years, although military operations were often defensive or counteroffensive in nature. There are already numerous programs in which various DoD components are involved with the Colombian military. Currently, the U.S. military presence in Colombia consists of about 200 trainers and about 200 other personnel providing reconnaissance support and leadership and planning guidance to the Colombian military.[99] Planning and Assistance Training Teams (PATTs) assist Colombian brigade and division and regional joint command headquarters in operational planning, logistics, communication, and intelligence. Other areas of training include support to counternarcotics brigades, helicopter flight and maintenance, oil pipeline protection, and riverine capabilities, among others.[100]

Partner-Country Capabilities. Because of this operational environment and training support, the Colombian armed forces, consisting of more than 360,000 soldiers and police, is a significant fighting force, probably the most capable in Latin America. However, as the Congressional Budget Justification notes, Colombian security forces still require significant U.S. assistance for counternarcotics and counterterrorism, especially in key areas of mobility, intelligence, sustainment, and training, due to the increased operational pace demanded by President Uribe's proactive military strategy.[101]

U.S. Air Force Support Role. The Air Force, and indeed all of DoD, have a continuing role to play in all these areas. Some potential areas of support for the Air Force include the following:

---

[99] Rhem (2005). Until early fiscal 2005, Congress had imposed a 400-troop cap on U.S. forces in Colombia. The cap is now 800 service members.

[100] Turner (2005).

[101] U.S. Department of State (2005e), p. 509.

Counternarcotics and Counterterrorism. Colombia's counternarcotics battalions already receive a great deal of training and support from the Army's 7th Special Forces Group. The Air Force has provided some highly specialized training by the 6th Special Operations Squadron (SOS). The 6th SOS conducted training in joint insertion and extraction missions with night-vision goggles (NVG). This was the first ever use of NVG capability in a joint combat search and rescue mission in Colombia.[102] Continued provision of sophisticated technology and capabilities would improve the Colombian military's ability to target and defeat illegal armed groups.

Mobility and Sustainment. The Air Force could provide analysis and know-how to improve the capability of the Colombian air force and army to train and equip personnel and sustain air activity. An Air Force review of current air bridges and flight coordination and planning could be essential in improving Colombian air mobility and sustainability. Because Colombian military successes since the late 1990s have depended on air-ground coordination to a large extent, contingency plans should be made to provide the Colombian military with countermeasures against surface-to-air missiles, should the FARC begin to deploy and use these weapons.

Intelligence. The Air Force could also help Colombia develop the best possible intelligence, surveillance, and reconnaissance (ISR) routes to support combat, counterdrug intervention, and border security.

Civil Affairs. As in the case of all civil conflicts, the dominant feature of the Colombian conflict is political. The government's strategy is to separate the insurgents from the population and to restore confidence in the government by establishing a tangible government presence in areas previously neglected by Bogotá. Civil affairs is a critical component of this strategy. The Colombian military is already providing medical support in various departments throughout the country as well as supporting construction of infrastructure. These efforts could be expanded. Greater linkages with local communities in areas of military operations could increase support for the Colombian government and military, bring about better cooperation, and facilitate force protection. Infrastructure development is also critical to crop substitution policies designed to wean the population in coca-growing areas from coca cultivation.

Interagency Coordination. The most common criticism of the military and the Colombian government in general is that they are unable to work together in a coordinated manner. Programs such as those that exist under the purview of Colombia's Coordination Center for Integrated Action could be expanded. Under the military's restructuring in the late 1990s, a joint operations construct was put in place to support better command, control, and coordination. However, this construct has not always yielded the desired results because of bureaucratic infighting and mistrust.

---

[102] Montgomery (2005).

CHAPTER THIRTEEN

Case Study: The Guatemala-Chiapas Border

Steven Boraz

Introduction

The border separating Guatemala and Mexico is a more than 600-mile-long frontier that is plagued by poverty, violence, corruption, and an overall lack of state presence. It represents an increasingly utilized and important transit zone for the smuggling of drugs, people, and other contraband that often reach the United States. Both Guatemala and Mexico face significant challenges in enforcing security in a region that is increasingly coming under the control of such nonstate actors as gangs, criminal organizations, and vigilante groups. These groups are able to exploit state weakness to increase their illicit activity and gain control of important transit zones. The potential for these criminal elements to achieve dominance in the border region appears to be far greater than that of either the central authorities in Guatemala City or Mexico City.

This chapter is organized in four parts. First, it provides a brief historical context in the region, with particular attention to the effects of Guatemala's internal armed conflict in the 1980s and 1990s. The second and third parts of this chapter evaluate the region's ungovernability and conduciveness to terrorist operations based on criteria developed in the introduction to this study and focusing on Guatemala as the weaker state. Finally, we present implications and recommendations for policy to support U.S. strategy in the region.

The border region encompasses the departments of San Marcos, Huehuetenango, Quiché, and Petén in Guatemala (Alta Verapaz is also very close to the border) and the states of Chiapas, Tabasco, and Campeche in Mexico (see Figure 13.1). The indigenous populations on both sides of the border have cultural, ethnic, and linguistic ties dating back to the Mayan civilization. During Spanish colonial rule, the region was a part of the Captaincy-General of Guatemala, a separately functioning entity within the viceroyalty of New Spain that stretched from Chiapas and part of the Yucatán south to Costa Rica. Until well into the twentieth century, the national governments in Mexico City and Guatemala City exercised tenuous control over the border area. Great Mayan rebellions broke out in the nineteenth century on the Mexican side of the border, the "caste wars" of Yucatán (1847–1901) and Chiapas (1867–1869). In

Figure 13.1
The Guatemala-Mexico Border Area

SOURCE: Microsoft MapPoint, © 2005 Microsoft Corp.
RAND *MG561-13.1*

more recent years, both sides of the border have seen conflict, most significantly on the Guatemalan side.

The antecedent of Guatemala's civil war was the overthrow of General Jorge Ubico's dictatorship by the democratic revolution of 1944. A civilian president, Juan José Arévalo, was elected in 1945 for a six-year term marked by social reform policies that were continued under the successive term of Colonel Jacobo Arbenz. Arbenz instituted an agrarian reform law and legalized the Communist Guatemalan Labor Party (PGT). Under Arbenz, the PGT extended its control to key labor unions, peasant organizations, and government sectors. A U.S.-backed coup deposed Arbenz in 1954, and successive military leaders continued increasingly autocratic rule. In 1960, a group of junior officers mounted a failed revolt against the government of General Miguel Ydígoras Fuentes. This group became the nucleus of the forces that were in armed insurrection against the government at various times over the next 36 years.

The insurgent groups that emerged from the failed 1960 revolt, the Revolutionary Armed Forces (FAR), Guerrilla Army of the Poor (EGP), and Revolutionary Movement November 13 (MR-13), engaged in kidnappings and violent tactics, and the government responded with selective and intense repression. According to the Commission for Historical Clarification, established by the United Nations in 1994 as part of the Guatemalan peace process, there were three sides of the conflict: the military government, the insurgent groups, and the various ethnic Mayan communities that were victimized by both. Beside the army, police, and rural and urban patrols (government-sanctioned paramilitary civilian groups), there were death squads involved in counter-insurgency operations. The insurgent groups were factionalized until their unification in 1981 as the National Guatemalan Revolutionary Unity (URNG). The indigenous peoples were mostly members of different subgroups of Maya speakers. They were generally sympathetic to the insurgents but were often forced into cooperation and victimized by both sides. Guerrillas requesting food and support or new members often used the threat of violence; the military, upon receiving any intelligence of cooperation with guerrillas, often massacred entire villages.[1]

By the mid-1980s, the guerrillas had been effectively defeated and the conflict entered a period of abatement.[2] In 1985, a new constitution was written and elections were held in which the Christian Democratic Party candidate, Vinicio Cerezo, won the presidency with 70 percent of the vote and took office in January 1986. These developments ushered in a slow process of reconciliation, which reached fruition in the signing of the Peace Accords between the government and the URNG in December 1996.

All told, the civil war took the lives of more than 200,000 people and displaced more than 1 million. Those living in the border regions were affected disproportionately (see Figure 13.2). Although the war ended nearly ten years ago, Guatemala is still coming to terms with the aftermath of the decades-long conflict.

In Mexico's most neglected state of Chiapas, the Zapatista Army of National Liberation (EZLN)[3] took over the state capital, San Cristóbal de las Casas, in January 1994, the day that the North American Free Trade Agrement (NAFTA) took effect. The Mexican government moved quickly to put down the rebellion, and the EZLN guerillas fled to the jungles of Chiapas. The EZLN leader and now folk hero, Subcommander Marcos, began an information campaign and forced the Mexican government into talks that lasted through 1998.[4] The conflict eventually resulted in the ratification by the Mexican congress of the so-called COCOPA law, which essentially banned

---

[1] See "The Peace Accord and the Commission for Historical Clarification" (undated).

[2] See Conflict Early Warning Systems (CEWS) (undated). According to the CEWS document, the rebels' new tactics aimed at obtaining international support. The military campaigns against the indigenous population and the support of the indigenous population for the rebels contributed to their acceptance by international groups and organizations.

[3] The Zapatistas take their name from revolutionary hero Emiliano Zapata who was from Morelos State, near Mexico City.

[4] See Ronfeldt et al. (1998).

Figure 13.2
Massacres per 10,000 Inhabitants

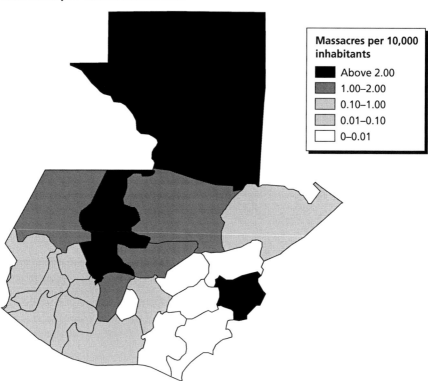

SOURCE: U.N. UNOSAT Guatemala maps, accessible online at http://unosat.web.cern.ch/
unosat/asp/prod_free.asp?id=20
NOTE: A massacre is defined in Guatemala as a killing of five or more persons in one
event.
RAND *MG561-13.2*

racism against Mexico's indigenous persons but fell well short of indigenous demands
for autonomy.[5]

The Guatemala-Chiapas Border as Ungoverned Territory

The Guatemala-Chiapas border region exhibits high levels of ungovernability, as
discussed throughout this section and summarized in Table 13.1. Scores are 1 = low;
2 = medium; and 3 = high.

---

[5]   This law was highly controversial. In its original form submitted by President Vicente Fox in 2001, it did call
for economic autonomous zones, increased legal rights, and reconciliation from the Mexican government, but it
was changed significantly by the Mexican congress before its passage. The controversy wound up in the supreme
court in 2002, and the court ruled that it would not overturn the modifications the congress made.

Table 13.1
Indicators of Ungovernability,
Guatemala-Mexico Border

Variable	Score
Lack of state penetration	
Absence of state institutions	3
Lack of physical infrastructure	3
Social and cultural resistance	2
Lack of monopoly of force	
Organized armed groups	3
Criminal networks	3
Population with access to arms	3
Lack of border controls	3
External interference	1

Lack of State Penetration

Absence of State Institutions

The Guatemala-Mexico frontier remains largely isolated from the central governments of both countries. Inhabitants of the border region live in extraordinary poverty, and their cities and town are awash in crime and corruption. Poor governance is endemic in Guatemala and more so in the rural border departments. A recent World Bank study notes that Guatemala performs at or near the bottom of several governance indicators, including political stability, government effectiveness, regulatory quality, rule of law, control of corruption, and accountability. Worse, government effectiveness and the rule of law have been on a steady decline since 2002.[6]

Though mentioned above, corruption is worthy of highlighting. The 2004 Global Corruption Perceptions Index ranked Guatemala 122nd out of 145 countries with a score of 2.2, continuing a downward trend. The populace does not trust the government or the security services, a legacy of the internal conflict and of rampant corruption. This lack of trust has severely hampered the growth of legitimate governmental institutions.

The crime that ravages Guatemala is by far the gravest threat to the country's stability and affects three out of every four citizens.[7] The government is virtually unable to prosecute anyone, so criminals act with impunity. According to the leading Guatemala City daily, 95 percent of crimes in 2003 did not result in any jail time for the perpetrators.[8] As the State Department noted in a travel warning:

---

[6] World Bank (2005b), p. 71.

[7] See Garzaro and Barillas (2005).

[8] Lara (2004).

There is little evidence of effective investigation or arrest and prosecution of the perpetrators. . . . The police suffer from corruption, inexperience and lack of funds and the judicial system is weak, overworked, and inefficient. . . . Criminals, at times armed with an impressive array of weapons, know there is little chance they will be caught and punished.[9]

One noteworthy statistic on the effect that crime has had on Guatemala is this: The material losses associated with it are close to 6.8 percent of GNP, the highest in Latin America. Moreover, "this estimate is conservative [as] it does not include indirect costs such as medical attention of the injured, the loss of capital, the negative impact to foreign investment and the costs of deterrence."[10]

Because of Guatemala's inability to control crime, private security firms have moved in to fill the void. Guatemalan sources note that there are at least 120 licensed security firms operating in Guatemala, another 119 awaiting certification, and an untold number of unlicensed firms. These firms employ about 60,000 personnel—by contrast, Guatemala's national police force (PNC) only employs slightly more than 18,000 and the military approximately 15,000.[11]

Beyond security issues, the lack of state presence is shown in numerous other indicators: Half the population suffers from chronic malnutrition; 56 percent live in poverty and 16 percent in extreme poverty; the average years of schooling are the lowest in Central America (3.5 years) and only 18 percent complete secondary school education.[12] In short, the entire country is bordering on "ungovernability" and even the United Nations notes that Guatemala has fallen into "lawlessness."[13]

On the Mexican side of the border, conditions are only marginally better. For the most part, Chiapas is a neglected state, and the central government has only recently attempted to exert greater authority and presence. Poverty is at the highest level in Mexico; children attend school for less than six years; illiteracy is at nearly 12 percent; and infrastructure services, such as sewage, water, garbage collection, highways, and electricity, are the worst in Mexico.[14] Corruption is also a significant problem in

---

[9]   U.S. Department of State (2005f).

[10]   World Bank (2005b), p. 84.

[11]   Guatemalan President Berger reduced the military from about 27,000 to 15,000 in 2004 in compliance with the Guatemalan Peace Accords. See Millman (2003), p. A.14; Seijo (2005a); and World Bank (2005b), p. 85.

[12]   Poverty is three times higher in rural areas. With respect to average years of schooling, Nicaragua is next-lowest in Central America at 4.6 years, and Panama has the highest rate at 8.6 years. Regarding the secondary education rate, Guatemala is exceptionally low by hemispheric standards: Paraguay is second lowest at 32 percent. Other comparisons include El Salvador at 55 percent, Panama at 58 percent, and Mexico at 68 percent. See World Bank (2005b), pp. vi, 2, 32–25, 120.

[13]   Quoted in Cirino, Elizondo, and Ward (2004), p. 42.

[14]   Fuentes and Montes (2003), pp. 12, 24.

Mexico, which was ranked 64th at 3.6 (holding steady for the previous three years) on Transparency International's Corruption Perception Index.

The prevalence of crime is an indicator of absence or lack of effectiveness of law enforcement institutions. Table 13.2 shows Guatemala's crime statistics in 2003. The murder rate, at 37.9 per 100,000 in 2003 has increased 50 percent since 2000. In Guatemala City, there were 2,397 murders in the six months from September 2004 to March 2005; that is a rate near 96 per 100,000. Of those, only 40 cases have been brought to trial, and only six perpetrators have seen the inside of a prison.[15]

Table 13.2
Crime Statistics in Guatemala, 2003

	Homicides	Attempted Homicides	Robberies/ Assaults	Sexual Assaults	Kidnappings
Totals	4,244	6,560	18,083	379	37

SOURCE: Guatemalan Instituto Nacional de Estadisticas at http://www.ine.gob.gt/.

Lack of Physical Infrastructure

Two major highways connect Guatemala and Mexico, and many lesser roads are crossing points. Overall, there are only about 14,000 kilometers of main and secondary roads in Guatemala, which represent about 1.3 kilometers per 1,000 people, the lowest rate in Central America. Roads are not available to 13 percent of the population, and even fewer are available in the areas around the border where poverty is highest. In the rural areas, only 56 percent of households have electricity and 44 percent have access to phone lines.[16]

Guatemala has four active ports: Santo Tomás de Castilla and Puerto Barrios on the Atlantic Coast, and Puerto Quetzal and Puerto Champerico on the Pacific Coast (though neither can handle deepwater traffic). In total, these ports handled 21 percent of commerce in Central America, second only to Panama at 38 percent. Puerto Barrios, which is run by a private firm, has been ranked as the second most reliable port in Central America.

Social and Cultural Resistance

The Guatemalan central authority's ability to govern is also complicated by complex topography and cultural and linguistic diversity—23 languages are spoken in this country of about 12.7 million, although Spanish is the official language. Indigenous peoples, primarily Mayas but also Xincas and Garífuna, make up between 40 percent

---

[15] Based on 2002 census from the Instituto Nacional de Estadística de Guatemala (Guatemalan National Institute of Statistics), the total population was 11.2 million and population in Guatemala City was 2.5 million. See "El mayor riesgo" (2004), p. 2; Erikson and Lapointe (2005); Seijo (2005b).

[16] World Bank (2005b), pp. 94, 104.

and 45 percent of the population.[17] The fact that so many of these people were the victims of violence during the armed conflict, their high level of social exclusion (poverty, lack of access to education, discrimination) and the ties within many indigenous communities to the Marxist insurgent group URNG, all contribute to social resistance to the government's efforts to extend its control.

Figure 13.3 shows the linguistic diversity and social exclusion areas in Guatemala. Note that the border departments are most affected.

This social resistance manifests itself in strikes and protests in which the populace comes into conflict with government forces. This activity included the March 2005 protests against the government's ratification of the Central American Free Trade Agreement (CAFTA). The protests originally lasted for more than a week but resurfaced later in the month, extending to 12 of the 22 departments in the country as well as Guatemala City. In June 2004, national strikes occurred against tax proposals, CAFTA, and government evictions of indigenous families from disputed lands,.[18] The government of President Oscar Berger, who was elected in 2003, is extremely unpopular: A recent poll indicated that 74 percent of the populace disapproved of his administration.[19] The reasons for Berger's lack of public support vary, but the poll results point to the larger issue of people's alienation from the central authorities.

Tax collection is another problem for the central government especially with regard to the country's elite, who have been historically averse to paying taxes.[20] The 1996 Peace Accords established targets for tax increases from approximately 8.0 percent of GDP in 1996 to 12 percent by 2004 (originally targeted for 2000), which is well below the 23 percent average paid in Latin America, the 19.5 percent paid in Mexico, and the 25.4 percent paid in the United States. However, the ratio had reached only 10.3 percent of

---

[17] Population figures based on the Instituto Nacional de Estadística de Guatemala (INE).

[18] See Garmendia (2004); Grupo Política y Poderes (2004); Daniel (2005); and del Cid (2005).

[19] "Saca Es El Presidente" (2005).

[20] Guatemala's tax system was reformed in May 2004. It includes a progressive income tax (ISR); a value added tax (IVA); an alternative income tax on businesses (IETAAP), which replaced the previous IEMA that was found to be unconstitutional (see note 24 below), as well as other import/export tariffs (DA) and various taxes on items such as gasoline, electricity, alcohol, etc. A reformed tax system was presented to the congress in May 2004. Guatemala is characterized by a high concentration of wealth, with 64 percent of the income in the hands of only 20 percent of the population. It is the second most unequal country in Latin America. See United Nations Development Programme (2005–2008).

Figure 13.3
Linguistic Communities in Guatemala and Social Exclusion

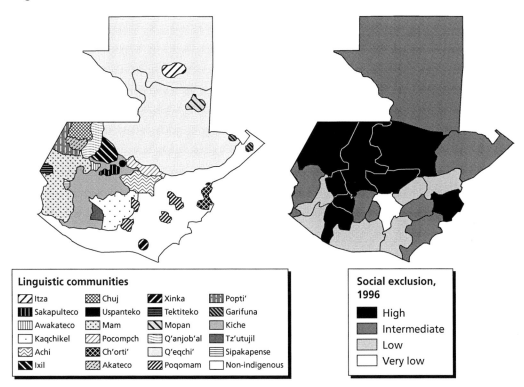

Linguistic communities

Itza	Chuj	Xinka	Popti'
Sakapulteco	Uspanteko	Tektiteko	Garifuna
Awakateco	Mam	Mopan	Kiche
Kaqchikel	Pocompch	Q'anjob'al	Tz'utujil
Achi	Ch'orti'	Q'eqchi'	Sipakapense
Ixil	Akateco	Poqomam	Non-indigenous

Social exclusion, 1996

- High
- Intermediate
- Low
- Very low

SOURCE: U.N. UNOSAT Guatemala maps, accessible online at http://unosat.web.cern.ch/unosat/asp/prod_free.asp?id=20

RAND *MG561-13.3*

GDP at the end 2004.[21] Guatemalan court decisions and poor administration in the tax collection agency (SAT) have also hampered the government's ability to collect revenue.[22]

---

[21] World Bank (2005b), p. 13; Canadian International Development Agency (2006).

[22] In 2003, Guatemala's supreme court called the IEMA unconstitutional and ruled against the states' ability to collect additional revenues from the VAT. These two decisions may have cost Guatemala about 2 percent of GDP in revenues for 2003. See USAID (2004). The government has worked hard at reimplementing the IEMA tax and has even received some support from the very conservative and powerful business trade association, CACIF. SAT was created in 1998, as a decentralized state entity, a status that gives it functional, economic, financial, technical and administrative autonomy. In 2001, SAT collected 97 percent of Guatemala's fiscal revenues. See World Bank (2005b), p. 100. Guatemala named a new SAT administrator, Willy Zapata, in 2004, who, by all accounts, has made headway in establishing credibility in the SAT.

Lack of Monopoly of Force

Organized Armed Groups and Criminal Networks

Gangs, or *maras,* as they are known throughout Central America, pose a staggering problem to security throughout the region, and Guatemala is no exception. The most often cited numbers originate from the Salvadoran national police. Their estimates total over 69,000 gang members, 14,000 of them in Guatemala, organized into 920 gangs in the region. However, some estimates range as high as 500,000 gang members in Central America. One Guatemalan NGO estimates that there are more than 180,000 gang members, 32,000 in the four border departments.[23] Although that estimate is undoubtedly high, even the low number provided by the Salvadoran National Police puts the gangs on nearly equal footing as the Guatemalan police.[24]

The most prominent organized gangs in the region and Guatemala are Mara Salvatrucha (MS-13) and Mara 18.[25] Interestingly, both gangs have their roots in the streets of Los Angeles. According to most figures, the civil wars in Central America displaced more than 2 million people from El Salvador, Guatemala, and Nicaragua, as well as Honduras (though not by war). As many of these young refugees arrived in the United States, they had to confront existing gangs, especially in Los Angeles. The Salvadorans, many of whom had military training and were excluded from the existing Latin gangs, including the 18th Street Gang, formed MS-13. Following the enactment of tough antigang laws in California, federal antimigration laws, and after the civil wars in El Salvador and Guatemala ended (in 1992 and 1996 respectively), arrested gang members began to be deported back to their home countries (after having served their prison sentences). In fact, between 2000 and 2004 an estimated 20,000 criminals were deported to the countries of their birth, in some cases having been stripped of their citizenship.[26] With no family or support structure to return to, these men started the organizations they had become comfortable in and associated with in the United States.

MS-13 found fertile recruiting ground in the staggering poverty of Central America. Now there are upward of 30,000–50,000 MS-13 members throughout Central America, chiefly in El Salvador, Guatemala, and Honduras. Mara 18, created in similar fashion and still part of the 18th St. Gang, is MS-13's chief rival; there are about 10,000–20,000 members in the Central American region. Gang membership in Gua-

---

[23] The source for these high numbers is Asociación para la Prevención del Delito (APREDE) a gang-rehabilitation NGO in Guatemala in "En búsqueda de la Gobernabilidad, aciertos y desaciertos del gobierno de GANA: Análisis de Coyuntura" (2004).

[24] See Swedish (2004).

[25] *Mara Salvatrucha* can best be translated as "gang of street-wise Salvadorans." Mara is a contraction of *marabunta,* a carnivorous, swarming variety of ant found in the jungles of Central America. *Trucha* means trout but is slang for street-wise. Mara 18 takes its name from the 18th St. Gang in Los Angeles.

[26] Arana (2005), p. 100.

temala and Mexico is growing because antigang laws that were instituted in Honduras and El Salvador have had the unintended consequence of pushing the Maras northward.[27]

The maras are not just a problem on the Guatemalan side of the border. In November 2004, maras attacked a school parade in Tapachala, Mexico, and were arrested. When other members of their clique threatened to avenge the arrests, most of the schools in the city of 200,000 closed, some for up to a week. A local university professor and human rights organizer notes, "[The maras] provide security to the drug smugglers and human traffickers . . . they are the army of these people. They have created a society of fear."[28] According to Mexican officials, MS-13 and Mara 18 operate in at least 25 states and Mexico City; the majority are in Chiapas, where a significant presence exists in the border towns of Ciudad Hidalgo and Talisman as well as the aforementioned Tapachula.[29]

The maras are exceptionally violent. MS-13 seems to pride itself on its brutality. In Chiapas, for example, as many as 200 murders were carried out by gang members in 2003, and "one-third of the victims were tortured or raped before they were killed."[30] MS-13 has advanced well beyond the typical street gang fighting for turf. In El Salvador, for instance the gang is "highly organized and disciplined . . . with semiclandestine structures and vertical commands."[31] It truly has a global reach, with affiliates in Canada, Mexico, Colombia, Bolivia, Australia, Western Europe, and throughout the United States. It runs car-theft rings and traffics in drugs, people, and arms. It also uses modern technology for communications, including cell phones and the Internet, and it has its own Web page.[32] In fact, MS-13 is such a threat to security in the United States that the FBI has organized a nationwide task force targeting it, the first of its type concentrating on a single street gang, and has also established an office in El Salvador to fight MS-13.[33]

Despite the grave security problem the maras present in Guatemala and increasingly in Mexico, especially Chiapas, these organizations are not the only elements in

---

[27] For example, El Salvador has passed laws known as *Mano Dura* and *Mano Superdura* (firm hand and super-firm hand) that allow authorities to arrest individuals simply for having tattoos. Gang members in Honduras are sent to prison to serve a 30-year term. Similarly harsh laws were put in place in Guatemala but were later struck down as unconstitutional.

[28] Sullivan (2005), p. A10.

[29] See Torre (2005). See also "Transnational Gangs in Mexico and Central America" (2004).

[30] Swedish (2004)

[31] Oscar Bonilla, Chairman of the National Council on Public Safety of El Salvador, cited in Campo-Flores (2005).

[32] MS-13's Web site is at www.salvatrucha13.com.

[33] There are an estimated 8,000–10,000 MS-13 members in at least 33 states. See Campo-Flores (2005); and Connell and Lopez (2005).

society that manifest criminal behavior. The maras have been singled out and targeted with harsh laws, such as Mano Dura in El Salvador;[34] and media, government, and other sources of information use terminology intimating that the maras are the cause of all society's problems.[35] The maras seem to make a convenient scapegoat; governments can blame them for nefarious activity for which the gangs may or may not be responsible. Police corruption in Guatemala and Mexico is a good example. The government-run Beta Group in Chiapas (beta groups are essentially protection houses for illegal migrants) estimates that 51 percent of crimes committed against migrants in Chiapas are at the hands of Mexican security forces, while just two of nine violations against migrants can be attributed to the maras.[36] In El Salvador, the country probably most affected by the maras, gangs were believed to be responsible for 60 percent of the 2,576 murders committed there in 2004; a very high rate, no doubt, but it shows that these groups are not the only source of the ills in the border region or beyond.[37]

Other illegal armed groups that present security issues in Guatemala are known as "clandestine groups" or "hidden powers."[38] The members of these groups have links to state agents and organized crime, providing them both political and economic resources. They carried out particularly ruthless operations in the early 1980s against URNG personnel and those they believed to be URNG sympathizers. They currently target journalists, witnesses, NGOs, and state functionaries, such as judges and forensic experts, and have generally operated with complete impunity.[39] They have also reoriented their operations toward moneymaking ventures, such as trafficking in arms, drugs, and humans, and are believed to have links to the maras as well.[40]

In 2003, Guatemala accepted a U.N. proposal to establish a Commission for the Investigation of Illegal Groups and Clandestine Security Organizations in Guatemala (known by the Spanish acronym CICIACS). CICIACS was chartered "to investigate the structure and activities of illegal groups and clandestine security organizations and their association with the State and organized criminal activities, as well as prosecute

---

[34] *Mano dura* is better translated as "iron fist." The law provides stiff penalties for antisocial behavior by gang members.

[35] Even legislation in the United States is targeted at gangs and gang violence as proposed in the Gang Deterrence and Community Protection Act of 2005 (H.R. 1279).

[36] The numbers attributed to the maras from this source may be deliberately low. There is no question that the maras are responsible for a great deal of violence along the border, but, as the report points out, not all of it. See "*Marafobia*" (2004).

[37] See Ribando (2005), p. 1.

[38] The term "hidden powers" is from Peacock and Beltrán (2003).

[39] For more on clandestine groups, see Peacock and Beltrán (2003); Amnesty International (2004); U.S. Department of State (2004a); and Human Rights Watch (2005a).

[40] Benítez Manaut (2005).

those persons responsible for the formation and operation of these entities."[41] Although President Berger has fully endorsed the Commission, the Guatemalan supreme court ruled against some of its key provisions in August 2004. The Guatemalan congress has yet to take action on the agreement to satisfy the court, leaving the U.N. ombudsman for Human Rights to note, "the State lacks the political will to combat the violence."[42]

Corruption in the police force—the very personnel who are supposed to provide for state security—is also a problem. For example, the Guatemalan Police's former Anti-Narcotics Operations Department (DOAN) stole twice as much cocaine as it interdicted in 2002 and held an entire village hostage, killing two residents, for 2,000 kilos of cocaine.[43] The U.S. State Department notes that "the historic problems of widespread corruption, acute lack of resources, poor leadership, and frequent personnel turnover in law enforcement and agencies continue to plague [Guatemala] and negatively affect their ability to deal with narcotrafficking and organized crime."[44]

MS-13's international reach, its use of sophisticated communications, and its increasingly political agenda have advanced it into a criminal network unto itself—what gang expert John P. Sullivan categorizes as a "third generation gang." These gangs "share networked organizational features that are difficult to counter" and "have honed their ability to co-opt, corrupt and challenge state institutions."[45]

Other lines between the maras, clandestine groups, and criminal networks, especially drug trafficking organizations, are opaque at best. The maras and clandestine groups, in fact, form many of the criminal networks—or at least provide them security and safe passage. Criminal organizations have flourished in the corrupt environment found in Guatemala. The Anti-Narcotics Analysis and Information Services (SAIA) estimate that 400 narcotrafficking groups are operating in Guatemala, primarily in the east, north, and south of the country. These 400 groups are dominated by six larger cartels, three of which operate in the border region: the Tecún Umán group in San Marcos, the Sayaxché in Petén, and Golfo in Alta Verapaz. Officials also note that an alliance exists with Mexican trafficking cartels.[46]

Criminal organizations and gangs also control considerable portions of the border networks that transport people, drugs, and weapons between the two countries. They

---

[41] See U.S. Department of State (2004a), Article I.

[42] Loder (2004).

[43] The DOAN was dismantled in November 2002 and replaced by the Anti-Narcotics Analysis and Information Services (SAIA).

[44] U.S. Department of State (2005c).

[45] Sullivan and Bunker (2000), pp. 82–96; Sullivan and Bunker (2002), p. 52.

[46] The SAIA has only about 200 personnel assigned to combat these DTOs. See López (2005).

have also moved into areas in the Petén, such as Sierra del Lacandón, Laguna del Tigre Park, and around Lake Izabal.[47]

The greatest threat these third-generation gangs and criminal organizations pose is becoming increasingly powerful in a weak state, turning it into a "narco-state" or criminal state. This process is under way in Guatemala; even the vice president of the country has noted, "I wouldn't hesitate to say that the "Colombianization" of Guatemala is under way. You're talking about a network of colossal proportions that wields formidable amounts of money."[48]

Population with Access to Arms

One Guatemalan monitoring agency notes that there are more than 400,000 weapons in Guatemala, while a recent World Bank study estimates the number of firearms to be between 1.5 and 1.8 million. Moreover, no limits are imposed on the number of arms an individual can own or the amount of ammunition one can buy. One telling statistic about the extensive availability of weapons is that more than 50 percent of Guatemalan crimes are carried out by armed perpetrators.[49]

Lack of Effective Border Control

The border between Mexico and Guatemala is poorly controlled. It has more than 200 crossing points, many without even a security checkpoint. On the Guatemalan side, one official estimated that there were no more than 100 police and 1,000 military personnel in the entire state of Petén, an area equal in size to that of El Salvador.[50] Those who guard the remainder of the Guatemalan side of the border are likely to be more involved in crime than they are in security.

The problems along the border are just as difficult for Mexico as they are for Guatemala. Mexican authorities have only 300 agents covering the border. In contrast, the maras were estimated to be at least 3,000 strong near the border at the end of 2003.[51] The municipal president of Ciudad Hidalgo, just across the Guatemalan border town of Tecún Umán, known as "little Tijuana" because of its rampant prostitution, corruption, and "unbridled lawlessness,"[52] notes "the Guatemalan border puts us in a compli-

---

[47] See Garzaro and Barillas (2005).

[48] Quoted in "Drug Smugglers Finding Central American Corridor Useful" (2004).

[49] See "Más de 200 mil armas ilegales en el país" (2004). See also World Bank (2005b), p. 84.

[50] Boraz correspondence with Dr. Thomas C. Bruneau following his interviews with personnel at the U.S. Military Group, April 12, 2005.

[51] Mark Stevenson (2003).

[52] Grayson (2002), p. 3.

cated and difficult situation. We've become vulnerable to every type of illicit activity."[53] A former Chiapas secretary of state is blunter: "The Mexican government is either unable or unwilling to really take this southern border as a major priority. . . . They have pretty much left it as an open border."[54]

There is an additional factor as well, which has been repeated throughout this book, an utter lack of coordination among government agencies to ensure security— what Raul Benítez calls "the incapacity of the distinct governmental agencies of both countries to control and legalize the border."[55]

Thus, Guatemala has become a particularly important entry point for drugs, weapons, and hundreds of thousands of migrants from all over the world who enter Mexico in hopes of reaching the United States. Aside from using many of the unmanned checkpoints, migrants also cross the frontier using the 100-mile-long Suchiate River that separates Chiapas from Guatemala. Numerous accounts discuss the armada of *balsas* (rafts), their wood planks on top of tire inner tubes, which await the migrant willing to pay a nominal fifty-cent fee for a comfortable ride across the river. Many others simply wade. All this occurs often under the watchful but indifferent gaze of Mexican security officials.

Migrants who do make it across the border seek the railheads in Ciudad Hidalgo or Tapachula to reach the United States. But first they must be prepared to suffer two indignities: they must bribe a Mexican official to continue their journey and they must somehow avoid the maras who rob and often beat them. In just one case, as many as 20 gang members hacked migrants with machetes and tossed some from moving trains.[56]

External Interference

In the introductory chapters, we discussed external interference as coming from an outside government that acts in a way that exacerbates the lack of governance or encroaches on the sovereignty of another nation. This is generally not the case on the Guatemala-Chiapas border. And while some might argue that Mexico's border and repatriation policies (discussed below) or the United States' overall influence in the region might impinge on Guatemala's sovereignty, neither has a sufficient effect on conditions on the border to rise to the level of external interference.[57]

---

[53] See Navarro (2005).

[54] Sullivan (2005).

[55] Benítez Manaut (2005).

[56] See Mark Stevenson (2003); and Dellios (2005), p. 3.

[57] Mexico is routinely singled out by human rights groups for having some of the most restrictive immigration policies in the world. Moreover, many criticize Mexico's "double standard" in demanding a just treatment for

Mitigating Factors

Both Guatemalan and Mexican authorities are aware of the problems along their shared border and have taken some steps to address them. In Guatemala, President Berger has instituted a plan to decentralize government institutions and regulations, revamp the national police and improve security, integrate Guatemala into the global economy, fight corruption, invest in rural development, and incorporate Guatemala's diverse ethnic population—and has publicly acknowledged their historic marginalization from the larger society. President Berger has appointed human rights activists to government positions and made good on the his commitment to cut the size of the military. He went even further by slashing the defense budget by nearly 50 percent. Nevertheless, human rights organizations still complain that the Berger administration has not gone far enough in combating human rights violations and impunity from prosecution.[58]

In fact, the Berger administration has pursued numerous public corruption cases against former public officials, army officers, and high-level police officials. The attorney general began corruption cases against the former vice president and finance minister, who both have been arraigned. The former president, Alfonso Portillo, fled to Mexico when it became evident he was about to be arrested, and many other officials are either in jail awaiting trial or have been sentenced to prison time.[59] Even former President Rios Montt is under house arrest, although he has not been charged with any crime by Guatemalan judicial authorities.

The government has also taken other steps to fight corruption. The aforementioned scrapping of the Treasury Police's Department of Anti-Narcotics Operations included the firing of more than 75 percent of the agency's personnel, and new hires into the narcotics police undergo a background investigation, polygraph exam, and urine testing. The program has been institutionalized and extended to the Anti-Corruption, Money Laundering, and Narcotics prosecutor's offices and includes the periodic retesting of all active members.[60] Still, corruption remains a significant hurdle to efficiency and good governance everywhere in Guatemala.

With respect to security, Guatemala has approved new antigang laws and is considering more, though not as draconian as those adopted recently in Honduras and El Salvador. Additionally, 4,000 army troops have been involved in supporting operations to increase government presence in troubled neighborhoods in Guatemala City.

---

undocumented Mexicans while Mexico City affords no such treatment for migrants crossing its southern border. See for example, Benítez Manaut (2005).

[58] See Loder (2004).

[59] U.S. Department of State (2005c).

[60] U.S. Department of State (2005c). This is not to say that the SAIA is free of corruption. These measures simply place some level of institutional transparency.

President Berger also appointed a new interior minister whose sole purpose is to fight crime.[61] Guatemala has also instituted some programs aimed at preventing crime and for assisting at-risk youth, especially former gang members.[62]

On the Mexican side, President Vicente Fox instituted Plan Sur (Southern Plan) in 2001, which increased surveillance and established joint police-military operations to close some of the border gaps. Deportations have risen sharply: Mexico returned 203,000 migrants in 2004, 141,000 in 2003, and 112,000 in 2002.[63] While these numbers seem to show signs of improved interdiction, immigration officials in Chiapas "concede that the higher figure represents not their success in stemming the flow, but evidence that more are making the journey."[64] Also, Beta groups, which were created in 1996 and are funded by the Mexican National Migration Institute (INM), provide food, lodging, protection, and legal representation to migrants, regardless of their status. Chiapas has only two Beta groups, however.[65]

Mexico has also instituted policies to combat the maras. Anticrime operations have deployed more than one thousand officials from Mexico's migration, security, and justice organizations to Tapachula, where the mara problem is most severe and have also targeted the rail routes from Ciudad Hidalgo.[66]

Bilateral and regional cooperation has been stepped up. In February 2005, Presidents Berger and Fox met to discuss the issues surrounding the border. They agreed to establish mechanisms to fight drug trafficking and the maras and established a High Level Group on Border Security to evaluate those mechanisms.[67] In addition, Guatemala's cooperation with other Central American nations in combating drug trafficking, violence, and crime is on the rise. In January 2004, Guatemalan, Salvadoran, Honduran, Nicaraguan, and officials from the Dominican Republic agreed to create a database on crimes to better track movements of criminal organizations. In March 2005, defense, security, and interior ministers of the seven Central American countries agreed to create a regional rapid response force to combat drug trafficking, terrorism, and other regional threats. A follow-up meeting took place in early April 2005 when Presidents Berger, Ricardo Maduro (Honduras), Tony Saca (El Salvador), Abel Pacheco

---

[61] Johnson and Muhlhausen (2005), p. 11.

[62] Ribando (2005), p. 4.

[63] Mexico's repatriation program sends migrants back to their countries of origin if they are caught by authorities. In the past, most of the migrants had been simply dropped off in Guatemala, but Mexico has recently been more stringent about sending migrants back to their home countries.

[64] Quoted in "Mexico's Immigration Problem: The Kamikazes of Poverty," (2004).

[65] Grayson (2002).

[66] See "Transnational Gangs in Mexico and Central America" (2004); and Torre (2005).

[67] Gómez Quintero (2005).

(Costa Rica), Enrique Bolaños (Nicaragua), and representatives from Mexico and the United States met at an "Anti-Mara Summit."[68]

Attributes of the Guatemala-Mexico Border Conducive to the Presence of Terrorist Groups

The border area exhibits some important aspects that may be conducive to terrorist operations, as summarized in Table 13.3. The greatest threat is most likely from continued neglect by the state and the activities of various criminal groups that are apt to carve out space to carry out their illegal activities. Although this region may not represent the most appealing area to Islamist terrorists, the region's lawlessness may be exploitable by terrorists. As one DEA official pointed out,

> If you can move drugs and you can move money, you can move people and you can move weapons and you can move a lot of other things, which is why Central America at that point becomes important because it is in effect the soft spot in our security apparatus, say, for a terrorist to exploit, not simply the drug traffickers. Because what is the difference in moving kilos or people or weapons? It's the same skill set.[69]

Table 13.3
Indicators of Conduciveness to Terrorist Presence, Guatemala-Mexico Border

Variable	Score
Adequacy of infrastructure	
Communications	1
Financial infrastructure	2
Transportation	1
Operational access	2
Income-producing activities	3
Favorable demographics	
Presence of extremist groups	3
Supporting social norms	1
Preexisting state of violence	2
Informal social networks	1
Criminal syndicates	3
Invisibility	2

---

[68] See "Central America Creates Security Force" (2005); and "Maras en Centroamérica (2005).

[69] "Drug Smugglers Finding Central American Corridor Useful" (2004).

Adequacy of Infrastructure and Operational Access

As pointed out earlier in this chapter, the infrastructure on both sides of the border is not very well developed. Telecommunications, an area that may be conducive to terrorist operations, are poorly developed too. In the Guatemala border region, only 56 percent of households have electricity, 44 percent have access to phone lines, and 3 percent have access to cellular phones. Internet usage throughout the entire country is the lowest in Central America, an estimated 1.2 percent of the population (although the rate increased by more than 2,000 percent from 2000 to 2003). Although there are banks, ATMs and access to cash are anything but ubiquitous.[70]

From the standpoint of access, however, Guatemala provides an important staging point for entry into the United States. The U.S. border patrol arrested about 1.1 million people trying to cross the border between Mexico and the United States in 2004. Of those, 65,814 other-than-Mexicans (or OTMs in the border patrol lexicon) were apprehended in 2004, nearly double the previous year's totals. And as noted above, Mexico continues to see the levels of migrants at the Guatemalan border increase. In fact, government and aid officials say the flow increased 25 percent in the first few months of 2005.[71]

A very high percentage of OTMs probably entered Mexico through Guatemala. And while the vast majority came from Honduras, Guatemala and Nicaragua, many others came from other areas in Latin America, China, and the Middle East.[72] They come to Guatemala knowing that the border with Mexico is porous, and they take advantage of the lack of security presence along the border. According to one source, once U.S.-bound foreigners slip into Mexico from Guatemala, they have a better-than-even chance of making it into California, Arizona, or Texas. In addition, the maras seem to have little problem in returning to the United States; an estimated 65 percent of those deported from the United States return here illegally.[73]

This ability of illegal migrants to enter the United States naturally concerns government officials. The former Deputy Secretary of Homeland Security noted, "Several al-Qaeda leaders believe operatives can pay their way into the [United States] through Mexico and also believe illegal entry is more advantageous than legal entry for operational security reasons."[74]

---

[70] World Bank (2005b), pp. 86–107.

[71] Kraul (2005), Part A, p. 1.

[72] An Egyptian man arrested by immigration and customs officials in July 2004 was using Guatemala as his base of operations to smuggle Egyptians and other Middle Easterners into the United States. See "Border Security: Ice Gets Major 'Special Interest' Smuggler" (2004). Also see Tuckman (2001).

[73] See Bruneau (2005); and Grayson (2005).

[74] Quoted in Sandoval (2005). Also see Bonner (2005).

Sources of Income

Despite the lack of adequate infrastructure, illegal business is booming on the frontier. Gangs, criminal syndicates, thieves, and (as noted previously) state entities are producing income from drug and human smuggling, money laundering, stolen cars, extortion, and other illicit activities.

According to the Department of State's Bureau for International Narcotics and Law Enforcement Affairs, Guatemala is the preferred transit point in Central America for shipment of cocaine to the United States. An estimated 400 metric tons of cocaine, about 60 percent of the world's trade, are shipped annually through the Central American corridor to Mexico and then on to the United States. While clearly not all the cocaine bound for the United States passes directly through Guatemala, even a conservative estimate of 300 tons could produce a street value of $600 million.[75]

Guatemalan law enforcement agencies, hampered by a lack of resources, interdicted only 4.5 metric tons of cocaine in 2004, down significantly from the previous year's 8.8 metric tons. Guatemala's fleet of A-37s was grounded in 2004 due to safety concerns, and only one Army helicopter is available to police to interdict drug traffickers (a second helicopter crashed in 2004 and has not been replaced).[76] Drug traffickers, however, do not lack resources. For example, they commonly crash-land aircraft in the Petén and then truck cocaine across the border into Mexico.

As a consequence of the poor economic conditions in the country, many Guatemalans participate in the drug economy. Fishermen look to win the "lottery" by finding bundles of cocaine that smugglers drop into the ocean. These men are later notified of a location from a local buyer and paid between $3,000 and $5,000 per kilo as a transportation fee. There is little law enforcement involvement either, because corruption affects counterdrug operations, which are generally compromised within hours either by an inside source or a spotter who radios that navy boats are about to leave port.[77]

Smuggling aliens is also an increasingly lucrative market for illegal groups. Individual smugglers charge between $3,000 and $5,000 to guide one person to the United States. And while more than 200,000 migrants were apprehended by the Mexican government last year, most estimates indicate that the number of migrants who are not caught is at least twice that of those who are. At the high end, the illegal migration business could generate as much as $1 billion annually. As noted previously, movement through Guatemala is on the rise, and so are profits.

---

[75] Based on the commonly quoted street value of $20 million per ton. The U. S. Military Group provided the 75 percent "conservative" estimate in a phone interview with Steven Boraz, May 26, 2005.

[76] Jordan (2004), p. A20; U.S. Department of State (2005c).

[77] "Drug Traffickers of Guatemala" (2004).

Money laundering is another large income-producing activity, and Guatemalan authorities estimate that $1 billion is "laundered" each year. Moreover, much of the activity occurs at the frontier with Mexico, where the chief of Guatemala's public ministry responsible for combating this crime notes: ". . . we don't have a physical presence."[78]

Networks in Guatemala also play a role in trafficking in stolen vehicles. Although we have found no data on income from stolen vehicles in Guatemala or Mexico, more than 1.2 million cars were stolen in the United States in 2003, and eight of the ten most plagued cities were in states bordering Mexico. Many of these vehicles clearly have made their way into Guatemala: As George W. Grayson remarked, "In El Carmen, Guatemala, just across the border from Talisman, Mexico, one can see literally hundreds of stolen vehicles from the United States."[79]

Finally, gangs and criminal syndicates generate profits from extortion and theft. The security business is growing significantly in Guatemala, generating more than $335 million in protection services in 2003. And while criminal organizations did not partake in all that profit (although some probably did because many security firms in Guatemala are unregistered), many enterprises still make payments to criminals in order conduct their business in peace.[80]

Favorable Demographics

Indicators of favorable demographics, such as the presence of extremist groups, a pre-existing state of violence, and the existence of criminal networks, are clearly evident on the frontier.

Supportive Social Norms

There is no particular set of social norms along the Guatemala-Mexico border—such as religious solidarity or traditions of safeguarding guests from the authorities—that might give terrorist groups an advantage. While antigovernment sentiment in Guatemala can mobilize thousands, as evinced by the protests against the government and CAFTA noted above, neither Mexico nor Guatemala could be considered a hotbed of radical Islam—or Islam in general, for that matter. There are only four mosques and Islamic centers in Mexico and two in Guatemala, none of them in the border departments. The overall Muslim population in both countries is insignificant.[81] Much atten-

---

[78] "Drug Traffickers of Guatemala" (2004).

[79] "Drug Traffickers of Guatemala" (2004).

[80] Millman (2003).

[81] According to the Mexican National Institute of Statistics, Geography and Information, there were about 1,400 Muslims living in Mexico in 2000 (out of a total population over 100 million). The number today is likely

tion was given to a group of about 300 Mayans in San Cristóbal de las Casas, Chiapas who converted to Islam in the mid-1990s, established a madrasa, and announced their solidarity with the EZLN. However, since their conversion in 1995, there have not been many more in the region accepting Islam as their faith.[82]

The Maras as Extremists

The maras themselves have been recently carrying out decidedly more terrorist-style[83] operations, especially where antigang laws have been instituted. In December 2004, gunmen killed 28 people, mostly women and children, in a bus in Honduras. The assailants left threatening messages for President Maduro and the current congressional president, Porfirio Lobo Sosa, who supports the death penalty and was a leading candidate for president in 2005. In February 2004, a dismembered body was found in Honduras with a message that warned if the government continued to target street gangs, more people would die. After his inauguration in January 2004, President Berger received a similar message on a note attached to the body of a dismembered dead man. In both cases, the notes were signed Mara Salvatrucha 13.[84]

Possible linkages between MS-13 members and al-Qaeda surfaced in statements by U.S. and Honduran officials, as well as various news sources. These accounts stemmed from an alleged meeting in Honduras in July 2004 between MS-13 members and Adnan G. El Shukrijumah, a known al-Qaeda member and suspect in the planning of 9/11.[85] Intelligence and security personnel are absolutely firm in their belief that no such meeting took place. In fact, Robert Clifford, who is director of the FBI's new MS-13 task force, unequivocally dismisses this theory: ". . . to have something as sophisticated as al-Qaeda overtly align and identify itself with a group of misfits [like MS-13] is improbable."[86]

There are two schools of thought on a potential tie between MS-13 and al-Qaeda. On one hand, there may be common interests: al-Qaeda would benefit from MS-13's transit routes, and MS-13 could earn notoriety, power, and money. On the other, the cost of doing business for both groups may be too high: MS-13 is increasingly involved

---

higher, but not significantly so. See *Mujeres y Hombres en Mexico* (2005), p. 490. Muslims in Guatemala probably total around 300, mostly Palestinian/Jordanian, out of more than 11 million people. The two mosques, one Sunni and one of an Indian sect, are in or near the capital. Email correspondence with Military Group Guatemala, April 29, 2005.

[82] "Mayans in Mexico's Chiapas Region Convert to Islam" (2005).

[83] Using the U.S. State Department definition of terrorism of "premeditated, politically motivated violence perpetrated against noncombatant targets by subnational groups or clandestine agents, usually intended to influence an audience."

[84] Weissert (2004). See also Cuevas (2004); and Domas (2006).

[85] See "Guatemala y México niegan vínculo de Maras con terrorismo" (2004); and Seper (2004).

[86] Quoted in Harman (2005), p. 1. Also see Cruz (2005).

in black-market (and some legitimate) ventures and a tie to al-Qaeda would certainly be bad for business; for al-Qaeda, having to travel through Mexico to the United States with no support structure hardly seems economical or sensible when operatives have ways of coming into the country through normal ports with false documentation. We believes that the argument for al-Qaeda seeking to access the United States through a route other than Mexico is the stronger one; however, what makes an organization like al-Qaeda so dangerous is that it could behave in an unpredictable and counterintuitive way.

Invisibility

As noted in the introduction to this study, invisibility manifests itself in terrorists' ability to blend in with populations and to remain outside the purview of central governments. With respect to blending into societies, the maras stand out because of their tattoos; in some cases, they are literally covered from head to toe. While some cliques have begun to use less-obvious markings, the local populace is not supportive of the maras or their methods. The same can generally be said for other organized criminal elements, who would stand out in border communities because they are often not indigenous or do not speak the local language. As pointed out throughout this chapter, however, the maras and other criminal groups can hide because there are few authorities to find them, especially in the border region, and they "terrorize and control neighborhoods in their territory to impede anyone from acting against them."[87]

U.S. Policy Toward the Region

U.S. policymakers have placed a low priority on regional security issues as well, although that is changing. The security problems in the border region are becoming ever more apparent in key U.S. policymaking circles as evinced in recent congressional testimony, policy decisions, and a bill proposed in the Senate called the North American Cooperative Security Act (NACSA), which tasks the State Department to provide a framework for enhanced security management, communication, and coordination among the United States, Canada, and Mexico and specifically cites the need for support to Mexico, Belize, and Guatemala to shore up their mutual border.[88] Successive U.S. Southern Command chiefs have highlighted the sophistication and brutality of the gangs operating across Central America and their ties to drug traffickers and organized crime. Former deputy Homeland Security Secretary Admiral James

---

[87] Savenije (2004).

[88] North American Cooperative Security Act (2005–2006).

Loy noted, "We assess that al-Qaeda continues to be the primary transnational threat group, although we are seeing the emergence of other threatening groups and gangs like MS-13 that will also be destabilizing influences."[89] The FBI added the aforementioned special task force on MS-13 and will also place agents in regional embassies as liaisons, including an office in San Salvador.[90]

In Guatemala, assistance requested in FY2006 is for almost $47 million—an increase of $1.5 million from the FY2005 request but a more than 15 percent reduction from 200—with the majority going to various economic and public assistance programs.[91] Military aid to Guatemala was "unfrozen" for the first time in 15 years, with an estimated $3.2 million targeted to improve Guatemala's ability to support air and naval interdiction of drug trafficking.[92] Table 13.4 shows funding for U.S. assisance programs in Guatemala. These programs are designed to improve and decentralize governance; repair the justice system; fight corruption and improve education (Economic Support Funds [ESA] and Development Assistance [DA]); support military reform education, professionalization, and management practices; and improve counternarcotics operations, capabilities, and interoperability (Foreign Military Financing, International Military Education and Training, and International Narcotics Control and Law Enforcement [INCLE] funds). Child Survival and Health (CSH) funds, PL-480 Title II funds, and Peace Corps funds are designed to support a variety of pro-

Table 13.4
U.S. Aid to Guatemala (thousands of U.S. dollars)

Account	FY 2004 Actual	FY 2005 Estimate	FY 2006 Request
ACI	—	992	—
CSH	11,400	11,600	9,896
DA	12,362	10,900	9,661
ESF	4,971	5,952	4,000
FMF	—	—	500
IMET	504	350	400
INCLE	3,000	—	2,500
P.L. 480 Title II	14,723	18,033	16,306
Peace Corps	3,601	3,727	3,589

SOURCE: U.S. Department of State (2005e), p. 519.

---

[89] Craddock (2005); Loy (2005).

[90] Campo-Flores (2005).

[91] Of the near $47 million in the FY2006 budget, only $3.4 million is targeted for IMET, FMF, and counternarcotics support. See U.S. Department of State (2005e), p. 519.

[92] It is more accurate to say the aid was "unfrozen" rather than restored because the $3.2 million was a one-time transfer of funds rather than a restored military aid program.

grams to create a healthier, better-educated population. In 2004, Guatemala signed four letters of agreement with the United States on control of organized crime and narcotics trafficking, law enforcement institution-building, and demand reduction.

Policy Implications and Recommendations

The dire situation throughout Guatemala, particularly on the border, gives the U.S. government and the U.S. military opportunities to develop military strategy and doctrine; to improve training, equipment and professionalization; and to change the way Guatemalan forces conduct counternarcotics operations. Opportunities for the U.S. government in fighting terrorism in Guatemala are apparent in virtually every sector of the government, economy, and civil society. As the National Intelligence Council's report points out, organized crime and illegal armed groups "do not want to see governments toppled but thrive in countries where governments are weak, vulnerable to corruption, and unable or unwilling to consistently enforce the rule of law.[93] Thus, the primary means of defeating the growing threat of Guatemala becoming a narco or criminal state is in shoring up its governance.

However, every step the United States might take in supporting a more stable, transparent Guatemala must include careful reflection on how policies may be perceived, buttressed by appropriate information campaigns developed in close coordination with the government of Guatemala. Policy development should include independent input as well and be monitored closely to deter corruption.

Recommendations for the U.S. Government

As noted above, there are ample areas where U.S. support could improve upon the situation in Guatemala, as well as along the border with Mexico. There is little doubt within U.S. policy circles that good governance–a functioning judiciary, a transparent political society, a plan to combat poverty and unemployment, and professional security forces—is paramount if Guatemala is going to stave off "Colombianization." Policies already supporting this effort should be reviewed and enhanced, especially those aimed at strengthening Guatemalan agencies involved in fighting crime, narcotics, and money laundering. The United States would do well to involve independent monitoring groups to report on Guatemalan progress in these issues. The human rights monitoring organizations of the Organization of American States and the UN have ample experience in the country to provide honest assessments.

The North American Cooperative Security Act is a positive step forward in supporting border security between Guatemala and Mexico. It should be enhanced to provide resources for Guatemalan operations to ensure that drugs, migrants, and other

---

[93] National Intelligence Council (2004), p. 97.

contraband are interdicted before they reach the Mexican border, much less that of the United States.

The United States should spend considerable human and economic capital to support a regional initiative to combat organized crime, interdict drugs, and support security. A potential initiative in this direction could be a regional headquarters (probably in El Salvador where the PNC has had the most success and most experience in combating the maras and where the FBI has established a liaison office) staffed by key members of each of the Central American countries and the United States. This central organization would have ties to local entities within each country's security organizations and the ability to deploy forces rapidly in response to drug shipments. These efforts should ensure that all the countries pass asset forfeiture laws so that captured illicit funds and equipment could be used to support further anticrime operations.[94]

Particularly in regard to the maras, it would be advisable to explore and when feasible implement so-called Mano Amiga plans that help to integrate former gang members into society.[95] As Los Angeles Police Chief William Bratton points out, simply sending gang members to jail "reinforces their loyalty to the gang. To them, prison is like going to finishing school."[96] USAID has already started a community-policing program in El Salvador and plans to start one in Guatemala. Also, USAID has proposed to create homes for disadvantaged youth, including former gang members, and provide more educational and employment opportunities for at-risk youth.[97]

In addition, there is a need for the United States and regional governments to develop a database and protocols to facilitate the sharing of information among intelligence and law enforcement agencies, as proposed in NACSA. The U.S. should work hard to incorporate into this effort police units in Boston, Los Angeles, San Diego, San Jose, and Washington D.C.—cities where the mara problem is most prevalent. Care should be taken not to deport a gang member from the United States to Central America without forwarding his criminal records to the country to which he is being returned.

In Guatemala and elsewhere in Central America, the intelligence organizations of the military and police could benefit greatly from restructuring, reform, and professionalization. Because these organizations focus on collecting information on the maras, there is a great need to ensure that applicable oversight is in place. Further,

---

[94] For example, in April 2003, Guatemalan forces captured $14 million in a raid that remains unavailable to their forces. This is five times the assistance the United States provides in its anticrime program. Ambassador Hamilton lamented the lack of legal precedent in a May 2005 interview. See Garzaro and Barillas (2005).

[95] *Mano Amiga* (friendly hand) is the name given to a Panamanian program passed in 2004 designed to provide alternatives to gang membership and prevent crime.

[96] Quoted in Arana (2005), p. 106.

[97] Ribando (2005), p. 5.

intelligence reform could greatly enhance joint efforts and the integration of information among public security sectors.

An integrated effort to improve governance along the Guatemala-Mexico border would involve addressing the economic and social problems of the region. While CAFTA will likely foster greater overall economic growth in Guatemala, some sectors of the population will be negatively affected, as has been the case in Mexico with the implementation of NAFTA. There is a need for an assessment of the likely impact of CAFTA on governance, particularly along the border region.

As the World Bank points out, "with a relatively low level of tax receipts, fiscal policy has few degrees of freedom to accommodate shocks and provide countercyclical stimulus when needed."[98] Thus, there is a need to reshape Guatemala's public finances to ensure that the Peace Accords target of at least 12 percent tax collection, in relation to GDP, is met. At the same time, it is important that tax policies do not become a disincentive for the expansion of private enterprise. USAID is already working to improve both public spending and the tax system and there is ample opportunity to coordinate efforts with the World Bank, the UNDP, and other national and international agencies. As revenues increase, a spending plan that targets education, poverty, health, and infrastructure along the border region would help to reduce the problems of lack of governance that we describe in this chapter.

In the area of law enforcement and judicial reform, a concerted effort to combat clandestine groups and to develop a functioning judiciary could go a long way in restoring civil society's faith in the government. A more proactive approach is needed to reduce illegal migration through means other than deportation. Governments in the region lament what has become a right of passage for youths to try to make the journey to the United States. As a Honduran official puts it, the trek to the United States "[has] become a passion among our youths, like soccer."[99]

There is justifiable concern that U.S. assistance to Guatemala has not been effective or could be diverted by corrupt officials. Nevertheless, U.S. security interests are better served by efforts to improve governance and increase transparency than the alternative, which would be to cede control to the maras and narco-traffickers. The bottom line is that the United States must have a short- and long-term strategy that supports regional security as well as democratic institution building.

Recommendations for the Defense Department and the U.S. Air Force: Controlling "Ungoverned Airspaces"

The Guatemalan military's recent restructuring and serious need for a focused military strategy and doctrine are areas where the Air Force, as well as other DoD components, can provide significant input to the Guatemalan military services to help them struc-

---

[98] World Bank (2005b), p. iii.

[99] Kraul (2005).

ture themselves to support security and democracy. Greater emphasis on professional training and an expansion of IMET funds would help Guatemala's future military leadership attend military postgraduate programs in the United States. Having officers spend time at U.S. institutions can go a long way in improving professionalization and a better understanding of the U.S. system of democratic civilian control of the military. Programs like this should also include civilian defense officials and experts.

The Guatemalan experience also illustrates the importance of addressing the problem of ungoverned airspaces. There is significant airborne drug trafficking from Colombia to the Petén region of Guatemala and thence to Mexico and the United States. The U.S. Air Force has begun to study applying the lessons of the Regional Airspace Initiative (RAI) for Europe to strengthen air sovereignty in Latin America. RAI's objective was to help Central and Eastern European countries after the collapse of the Soviet bloc to modernize and integrate their air traffic control and air defense systems and to build a framework for a regional air sovereignty network.[100] A similar approach could be used in Central and South America with the dual benefit of increasing national air sovereignties while decreasing airborne narcotics trafficking.

Guatemala is currently involved in narcotics eradication and interdiction under the Central Skies Operational framework[101] and participates in combined U.S.-Guatemalan counternarcotics exercises known as Mayan Jaguar. The United States has also established the Cooperating Nation Information Exchange System (CNIES), operated by USSOUTHCOM, to provide data to regional governments for the detection and monitoring of suspicious aircraft and vessels.[102]

The U.S. Air Force can provide a great deal of support to these activities, lending its expertise in restarting Guatemalan counternarcotics air operations. The equipment of the Guatemalan air force is in serious need of repair and its pilots are most assuredly in need of training. Reequipping the Guatemalan air force may also make sense because its adversaries have far better resources. For example, the narco-traffickers who use Guatemala's airways have high-speed aircraft and fly them at night to avoid detection. Guatemala's air force has no night flight capability and therefore is not in a position to interdict these narcotics runs.

The effectiveness of Guatemalan counternarcotics operations could be improved by simply making enough fuel available for the Guatemalan air force and navy to operate. Both organizations have participated in counternarcotics operations in which U.S. Air Force assets fly maritime patrols to spot possible drug and human smuggling

---

[100]See Planzer (2000).

[101] Central Skies is the code name for the air campaign led by the U.S. Army and DEA to interdict and eradicate drug cultivation in countries from Panama to Guatemala.

[102]Farrar (2005b).

vessels.[103] Interdiction of migrants and drugs at this level of the "supply chain" would be more effective and less expensive than at the U.S.-Mexican border or in the United States.

The Air Force and other DoD elements could improve the situation by lending their antiterrorism operational experience, an area in which Guatemala has been improving, as noted above, but could certainly use more assistance. Finally, the Air Force and DoD could provide equipment and training for increased communications capabilities for Guatemalan security forces.

---

[103] U.S. Military Group officials thought these missions were noteworthy not only for their success but also for the positive way in which both the Guatemalan air force and navy expressed a desire to work jointly. They also were impressed with the navy's willingness and capability to interdict vessels when resources, especially fuel, were available. Boraz interview, May 26, 2005.

Assessment of Ungovernability and Conduciveness Values for Ungoverned Territories

To lay the groundwork for a comparative analysis of ungoverned territories, we evaluate each of the regions on the basis of the variables and indicators of ungovernability and conduciveness described in Chapters One, Two, and Three. We do this by scoring each of the regions on these variables and indicators. The values are given as 1 = low, 2 = medium, and 3 = high. Thus, a value of 3 for lack of control over borders indicates that the state exercises very little control over its borders, while a 1 for lack of monopoly of force indicates that the state, in fact, exercises a monopoly on the use of force. These values, summarized in the tables that follow, are based on the analysis of the individual case studies in chapters Six through Thirteen. We show separate tables for three multicountry case studies: the Arabian Peninsula; the East Africa corridor; and West Africa. We also disaggregate the values for the component republics of the North Caucasus region.

Where we have a complex variable, that is, one composed of several indicators, we prefer not to aggregate the value of the indicators to arrive at an overall value for the variable, because the weight of the indicators may vary from region to region. Supportive social norms, for example, might have critical importance in some cases, but less so in others. The values assigned to each of these indicators are based on the data in the case studies. They reflect the informed judgment of the researchers involved in this project refined through an interative process that moved on two tracks: the development of the analytical framework for the project (Chapters One to Four) and research on the case studies (Chapters Six to Thirteen). To the extent possible, we tried to make the evaluation of the case studies uniform across the different regions, but we were constrained by the limitations of the data. For instance, police per square kilometer may not be a meaningful measure if the police are corrupt or in cahoots with criminal elements, as is the case in several of our case studies.

Nevertheless, with these caveats in mind, we believe it useful to attempt a comparative assessment of these ungoverned territories using the methodology discussed above. In applying it, we get the results in the following tables.

Table A.1
Summary of Indicators of Ungovernability

Variable	Pakistani-Afghan Border	Arabian Peninsula	Sulawesi/ Mindanao	East Africa	West Africa	North Caucasus	Colombia-Venezuela Border	Guatemala-Chiapas Border
Lack of state penetration		See Table A.3		See Table A.5	See Table A.7			
Absence of state institutions	2		2, 2			3	3	3
Lack of physical infrastructure	2		2, 2			2	3	3
Social and cultural resistance	3		1, 3			3	1	2
Lack of monopoly of force								
Organized armed groups	3		2, 3			3	3	2
Criminal networks	3		2, 3			3	3	3
Population with access to arms	3		2, 3			3	3	3
Lack of border controls	3		2, 3			3	3	3
External interference	1		1, 1			2	2	1

Table A.2
Summary of Indicators of Conduciveness to Terrorist/Insurgent Presence

Variable	Pakistani-Afghan Border	Arabian Peninsula	Sulawesi/Mindanao	East Africa	West Africa	North Caucasus	Colombia-Venezuela Border	Guatemala-Chiapas Border
Adequacy of Infrastructure		See Table A.4		See Table A.6	See Table A.8			
Communications	2		1, 2			2	2	1
Financial transactions	2		2, 2			2	2	2
Transportation	2		2, 2			2	1	1
Operational access	2		1, 2			3	1	2
Favorable demographics								
Presence of extremist groups	3		2, 3			3	3	3
Supportive social norms	3		2, 3			3	1	1
Preexisting state of violence	2		3, 3			3	3	2
Criminal syndicates	2		2, 2			2	3	3
Sources of income	3		2, 2			3	3	3
Invisibility	2		2, 3			3	2	2

Table A.3
Indicators of Ungovernability, Arabian Peninsula

Variable	Saudi Arabia	Oman	UAE	Bahrain	Qatar	Yemen	Kuwait	Jordan[a]
Lack of state penetration								
Absence of state institutions	2	2	1	1	1	3	1	2
Lack of physical infrastructure	2	1	1	1	1	3	1	1
Social/cultural resistance	2	2	1	2	1	3	2	2
Lack of monopoly of force	2	1	1	2	1	3	2	2
Organized armed groups	3	2	1	2	1	3	2	2
Criminal networks	2	1	3	1	1	3	1	3
Population with access to arms	3	2	1	1	1	3	2	3
Lack of border controls	2	1	1	1	1	3	2	3
External interference	2	1	1	1–2	1	2	2	3

[a] Because this country borders Saudi Arabia.

Table A.4
Indicators of Conduciveness to Terrorist Presence, Arabian Peninsula

Variable	Saudi Arabia	Oman	UAE	Bahrain	Qatar	Yemen	Kuwait	Jordan[a]
Adequacy of Infrastructure	2	2	3	3	3	1	2	2
Operational access	3	1	1	2	2	2	3	3
Favorable demographics	3	1	1	2	2	2	2	2
Sources of Income[b]	1	1	1	1	1	2	1	1
Invisibility	3	2	1	2	2	3	2	2

[a] Because this country borders Saudi Arabia.
[b] Difficult to determine directly due to lack of reliable data.

Table A.5
Indicators of Ungovernability, East Africa

Variable	Somalia	Sudan	Kenya	Tanzania	Mozambique	Zimbabwe
Lack of state penetration						
Absence of state institutions	3	2	2	2	2	1
Lack of physical infrastructure	3	2	1	1	2	2
Social/cultural resistance	3	3	1	2	1	3
Lack of monopoly of force	3	3	1	1	2	1
Armed groups	3	3	1	1	1	1
Criminal networks	3	2	2	1	2	2
Population with access to arms	3	3	1	1	2	1
Lack of border controls	3	3	2	2	2	1

Table A.6
Indicators of Conduciveness to Terrorist Presence, East Africa

Variable	Somalia	Sudan	Kenya	Tanzania	Mozambique	Zimbabwe
Adequacy of infrastructure	1	1	3	3	2	2
Financial infrastructure	1	2	3	3	2	2
Transportation and communications	1	1	3	3	2	2
Operational access	2	2	3	3	2	2
Sources of income	2	1	2	2	2	2
Favorable demographics	2	2	1	1	1	1
Invisibility	2	2	1	1	3	3

Table A.7
Indicators of Ungovernability, West Africa

Variable	Benin	Ghana	Guinea	Togo	Burkina Faso	Nigeria	Liberia	Sierra Leone	Cote d'Ivoire	Guinea-Bissau
Lack of state penetration										
Absence of state institutions	2	2	2	2	3	2	3	3	2	3
Lack of physical infrastructure	3	3	3	3	3	2	3	3	3	3
Social/cultural resistance	2	2	2	2	3	2	3	2	3	3
Lack of monopoly of force										
Illegal armed groups	1	1	1	1	2	2	3	3	2	2
Criminal networks	2	2	2	2	3	3	3	3	3	3
Population with access to arms	3	3	3	3	3	3	3	3	3	3
Lack of border controls	3	3	3	3	3	3	3	3	3	3
External interference	2	2	3	2	3	2	3	3	3	3

Table A.8
Indicators of Conduciveness to Terrorist Presence, West Africa

Variable	Benin	Ghana	Guinea	Togo	Burkina Faso	Nigeria	Liberia	Sierra Leone	Cote d'Ivoire	Guinea-Bissau
Adequacy of infrastructure										
Financial infrastructure	2	2	1	2	1	1	2	2	2	1
Transportation and communications	2	2	1	2	1	2	1	1	1	1
Operational access	1	1	2	1	2	3	2	2	2	2
Sources of income	—	—	—	—	—	3	3	3	2	2
Favorable demographics	2	2	3	2	3	3	3	3	3	3
Invisibility	3	3	3	3	3	2	3	2	3	3

We can now begin to identify relationships among these variables and patterns across varying conditions. A high value on the presence of organized armed groups outside the state's control is a common characteristic of three of the single and two-country cases (the Pakistani-Afghan border, Mindanao, and the Colombian-Venezuelan border); two cases in the Arabian Peninsula (Saudi Arabia and Yemen); and two cases in East Africa (Somalia and Sudan). Regions that score high on the presence of armed groups also score medium or high on absence of state institutions, as is to be expected, but what is most interesting is that they show a very high relationship to lack of border control. This suggests that lack of border control is a key variable in explaining ungoverned territories and may be a strategic factor in reducing their scope.

Interference by external states does not appear to be an important factor, except to the extent that Russian is an "external state" in some parts of the North Caucasus. Venezuela's interference has the potential to influence the course of the Colombian conflict, but that level of interference has not yet materialized. Similarly, Iran may have the potential to destabilize some of the Gulf states—Tehran tried and failed after the 1979 revolution—but that has not yet occurred. On the other hand, as noted in the discussion of external interference in Chapter Two, in cases where political systems are not completely aligned with state institutions and national boundaries, i.e., where power is exercised through transnational networks, the distinction between state interference and the interference of foreign networks (e.g., Saudi "charities" in Somalia, Bosnia, and the Caucasus) might be blurred.

Levels of social and cultural resistance are very closely related to supportive social norms, a key indicator of favorable demographics that can be exploited by terrorists. The following territories register high on both indicators: the Pakistani-Afghan border, the North Caucasus, and Mindanao. This combination of social and cultural resistance and supportive social norms is characteristic of a class of ungoverned territories that we denominate as cases of contested governance. These territories are also among the areas of highest concern with regard to their potential for becoming sanctuaries for international terrorist groups.

In contrast, the two Latin American cases (the Colombian-Venezuelan and Guatemala-Chiapas border regions), West Africa, and the East African cases outside Sudan and the Horn of Africa score low or medium on social and cultural resistance and supportive social norms (although some score high on other aspects of favorable demographics, such as presence of criminal syndicates). This suggests a different class of ungoverned territories, where "ungovernability" derives less from local resistance than from state neglect or incompetence.

Using these two variables, social and cultural resistance and supportive social norms, also highlights an importance difference between the Sulawesi and Mindanao components of the Southeast Asia case study. While we initially believed that the two constituted a single case, because of cultural and historical ties between the two regions, we found that while sociocultural resistance is low in Sulawesi, it is high in Mindanao. Similarly, we rate supportive social norms as high in Mindanao, but medium in Sulawesi. This suggests that the two regions represent two different types of ungoverned territories and require different approaches to defeating embedded terrorists.

Bibliography

Abedin, Mahan, "Al-Qaeda: In Decline or Preparing for the Next Attack: An Interview with Saad al-Faqih," *Spotlight on Terror,* The Jamestown Foundation, Vol. 3, No. 5, June 15, 2005. As of September 21, 2005:
http://jamestown.org/terrorism/news/article.php?articleid=2369721

Abha Al-Watan, December 8, 2004, FBIS GMP20041208000168.

Abinales, Patricio N., *Making Mindanao: Cotabato and Davao in the Formation of the Philippine Nation-State,* Quezon City: Ateneo de Manila University Press, 2000.

Abizaid, General John P., "Statement of General John P. Abizaid, United States Army Commander, United States Central Command, Before the House Armed Services Committee on the 2005 Posture of the United States Central Command," March 2, 2005.

AbuKhalil, As'ad, *The Battle for Saudi Arabia: Royalty, Fundamentalism, and Global Power,* New York: Seven Stories Press, 2004.

"Abu Sayyaf Kicked out of MILF Turf—Military Commander," *Philippine Daily Inquirer,* July 6, 2005.

Abuza, Zachary, *Funding Terrorism in Southeast Asia: The Financial Network of Al-Qaeda and Jemaah Islamiya,* National Bureau of Asian Research, NBR Analysis, December 2003a.

———, *Militant Islam in Southeast Asia: Crucible of Terror,* London: Lynne Rienner, 2003b.

"Accommodating the Urban Informal Sector in the Public Policy Process: A Case Study of Street Enterprises in Bandung Metropolitan Region (BMR), Indonesia," briefing, 2003 International Policy Fellowship.

Adebajo, Adekeye, *Liberia's Civil War: Nigeria, ECOMOG and Regional Security in West Africa,* Boulder, Colo.: Lynne Rienner, 2002.

Adil, Adnan, "JeM, Al-Omer Agents of al-Qaeda," *Tribune* (India), June 14, 2002.

"Africa and the War on Global Terrorism," hearing before the House International Relations Committee Subcommittee on Africa, United States Congress, Washington D.C., November 15, 2001.

Africa Center for Strategic Studies, "About the Africa Center," undated. As of March 7, 2007:
http://www.africacenter.org/Dev2Go.web?id=243352&rnd=31907

Ahmad, Mansoor, "Regulations to Curb Smuggling, Under-Invoicing a Must," *Nation* (Pakistan), July 13, 2004.

Ahmed, A. S., *Resistance and Control in Pakistan,* New York: Routledge, 1991.

Ahmed, Samina, and Andrew Stroehlein, "Pakistan: Still Schooling Extremists," *Washington Post,* July 17, 2005.

Akhmadov, Ilyas, "Chechnya: Russia's Forgotten War," *Boston Globe,* February 25, 2005.

Akhmadov, Yavus Z., Stephen R. Bowers, Marion T. Doss, Jr., and Valeria Ciobanu, *Religious Brotherhoods in Chechnya: Their Relevance for the Chechen Conflict,* Harrisonburg, Va.: William R. Nelson Institute for Public Affairs, 2000.

Akhmadov, Yavus, Stephen R. Bowers, Marion T. Doss, Jr., and Liuli Kurnosov, *Islam in the North Caucasus: A People Divided,* William R. Nelson Institute for Public Affairs, James Madison University, 2001.

Alcala, Gustavo Azocar, "No es culpa de la FAN," *El Universal* (Venezuela), January 30, 2005. As of January 31, 2007:
http://archivo.eluniversal.com/2005/01/30/pol_art_expe01.shtml

Al-Jazirah, November 25, 2003, FBIS GMP20031124000208.

"Allowing Crime and Recruiting Those Who Have Strayed: Deep-Rooted Principles in the Thinking of the Misguided; the Addict and the Thief in the Terrorism Organization," *Ukaz,* June 17, 2005, FBIS GMP20050617514005.

Al-Musfir, Muhammed Saleh, "The GCC States: Internal Dynamics and Foreign Policies," in Joseph Kechichian, ed., *Iran, Iraq, and the Arab Gulf States,* New York: Palgrave, 2001.

Al Qaida in the Arabian Peninsula: Shooting, Hostage Taking, Kidnapping Wave—May/June 2004, Alexandria, Va.: Intelcenter (AQAP-SHK-WMJ04), Vol. 1, July 10, 2004.

Al-Shishani, Murad Batal, "The Amman Bombings: A Blow to the Jihadists?" Jamestown Foundation, *Terrorism Focus*, Vol. 2, Issue 22, November 29, 2005.

Alvarado, Jorge A. Lozada, "Small Arms and Light Weapons in Colombia," *International Action Network on Small Arms (IANSA) 2003 Global Week of Action Report,* June 2003. As of January 31, 2007:
http://www.iansa.org/newsletter/june2003/june2003.pdf

Amnesty International, *The Russian Federation: Denial of Justice, 2002.* As of January 12, 2007:
http://web.amnesty.org/aidoc/ai.nsf/afec99eadc40eff880256e8f0060197c/
926470531af8183580256c36005337be/$FILE/denial_of_justice.pdf

———, "Guatemala Country Report 2004." As of March 20, 2007:
http://web.amnesty.org/report2004/gtm-summary-eng/

———, "Conflict Diamonds: Did Someone Die for That Diamond?" March 19, 2005. As of January 31, 2007:
http://www.amnestyusa.org/diamonds/

Andrabi, Tahir, et al., *Religious School Enrollment in Pakistan: A Look at the Data,* Washington, D.C.: The World Bank Policy Research Working Paper 3521, March 2005.

Aragon, Lorraine V., "Communal Violence in Poso, Central Sulawesi: Where People Eat Fish and Fish Eat People," *Indonesia,* Vol. 72, October 2001. As of March 20, 2007:
http://cip.cornell.edu/Dienst/UI/1.0/Summarize/seap.indo/1106940647

———, "Waiting for Peace in Poso," *Inside Indonesia,* April–June 2002.

Arana, Ana, "How the Street Gangs Took Central America," *Foreign Affairs,* Vol. 84, No. 3, May/June 2005.

Arquilla, John, and Theodore Karasik, "Chechnya: A Glimpse of Future Conflict?" *Studies in Conflict & Terrorism,* Vol. 22, 1999, pp. 207–229.

"Article Discusses Number, Motives of Saudi Combatants in Iraq," May 24, 2005, FBIS FEA20050524003471.

"As Africans Join Iraqi Insurgency, U.S. Counters with Military Training in Their Lands," *New York Times,* June 10, 2005.

"Azahari Death 'May Spark Revenge,'" *Australian,* December 28, 2005.

Bagley, Bruce, "Globalization and Transnational Organized Crime: The Russian Mafia in Latin America and the Caribbean," conference paper, October 31, 2002. As of January 5, 2007:
http://www.mamacoca.org/feb2002/art_bagley_globalization_organized_crime_en.html

Bakre, Owolabi M., "Tax Avoidance, Capital Flight and Poverty in Nigeria," 2005. As of January 23, 2007:
http://visar.csustan.edu/aaba/Bakre2006.pdf

"Baloch Will Resist Military Offensive, Warns Senator," *Daily Times* (Pakistan), January 16, 2005.

Beattie, Hugh, *Imperial Frontier: The Tribe and State in Waziristan,* Richmond, Surrey: Curzon, 2002.

Behar, Richard, "Kidnapped Nation," *Fortune,* Vol. 145, No. 9, April 2002.

Behn, Sharon, "Foreign Strategists Aid U.S. on Terror," *Washington Times,* January 5, 2005.

Benítez Manaut, Raúl, "Seguridad nacional y fronteras ilegales e inestables," paper presented to the conference Seguridad y Nuevos Desafíos de las Fronteras de México, in Tapachula, Mexico, April 2005.

Bergin, Peter, *Holy War Inc.: Inside the Secret World of Bin Laden,* New York: The Free Press, 2001.

"Big Issue, Big Problem? MANPADS," *Small Arms Survey 2004: Rights at Risk, 2004,* Chapter 3. As of January 31, 2007:
http://www.smallarmssurvey.org/files/sas/publications/year_b_pdf/2004/2004SASCh3_full_en.pdf

Bin-Falah, Abdallah, "Security Campaign in Riyadh Shift to Sultanah," *Al-Watan,* June 6, 2005, FBIS GMP20050606514004.

Blandy, C. W., *Dagestan: The Gathering Storm,* Shrivenham, UK: Conflict Studies Research Centre, June 1998.

Blank, Jonah, "Kashmir-Fundamentalism Takes Root," *Foreign Affairs,* Vol. 78, No. 6, November–December 1999.

"Blast Hits Pakistan Luxury Hotel," BBC Online News, 28 October, 2004. As of March 20, 2007:
http://news.bbc.co.uk/1/hi/world/south_asia/3963243.stm

Block, R., and Daniel Pearl, "Bin Laden Is Backed by Rare Blue Gem Called Tanzanite," *Wall Street Journal,* November 16, 2001.

"Bombing: Theories Abound," *Tempo,* June 14–20, 2005.

Bonner, Raymond, and Carlos Conde, "U.S. and Philippines Join Forces to Pursue Terrorist Leader," *New York Times,* July 23, 2005.

Bonner, Robert C., Commissioner of U.S. Customs and Border Protection, "Statement Before the House Appropriations Committee, Subcommittee on Homeland Security," March 15, 2005.

"Border Security: ICE Gets Major 'Special Interest' Smuggler," *U.S. Immigration and Customs Enforcement: Inside ICE,* Volume 1, Issue 7, July 19–August 2, 2004. As of January 31, 2007: http://www.ice.gov/pi/news/insideice/articles/insideice_071904_Web5.htm

Bose, Sumantra, *The Challenge in Kashmir: Democracy, Self-Determination and a Just Peace,* New Delhi: Sage Books, 1997.

Bradley, John, *Saudi Arabia Exposed,* New York: Palgrave Macmillan, 2005.

Brass, Paul, *Ethnicity and Nationalism: Theory and Comparison,* New Delhi: Sage, 1991.

"Briefing Notes on Islam, Society, and Politics," *CSIS,* Vol. 5, No. 1, December 2002, p. 6.

Bruneau, Thomas C., "The Maras and National Security in Central America," draft paper, April 2005.

Brzezinski, Mark, "Surreal Politik," *Washington Post Magazine,* March 20, 2005, p. 16.

Buse, Uwe, et al., "Putin's Ground Zero," *Der Spiegel,* December 27, 2004, pp. 65–101, FBIS EUP20050228000220.

"Bush Presses Putin on Democracy," BBC News UK Edition, February 24, 2005. As of September 20, 2005: http://news.bbc.co.uk/go/pr/fr/-/1/hi/world/europe/4292807.stm

Buzan, Barry, *People, States and Fear: An Agenda for International Security Studies in the Post-Cold War Era,* Boulder, Colo.: Lynne Rienner, 1991.

Byman, Daniel L., and Jerrold D. Green, *Political Violence and Stability in the States of the Northern Persian Gulf,* Santa Monica, Calif.: RAND Corporation, MR-1021-OSD, 1999. As of September 21, 2005: http://www.rand.org/pubs/monograph_reports/MR1021

Campo-Flores, Arian, "The Most Dangerous Gang in America," *Newsweek,* March 28, 2005. As of January 31, 2007: http://www.msnbc.msn.com/id/7244879/site/newsweek/

Canadian International Development Agency, *Guatemala, Bilateral Programming,* December 1, 2006. As of February 28, 2007: http://www.acdi-cida.gc.ca/CIDAWEB/acdicida.nsf/En/NIC-22312396-NQ3

Canadian Immigration and Refugee Board, Country of Origin Research, "Venezuela: Kidnapping and extortion in rural and urban areas, particularly in Caracas, and state protection available to victims" (2003–March 2005), March 16, 2005. As of March 20, 2007: http://www.irb-cisr.gc.ca/en/research/rir/?action=record.viewrec&gotorec=446474

Castro, Giovanni Moreno, "El conflicto colombiano: Expansión de sus protagonistas hacia las fronteras," *Revista Arcanos,* No. 10, undated. As of January 31, 2007: http://www.nuevoarcoiris.org.co/local/infogeneral1003.htm

Ceasar, Mike, "Fill'er up: President Hugo Chavez holds down gasoline prices, creating a black market and costing his government billions," *Latin Trade,* July 2004. As of March 20, 2007: http://findarticles.com/p/articles/mi_m0BEK/is_7_12/ai_n6183859

Cellular News, "Infrastructure Contracts Awarded this Month," undated. As of March 20, 2007: http://www.cellular-news.com/infrastructure_contracts

Center for Arms Control and Non-Proliferation, "Global Peace Operations Initiative: Future Prospects" (October 21, 2004). As of April 25, 2007: http://armscontrolcenter.org/archives/000911.php

"Central America Creates Security Force," *Guardian* (London), March 4, 2005. As of May 2005: http://www.guardian.co.uk/worldlatest/story/0,1280,-4840032,00.html

Chalk, Peter, "The Davao Consensus: A Panacea for the Muslim Insurgency in Mindanao?" *Terrorism and Political Violence,* Vol. 9, No. 2, 1997.

———, "The Liberation Tigers of Tamil Eelam (LTTE) International Organization and Operations: A Preliminary Analysis," *Commentary,* No. 77, Canadian Security Intelligence Service March 17, 2000a. As of March 20, 2007: http://www.fas.org/irp/world/para/docs/com77e.htm

———, "Maritime Piracy: A Global Overview," *Jane's Intelligence Review,* August 2000b.

———, *Non-Military Security and Global Order: The Impact of Extremism, Violence and Chaos on National and International Security,* London: Macmillan, 2000c.

———, "Africa Suffers Wave of Maritime Violence," *Jane's Intelligence Review,* April 2001, pp. 44–45.

———, "Threats to the Maritime Environment: Piracy and Terrorism," presentation given before the RAND Stakeholder Consultation Meeting, Ispar, Italy, October 28–30, 2002.

———, "Non-Military Security in the Wider Middle East," *Studies in Conflict and Terrorism,* Vol. 26, No. 3, May–June 2003a, pp. 197–205 and 209–214.

———, "Countering Nigerian Organized Crime," *Jane's Intelligence Review,* September 2003b.

———, "Islam in West Africa: The Case of Nigeria," in Angel Rabasa et al., *The Muslim World After 9/11,* Santa Monica, Calif: RAND Corporation, MG-246-AF, 2004. As of January 31, 2007: http://www.rand.org/pubs/monographs/MG246/

———, "North and West Africa: The Global War on Terror and Regional Collaboration," The Jamestown Foundation, Terrorism Monitor, Vol. 3, No. 15, July 28, 2005. As of March 21, 2007: http://jamestown.org/terrorism/news/article.php?issue_id=3418

Chandrasekeran, Rajiv, "Muslim World Moves Money Without Trace," *Washington Post,* November 10, 2001.

Chandrasekeran, Rajiv, and Rama Lakshmi, "New Delhi Lays Blame," *Washington Post,* December 29, 2001.

Chouvy, Pierre-Arnaud, "The Dangers of Opium Eradication in Asia," *Jane's Intelligence Review,* January 2005.

"Cheap and Trusted," *Economist,* November 24, 2001.

"Chechens in Theater Raid Linked to Turkish Foundations, Russians Say," Associated Press, October 30, 2002.

CIA World Factbook, 2005. As of September 21, 2005: http://www.cia.gov/cia/publications/factbook/index.html

Cirino, Julio A., Silvana L. Elizondo, and Geoffrey Ward, "Latin America's Lawless Areas and Failed States: An Analysis of the 'New Threats,'" in Paul D. Taylor, ed., *Latin American Security Challenges: A Collaborative Inquiry from North and South,* Newport, R.I.: U.S. Naval War College Press, 2004.

Citizens for Global Solutions, "Global Peace Operations Initiative." As of February 2, 2006: http://oldsite.globalsolutions.org/programs/peace_security/peace_ops/peace_ops_home.html

Cohen, Stephen, *The Idea of Pakistan,* Washington, D.C.: The Brookings Institution Press, 2004.

"Cole Bombers Identified as Veterans of Afghan War," *Washington Post,* November 17, 2000.

Collier, Paul, "On the Economic Consequences of Civil War," Oxford Economic Papers, No. 51, 1999, pp. 168–183.

————, "Economic Causes of Civil Conflict and Their Implications for Policy," in Chester A. Crocker and Fen Osler Hampson with Pamela Aall, eds., Managing Global Chaos, Washington. D.C.: U.S. Institute of Peace, forthcoming.

Collier, Paul, and Anke Hoeffler, "Greed and Grievance in Civil War," World Bank Policy Research Working Paper, 2001. As of January 3, 2006: http://www.worldbank.org/research/conflict/papers/greedgrievance_23oct.pdf

Colombia: Country Profile, Washington, D.C.: Library of Congress, December 2004.

Colombia Forum, No. 37, October 2004–mid-February 2005. As of March 20, 2007: http://usofficeoncolombia.org/coloforum/cf37.pdf

"Colombia Makes 'Record Arms Haul,'" BBC News, May 30, 2005. As of January 31, 2007: http://news.bbc.co.uk/2/hi/americas/4592649.stm

"Combined Joint Task Force—Horn of Africa," Global Security.org, undated. As of January 31, 2007: http://www.globalsecurity.org/military/agency/dod/cjtf-hoa.htm

Conflict Early Warning Systems (CEWS), "Coding the Guatemalan Conflict," Coding Notes, Guatemala '51–'96, undated, CEWS Conflict Database. As of January 30, 2007: http://www.usc.edu/dept/LAS/ir/cews/database/Guatemala/codenotes.doc

Congressional Research Service, "Pakistan-U.S. Relations," CRS Brief for Congress, updated November 14, 2005.

Connell, Rich, and Robert J. Lopez, "Gang Sweeps Result in 103 Arrests," Los Angeles Times, March 15, 2005.

Cornwell, Richard, ed., Zimbabwe's Turmoil: Problems and Prospects, Pretoria, South Africa: Institute for Security Studies Monograph 87, September 2003.

Corr, Edwin G., "Introduction," in Max G. Manwaring, ed., Gray Area Phenomena: Confronting the New World Disorder, Westview Studies in Regional Security, Boulder, Colo.: Westview Press, Inc., 1993.

"Corruption Fuels Epidemic of Illegal Logging in Indonesia," Endonesia, February 20, 2002. As of January 31, 2007: http://www.endonesia.net/mod.php?mod=publisher&op=viewarticle&artid=107

Cowell, Alan, "8 Are Detained in Britain as a Wider Search for Suspects," New York Times, August 1, 2005.

Craddock, General Bantz J., United States Army Commander, United States Southern Command, "Posture Statement Before the House Armed Services Committee, 109th Congress," March 9, 2005.

Cragin, Kim, and Bruce Hoffman, Arms Trafficking and Colombia, Santa Monica, Calif.: RAND Corporation, MR-1468, 2003. As of January 5, 2007: http://www.rand.org/pubs/monograph_reports/MR1468/

"Crime Watch: Crime Rate Drops by 50 Percent," Saudi Gazette, May 25, 2005, FBIS GMP20050525514013.

Cruz, Carlos Mauricio Pineda, "Al-Qaeda's Unlikely Allies in Central America," The Jamestown Foundation, Terrorism Monitor, Vol. 3, No. 1, January 13, 2005.

Cuevas, Freddy, "Honduras Gangs Leave Grisly Warning," Associated Press, February 22, 2004.

"Dagestan Incursions—August–September 1999," GlobalSecurity.org. As of September 13, 2005: http://www.globalsecurity.org/military/world/war/chechnya2-2.htm

"Dagestan in the Run-Up to an Islamic Revolution," *Baku Ekspress,* December 28, 2004, FBIS CEP20050121000292.

Daniel, Frank Jack, "Guatemalan Protesters, Police Clash over Trade Pact," Reuters, March 17, 2005.

Danilov, Dmitry, Sergei Karaganov, Dov Lynch, Alexey Pushkov, Dmitri Trenin, and Andrei Zagorski, *What Russia Sees,* Paris: EU Institute for Security Studies, Chaillot Paper No. 74, Dov Lynch, ed., January 2005. As of September 19, 2005: http://www.iss-eu.org/chaillot/chai74.pdf

"Dark Days for a Black Market," *Businessweek Online,* October 15, 2001. As of April 2005: http://businessweek.com/magazine/content01_42/b3753016.htm

Darling, Miranda, "Action Needed on al-Qa'ida's Hiding Place," *Australian,* January 17, 2005. As of January 31, 2007: http://cis.org.au/exechigh/Eh2005/EH24805.htm

Davies, Victor A.B., "Explaining African Economic Growth Performance: Sierra Leone Case Study," African Economic Research Consortium Collaborative Research Project (Interim Report), October 2001. As of January 23, 2007: http://www.gdnet.org/pdf/davies.pdf

"Deadly Connections: The War/Disease Nexus Workshop Report," Vancouver, British Columbia, Canada: Human Security Centre, March 22–23, 2004.

"Defense of the Realm," *Middle East Economic Digest,* January 28–February 3, 2005.

DeGrasse, Beth, David Dickson, and Michael Dziedzic, "Global Peace Operations Initiative: Future Prospects," U.S. Institute of Peace briefing, October 21, 2004, As of January 18, 2007: http://www.usip.org/pubs/usipeace_briefings/2004/1021_nbgpoi.html

Del Cid, Marvin, "Amenazan con más protestas," *Prensa Libre,* March 29, 2005. As of January 31, 2007: http://www.prensalibre.com/pl/2005/marzo/29/110843.html

Delgado, Eleonora, "Ejército desconoce enfrentamientos entre el ELN y las FARC en la frontera," *El Nacional* (Venezuela), April 2, 2005. As of January 31, 2007: http://www.serviciojesuitaarefugiados-vzla.org/noticias_anteriores/2-abril05.html

Dellios, Hugh, "Mexico Urged to Tighten South Border," *Chicago Tribune,* March 5, 2005. As of January 31, 2007: http://dehai.org/archives/dehai_news_archive/feb-mar04/0655.html

Denning, Mike, "A Prayer for Marie: Creating an Effective African Standby Force," *Parameters,* Vol. 34, 2004.

Department of the Air Force, International Affairs Office (SAF/IA), *USAF Security Cooperation Strategy,* October 2004.

Dewan, Ashish, and Sabrina Saccoccio, "Money-Transfer Systems, Hawala Style," CNN Online News, November 13, 2001.

Dhanapala, Jayantha, et al., eds., *Small Arms Control: Old Weapons, New Issues,* Aldershot: Ashgate Books, 1999.

Diaz, Patricio P., *Understanding Mindanao Conflict,* Davao City: MindaNews Publications, 2003.

Dictaan-Bang-oa, Eleanor, "The Question of Peace in Mindanao, Southern Philippines," in Chandra K. Roy, Victoria Tauli-Corpuz, and Aanda Romero-Medina, eds., *Beyond the Silencing of the Guns,* Baguio City, Philippines: Tebtebba Foundation, 2004.

Domas, Shelly Feuer, "America's Most Dangerous Gang," *Police, the Law Enforcement Magazine,* June 5, 2006. As of January 31, 2007:
http://www.apfn.org/APFN/MS-13.HTM

"Dos GN heridos durante enfrentamientos en la frontera," *El Universal* (Venezuela), June 18, 2004.

"Double Whammy: One ID'd in Cole Attack; 5 Indicted for Embassy Bombing," ABCNews.com, December 21, 2000.

Douthat, Ross, "A Muslim Europe," *Atlantic,* Vol. 295, No. 1, January–February, 2005.

Doyle, Mark, "UN's Liberia 'Honeymoon' to End," BBC News, January 23, 2004. As of January 23, 2007:
http://news.bbc.co.uk/1/hi/world/africa/3423215.stm

"Drug Smugglers Finding Central American Corridor Useful," National Public Radio Morning Edition, October 20, 2004.

"Drug Traffickers of Guatemala," National Public Radio Morning Edition, October 21, 2004.

"The Drugs Connection in the Terror Hunt at Coast," *Nation* (Kenya), December 9, 2002.

Dukuly, Abdullah, "Politics-Liberia: Policing the Police," Inter-Press Service News Agency, August 2, 2005. As of January 22, 2007:
www.ipsnews.net/africa/interna.asp?idnews=24904

"Editorial: Retreating on the Madrassas," *Daily Times* (Pakistan), August 5, 2002.

Ehteshami, Anoushiravan, "Iran's International Posture After the Fall of Baghdad," *Middle East Journal,* Vol. 58, No. 2, Spring 2004.

Elbe, Stefan, *Strategic Implications of HIV/AIDS,* Adelphi Paper 357, Oxford: OUP-IISS, 2003.

"El mayor riesgo de ser victima de homicidio en Costa Rica, Guatemala y El Salvador," Fundacion Genero y Sociedad (GESO), San José, October 2004.

El Qorchi, Mohammed, Samuel Munzele Maimbo, and John F. Wilson, *Informal Funds Transfer Systems: An Analysis of the Hawala System,* World Bank and International Monetary Fund, December 18, 2000. As of January 31, 2007:
http://www.imf.org/external/pubs/nft/op/222/index.htm

Embassy of Indonesia, Ottawa, Canada, "News on Trade and Investment in Indonesia," January 10, 2005. As of January 31, 2007:
http://www.indonesia-ottawa.org/economy/Economicissues/Trade-inv-news-10-jan-05.htm

Embassy of the Philippines, "Status of the GRP-MILF Peace Process," Washington, D.C., February 8, 2005.

"En búsqueda de la Gobernabilidad, aciertos y desaciertos del gobierno de GANA: Análisis de Coyuntura," January–March 2004, Guatemala, April 22, 2004. As of January 30, 2007:
http://www.incep.org/analisisabril.pdf

"Enemies Everywhere," *Economist,* September 29, 2005.

Erikson, Daniel P., and Michelle Lapointe, "Guatemala Emerging from the Darkness," *Miami Herald,* March 20, 2005. As of January 30, 2007:
http://www.thedialogue.org/publications/oped/mar05/erikson_0320.asp

Esty, Daniel C., Jack Goldstone, Ted Robert Gurr, Barbara Harff, Pamela Surko, Alan N. Unger, and Robert S. Chen, "The State Failure Project: Early Warning Research for U.S. Foreign Policy Planning," in John L. Davies and Ted Robert Gurr, eds., *Preventive Measures: Building Risk Assessment and Crisis Early Warning Systems,* Lanham, Md.: Rowman & Littlefield Publishers, Inc. 1998.

Ethnic Compositions from WorldGeo. As of September 20, 2005:
http://wgeo.ru/russia/okr_ugn.shtml

Europa World Plus, subscription-based database. As of May 13, 2005:
http://www.europaworld.com/entry/ru

Evans, Alexander, "The Kashmir Insurgency: As Bad As It Gets," *Small Wars and Insurgencies,* Vol. 11, Spring 2000.

"Ex guerrilleros acusan a la GN," *El Universal* (Venezuela), January 28, 2005. As of January 31, 2007:
http://www.eluniversal.com/2005/01/28/pol_art_28186A.shtml

Fair, Christine, "Islam and Politics in Pakistan," in Angel Rabasa et al., eds., *The Muslim World After 9/11,* Santa Monica, Calif: RAND Corporation, 2004a. As of January 31, 2007:
http://www.rand.org/pubs/monographs/MG246/

———, "Militant Recruitment in Pakistan," *Studies in Conflict and Terrorism,* Vol. 27, No. 6, 2004b.

Fair, C. Christine, and Peter Chalk, "Domestic Disputes: Pakistani Internal Security," *Georgetown Journal of International Affairs,* Summer/Fall, 2004.

———, *Fortifying Pakistan: The Role of U.S. Internal Security Assistance,* Washington, D.C.: U.S. Institute of Peace, 2006.

Farah, Douglas, "Al-Qaida Tied to Africa Diamonds Trade," *Washington Post,* December 30, 2002.

———, "Draining Terror's Financial Swamps," *Middle East Forum,* November 4, 2004a. As of January 23, 2007:
http://netwmd.com/articles/article770.html

———, *Blood from Stones: The Secret Financial Network of Terror,* New York: Broadway, 2004b.

"Farc y Eln combaten en frontera venezolana," *El Tiempo* (Colombia), March 3, 2005.

Farrar, Jonathan D., Deputy Assistant Secretary of State, Bureau For International Narcotics and Law Enforcement Affairs, "Testimony before the Committee on International Relations U.S. House of Representatives, 'Plan Colombia: Major Successes and New Challenges,'" May 11, 2005a.

———, "Statement before the House International Relations Committee, Subcommittee on the Western Hemisphere," November 9, 2005b. As of January 31, 2007:
http://www.foreignaffairs.house.gov/archives/109/24517.pdf

Federation of American Scientists, "Europe and Eurasia." As of January 6, 2007:
http://www.fas.org/asmp/profiles/aid/fy2003part9.pdf

Feith, Douglas J., Under Secretary of Defense for Policy, "Strengthening U.S. Global Defense Posture: Report to Congress," September 2004.

Finn, Peter, "Al Qaeda Arms Traced to Saudi National Guard," *Washington Post,* May 19, 2003.

"Flintlock," GlobalSecurity.org, 2005. As of January 23, 2007:
http://www.globalsecurity.org/military/ops/flintlock.htm

"For a Few Dollars More," Global Witness, April 2003. As of January 31, 2007: http://www.globalwitness.org/media_library_detail.php/109/en/for_a_few_dollars_more

Forero, Juan, "Rightist Militias Are a Force in Colombia's Congress," *New York Times,* November 10, 2004, Section A, p. 3.

Four Corners, Investigative Journalism, "Interview with Sidney Jones," 2003. As of January 16, 2007: http://www.abc.net.au/4corners/content/2003/20031103_still_at_large/int_jones.htm

"Four Explosions Rock Balochistan," *Daily Times* (Pakistan), April 20, 2005.

"14 Detained Over Tentena Bombings," Laksamana.net, June 3, 2005. As of March 20, 2007: http://www.laksamana.net/vnews.cfm?news_id=8172

Franchetti, Mark, "Saudi Killer Spearheads Chechen War," *Times Online,* March 13, 2005. As of September 19, 2005: http://www.timesonline.co.uk/tol/news/world/article426320.ece

Fuentes, Ricardo, and Andrés Montes, *Mexico: Country Case Study Towards the Millennium Development Goals at the Sub-National Level,* United Nations Development Program, Human Development Report Office, Background Paper for Human Development Report 2003. As of January 30, 2007: http://hdr.undp.org/docs/publications/background_papers/2003/Mexico/Mexico_2003.pdf

Fuerzas Militares de cara al Siglo XXI: Reestructuration Fuerzas Militares, Bogotá: Comando General, Fuerzas Militares, 1998–2001.

Fuller, Liz, "Analysis: The Warlord and the Commissar," RFE/RL, January 15, 2005. As of April 27, 2007: http://www.eurasianet.org/departments/civilsociety/articles/pp011505.shtml

Fuller, Liz, and Julie Corwin, "Putin Reinvents the North Caucasus Wheel," RFE/RL, September 15, 2004.

Fundación Seguridad y Democracia, "Observatorio de Seguridad Suramericano," reporte del 1 al 31 de diciembre de 2004. As of March 20, 2007: http://www.seguridadregional-fes.org/cgi-bin/showdocs.asp?ISBN=1591

———, *Colombia: Balance de Seguridad*, boletín No. 7 (October–December 2004), February 17, 2005. As of January 30, 2007: http://www.seguridadydemocracia.org/docs/pdf/boletin/boletin%207%20completo.pdf

Galeotti, Mark, "Central Asian Republics Increase Cooperation on Organised Crime," *Jane's Intelligence Review,* February 2005.

Gall, Carlotta, "Afghan Poppy Growing Reaches Record Level, U.N. Says," *New York Times,* November 19, 2004.

———, "Armed and Elusive, Afghan Drug Dealers Roam Free," *New York Times,* January 2, 2005.

Ganguly, Sumit, *The Crisis in Kashmir,* Washington D.C.: Woodrow Wilson Press, 1997.

Garamone, Jim, "Flintlock Exercise Trains Africans to Handle Defense," American Forces Press Service, June 20, 2005. As of January 23, 2007: http://www.eucom.mil/english/FullStory.asp?art=583

Garmendia, Maite, "Jornada de Protestas," *Prensa Libre* (Guatemala), June 8, 2004. As of January 31, 2007: http://www.prensalibre.com.gt/pl/2004/junio/08/90212.html

Garrett, Laurie, *HIV and National Security: Where are the Links?* New York: Council on Foreign Relations, 2005.

Garzaro, Michelle, and Byron Barillas, "Situación es peor en narcotráfico," *Siglo XXI* (Guatemala), May 26, 2005. As of May 2005:
http://www.sigloxxi.com/detallesnews.asp?pag=nl1eia01.txt

Gause, F. Gregory, III, *Oil Monarchies: Domestic and Security Challenges in the Arab Gulf States,* New York: Council on Foreign Relations Press, 1994.

Geneva Centre for Democratic Control of Armed Forces, International Advisory Board for Border Security, "Lessons Learned from the Establishment of Border Security Systems—General Project Information on Past, Present and Future Activities," October 12, 2004.

Ghafour, Hamid, "Spicy Solution to the Afghan Poppy Problem," *Los Angeles Time*s, April 5, 2004.

Glasser, Susan B., "Martyrs in Iraq Mostly Saudis," *Washington Post,* May 15, 2005.

A Global Overview of Narcotics-Funded Terrorist and Other Extremist Groups, A Report Prepared by the Federal Research Division, Library of Congress Under an Interagency Agreement with the Department of Defense, Washington, D.C.: May 2002. As of January 30, 2007:
http://www.loc.gov/rr/frd/pdf-files/NarcsFundedTerrs_Extrems.pdf

Global Witness Limited—ReliefWeb, "Timber, Taylor, Soldier, Spy: How Liberia's Uncontrolled Resource Exploitation, Charles Taylor's Manipulation and the Re-recruitment of Excombatants Are Threatening Regional Peace," June 15, 2005. As of January 23, 2007:
http://new.reliefweb.int/rw/RWB.NSF/db900SID/RMOI6DE4Z3?OpenDocument&rc=1&emid=ACOS-635PLK

"Gobernadores apoyan erradicación manual de cultivos ilícitos," *Diario del Sur,* May 29, 2005. As of June 2005:
http://www.diariodelsur.com.co/mayo/29/putumayo.php

Goldschmidt, Arthur, Jr., *A Concise History of the Middle East,* Boulder, Colo.: Westview Press, 1991.

Gomez Quintero, Natalia, "México y Guatemala van contra 'maras,'" *El Universal* (Mexico), February 22, 2005. As of January 31, 2007:
http://www2.eluniversal.com.mx/pls/impreso/noticia.html?id_nota=122110&tabla=Nacion_H

Goss, Porter J., Director of Central Intelligence, U.S. Senate Armed Services Committee, "Statement before the U.S. Senate Armed Services Committee, Hearing on Threats to U.S. National Security," March 17, 2005.

Government Accounting Office (GAO), "Drug Control: Coca Cultivation and Eradication Estimates in Colombia," January 8, 2003. As of January 30, 2007:
http://www.gao.gov/new.items/d03319r.pdf

Government of Pakistan, *The 1998 Provincial Census Report of NWFP,* Islamabad: Population Census Organization (Statistics Division), October 2000.

———, *The 1998 Provincial Census Report of Balochistan,* Islamabad: Population Census Organization (Statistics Division), November 2001.

Government of Sierra Leone, "Annual Statistical Digest 2001," December 2001. As of January 30, 2007:
www.sierra-leone.org/cso2001-index.html

Grant, Bruce, "The Good Russian Prisoner: Naturalizing Violence in the Caucasus Mountains," *Cultural Anthropology,* Vol. 20, No. 1, 2005.

Grayson, George W., "Mexico's Forgotten Southern Border: Does Mexico Practice at Home What It Preaches Abroad?" Washington, D.C.: Center for Immigration Studies, July 2002. As of January 31, 2007:
http://www.cis.org/articles/2002/back702.html

———, Foreign Policy Research Institute E-Note: "Mexico's Southern Flank: A Crime-Ridden 'Third U.S. Border,'" March 22, 2005. As of January 31, 2007:
http://www.fpri.org/enotes/20050322.latin.grayson.mexicosouthernflank.html

Greenberg, Bruce, "Combating Terrorism in Africa Makes America More Secure," Washington, D.C.: U.S. Department of State, April 21,2004. As of January 23, 2007:
http://www.borrull.org/e/noticia.php?id=31634

Greenberg, Bruce, and Daniel Cain, "U.S.-Africa Partnerships Key to Waging War on Terrorism," March 14, 2005. As of January 23, 2007:
http://usinfo.state.gov/af/Archive/2005/Mar/15-904874.html

Grupo Política y Poderes, "Protestas terminan en acuerdo Gobierno asume compromisos y organizaciones no manifestarán por los mismos temas en 90 días," *PrensaLibre.com,* June 9, 2004. As of January 30, 2007:
http://www.prensalibre.com.gt/pl/2004/junio/09/90342.html

"Guatemala y México niegan vínculo de Maras con terrorismo," *El Heraldo* (Honduras), October 12, 2004.

Guatemalan Instituto Nacional de Estadisticas. As of March 20, 2007:
http://www.ine.gob.gt/

"Guatemalans to Step Up Protests," BBC News, March, 16 2005. As of January 31, 2007:
http://news.bbc.co.uk/1/hi/world/americas/4355999.stm

"Guerrilla venezolana antiyanqui," *La Semana*, April 20, 2005. As of March 7, 2007:
http://www.semana.com/wf_InfoArticulo.aspx?IdArt=85829

"Gujarat Raid for Qaeda: South Africa Wants Access to Held Nationals," *Daily Times* (India), November 7, 2004.

Gunaratna, Rohan, "Illicit Transfer of Conventional Weapons: The Role of State and Non-State Actors in South Asia," in Jayantha Dhanapala et al., eds., *Small Arms Control: Old Weapons, New Issues,* Aldershot, U.K.: Ashgate Books, 1999.

Habtar, Nasir, "Interview with Lt. Gen. Talal Anqawi," *Abha Al-Watan,* January 18, 2005, FBIS GMP20050118000180.

Haqqani, Hussain, et al., *Countries at the Cross-Roads: Country Profile of Pakistan, 2004.* As of January 10, 2007:
http://unpan1.un.org/intradoc/groups/public/documents/NISPAcee/UNPAN016204.pdf

Harman, Danna, "FBI Confronts New Gang Threat," *Christian Science Monitor WORLD,* February 24, 2005.

Hart, David M., *Guardians of the Khaibar Pass: The Social Organisation and History of the Afridis of Pakistan,* Lahore: Vanguard Books, 1985.

The Hashemite Kingdom of Jordan, Department of Statistics (DOS), "Economic Surveys: Employment in Establishments," World Development Indicators Online Database, 2003. As of September 20, 2005:
http://www.dos.gov.jo/sdb_ec/sdb_ec_e/index.htm

Haven, Paul, "Al-Qaida's No. 3 Man Arrested in Pakistan," *Guardian* (London), May 4, 2005.

Henley, Jon, "Al-Qaeda Terror Plot Foiled, Say French Police," *Guardian* (London), January 12, 2004.

Herbst, Jeffrey, "African Militaries and Rebellion: The Political Economy of Threat and Combat Effectiveness," *Journal of Peace Research,* Vol. 41, No. 3, 2004, pp. 357–369.

Hill, Fiona, "Islam and the Caucasus: A Look at Chechnya," Center for Strategic and International Studies panel discussion, May 10, 2004.

Hirschkorn, Phil, "Trial Spotlights America's Top Terrorist Threat," *The Journal of Counterterrorism and Security International,* Vol. 7, No. 4, Summer 2001.

Hoge, Warren, "Unpaid Aid Pledges Endanger Sudan Peace Pact, U.N. Says," *New York Times,* March 7, 2005.

Holsti, Kal, *The State, War and the State of War,* Cambridge: Cambridge University Press, 1995.

Holt, Andrew, "South Africa in the War on Terror," The Jamestown Foundation, *Terrorism Monitor,* Vol. 2, No. 23, December 2, 2004a. As of March 21, 2007:
http://www.jamestown.org/publications_details.php?volume_id=400&&issue_id=3161

———, "Will Zimbabwe Become a-Qaeda's Newest Hub?" The Jamestown Foundation, *Terrorism Monitor,* Vol. 2, No. 21, November 2004b. As of March 21, 2007:
http://www.jamestown.org/publications_details.php?volume_id=400&&issue_id=3131

"Home-Grown Terrorism," *Sydney Morning Herald,* October 2, 2004. As of January 31, 2007:
http://www.smh.com.au/articles/2004/10/01/1096527940768.html?from=storylhs

"Homeland Defense and Consequence Management," The Institute for Foreign Policy Analysis (IFPA), undated. As of September 27, 2005:
http://www.ifpa.org/projects/homeland.htm

Honwana, Joao, and Guy Lamb, *Small Arms Proliferation and Drug Trafficking in Southern Africa,* Cape Town: University of Cape Town Centre for Conflict Resolution, 1998.

Hourani, Albert, *A History of the Arab Peoples,* Cambridge: Harvard University Press, 1991.

Hubschle, Annette, *An Unholy Alliance? Assessing the Links Between Organized Criminals and Terrorists in Southern Africa,* Pretoria: Institute for Security Studies, October 2004.

Hugo, G. J., "International Labour Migration and the Family: Some Observations from Indonesia," *Asian and Pacific Migration Journal,* Vol. 4, Nos. 2–3, 1995.

Human Rights Violations in Chechnya, "Rights Activist: Kadyrovtsy Are Chechnya's Main Problem," 2005. As of January 31, 2007:
http://www.hrvc.net/news2005/10-2-05.html

Human Rights Watch, *Indonesia: Breakdown: Four Years of Communal Violence in Central Sulawesi,* December 2002. As of January 31, 2007:
http://www.hrw.org/reports/2002/indonesia/indonesia1102.pdf

———, "Human Rights Overview: Guatemala," 2005a. As of January 31, 2007:
http://hrw.org/english/docs/2005/01/13/guatem9849.htm

———, "History of Policing in Pre-Colonial and Colonial Nigeria," July 2005b. As of January 21, 2007:
http://www.hrw.org/reports/2005/nigeria0705/4.htm

————, "Liberia at a Crossroads: Human Rights Challenges for the New Government"—A Human Rights Watch Briefing Paper, September 30, 2005c. As of March 20, 2007:
http://hrw.org/backgrounder/africa/liberia0905/

Husby, Gorrill, "Islam Gains Ground in East Africa," *Jane's Intelligence Review,* May 2003.

Hussain, Iftikhar, *Some Major Pukhtoon Tribes Along the Pak-Afghan Border,* Peshawar: Area Study Centre and Hanns Seidel Foundation, 2000.

Hussain, Zahid, "Thousands of Pakistani Troops Hunt for Bin Laden," *Times* (UK), February 23, 2004.

ICG—*See* International Crisis Group.

IDMC—*See* Internal Displacement Monitoring Centre.

Idris, Iffat, "Point of No Return?" *Al-Ahram Weekly,* June 24–30, 2004. As of April 27, 2007:
http://weekly.ahram.org.eg/2004/696/in2.htm

IMF—*See* International Monetary Fund.

"IMF Asks Pakistan to Reduce Corruption," *News* (Pakistan), October 29, 2003.

Index of Economic Freedom, 2005. As of September 20, 2005:
http://www.heritage.org/research/features/index/countries.cfm

"India Timeline—Year 2003," South Asia Terrorism Portal. As of September 20, 2005:
http://www.satp.org/satporgtp/countries/india/timeline/2003.htm

Infoplease, Web site (2005). As of January 23, 2007:
http://www.infoplease.com/ipa/A0107718.html

Institute for Foreign Policy Analysis, "Homeland Defense and Consequence Management," As of January 15, 2007:
http://www.ifpa.org/projects/homeland.htm

Institute for Strategic Studies (Pretoria), "Nigeria Security Information," undated. As of January 23, 2007:
http://www.iss.org.za/AF/profiles/nigeria/SecInfo.html

————, "Sierra Leone Security Information," undated. As of January 23, 2007:
http://www.iss.org.za/AF/profiles/sieraleone/SecInfo.html

Instituto Nacional de Estadística de Guatemala, Web site (undated). As of January 30, 2007:
http://www.ine.gob.gt/

Internal Displacement Monitoring Centre, Internally Displaced Persons Project, "Sudan," undated. As of April 25, 2007:
http://www.internal-displacement.org/8025708F004CE90B/(httpCountries)/
F3D3CAA7CBEBE276802570A7004B87E4?OpenDocument

International Crisis Group (ICG), *Colombia's Elusive Quest for Peace,* Latin America Report No. 1, March 26, 2002a.

————, *Indonesia Backgrounder: How the Jemaah Islamiyah Terrorist Network Operates,* Brussels and Jakarta, December 11, 2002b.

————, "Latin America Briefing, Colombia: Will Uribe's Honeymoon Last?" December 19, 2002c.

————, "The Challenge of Political Reform: Jordanian Democratisation and Regional Instability," Middle East briefing, Amman/Brussels, October 8, 2003a.

———, *Colombia: Negotiating with the Paramilitaries,* Latin America Report No. 5, September 16, 2003b.

———, *Jemaah Islamiyah in South East Asia: Damaged But Still Dangerous,* Asia Report No. 63, Jakarta/Brussels, August 26, 2003c.

———, "Red Alert in Jordan: Recurrent Unrest in Maan," Middle East Briefing, Amman/Brussels, February 19, 2003d.

———, *Sierra Leone: The State of Security and Governance,* Africa Report No. 67, September 2, 2003e.

———, *Yemen: Coping with Terrorism and Violence in a Fragile State,* Middle East Report No. 8, January 2003f.

———, *Building Judicial Independence in Pakistan,* Islamabad/Brussels, Asia Report No. 86, November 10, 2004a.

———, *Colombia's Borders: The Weak Link in Uribe's Security Policy,* Latin America Report No. 9, September 23, 2004b.

———, *Demobilizing the Paramilitaries in Colombia: An Achievable Goal?* Latin America Report No. 8, August 5, 2004c.

———, *Indonesia Backgrounder: Jihad in Central Sulawesi,* Asia Report No. 74, February 3, 2004d.

———, *Pakistan: Reforming the Education Sector,* Islamabad/Brussels, Asia Report No. 84, October 7, 2004e.

———, *Somalia: Continuation of War by Other Means?* Africa Report No. 88, Nairobi/Brussels, December 21, 2004f.

———, *Southern Philippines Backgrounder: Terrorism and the Peace Process,* Asia Report No. 80, July 13, 2004g.

———, "Sudan's Dual Crises: Refocusing on IGAD," Africa Briefing, Nairobi/Brussels, October 5, 2004h.

———, *Zimbabwe: In Search of a New Strategy,* Nairobi/Brussels: ICG Africa Report No. 78, April 19, 2004i.

———, *Counter-Terrorism in Somalia: Losing Hearts and Minds?* Nairobi/Brussels: ICG Africa Report No. 95, July 11, 2005a.

———, CrisisWatch No. 21, May 1, 2005b.

———, *War and Drugs in Colombia,* Latin America Report No. 11, January 27, 2005c.

International Helsinki Federation for Human Rights, "Russian Federation," in *Human Rights in the OSCE Region: Europe, Central Asia and North America,* Report 2004 (Events of 2003), 2004.

International Monetary Fund (IMF), Country Report No. 05/154, 2005a. As of January 29, 2007: http://www.imf.org/external/pubs/ft/scr/2005/cr05154.pdf

———, "Colombia: 2005 Article IV Consultation and Fourth Review Under the Stand-By Arrangement, Requests for Waiver of Nonobservance of Performance Criteria and the Completion of the Fourth Review and Request for Stand-By Arrangement—Staff Report," April 14, 2005b. As of January 29, 2007:
http://ideas.repec.org/p/imf/imfscr/05-154.html

"Interview with Director-General of the Saudi Border Guard, Lt. Gen. Talal Bin-Muhsin al-Anqawi," *Ukaz,* December 21, 2004, FBIS GMP20041221000078.

"Iran's Muscle Flexing Slows Taliban Drug Trade," *Australian,* September 8, 1998.

IRINnews.org, "Nigeria: Muslim Fundamentalist Uprising Raises Fears of Terrorism," January 25, 2004. As of January 23, 2007:
http://www.globalsecurity.org/military/library/news/2004/01/mil-040125-irin02.htm

Iskandryian, Alexander, *Wahhabism and Islamic Trends in the North Caucasus,* William R. Nelson Institute for Public Affairs, James Madison University, 2002.

"Islam by Country," Wikipedia. As of January 23, 2007:
http://en.wikipedia.org/wiki/Islam_by_country

"Islam, Jihadism and Terrorism in Sudan," 2004. As of March 19, 2007:
http://www.aei.org/docLib/20040809_SANDEEremarks.pdf

"Islamic Nerves," *Economist,* October 14, 2000.

"Izvestiya Interview with OSCE Chairman-in-Office Dr. Dimitrij Rupel," 2005. As of September 13, 2005:
http://www.osce.org/documents/cio/2005/02/4216_en.pdf

Jackson, Robert, *Personal Rule in Black Africa: Prince, Autocrat, Prophet, Tyrant,* Berkeley, Calif.: University of California Press, 1982.

———, "Quasi States, Dual Regimes and Neoclassical Theory: International Jurisprudence and the Third World," *International Organization,* Vol. 41, No. 4, Autumn 1987, pp. 519–549.

———, *Sovereignty, International Relations and the Third World,* Cambridge: Cambridge University Press, 1995.

Jackson, Robert, and Carl Rosberg, "Why Africa's Weak States Persist: The Empirical and the Juridicial in Statehood," *World Politics,* No. 35, October 1982, pp. 1–24.

Jackson, Steve, "West African Organized Crime in Focus," *Platypus Magazine,* No. 74, March 2002.

Jacoby, Vice Admiral Lowell E., Director, Defense Intelligence Agency, "Statement Before the U.S. Senate Armed Services Committee, Hearing on Threats to U.S. National Security," March 17, 2005.

The Jamestown Foundation, "Rights Activists: Kadyrovtsy Are Chechnya's Main Problem," *Chechnya Weekly,* Vol. 6, No. 6, February 9, 2005.

Jane's Information Group, "Jordan," Jane's Sentinel Security Assessments [Eastern Mediterranean], October 21, 2004a. As of September 20, 2005:
http://sentinel.janes.com/docs/sentinel/EMEDS_country.jsp?Prod_Name=EMEDS&Sent_Country=Jordan&

———, "Sudan Country Report," Jane's Terrorism and Insurgency Centre, December 15, 2004b. As of January 31, 2007:
http://catalog.janes.com/catalog/public/index.cfm

———, "Yemen," Jane's Sentinel Security Assessments [The Gulf States], June 8, 2004c. As of September 20, 2005:
http://sentinel.janes.com/docs/sentinel/GULFS_countryjsp?Prod_Name=GULFS&Sent_Country=Yemen&

———, "A New Front in Sudan's Eternal War," Jane's Terrorism and Insurgency Centre, June 23, 2005a. As of January 31, 2007:
http://catalog.janes.com/catalog/public/index.cfm

———, "Russia and the CIS," Jane's Sentinel Security Assessments, Jane's Online subscription-based database. As of May 25, 2005b:
http://www2.janes.com/

———, North Africa," Jane's Sentinel Security Assessments, January 2007. As of January 18, 2007:
http://sentinel.janes.com/docs/sentinel/north_africa.jsp?refreshSession=true&SORT=PostDate+
desc&ResultCount=20&CONTENT=CURRENT&SubscribedSelection=NAFRS&branchNo=86

Job, Brian, ed., *The Insecurity Dilemma: National Security of Third World States,* Boulder, Colo.: Lynne Rienner, 1992.

Johnson, Kevin, and John Diamond, "Embassy Bombings Suspect Captured in Pakistan," *USA Today,* July 30, 2004.

Johnson, R. W., "Al-Qaeda and the Zimbabwe Nexus," *Focus,* Vol. 34, June 2004.

Johnson, Stephen, and David B. Muhlhausen, "North American Transnational Youth Gangs: Breaking the Chain of Violence," Heritage Foundation Backgrounder, No. 1834, March 21, 2005.

Joint Staff, *DOD Dictionary of Military and Associated Terms,* August 8, 2006. As of January 2, 2007:
http://www.dtic.mil/doctrine/jel/doddict/

Jones, Lucy, "Al-Qaeda Traded 'Blood Diamonds,'" BBC Online News, February 20, 2003. As of January 31, 2007:
news.bbc.co.uk/1/hi/world/africa/2775763.stm

Jones, Toby Craig, "The Clerics, the Sahwa and the Saudi State," *Strategic Insights,* Vol. 4, No. 3, March 2005.

Jordan, Mary, "Pit Stop on the Cocaine Highway," *Washington Post,* p. A20, October 6, 2004.

"Jordan Set to Launch Youth Strategy," *Choices,* Vol. 13, No. 3, September 28, 2004.

Jost, Patrick M., and Harjit Singh Sandhu, *The Hawala Alternative Remittance System and Its Role in Money Laundering,* Lyon, France: Interpol. As of January 16, 2007:
http://www.interpol.int/Public/FinancialCrime/MoneyLaundering/hawala/default.asp

Kailani, Wasfi, "Chechens in the Middle East: Between Original and Host Cultures," seminar at the Kennedy School of Government hosted by The Caspian Studies Program, September 18, 2002.

Kaplan, David, and Stefan Lovgren, "On Terrorism's Trail: How the FBI Unraveled the Africa Embassy Bombings," *US News and World Report,* Vol. 125, No. 50, November 1998.

Kavkazcenter.com, Web site, January 2, 2004.

Khan, Ilyas, "Inside the MMA," *Herald Magazine* (Pakistan), November, 2002a.

———, "Meet the Maulanas," *Herald Magazine* (Pakistan), November, 2002b.

———, "Back to the Hills," *Herald Magazine* (Pakistan), September 2004a.

———, "Inside Waziristan," *Herald Magazine* (Pakistan), March 2004b.

———, "Who Are These People?" *Herald Magazine* (Pakistan), April 2004c.

Khan, M. Ghazanfar Ali, "Most Child Beggars Are Saudis, Study Shows," *Arab News,* September 1, 2002.

Khan, Muhammad Shahedul Anam, "Linkages Between Arms Trafficking and the Drug Trade in South Asia," in Jayantha Dhanapala et al., eds., *Small Arms Control: Old Weapons, New Issues,* Aldershot, U.K.: Ashgate Books, 1999.

Knights, Michael, "Jeddah Attack Underscores Fall in Capabilities of Saudi Militants," Washington Institute for Near East Policy, January 2005a. As of January 30, 2007: http://www.washingtoninstitute.org/templateC06.php?CID=767

———, "US Regional Commands Diversify Across the 'Arc of Instability,'" *Jane's Intelligence Review,* Vol. 17, No. 9, September 2005b.

Knights, Michael, and Anna Solomon-Schwartz, "The Broader Threat from Sunni Islamists in the Gulf," *Policywatch,* The Washington Institute for Near East Policy, No. 883, July 19, 2004. As of September 20, 2005: http://www.washingtoninstitute.org/templateC05.php?CID=1761

Koch, Andrew, "U.S. Steps Counterterrorism Training in the Sahel," *Jane's Intelligence Review,* November 2004.

Korteweg, Rem, and David Ehrhardt, *Terrorist Black Holes: A Study into Terrorist Sanctuaries and Governmental Weakness,* The Hague: Clingendael Centre for Strategic Studies, 2005.

Kramer, Franklin D., and C. Richard Nelson, *Global Futures and Implications for U.S. Basing,* Atlantic Council of the United States, Working Group Report, June 2005.

Kraul, Chris, "A Surge South of Mexico; Illegal Immigration from Central America Has Spiked. Deprivation at Home and a Growing Support Network in the U.S. Are Factors," *Los Angeles Times,* May 1, 2005.

Kronstadt, Alan, and Bruce Vaughn, *Terrorism in South Asia,* Washington D.C.: Congressional Research Service Report No. RL32259, updated January 3, 2007.

Krinks, Peter, *Peasant Colonization in Mindanao,* Ph.D. dissertation, Australian National University, 1970.

Krott, Rob, "Guns of the Outer Frontier," *Soldier of Fortune,* January 2000.

Kulikov, General Anatoliy, *Trouble in the North Caucasus,* Fort Leavenworth, Kan.: Foreign Military Studies Office. Originally published in *Military Review,* July–August 1999.

Lacey, Marc, "Kenya: US Suspends Anti-Corruption Aid," *New York Times,* February 9, 2005a.

———, "Where Refugees Cower at the Latest London Bombing," *New York Times,* August 1, 2005b.

Lacey, Marc, and Dexter Filkins, "Kenya's Porous Borders Lies Open to Arms Smugglers," *New York Times,* December 4, 2002.

Lafraniere, Sharon, "How Jihad Made Its Way to Chechnya: Secular Separatist Movement Transformed by Militant Vanguard," *Washington Post,* April 26, 2003.

Lancaster, John, and Kamran Khan, "Investigation of Attacks on Musharraf Points to Pakistani Group," *Washington Post,* January 14, 2004.

Lara, Julio, "95% de Crímenes Sin Sentencia," *Prensa Libre* (Guatemala), February 9, 2004. As of January 30, 2007: http://www.prensalibre.com/pl/2004/febrero/09/lectura_nac.html#80867

LatinWorld.com, "Cybercafés in the LatinWorld," undated. As of February 28, 2007: http://www.latinworld.com/special/cybercafes.html

Lavrov, Alexei M., and Alexei G. Makushkin, *The Fiscal Structure of the Russian Federation: Financial Flows Between the Center and the Regions,* New York: EastWest Institute, 2001.

Leader, Stefan, and David Wiencek, "Drug Money: The Fuel for Global Terrorism," *Jane's Intelligence Review,* February 2000.

"Liberia: AFL Goes Amok Again!" *Analyst* (Monrovia), June 15, 2005. As of April 25, 2007:
http://allafrica.com/stories/200506150556.html

LeMiere, Christian, "Military Offensives Threaten Waziristan Stability," *Jane's Intelligence Review,* November 2004.

Loder, Julie, "One Year In, Berger's Human Rights Report Card," *EntreMundos,* Issue 19, November–December 2004. As of January 31, 2007:
http://www.entremundos.org/index.php?option=com_content&task=view&id=43&Itemid=34

Lonely Planet Guide, *Africa on a Shoestring,* Oakland, Calif.: Lonely Planet Publications, 2004.

Long, David E., "The Hajj and Its Impact on Saudi Arabia and the Muslim World," Saudi-U.S. Relations Information Service, January 19, 2005.

Looney, Robert, "Strategic Insight—A U.S. Strategy for Achieving Stability in Pakistan: Expanding Educational Opportunities," September 2, 2002. As of January 31, 2007:
http://www.ccc.nps.navy.mil/rsepResources/si/sept02/SouthAsia.asp

López, Olga, "SAIA busca recuperar credibilidad," *Prensa Libre,* April 23, 2005. As of January 31, 2007:
http://www.prensalibre.com/pl/2005/abril/23/112761.html

Loy, Admiral James, Deputy Secretary of Homeland Security, "Testimony Before the Senate Select Committee on Intelligence," February 16, 2005.

Luce, Edward, and Khozem Merchant, "India Counts the Cost of a New Breed of Terrorists," *Financial Times* (UK), September 11, 2003.

Mackintosh-Smith, Tim, *Yemen: The Unknown Arabia,* New York: Overlook Press, 2000.

Magyar, Karl P., ed., *Peacekeeping in Africa: ECOMOG in Liberia,* London: Palgrave Macmillan, 1998.

Maharaj, D., "The World Gem Tied to Terror Loses Sparkle, East Africa: Reports That al-Qaeda Controlled Part of the Tanzanite Trade Have Sent the Stone's Price Plunging and Left Miners in the Lurch," *Los Angeles Times,* March 20, 2002.

Malashenko, Alexey, *Islamic Factor in the Northern Caucasus,* Carnegie Moscow Center, Carnegie Endowment for International Peace, March 2001.

Malik, Nadeem, "15 to 20 pc Madaris Impart Military Training: WB," *News International* (Pakistan), August 2, 2002.

Marafobia, Boletín Chiapas al Día, Centro de Investigaciones Económicas y Políticas de Acción Comunitaria (CIEPAC) No. 442, December 1, 2004. As of January 31, 2007:
http://www.ciepac.org/archivo/bulletins/301-%20500/bolec442.htm

"Maras en Centroamérica: de las guerras civiles a la ultraviolencia callejera," *La Hora* (Guatemala City), March 30, 2005. As of January 31, 2007:
http://www.lahora.com.gt/05/03/30/paginas/nac_4.htm#n3

Marzuk, Moshe, *Radical Islamic Organizations Announce Merger with al-Qaida,* International Policy Institute for Counterterrorism, October 3, 2003. As of September 20, 2005:
http://www.ict.org.il/spotlight/det.cfm?id=933

Mason, Ann C., "Constructing Authority Alternatives on the Periphery: Vignettes from Colombia," *International Political Science Review,* Vol. 26, No. 1, 2005, pp. 37–54.

Masood, Salmon, "Musharraf Vows Crackdown," *National Post* (Canada), December 26, 2003.

Matri, Shimaila, "Hard Time Hotels," Newsline, September 2002. As of January 30, 2007:
http://www.newsline.com.pk/NewsSep2002/industry2002.htm

"Más de 200 mil armas ilegales en el país," *La Hora,* June 3, 2004. As of January 31, 2007:
http://www.lahora.com.gt/04/06/03/paginas/nac_1.htm#n4

May, R. J., "The Wild West in the South: A Recent Political History of Mindanao," in Mark Turner, R. J. May, and Respall Lulu Turner, eds., *Mindanao: Land of Unfulfilled Promise,* Quezon City, Philippines: New Day Publishers, 1992.

"Mayans in Mexico's Chiapas Region Convert to Islam," Deutsche Presse-Agentur, February 2005. As of January 31, 2007:
http://www.banderasnews.com/0502/nr-mayanislam.htm

Mazrui, Ali, "Blood of Experience: The Failed State and Political Collapse in Africa," *World Policy Journal,* Vol. 9, No. 1, 1995, pp. 28–34.

McDermott, Jeremy, "An Interview with Jorge Noguera, Director of Colombia's Administrative Department of Security," *Jane's Intelligence Review,* June 1, 2003.

McElroy, Damien, "Sahara: A New Terror Front," *Sunday Telegraph* (UK), June 7, 2004.

———, "US Forces Hunt Down al-Qa'eda in Sudan," *Daily Telegraph* (UK), July 7, 2005.

McGirk, Tim, "Terrorism's Harvest," *Time Asia,* August 9, 2004.

McKenna, Thomas, *Muslim Rulers and Rebels: Everyday Politics and Armed Separatism in the Southern Philippines,* Berkeley, Calif.: University of California Press, 1998.

Meisburger, Tim, ed., *Democracy in Indonesia: A Survey of the Indonesian Electorate in 2003,* Jakarta: The Asia Foundation, 2003.

Memorial Institute for the Prevention of Terrorism (MIPT), Terrorism Knowledge Base. As of May 18, 2005:
http://www.tkb.org

Méndez Viallasenor, Claudia, "Difícil Combate de Lavado," *Prensa Libre* (Guatemala), January 17, 2005. As of January 30, 2007:
http://www.prensalibre.com.gt/pl/2005/enero/17/105671.html

Menkhaus, Ken, *Somalia: State Collapse and the Threat of Terrorism,* Oxford, UK: Oxford University Press, 2004.

"Mexico's Immigration Problem: The Kamikazes of Poverty," *Economist,* January 29, 2004. As of January 30, 2007:
http://www.freerepublic.com/focus/f-news/1067707/posts

Migdal, Joel, *Strong States and Weak Societies: State-Society Relations and State Capabilities in the Third World,* Princeton: Princeton University Press, 1988.

———, *Boundaries and Belonging: States and Societies in the Struggle to Shape Identities and Local Practices,* New York: Cambridge University Press, 2004.

Miller, Derek B., "Demand, Stockpiles, and Social Control: Small Arms in Yemen," *Small Arms Survey,* Occasional Paper No. 9, May 2003. As of January 31, 2007:
http://www.smallarmssurvey.org/files/sas/publications/o_papers_pdf/2003-op09-yemen.pdf#search=

Millman, Joel, "Gangs Plague Central America," *Wall Street Journal,* December 11, 2003.

Mills, Greg, "Africa's New Strategic Significance," *Washington Quarterly,* Autumn 2004, pp. 147–169.

"MMA Opposes Pak-US Military Drive," *News* (Pakistan), June 24, 2003.

"MMA Says Check on Seminaries to Be Resisted," *Dawn* (Pakistan), November 11, 2003.

Molinski, Dan, "Colombia Rebels Attack Town Twice in Week," Associated Press, April 18, 2005. As of January 31, 2007:
http://www.freerepublic.com/focus/f-news/1386298/posts

Montgomery, Capt. Tom, "Training Foreign Forces in Air Force Special Ops," Air Force Link, July 13, 2005. As of January 30, 2007:
http://www.af.mil/news/story.asp?storyID=123011035

MOST Ethno-Net Africa Database, 2004. As of January 23, 2007:
http://www.ethnonet-africa.org/data/

Mujeres y Hombres en Mexico, Aguascalientes, Mexico: Instituto Nacional de Estadística, Geografía e Informática, 2005.

Murphy, Kim, "Saudis' Quicksand of Poverty," *Los Angeles Times,* May 16, 2003.

Murphy, Paul, *The Wolves of Islam,* Washington, D.C.: Brassey's, Inc., 2004.

"Musharraf Survives Second Assassination Attempt in Two Weeks," CBC News, December 25, 2003. As of January 31, 2007:
http://cbc.ca/story/world/national/2003/12/25/musharraf031225.html

Myers, Lisa, and the NBC Investigative Unit, "Saudi Clerics Still Encouraging Jihad," MSNBC.com, March 31, 2005. As of September 27, 2005:
http://www.msnbc.msn.com/id/7347417/

Nabi, Abdullaev, "Chechen Statehood: Is Islam an Obstacle," event report, Caspian Studies Seminar at Belfer Center for Scientific and International Affairs, Harvard University, September 24, 2003.

Naik, Niaz A., "Light Weapons Flows to and from Afghanistan," in Jayantha Dhanapala et al., eds., *Small Arms Control: Old Weapons, New Issues,* Aldershot, U.K.: Ashgate Books, 1999.

National Commission on Terrorist Attacks Upon the United States, *The 9/11 Commission Report,* New York: W. W. Norton, 2004. As of January 2, 2005:
http://www.gpoaccess.gov/911/

National Integrity Systems, *Transparency International Country Study Report—Pakistan 2003.* As of January 31, 2007:
http://www.transparency.org.pk/CSR.pdf

National Intelligence Council, *Mapping the Global Future: Report of the National Intelligence Council's 2020 Project,* NIC-2004-13, December 2004.

NationMaster.com, 2005. As of April 2005:
http://www.nationmaster.com/

Navarro, Julio, "Pandillas binacionales," *Noticieros Televisa,* May 11, 2005. As of January 31, 2007:
http://www.esmas.com/noticierostelevisa/investigaciones/445192.html

Nesser, Petter, presentation before RAND Institute for Middle East Youth (IMEY) Conference on Positive Options to Deter Youth Radicalism, Washington, D.C., September 22, 2005.

"Nigeria Police Force," Globalsecurity.org. As of January 31, 2007:
http://www.globalsecurity.org/intell/world/nigeria/npf.htm

Niksch, Larry, "Southeast Asian Terrorism in U.S. Policy," in *Fighting Terrorism on the Southeast Asian Front,* Asia Program Special Report No. 112, The Woodrow Wilson International Center for Scholars, Washington, D.C., June 2003.

9/11 Commission Report—See National Commission on Terrorist Attacks Upon the United States.

1903 Census of the Philippine Islands. As of January 17, 2007:
http://books.google.com/books?id=iKQJAAAAIAAJ&dq=1903+Census+of+the+Philippine+Islands

Nir, Ori, "Saudi Jihadists Play a Growing Part in Iraq Insurgency, U.S. Generals Say," *Jewish Daily Forward,* June 17, 2005. As of April 27, 2007:
http://www.forward.com/articles/saudi-jihadists-play-a-growing-part-in-iraq-insurg/

"No Connections: Bin Laden Denies Link to Cole Blast, Kuwait Plot," ABCNews.com, November 13, 2000.

Noriega, Roger F., Assistant Secretary for Western Hemisphere Affairs, "Statement Before the House International Relations Committee, 'Plan Colombia Major Successes and New Challenges,'" Washington, D.C., May 11, 2005.

North American Cooperative Security Act (S. 853), 109th U.S. Congress (2005–2006). As of January 31, 2007:
http://www.govtrack.us/congress/bill.xpd?bill=s109-853

O'Brien, Kevin A., "HIV-AIDS Pandemic Threatens Africa's Stability & Security (Part I)," *Jane's Intelligence Review,* December 2005.

———, "AIDS & African Stability—Fighting a Losing War (Part II)," *Jane's Intelligence Review,* January 2006**.**

Ochmanek, David, *Military Operations Against Terrorist Groups Abroad: Implications for the United States Air Force,* Santa Monica, Calif.: RAND Corporation, MR-1738-AF, 2003. As of January 5, 2007:
http://www.rand.org/pubs/monograph_reports/MR1738/

Office of the Coordinator for Counterterrorism, *Patterns of Global Terrorism, 2002,* Washington D.C.: U. S. Department of State, 2003.

Offoaro, Godson, "I Am Now a Smuggler, Part I," *Nigeriaworld,* May 30, 2005. As of January 23, 2007:
http://nigeriaworld.com/columnist/offoaro/053005.html

"OFW Remittances Up 5.1%: Central Bank," *Philippine Daily Inquirer,* July 15, 2005.

Olukoya, Sam, "Crime War Rages in Nigeria," BBC News, February 20, 2003. As of January 23, 2007:
http://news.bbc.co.uk/1/hi/world/africa/1443902.stm

"One Sheik's Mission: To Teach the Young to Despise Western Culture," *New York Times,* December 17, 2000.

Oosterhout, A. von, "Spatial Conflicts in Rural Mindanao, the Philippines," *Pacific Viewpoint,* May-June 1983.

"Orders from Osama; Sources: Cole Suspect Believes Orders Came from Bin Laden," ABCNews.com, January 8, 2001.

Organized Crime News. As of May 16, 2005:
http://www.iasoc.net/news/htm

Owens, Roger, *State, Power and Politics in the Making of the Modern Middle East,* London: Routledge, 1993.

"Pakistan Bombing Bears Stamp of Bin Laden," *People's Daily,* May 9, 2002. As of January 31, 2007:
http://english.people.com.cn/200205/09/eng20020509_95347.shtml

"Pan Sahel Initiative (PSI)," GlobalSecurity.org, undated. As of January 23, 2007:
http://www.globalsecurity.org/military/ops/pan-sahel.htm

Pasha, Tahir Anwar, "Current Problems in the Combat of Transnational Organized Crime." As of January 7, 2007:
http://72.34.34.34/~wjinabt/library/Pubs/2271.pdf

Paul, Rich, "Al Qaida and the Radical Islamic Challenge to Western Strategy," *Small Wars & Insurgencies,* Vol. 14, No. 1, 2003.

Pax Christi-International (Netherlands), *The Kidnap Industry in Colombia,* The Hague, November 2001. As of March 2005:
http://semana2.terra.com.co/imagesSemana/documentos/Antiontvoeringsrapport.doc

"The Peace Accord and the Commission for Historical Clarification," Nativeplanet.org. undated. As of January 30, 2007:
http://www.voicenet.co.jp/~jeanphi/countries/guatemala/truth.htm

Peacock, Susan C., and Adriana Beltrán, *Hidden Powers: Illegal Armed Groups in Post-Conflict Guatemala and the Forces Behind Them,* Washingon, D.C.: The Washington Office on Latin America, September 2003.

Percival, Bronson, "Indonesia and the United States: Shared Interests in Maritime Security," Washington, D.C.: United States-Indonesia Society (USINDO), June 2005, pp. 28–29.

Peters, John E., James Dickens, Derek Eaton, C. Christine Fair, Nina Hachigian, Theodore W. Karasik, Rollie Lal, Rachel M. Swanger, Gregory F. Treverton, and Charles Wolf, Jr., *War and Escalation in South Asia,* Santa Monica, Calif.: RAND Corporation, MG-367-1-AF, 2006. As of January 31, 2007:
http://www.rand.org/pubs/monographs/MG367-1/

Planzer, Neil, "Regional Airspace Initiatives in Europe," *Journal of Air Traffic Control,* April–June 2000. As of March 20, 2007:
http://www.thefreelibrary.com/Regional+Airspace+Initiatives+in+Europe-a078803063

"Policía confirma que detenido en Venezuela la semana pasada sí es guerrillero de las Farc," *El Tiempo.com,* February 26, 2005. As of May 2005:
http://eltiempo.terra.com.co/coar/ACC_JUDI/accionesjudiciales/articulo-web_nota_interior-1989875.html

"A Poisonous Plot," *Time Europe,* January 20, 2005.

"Politics, Drugs and the Gun," *Economist,* April 28, 2005. As of May 2005:
http://www.economist.com/world/la/displayStorycfm?story_id=3915056

Política de Defensa y Seguridad Democrática, Bogotá: Presidencia de la República, Ministerio de Defensa Nacional, República de Colombia, 2003. As of January 29, 2007:
http://alpha.mindefensa.gov.co/dayTemplates/images/seguridad_democratica.pdf

Politkovskaya, Anna, and John Crowfoot, *A Dirty War: A Russian Reporter in Chechnya,* London: Harvill Press, 2001.

Pope, William, "Opening Remarks," speech before the East Africa Counterterrorism Initiative Conference, Kampala, Uganda, April 21, 2004. As of January 31, 2007: http://www.state.gov//s/ct/rls/rm/2004/31731.htm

———, "Eliminating Terrorist Sanctuaries: The Role of Security Assistance," testimony before the House International Relations Committee, Subcommittee on International Terrorism and Nonproliferation, Washington, D.C., March 10, 2005. As of January 23, 2007: www.eucom.mil/english/transcripts/20050310a.asp

Posner, Gerald, *Secrets of the Kingdom: The Inside Story of the Saudi-U.S. Connection,* New York: Random House, 2005.

"Presidente Colombia Visita Frontera con Venezuela en Medio de Crisis," Terra/AP, January 28, 2005. As of January 31, 2007: http://www.terra.com/actualidad/articulo/html/act190025.htm

Prestupnost' i Pravoporiadok v Rossii (Crime and Law & Order in Russia), 2003. EastView, subscription-based database. As of June 3, 2005: http://udbstat.eastview.com/

"Profile: ECOMOG," BBC News, June 7, 2004. As of January 31, 2007: http://news.bbc.co.uk/2/hi/africa/country_profiles/2364029.stm

"Qatar to Host GCC Conference of Military Medicine and Protection Against WMD," *Peninsula,* October 9, 2002, FBIS GMP20021010000018.

"The Quiet US Front in the War of Terrorism," *Stratfor,* September 25, 2004.

Rabasa, Angel, *Political Islam in Southeast Asia: Moderates, Radicals and Terrorists,* International Institute for Strategic Studies, Adelphi Paper 358, 2003.

Rabasa, Angel, and Peter Chalk, *Colombian Labyrinth: The Synergy of Drugs and Insurgency and Its Implications for Regional Stability,* Santa Monica, Calif: RAND Corporation, MR-1339-AF, 2001. As of January 31, 2007: http://www.rand.org/pubs/monograph_reports/MR1339/

Rabasa, Angel, Peter Chalk, Kim Cragin, Sara Daly, Heather Gregg, Theodore Karasik, Kevin O'Brien, and William Rosenau, *Beyond al-Qaeda: Part 1, The Global Jihadist Movement,* Santa Monica, Calif.: RAND Corporation, MG-429-AF, 2006a. As of January 31, 2007: http://www.rand.org/pubs/monographs/MG429/

———, *Beyond al-Qaeda: Part 2, The Outer Rings of the Terrorist Universe,* Santa Monica, Calif.: RAND Corporation, MG-430-AF, 2006b. As of January 31, 2007: http://www.rand.org/pubs/monographs/MG430/

Rahman, B., "Balochistan Continues to Haunt Musharraf," South Asia Analysis Group Topical Paper No. 1205, December 12, 2004. As of January 31, 2007: http://www.saag.org/papers13/paper1205.html

Ram, Harsha, *Prisoners of the Caucasus: Literary Myths and Media Representations of the Chechen Conflict,* Berkeley Program in Soviet and Post-Soviet Studies, working paper, Summer 1999.

Rashid, Ahmed, *Taliban: Islam, Oil and the New Great Game in Central Asia,* London: I. B. Tauris, 2000.

———, "Islamists Impose Taliban-Type Moral Monitors," *Daily Telegraph* (UK), June 3, 2003a.

———, "The Wild Frontier," *Economist,* April 12, 2003b.

Ratnesar, Romesh, "Confessions of an Al-Qaeda Terrorist," *Time,* September 23, 2002.

Reeve, Richard, "Islamic Militants Establish Lake Chad Networks," *Jane's Intelligence Review,* November 2004.

Regiony Rossii—sotsial'no-ekonomicheskii pokazateli 2004 (Regions of Russia—Socioeconomic indicators 2004). EastView, subscription-based database. As of June 3, 2005: http://udbstat.eastview.com/

"Relaciones peligrosas, Escándalo en Venezuela y Colombia por la aparición de evidencias de los nexos entre el gobierno de Hugo Chávez y las FARC," *Semana.com.* As of February 26, 2002: http://semana2.terra.com.co/opencms/opencms/Semana/articulo.html?id=21100

Republic of Colombia, Office of the Vice-President, *Observatorio de Derechos Humanos,* 2005. As of January 31, 2007: http://www.derechoshumanos.gov.co/observatorio/departamentos/

Rhem, Kathleen T., "U.S. Helping Colombian Military Cope with Drug War's Legacy," Armed Forces Information Service, November 29, 2005. As of January 30, 2007: http://www.defenselink.mil/news/Nov2005/20051129_3467.html

Reno, William, "African Weak States and Commercial Alliances," *African Affairs,* Vol. 96, 1997.

———, *Warlord Politics and African States,* Boulder, Colo.: Lynne Rienner, 1999.

———, "The Empirical Challenge to Economic Analyses of Conflicts," paper presented at the SSRC-sponsored conference "The Economic Analysis of Conflict: Problems and Prospects," Washington, D. C., April 19–20, 2004.

Ribando, Clare, "Gangs in Central America," Congressional Research Service, May 10, 2005. As of January 31, 2007: http://fpc.state.gov/documents/organization/47140.pdf

Risen, James, and David Rohde, "Mountains and Border Foil Quest for Bin Laden," *New York Times,* December 13, 2004.

Rizvi, Hasan-Askari, "Political Parties and Wanna Operation," *Daily Times* (Pakistan), May 7, 2004.

———, "A Moderate and Enlightened Pakistan," *Daily Times* (Pakistan), January 17, 2005.

Robinowitz, Anna, "Terror at the Hajj," PolicyWatch/PeaceWatch, Washington Institute for Near East Policy, PeachWatch No. 446, March 3, 2004. As of January 15, 2007: http://www.washingtoninstitute.org/templateC05.php?CID=2137

Robinson, Linda, "Terror Close to Home," *U.S. News and World Report,* Vol. 135, No. 11, October 6, 2003.

———, "The Colombian War and U.S. Special Forces: A Case Study in 21st Century Conflict," Adelphi Paper, International Institute for Strategic Studies (forthcoming).

Ronfeldt, David, John Arquilla, Graham Fuller, and Melissa Fuller, *The Zapatista Social Netwar in Mexico,* Santa Monica, Calif: RAND Corporation, MF-944/A, 1998. As of January 31, 2007: http://www.rand.org/pubs/monograph_reports/MR994/

Rood, Steven, *Forging Sustainable Peace in Mindanao: The Role of Civil Society,* Washington, D.C.: East-West Center, Policy Studies, No. 17, 2005.

Rosenau, William, "Al-Qa'ida Recruitment Trends in Kenya and Tanzania," *Studies in Conflict and Terrorism,* Vol. 28, No. 1, January–February 2005.

Rossiiskaya Gazeta, June 24, 2004.

Rotberg, Robert, "Failed States in a World of Terror," *Foreign Affairs,* Vol. 81, No. 4, July/August 2002, pp. 127–140.

Rotella, Sebastian, "Jihad's Unlikely Alliance," *Los Angeles Times,* April 5, 2004.

Roth, John, Douglas Greenburg, and Serena Wille, *Monograph on Terrorist Financing,* Washington, D.C.: National Commission on Terrorist Attacks Upon the United States, 2004. As of January 5, 2007:
http://www.9-11commission.gov/staff_statements/911_TerrFin_Monograph.pdf

Royal United Services Institute (RUSI), "The Tribal Areas of Pakistan: A Haven for Terrorists?" conference proceedings, London: RUSI, January 19, 2005.

"The Russian Federation," *Europa World Plus,* subscription-based database. As of May 13, 2005:
http://www.europaworld.com/entry/ru

"Russia's Caucasian Nightmare," *Jane's Islamic Affairs Analyst,* September 1, 1999.

Ryan, Curtis R., and Jillian Schwedler, "Return to Democratization or New Hybrid Regime? The 2003 Elections in Jordan," *Middle East Policy,* Vol 11, No. 2, Summer 2004, pp. 138–151.

"Saca Es El Presidente Más Popular De Centroamérica," AP Spanish Worldstream, May 25, 2005. As of January 5, 2007: ,
http://www.terra.com.hn/noticias/nacionales/articulo/html/nac38462.htm

Sanchez, Fabiola, "Venezuela, Colombia Ease Diplomatic Spat," Associated Press Latin America, February 15, 2005. As of May 2005:
http://abcnews.go.com/International/wireStory?id=502471

Sandoval, Ricardo, "A perfect storm at the border," *U.S. News and World Report,* March 28, 2005. As of January 5, 2007:
 http://www.usnews.com/usnews/news/articles/050328/28mexico.htm

Saratov Center for the Study of Organized Crime and Corruption Problems Web site, 2003. As of April 18, 2005:
http://sartraccc.sgap.ru/index2.htm

"Saudi Arabia Faces Instability," *Jane's Intelligence Review,* July 2004.

"Saudi Arabia: A Show of Force," *Middle East Economic Digest,* Vol. 48, No. 13, March 26, 2004, pp. 29–56.

"Saudis have intercepted 100,000 infiltrators this year," *Worldtribune.com,* October 11, 2004. As of September 20, 2005:
http://216.26.163.62/2004/me_saudis_10_10.html

Savenije, Wim, "La Mara Salvatrucha y el Barrio 18 St. Fenómenos sociales trasnacionales, respuestas represivas nacionales," *Foreign Affairs En Español,* Abril–Junio 2004. As of January 5, 2007:
http://www.foreignaffairs-esp.org/20040401faenespessay040205/wim-savenije/la-Mara-salvatrucha-y-el-barrio-18-st-fenomenos-sociales-trasnacionales-respuestas-represivas-nacionales.html

Scarborough, Rowan, "Osama Bin Laden a 'Narco-Terrorist,'" *Washington Times,* January 22, 2004.

Schaffer, Teresita, *Pakistan's Future and U.S. Policy Options: Law Enforcement and Internal Security in Pakistan,* Washington D.C.: Center for Strategic and International Studies (CSIS), March 2004.

Schmidt, Susan, and Dana Priest, "Alleged USS Cole Plotter Caught," *Washington Post,* November 22, 2002. As of September 21, 2005:
http://www.washingtonpost.com/ac2/wp-dyn/A23656-2002Nov21?language=printer

Schofield, Clive, "Horn of Africa Conflicts Threaten US Anti-Terrorism Efforts," *Jane's Intelligence Review,* Vol. 16, No. 6, June 2004, p. 46.

Schofield, Richard, "Down to the Usual Suspects," in Joseph Kechichian, ed., *Iran, Iraq and the Arab Gulf States,* New York: Palgrave, 2001.

Seijo, Lorena, "Muertes, sin castigo," *Prensa Libre* (Guatemala), May 18, 2005. As of January 30, 2007:
http://www.prensalibre.com/pl/2005/mayo/18/114581.html

————, "Depuración de empresas de seguridad," *Prensa Libre* (Guatemela), May 26, 2005. As of May 2005:
http://www.prensalibre.com.gt/pl/2005/mayo/26/index.html

Seper, Jerry, "Al Qaeda seeks tie to local gangs," *Washington Times,* September 28, 2004.

Seraphin, Brad, "Cubic Participates in Anti-Terrorism Training Efforts," *Daily Transcript,* June 14, 2005.

Shahzad, Syed Saleem, "Pakistan Nears Endgame in al-Qaeda Hunt," *Asia Times Online*, August 25, 2004. As of January 31, 2007:
http://www.atimes.com/atimes/South_Asia/FH25Df03.html

Sharp, Jeremy, *The Middle East Partnership Initiative: An Overview,* CRS Report for Congress, Washington, D.C., February 8, 2005.

Shaw, Mark, "West African Criminal Networks in South and Southern Africa," *African Affairs,* Vol. 101, 2002.

Shimaila, Martin, "Hard Times Hotels," Newsline, September 2002. As of April 27, 2007:
http://www.newsline.com/pk/NewsSep2002/industry2002.htm

"Sierra Leone Security Information," Institute for Strategic Studies (Pretoria). As of January 22, 2007:
http://www.iss.org.za/AF/profiles/sieraleone/SecInfo.html

Singer, P. W., "AIDS and International Security," *Survival,* Vol. 44, No. 1, Spring 2002, pp. 145–158.

Singer, Peter, *Pakistan's Madrassahs: Ensuring a System of Education Not Jihad,* Washington, D.C.: The Brookings Institution, analysis paper 41, 2001.

SITE Institute, "The Mujahideen Shura Council in Chechnya Announces the Martyrdom of Chechen Rebel President Abdul Khalim Sadulayev," June 19, 2006. As of January 25, 2007:
http://siteinstitute.org/bin/articles.cgi?ID=publications186806&Category=publications&Subcategory=0

"Six Blasts Rock Pakistan," *Australian,* February 4, 2005.

Smirnov, Andrei, "Protesters Vacate Presidential Office in Cherkessk," The Jamestown Foundation, *Eurasia Daily Monitor,* Vol. 1, No. 134, November 24, 2004. As of March 21, 2007:
http://www.jamestown.org/publications_details.php?volume_id=401&issue_id=3151&article_id=2368900

————, "Dagestan's Insurgents Regroup As New 'Sharia Jamaat' Organization," The Jamestown Foundation, *Eurasia Daily Monitor,* Vol. 2, No. 3, January 19, 2005a. As of May 11, 2007:
http://www.jamestown.org/publications_details.php?volume_id=407&issue_id=3202&article_id=2369112

————, "Insurgents in Dagestan and Kabardino-Balkaria Ready for Summer Campaign," The Jamestown Foundation, *Eurasia Daily Monitor,* March 17, 2005b. As of March 20, 2007: http://jamestown.org/edm/article.php?volume_id=407&issue_id=3266&article_id=2369433

Smith, Chris, *The Diffusion of Small Arms and Light Weapons in Pakistan and Northern India,* London: Centre for Defense Studies, 1993.

————, "Africa: The Challenge of Light Weapons Destruction During Peacekeeping Operations," Basic Papers on International Security, Issue 23, December 1997.

Smith, Chris, and David Vines, *Light Weapons Proliferation in Southern Africa,* London: Centre for Defense Studies, November 1997.

Smith, Chris, Peter Batchelor, and Jakkie Potgieter, *Small Arms Management and Peacekeeping in Southern Africa,* New York: United Nations Institute for Disarmament Research, 1996.

Social Weather Stations, "Violence in ARMM Mostly Due to Family or Clan Conflict," media release, February 24, 2005a. As of January 16, 2007: http://www.sws.org.ph/

————, *The 2005 SWS Survey of Enterprises on Corruption, Transparent Accountable Governance Project: USAID and Asia Foundation,* July 26, 2005b. As of January 17, 2007: http://www.tag.org.ph/pdf/SWS_2005th_Survey.pdf

Sorongan, Arturo, *A Special Study of Landed Estates in the Philippines,* Manila: ICA, 1955.

South Asia Terrorism Portal, *South Asia Intelligence Review, Weekly Assessments & Briefings,* Vol. 1, No. 22, December 16, 2002. As of January 15, 2007: http://www.satp.org/satporgtp/sair/archives/1_22.htm

————, *India Timeline Year 2003.* As of January 15, 2007: http://www.satp.org/satporgtp/countries/india/timeline/2003.htm

"Southwest Asia," *Bulletin for International Narcotics and Law Enforcement Affairs,* 2004.

Spain, James W., *The Pathan Borderland,* The Hague: Moulton & Co., 1963.

"Special Trade Regimes in Colombia," undated. As of January 31, 2007: http://www.coltrade.org/traderegimes.htm

Spooner, Brian, "Insiders and Outsiders in Baluchistan: Western and Indigenous Perspectives on Ecology and Development," in P. Little, M. Horowitz, and E. Nyerges, eds., *Lands at Risk in the Third World: Local-Level Perspectives,* Boulder, Colo.: Westview Press, 1987.

————, "Baluchistan: Geography, History and Ethnography," in Ehsan Yarshater, ed., *Encyclopedia Iranica,* Vol. 3, London: Routledge, 1998, pp. 598–632.

Stack, Megan, and John Hendren, "Rockets Miss U.S. Ships at Port in Jordan," *Los Angeles Times,* August 20, 2005.

"Statistical Review—Bomb Blasts in Bangladesh, 2000–2002," *South Asia Intelligence Review: Weekly Assessments & Briefings,* Vol. 1, No. 22, December 16, 2002. As of September 20, 2005: http://www.satp.org/satporgtp/sair/archives/1_22.htm

"Stereotypes and Political Styles: Islamists and Tribefolk in Yemen," *International Journal of Middle East Studies,* Vol. 27, No. 4, November 1995.

Stern, Jessica, "Pakistan's Jihad Culture," *Foreign Affairs,* Vol. 79, No. 6, November/December 2000.

Steul, Willi, *Paschtunwali,* Wiesbaden: Steiner, 1981.

Stevenson, Jonathan, "Africa's Growing Strategic Resonance," *Survival,* Vol. 45, No. 4, Winter 2003–2004.

Stevenson, Mark, "Crackdown on Gangs Brings Mexico Violence," Associated Press, December 10, 2003. As of March 2005:
http://www.aberdeennews.com/mld/aberdeennews/news/nation/7456423.htm

Sullivan, John P., and Robert J. Bunker, "Drug Cartels, Street Gangs, and Warlords," in Robert J. Bunker, ed., *Small Wars and Insurgencies, Special Issue: Non-State Threats and Future Wars,* Vol. 13, No. 2, Summer 2002.

———, "Urban Gangs as Criminal Netwar Actors," *Small Wars and Insurgencies,* Vol. 11, No. 1, Spring 2000.

Sullivan, Kevin, "Mexico Battles Influx of Violent Gangs," *Washington Post,* January 21, 2005, p. A10.

"Sulawesi: Actors," *Building Human Security in Indonesia,* Program on Humanitarian Policy and Conflict Research, The President and Fellows of Harvard College, 2001. As of January 31, 2007:
http://www.preventconflict.org/portal/main/maps_sulawesi_actors.php

"Sulawesi (Palu)," undated. As of February 2007:
http://www.1000traveltips.org/index.htm

"Survey: The Importance of Going Straight," *Economist,* Vol. 373, No. 8405, December 11, 2004.

Suryadinata, Leo, Evi Nurvidya Arifin, and Aris Ananta, *Indonesia's Population: Ethnicity and Religion in a Changing Political Landscape,* Singapore: Institute of Southeast Asian Studies, 2003.

Swedish, Margaret, "Regions' Governments Sign Anti-Gang Pact," *Central America/Mexico Report,* May–June 2004. As of January 2005:
http://www.rtfcam.org/report/volume_24/No_1/article_1.htm

Sweig, Dr. Julia E., "Statement before the United States Senate Foreign Relations Committee, 108th Congress," October 29, 2003.

Tan, Andrew, "The Indigenous Roots of Conflict in Southeast Asia: The Case of Mindanao," in Kumar Ramakrishna and See Seng Tan, eds., *After Bali: The Threat of Terrorism in Southeast Asia,* Singapore: Institute of Defence and Strategic Studies, 2003.

Tan, Samuel K., "The Socio-Economic Dimension of Moro Secessionism," Mindanao Studies Reports No. 1, 1995, cited in Amina Rasul, *The Road to Peace and Reconciliation: Muslim Perspectives on the Mindanao Conflict,* Makati City, Philippines: Asian Institute of Management Policy Center, 2003.

Taylor, Paul D., ed., *Latin American Security Challenges: A Collaborative Inquiry from North and South,* Newport, R.I.: U.S. Naval War College Press, 2004.

"Terrorist Money Impossible to Stop," Associated Press, July 9, 2003.

Terzieff, Juliette, "Assassination Tries Linked to al-Qaeda," *San Francisco Chronicle,* January 16, 2004.

The Time of the South: Russia in Chechnya, Chechnya in Russia (English summary). Carnegie Moscow Center, September 2002. As of September 19, 2005:
http://pubs.carnegie.ru/english/books/2002/09am-dt/default.asp?n=summary.asp

Titus, Paul, "Honor the Baluch, Buy the Pashtun: Stereotypes, Social Organization and History in Western Pakistan," *Modern Asian Studies,* Vol. 32, No. 3, July 1998.

Tlisova, Fatima, "Kabardino-Balkaria Fears Spread of Terror," Institute for War and Peace Reporting, CRS No. 255, September 29, 2004. As of September 19, 2005:
http://www.iwpr.net/index.pl?archive/cau/cau_200409_255_1_eng.txt

"Tonne of Heroin Worth $8.4 Million Seized in Pakistan," Reuters, November 13, 2003.

Toothaker, Christopher, "Venezuela Ends U.S. Military Exchange," Associated Press, April 22, 2005. As of April 2005:
http://www.kansascity.com/mld/kansascity/news/world/11465728.htm

"Top Terror Suspect Noordin Behind Gem Shop Heist: Police," Channel NewsAsia, December 30, 2005. As of January 31, 2007:
http://www.channelnewsasia.com/stories/afp_asiapacific/view/185979/1/.html

Torre, Armando Salinas, Secretario Particular del C. Subsecretario Subsecretaría de Población, "Migración y Asuntos Religiosos, January 5, 2005," *Gaceta Parlamentaria,* No. 88, February 8, 2005. As of January 31, 2007:
http://www.senado.gob.mx/sgsp/gaceta/?sesion=2005/02/08/1&documento=6

Trans-Sahara Counterterrorism Initiative [TSCTI], GlobalSecurity.org, undated. As of January 23, 2007:
http://www.globalsecurity.org/military/ops/tscti.htm

"Transnational Gangs in Mexico and Central America," briefing charts, U.S. Southern Command (USSOUTHCOM) Foreign Military Studies Office, December 2004.

Transparencia Por Colombia, Edición 2004–5, "Índice de Integridad de Gobiernos, Asambleas y Contralorías Departamentales." As of March 2005:
http://www.transparenciacolombia.org.co/src/client/scripts/informacion2.php?cat_id=145

Transparency International, "Pakistan's Anti-Corruption Program: Observations and Recommendations," May 2002. As of January 8, 2007:
http://unpan1.un.org/intradoc/groups/public/documents/APCITY/UNPAN019877.pdf

———, *National Integrity Systems, Country Study Report—Pakistan,* 2003a. As of January 31, 2007:
http://www.transparency.org.pk/CSR.pdf

———, "Nine Out of Ten Developing Countries Urgently Need Practical Support to Fight Corruption, Highlights New Index," 2003b. As of January 8, 2007:
http://www.transparencykazakhstan.org/english/cpi2003.htm

———, *Corruption Perception Index 2004.* As of January 31, 2007:
http://www.transparency.org/policy_research/surveys_indices/cpi/2004

———, *Global Corruption Report 2005.* As of March 20, 2007:
http://www.transparency.org/publications/gcr/download_gcr/download_gcr_2005

Trenin, Dmitri, "Putin Must Secure Russia's Far East," *Financial Times,* March 1, 2005.

"Tribunal Supremo de Venezuela Aprobó la Extradición de Guerrillero de Las FARC a Colombia," *El Tiempo,* April 12, 2005. As of April 2005:
http://eltiempo.terra.com.co/inte/latin/noticias/articulo-web_nota_interior-2034455.html

Tuckman, Jo, "Mexican Detention Center Holds Would-be Migrants from 39 Countries," Associated Press, August 16, 2001.

Tully, Andrew F., "Russia: U.S. Says It Isn't Easing Criticism of Moscow over Chechnya," *CDI Weekly,* No. 215, 2003. As of January 28, 2007:
http://www.cdi.org/russia/215-3.cfm

Turnbull, Wayne, *A Tangled Web of Southeast Asian Islamic Terrorism: The Jemaah Islamiyah Terrorist Network,* Monterey, Calif.: Monterey Institute of International Studies, 2003.

Turner, Captain Edmund, U.S. Navy Deputy Director of Operations, U.S. Southern Command, "Written statement before the House Government Reform Committee, Subcommittee on Criminal Justice, Drug Policy, and Human Resources," May 10, 2005. As of January 30, 2007: http://www.defenselink.mil/dodgc/olc/docs/test05-05-10Turner.doc

Tyson, Ann Scott, "U.S. Pushes Anti-Terrorism in Africa," *Washington Post,* July 26, 2005. As of January 23, 2007: http://www.washingtonpost.com/wp-dyn/content/article/2005/07/25/AR2005072501801.html

Ulph, Stephen, "Jihadist Overtones in Sudan," *Jane's Terrorism Focus,* Vol. 2, August 2004.

UNAIDS, "AIDS Epidemic Update—December 2004, Sub-Saharan Africa: HIV and AIDS Statistics and Features." As of March 20, 2007: http://www.ntahc.org.au/EpiUpdate04_en.pdf

UNHCR—*See* United Nations High Commissioner for Refugees.

United Nations, *Human Development Report, 2004,* New York: Human Development Report Office, 2004.

United Nations Development Programme (UNDP), "Country Programme Document 2005–2008—Draft."

United Nations Environment Programme—Global Resource Information Database, "African Population Database Documentation," September 2004. As of May 11, 2007: http://grid2.cr.usgs.gov/globalpop/africa/

United Nations High Commissioner for Refugees (UNHCR), *International Protection Considerations Regarding Colombian Asylum-Seekers and Refugees,* Geneva: UNHCR, March 2005.

United Nations Office on Drugs and Crime, *Seventh United Nations Survey of Crime Trends and Operations of Criminal Justice Systems, Covering the Period 1998–2000,* 2001. As of September 27, 2005: http://www.unodc.org/pdf/crime/seventh_survey/7pc.pdf

———, *Colombia Coca Cultivation Survey 2003,* June 2004. As of January 30, 2007: http://www.unodc.org/pdf/colombia/colombia_coca_survey_2003.pdf

United States of America v Usama Bin Laden et al., SD (7) 98 Cr. 1023, Southern District Court of New York, February 15, 2001.

UNODC—*See* United Nations Office on Drugs and Crime.

U.S. Agency for International Development, "Guatemala Tax and Investment Policy Reform Program" (2004). As of January 30, 2007: http://www.fiscalreform.net/buy_ins/pdfs/scope_of_work_guatemala%20_webversion.pdf

———, "Democracy and Governance: West Africa Regional Program," excerpted from the *2006 Congressional Budget Justification for West Africa Regional Program (WARP),* June 14, 2005a. As of January 23, 2007: http://www.usaid.gov/policy/budget/cbj2006/afr/warp.html

———, "USAID Budget: Colombia," 2005b. As of January 29, 2007: http://www.usaid.gov/policy/budget/cbj2005/lac/co.html

———, "USAID Business," March 15, 2006. As of January 5, 2007: http://www.usaid.gov/business/

USAID—*See* U.S. Agency for International Development.

"U.S. Ambassador Thanks Marines, GTEP Cadre, Embassy of the United States, Georgia," April 21, 2004. As of September 20, 2005:
http://georgia.usembassy.gov/events/event20040421milesgtep.htm

U.S. Central Command, "U.S. Air Force Pakistan Relief Summary," news release, November 3, 2005. As of January 31, 2007:
http://www.globalsecurity.org/military/library/news/2005/11/mil-051103-centcom01.htm

U.S. Department of Defense, "CENTCOM Theater Security Cooperation Implementation Plan," FY05.

———, *Quadrennial Defense Review,* Washington, D.C.: Office of the Under Secretary of Defense for Policy, 2006.

U.S. Department of Energy, "World Crude Oil and Natural Gas Reserves," January 1, 2005a. As of January 12, 2007:
http://www.eia.doe.gov/emeu/aer/txt/ptb1104.html

———, Energy Information Administration, "Saudi Arabia Country Analysis Brief," August 2005b. As of January 15, 2007:
http://www.eia.doe.gov/emeu/cabs/saudi.htm

U.S. Department of Homeland Security, *Paradise Hotel Bombing,* Draft Working Paper, Washington D.C.: United States Department of Homeland Security, October, 2004.

U.S. Department of the Interior, Fish and Wildlife Service, "Endangered and Threatened Wildlife and Plants: Final Determination of the Threatened Status of the Beluga Sturgeon," in "Rules and Regulations," *Federal Register*, Vol. 69, No. 77, April 21, 2004, pp. 21425–21438. As of September 13, 2005:
http://www.sturgeonaquafarms.com/BelugaESA/2004%20Federal%20Register%201.htm

U.S. Department of Justice, *National Drug Threat Assessment 2005,* February 2005, Washington, D.C.: National Drug Intelligence Center. As of January 30, 2007:
http://www.usdoj.gov/ndic/pubs11/12620/12620p.pdf

U.S. Department of State, *African Crisis Response Initiative,* October 10, 2000. As of January 31, 2007:
http://usinfo.state.gov/regional/af/acri/

———, "U.S.-Pakistan Joint Working Group on Counterterrorism and Law Enforcement," Washington, D.C., May 8, 2002. As of March 21, 2007:
http://www.state.gov/r/pa/prs/ps/2002/10019.htm

———, "Agreement Between the United Nations and the Government of Guatemala for the Establishment of a Commission for the Investigation of Illegal Groups and Clandestine Security Organizations in Guatemala (CICIACS)," 2004a. As of January 31,2007:
http://www.state.gov/p/wha/rls/31015.htm

———, *Country Reports on Terrorism,* 2004b. As of September 27, 2005:
http://www.state.gov/documents/organization/45322.pdf

———, "Guatemala: Country Report on Human Rights Practices," February 25, 2004c. As of January 31, 2007:
http://www.state.gov/g/drl/rls/hrrpt/2003/27900.htm

————, *International Religious Freedom Report for 2004,* "Africa," September 15, 2004d. As of January 23, 2007:
http://www.state.gov/g/drl/rls/irf/2004/c12778.htm

————, *Foreign Military Training: Joint Report to Congress, Fiscal Years 2004 and 2005,* III. State Foreign Policy Objectives—South Asia Region, April 2005a. As of March 21, 2007:
http://www.state.gov/t/pm/rls/rpt/fmtrpt/2005/45676.htm

————, "Key U.S. Government Assistance Programs for Africa," June 15, 2005b. As of January 24, 2007:
http://www.state.gov/r/pa/scp/2005/47996.htm

————, *International Narcotics Control Strategy Reports, 2001–2005,* Washington D.C.: Bureau for International Narcotics and Law Enforcement Affairs, 2005c. As of January 30, 2007:
http://www.state.gov/p/inl/rls/nrcrpt/

————, Remarks of Secretary of State Condoleezza Rice with Colombian Foreign Minister Carolina Barco, April 27, 2005d. As of January 29, 2007:
http://www.state.gov/secretary/rm/2005/45280.htm

————, *Congressional Budget Justification for FY06 Foreign Operations, Western Hemisphere,* March 2005e. As of January 30, 2007:
http://www.state.gov/documents/organization/42255.pdf

————, "Guatemala Travel Warning," May 3, 2005f. As of March 2, 2005:
http://www.tandt.com/.%5Ctravel_update_20050505.asp

————, "Middle East Partnership Initiative" (undated-a). As of March 21, 2007:
http://mepi.state.gov/mepi/

————, "Military Assistance" (undated-b). As of March 21, 2007:
http://www.state.gov/documents/organizations/42247.pdf

"U.S. Navy Seizes Scores of Militants in Gulf," Reuters, March 14, 2005.

"USS Cole Suspect Involved in US Embassy Blast in Nairobi," *Yemen Times,* Vol. 10, No. 47, November 20–26, 2000. As of September 27, 2005:
http://www.yementimes.com/00/iss47/front.htm

"US Soldiers Arrested for Arms Smuggling," Reuters, May 5, 2005.

"U.S. Soldiers Arrested for Colombian Cocaine Plot," Reuters, April 1, 2005. As of March 20, 2007:
http://abcnews.go.com/US/print?id=632570

"US Support to African Capacity for Peace Operations: The ACOTA Program," The Henry L. Stimson Center, Washington, D.C., 2005. As of January 23, 2007:
http://se1.isn.ch:80/serviceengine/FileContent?serviceID=PublishingHouse&fileid=93B31F64-26B7-04F6-6FFF-C032FF04256D&lng=en

"U.S.: Top al Qaeda Operative Arrested," CNN.com, November 22, 2002. As of September 21, 2005:
http://archives.cnn.com/2002/US/11/21/alqaeda.capture/

"US Trying to Destabilize Pakistan, Iran: MMA," *Dawn* (Pakistan), November 4, 2003.

Van Creveld, Martin, *The Rise and Decline of the State,* Cambridge: Cambridge University Press, 1999.

Van Dongen, Rachel, "Colombia's Ambitious Peace Plan Hits Roadblocks," *Christian Science Monitor,* February 7, 2005. As of January 31, 2007:
http://www.latinamericanstudies.org/auc/roadblocks.htm

Varase, Sebastiana, "Como y donde funciona la guerrilla en la frontera," *Quinto Día Online*, No. 427, January 21–28, 2005. As of January 31, 2007:
http://www.quintodia.com/archivos/427/edicion/index.php?dir=columnas&pag=sebastiana_1

Varshney, Ashutosh, "India, Pakistan and Kashmir: Antinomies of Nationalism," *Asian Survey,* November 1991.

"Venezuela deporta hacia Colombia 17 personas, entre ellas 8 presuntosguerrilleros de las FARC," *El Tiempo,* June 20, 2004.

"Venezuela Refuerza su Frontera con Colombia," Associated Press, December 13, 2004. As of January 31, 2007:
http://www.esmas.com/noticierostelevisa/internacionales/412621.html

Vick, Alan, Adam Grissom, William Rosenau, Beth Grill, and Karl P. Mueller, *Air Power in the New Counterinsurgency Era: The Strategic Importance of USAF Advisory and Assisssstance Missions,* Santa Monica, Calif.: RAND Corporation, MG-509-AF, 2006. As of January 6, 2007:
http://www.rand.org/pubs/monographs/MG509/

Vick, Karl, "Alleged USS Cole Plotter Caught," *Washington Post,* November 17, 2000.

Villamizar, Andrés, *La Reforma de la Inteligencia: Un Imperativo Democrático,* Bogotá, Colombia: Fundación Seguridad y Democracia, 2004.

Vines, Alex, "The Struggle Continues: Light Weapons Destruction in Mozambique," *Basic* Papers on International Security, Issue 25, April 1998.

Vitug, Maritess, "People Power, MILF Style," Newsbreak: Inside Stories, June 23, 2005.

Vitug, Maritess, and Glenda Gloria, *Under the Crescent Moon: Rebellion in Mindanao,* Manila: CSPPA-IPD, 2000.

Waldman, Amy, "Pakistan Arrests Militant with Ties to Taliban," *New York Times,* August 9, 2004.

Walker, Edward W., *Islam in Chechnya: Conference Summary,* Berkeley Program in Soviet and Post-Soviet Studies, Berkeley: University of California, March 13, 1998.

Ware, Robert Bruce, "Will Southern Russian Studies Go the Way of Sovietology?" *Journal of Slavic Military Studies,* Vol. 16, No. 4, December 2003.

"Washington Revisits Africa's Strategic Importance," JINSA Online, May 14, 2004. As of January 31, 2007:
http://www.jinsa.org/articles/print.html/documentid/2497

"Web of Terror: Jemaah Islamiah Forged Links with Regional Groups," *Straits Times,* September 20, 2002.

Weber, Robert, Heiko Faust, and Werner Kreisel, "Colonial Interventions on Cultural Landscape of Central Sulawesi by 'Ethical Policy': Impacts of the Dutch Rule in Palu and Kuwali Valley, 1905–1942," STORMA Discussion Papers, No. 2, April 2002. As of March 20, 2007:
http://www.geogr.uni-goettingen.de/kus/sfb552/SDP2_110402.pdf

Webb-Vidal, Andy, "FARC Poised for New Battle in Long War," *Financial Times,* April 10, 2005. As of January 31, 2007:
http://www.freerepublic.com/focus/f-news/1381417/posts

Weissert, Will, "Debate Rising over Whether al-Qaida Is Recruiting Latin American Gangs," *Associated Press*, October 22, 2004. As of April 27, 2007:
http://www.dailytexanonline.com/media/paper410/news/2004/10/22/

West, James, "AFL Soldiers Demand Pay, Set Up Road Blocks Near Defense Ministry," *Liberian Observer* (Monrovia), June 15, 2005.

"West Africa," Wikipedia. As of October 6, 2005:
http://en.wikipedia.org/wiki/West_Africa

Wilhelmsen, Julie, "Between a Rock and a Hard Place: The Islamisation of the Chechen Separatist Movement," *Europe-Asia Studies,* Vol. 57, No. 1, January 2005, pp. 35–59.

Williams, Brian Glyn, "Jihad and Ethnicity in Post-Communist Eurasia: On the Trail of Islamic Holy Warriors in Kashmir, Afghanistan, Central Asia, Chechnya and Kosovo," *Global Review of Ethnopolitics,* Vol. 2, Nos. 3–4, March/June 2003, pp. 14–22.

Winchester, Mike, "Ship of Fools: Tamil Tigers' Heist of the Century," *Soldier of Fortune,* August 1998.

Wines, Michael, "Arrests and Plots Give South Africans a New Problem," *New York Times,* August 9, 2004.

Wirsing, Robert, *India, Pakistan and the Kashmir Dispute,* London: Macmillan, 1994.

World Bank, *Social Assessment of Conflict-Affected Areas in Mindanao,* March 3, 2003. As of May 7, 2007:
http://lnweb18.worldbank.org/ESSD/sdvext.nsf/67ByDocName/
Socialassessmentconflict-AffectedAreasinMindanao/$FILE/Mindanao.pdf

———, "Colombia Public Expenditure Review," April 2005a. As of June 2005:
http://www.wds.worldbank.org/servlet/WDSContentServer/WDSP/IB/2005/05/18/000160016_
20050518163008/Rendered/PDF/251630CO.pdf

———, *Guatemala Country Economic Memorandum (CEM): Challenges to Higher Economic Growth,* March 9, 2005b. As of January 30, 2007:
http://web.worldbank.org/WBSITE/EXTERNAL/COUNTRIES/LACEXT/GUATEMALAEXTN/
0,,contentMDK:20387031~pagePK:1497618~piPK:217854~theSitePK:328117,00.html

World Health Organization, Country Health Indicators, "Nigeria." As of January 23, 2005:
http://www.who.int/countries/nga/en/

———, Country Health Indicators, "Sierra Leone." As of January 23, 2005:
http://www.who.int/countries/sle/en/

"World News Quick Take, Colombia: Mayors Under Pressure," *Taipei Times,* October 29, 2004. As of January 30, 2007:
http://www.taipeitimes.com/News/world/archives/2004/10/29/2003208840

World 66.com, "Cyberstudio," undated. As of February 28, 2007:
http://www.world66.com/southamerica/venezuela/maracaibo/internetcafes/cyberestudio

Wriston, Walter B., *The Twilight of Sovereignty,* New York: Charles Scribner's Sons, 1992.

"Yemen Feels the Backlash," *Jane's Defence Weekly,* Vol. 38, No. 16, October 16, 2002.

"Yemen Quakes in Cole's Shadow," *Christian Science Monitor,* September 21, 2001.

Zaidi, Mubashir, "Militant Flourishes in Plain Sight," *Los Angeles Times,* January 25, 2004.

Zartman, I. William, ed., *Collapsed States: The Disintegration and Restoration of Legitimate Authority,* Boulder, Colo.: Lynne Rienner, 1995.

Zoller, Barbara, "Karachay-Cherkessia, in the Middle of Russia's Powder Keg," September 1999. As of September 13, 2005:
http://observatori.barcelona2004.org/observatorio/dossierCompleto_i.htm?num_dossier=67

Index